I0866684

All That Glitters

The Life and Times
of
Joe Ladue
Founder of Dawson City

Ed and Star Jones

WOLF CREEK BOOKS
Whitehorse

Copyright © 2005 Ed and Star Jones
ISBN 0973268395
All That Glitters
The Life and Times of Joe Ladue
Founder of Dawson City

All rights reserved. No part of this publication may be reproduced, stored in a retrieval system, or transmitted in any form or by any means, electronic, mechanical, photocopying, recording or otherwise, without prior written permission of the publisher, except by a reviewer, who may quote brief passages in a review to print in a magazine or newspaper or broadcast on radio or television.

Cover Photograph: Deadwood street scene (Nebraska State Historical Society.)
Book Editor: Ann Chandonnet
Copy Editor: Colleen Anderson
Book Design and Production: Graham Wilson
Project Management: Sofia Fortin
Printed and Bound in Canada by Friesens, Altona, Manitoba

WOLF CREEK BOOKS

Box 31599,
Whitehorse, Yukon
Y1A 6L2
info@wolfcreek.ca
www.wolfcreek.ca

To the Memory of
Joseph Francis Ladue II
"…a promise made is a debt unpaid,…"

Table of Contents

Foreword

In my childhood and teenage years in Dawson City I have to admit that I had never heard of Joe Ladue, although his name appeared in faded block letters on a building—a sawmill I suspect, —on Front Street.

We lived on Harper Street in the twenties and early thirties but I had no idea who Harper was. It was only when I began to do research on the gold rush, a generation later, that I realized that he and Ladue, besides being partners, were also the true pioneers of my home town.

I learned nothing about them at school or about the other great figures from their past—Jack McQuesten, Ed Schieffelin, Al Mayo, George Holt, or Kate Carmack. Chester Henderson was a schoolmate of mine but I had no more than a vague idea that his grandfather was the co-discoverer of the Klondike gold.

We studied all the kings and queens of England and some of the great figures of the British Empire but we learned very little about our own northern heritage.

That is why this book is so important. Its strength lies in the details that the authors have uncovered after much painstaking research. It is bound to re-awaken interest in the story of the Yukon in the years before the great stampede, and in the men and women who helped to give it birth. For Joe Ladue, and for all of them, this is their monument.

Pierre Berton
January 5, 2004

Acknowledgments

Our thanks to the librarians, archivists, historians and people who gave us directions to the sites we visited in the United States and Canada, and to all who so willingly shared information, materials and photographs. And particular thanks to the Ladue family members whose assistance, materials and encouragement have made this work possible. Some of the names may have faded from memory over the years, but here are several:

New York: the late Joseph Francis Ladue (II), the late Emily McMasters, Velma Newton, granddaughter of Ellis Turner, Sharon Bandhold, reference librarian, Plattsburgh Public Library, Addie Shields, Clinton County historian and her staff, the Clinton County Clerk's Office, Gloria Pratt, Northern New York-Canadian Genealogical Society, Wayne Miller at the Feinberg Library, State University of New York, Plattsburgh, Suellen Botsford and Dick Ward, Plattsburgh, Joseph Francis Ladue (III), Highland, Byron Schenk (present owner of Ladue's house), Schuyler Falls, Marie Gennett, historian, town of Chazy.

Oregon: Keith La Due, great nephew of Joseph Ladue, Don Miller and Katie Miller, great-granddaughter of Jack McQuesten, Lake Oswego.

Iowa: Rosemary Rockhill, Center Point, who shared in the search and discovery of the grave marker of Francois Ladue and Scott Hendryx, great-nephew of Joseph Ladue, Center Point.

California: Donald Chaput, curator emeritus of history at the Natural History Museum of Los Angeles, who shared with us his entire research file on Ladue.

Alaska: Gladi Kulp, reference librarian, Alaska State Library, Ken Graham, great-great nephew of Charles O. Farciot, Girdwood, Yvonne Mozee, granddaughter of Arthur, Sitka, Candy Waugaman who shared wonderful items from her extensive Klondike collection, Fairbanks, Barbara, great-granddaughter of Alfred Mayo, Fairbanks, Dee Longenbaugh, researcher, historian, author and owner of an antiquarian bookstore, Juneau.

South Dakota: the staff of the Adams Museum, Deadwood.

New Mexico: Marc Simmons, Cerrillos, Robert Eveleth, New Mexico School of Mines, Socorro, Jeff Carbajal, county clerk, Grant

County, Silver City, Marisa Castrillo, second deputy clerk, Grant County, Silver City, Glinda Lobdell, Placitas, Peter Burman, John and Gisele Chapman, Santa Fe, Dick and Julie Kavet, Albuquerque.
Yukon: Suzanne Saito, who shared her genealogical study of the Ladue family, John Gould, Dawson City, Paul Thistle, former director of the Dawson City Museum and Klondike History Library, Cheryl Thompson, Dawson City Museum and Klondike History Library, Michael Gates, Whitehorse.
British Columbia: Christopher Hanna, Victoria.
Washington State: Joanne Sanchez, great-niece of Emilie Tremblay.
Manitoba: John Richthammer, Winnipeg.
New Hamphshire: Ruth Huckins.
Ontario: Donna, great-niece of Joseph Ladue, Barrie, Mrs. Ann Byers, great-niece of George M. Dawson, Ottawa, John Eidt and Jane Lind, Etobicoke.
Florida: James and Joan Wheaton, granddaughter of Tappan Adney, Largo.
Ohio: Bob Majni, Macedonia, Dr. Jerry Green, Department of Geography, Miami University.
Quebec: Hazel Harrington, who shared her knowledge of the George Dawson family.
Pennsylvania: James A. McQuiston, North East, Louise Arnold-Friend, Historical Services Division, U.S. Department of the Army, U.S. Army War College and Carlisle Barracks, Carlisle.
Texas: George Kirkpatrick, great-nephew of Thomas W. Kirkpatrick, Smithville.
Arizona: Donald Langlois, history librarian, Arizona State Library, Phoenix, Art Austin, park manager, Tombstone Courthouse State Historic Park, Marilyn Butler, editor of Destination Tombstone, the diary of Edward L. Schieffelin, Sun Lakes, and our friends on the road, Bud and Elaine Hamm.

Special thanks to:
Our friends and neighbors Mike and Maureen Rene and Margaret O'Brien Ph.D and Neil O'Brien for giving their time, computer skills and patience to the completion of this project.

Diane Duguay and Isabel Rinquet of the National Archives of

Canada, and the superb staff at Yukon Archives and the New Mexico State Library.

John Small and Graham Wilson, Wolf Creek Books. A lucky telephone call led us to them and they, in turn, had the courage to review and accept this manuscript.

Ann Chandonnet of Juneau and Colleen Anderson of Vancouver who skillfully led us through our first editing experience

And, finally, we shall always be grateful to Alan Innes-Taylor (1900-1983), our friend, whose love of the Yukon Territory, the rivers and its people has inspired not only our interest in Joseph Ladue, but also in the many men and women who ventured into that vast and beautiful land when it was still remote and unknown and where they were certain gold could be found.

We very much appreciate the many individuals who have helped us with this project. We apologize if anyone has been overlooked.

Prologue

When we first saw Dawson City in the fall of 1962 all was still, the streets empty, the buildings appearing old, tired, colorless. Mysteriously, it has held our interest for the past 40 years. By early August 1963 we were living on Sisters' Island, purchased from the Catholic order of the Sisters of St. Ann, who left the Yukon the following week. The island is located three miles downriver from Dawson and across from Moosehide Village. On numerous mornings the northern view was of fog resting over the Fort Reliance site where Joe Ladue spent his first winter in the Yukon in 1882.

Beginning the summer of 1964 we operated boat tours taking visitors past the decaying remains of the riverboats *Julia B*, *Seattle No. 3* and the *Schwatka* that had been taken out of service and pulled from the water in 1928. After a visit to the abandoned Indian village of Moosehide, we crossed the river to Sisters' Island with our fishwheel operating in the channel behind it. In the barn on the island we developed a museum featuring machinery that had been used on the property and an archival photo display of Indian people, early traders and prospectors, riverboats and events of the Klondike Gold Rush. Among the displays were mastodon tusks and our collection of bottles dug from cabin sites on the creeks. In the museum gift shop only locally made items were sold, primarily Indian crafts, wild berry jams and jewelry. The tour business was sold after several years, but we spent most summers for the next two decades living on that beautiful, pristine 42 acres of wilderness.

In 1965 we spent our first winter in Dawson and became interested in its founder, Joseph Ladue, whose name was recognized by few and about whom little was known. When we contacted historian Emily McMasters, a resident of his birthplace, Clinton County, New York, she sent us photos of Joe and his wife, Kittie, with a note that "no one around here cares about him." In 1971 we visited his son in Chazy, New York. Francis showed us Joe's 40-star American flag that had flown in the Yukon before the Gold Rush, his watch and some gold nuggets from the Klondike. Francis had a keen interest in his father and asked if we would look for the truth about his life and "write a book." We promised we would—little knowing what it would take to keep that promise.

In the intervening years we have traveled thousands of miles to all the places Joe had been: his hometown of Schuyler Falls, neighboring Plattsburgh and Lake George, New York, Iowa, South Dakota, southwestern New Mexico, Arizona, San Francisco, Juneau, Dyea and Skagway. We traveled down the Yukon River to Fort Selkirk, Sixty Mile Island, Fort Reliance, Forty Mile (where we walked over the sites of Fort Constantine and Fort Cudahy), Belle Isle (Eagle, Alaska), Circle City and Fort Yukon. Because we arrived in the Yukon just after the end of the riverboat era, we made a special journey to Hannibal, Missouri, where we finally boarded a stern-wheeler and heard the churning of a paddle wheel in the muddy waters. We visited Ladue descendants in New York, Iowa and Oregon.

From libraries, archives, museums, historical societies, government offices and churches and from a former driver of the Williston Stage in the Black Hills, we slowly gleaned the amazing story of a man from humble beginnings who went west to search for gold and became the president of a huge gold mining and development company in the Klondike, and was received by an American president. Yet he remained unassuming, kind, generous and respected by all who knew him.

Joe Ladue was a shy, quiet man seeking to rise above the limitations and poverty of his childhood. He left a record of the places he went and many of the things he did, but said nothing of the great dangers that swirled around him. In the Black Hills of Dakota Territory, the Sioux regularly killed miners on their solitary claims, while in southwestern New Mexico, the Chiracahua Apaches raided mining camps and attacked prospectors and miners in the hills. In Tombstone the Clantons and the Earps shot it out at the OK Corral and other gunmen walked the streets.

The Yukon presented other challenges. It was a remote wilderness with long, unrelenting, dark winters when temperatures could fall to 70 below, and treacherous rivers that could easily claim the lives of the careless. Starvation was an ever-present danger.

Joe's letters from the Black Hills, Arizona, New Mexico and the Yukon to his friends the Lobdells were destroyed in a house fire. He never expressed publicly how he felt about his life, the amazing people he knew or the historical impact of events unfolding during the

last half of the nineteenth century. Nevertheless, we have diligently attempted to document the facts of Joe's life and times, and hope they are portrayed here realistically and that finally he is receiving richly deserved recognition as a man of intelligence, great courage and integrity.
Ed and Star Jones

Introduction

In William Shakespeare's, Merchant of Venice, the prince of Morocco, a suitor competing for the hand of Portia, discovered that the glittering casket of gold did not contain the treasure he sought. Rather, in the unadorned, lead casket rested the prize, her portrait, signifying Bassanio's wise choice, leading to their happy marriage.

The seduction of treasure glitters still in the human spirit. To hundreds of thousands of men who heard about the gold "like slices of cheese in a sandwich" found in 1896 in the remote Klondike, easy wealth beckoned.

Joe headed west as a young man, and when his prospects there didn't pan out, he headed north to the Yukon River and its creeks. He was already an established trader and entrepreneur in the Yukon when George Carmack, his wife, Kate, Skookum Jim and Tagish Charlie came upon Rabbit Creek.

Joe was a quiet man, typically shunning publicity, but he was restless, versatile, vigorous, adventurous and, above all, persistent. This is the story of one man's life and times and his pursuit of "all that glitters."

Roots: 1850-1876
Quebec, New York and Iowa

The dreary winter of 1865 was mercifully turning to spring and the bloody, divisive American Civil War was coming to an end. America would soon begin the slow healing process from the brutal four-year conflict and the chaos of economic ruin. A new industrial age was beginning. The mood was hopeful and, while loved ones waited for the return of husbands, fathers and sons, the surviving soldiers simply wanted to go home and plant their early crops.

But in a small frame house in the village of Schuyler Falls, New York, the month of March brought grief and despair to the young family of Francois Ladue. An epidemic of scarlet fever surging through the area had descended upon the household. Death had taken three members of the family. Eight-year-old Celina was the first to die on March 19, followed by the newest family member, two-month-old Francis, on March 21. Still recovering from giving birth for the eighth time in 15 years, their mother, Marie, succumbed on March 23. The children were buried on either side of Marie in a far corner of the Irish Settlement Cemetery in Schuyler Falls. Modest stones, spelling the surname "Ladou," mark their final resting places.[1]

The other children—Elmire, 12; Joseph, 10; Pierre, 7; and Andre, 5—survived the epidemic that year, but three-year-old Marie Catherine was left without hearing and spent the remainder of her long life in silence, never learning to speak.[2] One year later, Pierre died, perhaps weakened by his bout with the fever.[3] The future of the Ladue family was changed forever.

Francois Ladue and Marie Pelletier, natives of the Canadian province of Quebec, had been married on November 2, 1850, in St. Antoine sur le Richlieux in the region of St. Bernard.[4] Their first child, John, was born the following year, but died at the age of six months.[5] Soon after his death the couple emigrated to northeastern New York state, to the village of Schuyler Falls, a few miles from bustling Plattsburgh on the western shore of Lake Champlain. Here Francois hoped to find work as a bricklayer.[6]

The area of the Adirondack Mountains where they chose to settle was one of great natural beauty. Winters were severe with temperatures frequently dropping far below zero, and blizzards depositing snowdrifts up to the eaves of one-story farmhouses. The Saranac and Salmon Rivers provided generous supplies of power for mills and factories.[7] Dairy farms, rolling meadows and woodlands where maple, beech and oak trees painted the landscape each fall surrounded the small villages. Fish and game were plentiful. The red brick town of Plattsburgh had been founded in 1785 and had famously repulsed a British invasion in 1814. It was rapidly maturing, although a vestige of earlier days was evident in the mercantile establishments that still accepted farm produce and furs in trade.

When the Ladues crossed the border from Canada in 1851, the United States was on the cusp of the original colonial frontier, rapidly making the transition from its post-war industrial age of trade expansion, railroad construction and mass western migration. The Oregon and Santa Fe Trails had been beckoning settlers and trade goods away from the Mississippi for several decades, but many men who felt the crush of civilization still looked to the West for elbow room and a new start. Railroads and canals carried passengers and goods to parts of the country ripe for settlement and opened new markets.

The Nineteenth Century brought an explosion of new ways of thinking. In western New York State, for example, Joseph Smith (1805-44) declared he had discovered gold tablets that gave birth to a new religious movement, The Church of Jesus Christ of Latter Day Saints or Mormons. Geneva, New York, hosted a convention promoting the abolition of slavery as well as suffrage rights for women, creating revolutions of their own. Great social and religious experiments in communal living, such as Oneida Community, sprang up. The Women's Christian Temperance Union sent disciples into the fields, frequently speaking from portable lecterns, to preach the wisdom of abstinence from alcohol. All who would listen were warned of the dangers of consuming spirits and urged to sign pledges if they were truly willing to turn their backs on "demon rum" forever. The Chautauqua "enlightenment" movement found its birthplace at an 1874 camp meeting in southwest New York, in the town of the same name. Soon communities around the country hosted Chautauqua lecturers and established summer schools and weekly reading circles.

Schuyler Falls was named after Phillip John Schuyler, a general in the French and Indian War and a member of the second Continental Congress. Schuylerville and Schuyler Lake are also named for him. In 1794, Ezra Turner, one of Plattsburgh's original settlers, moved from there "seven miles into the wilderness,"[8] to the place that became Schuyler Falls. On April 4, 1848, the legislature of New York State passed an act separating Schuyler Falls from Plattsburgh.

Schuyler Falls enjoyed a flourishing and varied economy that embraced a carding mill, gristmill, two potato starch factories, blacksmiths and leather shops.[9] These enterprises provided employment not only for the large number of French Canadians crossing the border, but also for Irish immigrants searching for relief from religious persecution and the devastating potato famines of their homeland. Competition for jobs was fierce.

Like most families of the time, the Ladue family grew: Elmire (Almira) was born June 9, 1852; Joseph (Joe), July 28, 1854; Celina, June 21, 1856; Pierre (Peter), May 26, 1858; Andre (Andrew), August 1, 1859; Marie Catherine (Mary), September 15, 1861; and Francis, January 19, 1865.[10]

The breadwinner of the family, Francois was hard working and thrifty and enjoyed the respect of his neighbors, many of whom were godparents to the Ladue children. By May 1857 Francois and Marie were able to purchase a modest house on three-quarters of an acre of land for $350 from their good friend, Joseph Rock, godfather to their son, Joe.[11] It was under this roof that most of the children were born. The family eked out a living with earnings from Francois' work as a bricklayer[12] and by cultivating a vegetable garden. There was no extra money, however, and no record that the Ladue children attended the District No.1 Schoolhouse nearby. Since immunizations were not available, the children were subjected to, and survived, the usual childhood illnesses: measles, chicken pox and mumps. However, when scarlet fever struck in 1865, it had a devastating effect. Many illnesses killed by fever alone, as aspirin had not been invented.

After burying Marie, Celina and Francis that spring day, Francois was faced with managing a household of five young children while working to support them. Like generations of motherless girls before her, Almira, 12 years old, assumed the endless household chores and the care of her younger siblings.

When Andrew Ladue was baptized in 1860 at St. Peter's Church, his godparents were Andre Burke-Laliberte and his wife, Philomen (nee Favreau)[13] Burke-Laliberte. But tragedy fell upon the Laliberte household, too, and Andre died in early 1866 leaving Philomen a young widow with three children: Joseph, six; Rose Delima, seven; and Philomen, ten.[14]

The widower and the widow joined forces. On April 29, 1866, Francois Ladue married Philomen Burke-Laliberte in St. Peter's Church, Plattsburgh,[15] and she and her three children moved into Ladue's tiny house in Schuyler Falls. Four months later, Pierre Ladue, the eight-year-old son of Francois and the deceased Marie, died.[16] (No grave marker for Pierre could be found in the Irish Settlement Cemetery.) Now the household consisted of Francois, Philomen, seven children and Gabriel Ladue, Francois' father.

Two months prior to his marriage to Philomen, Francois had purchased 38 acres of land adjacent to his three-quarters of an acre from his neighbor, A. P. Brand[17] for $975. Other farms in the neighborhood were those of Abel Turner and Orrin D. Hilliard. Francois and Philomen now had enough land on which to grow food for their large combined family, as well as hay for their horse. There may even have been sufficient land to raise cash crops or even to rent out for additional income.

The first child of Francois and Philomen was born April 14, 1867, and they named her Clemence Thais. Her unusual middle name was that of her rather obscure patron saint, a penitent who lived and died in Egypt in the 4th Century C. E. The family knew her as "Nina." On April 11, 1869, Marie Adele was born, called "Ida" by her mother, as there was already a child named "Mary" (Catherine Marie) in the household. Like all other Laliberte and Ladue children, they were baptized in St. Peter's Church in Plattsburgh.[18]

The massive flow of European immigrants into New York Harbor that had begun in the 1850s continued and now posed a serious threat to employment for established residents. The particular threat to Francois was the arrival of stone masons and bricklayers from Ireland. After much discussion with family and friends, on March 12, 1869, Francois and Philomen sold their farm to Nathan Lobdell for $1, 500[19] and soon became emigrants heading West.

The Ladues chose Center Point, Iowa, as their new home. Their Schuyler Falls neighbor, Orrin D. Hilliard, had a relative, Brunson M. Hilliard, who had moved to Center Point from Schuyler Falls in 1864 with his father-in-law, Mr. Soper, where they established a successful mercantile business.[20]

The Ladue family arrived in Iowa in 1870 and purchased a farm in Denison Bottoms, between the hamlets of Center Point and Urbana. Their neighbors were the Manleys and Denisons. The Ladue household consisted of: Francois, Philomen and her Laliberte children: Philomen, Rose Delima "Delia" and Joseph; the children of Francois and Marie: Andrew and Mary Catherine; and the daughters of Francois and Philomen: Clemence Thais "Nina" or "Climma," Marie Adele "Ida," and grandfather, Gabriel Ladue.[21]

Some time before the move to Iowa, the decision had been made that the two oldest Ladue children would not accompany the family. Almira and Joe remained in Schuyler Falls employed on neighboring farms. The 1870 U.S. Census for New York State lists Almira in the household of A. Brand and his wife, Miranda, with their five children, and Mrs. Fannie Brand, age 83. Almira Ladue and Sally Walker were recorded as "domestic servants." The Brands were successful farmers, with real property valued at $6,000 and personal property at $3,000, who had sold the 38 acres of land to Francois in 1866.[22]

Although the same census listed Joe in the household of Jerome and Fidelia Lobdell, he had been left in the care of Jerome's brother, James Henry, as a "protectory boy."[23] It is likely that Joe was helping out on Jerome's farm the day the census taker stopped by, since the brothers owned adjoining properties.[24] The census form provided no column for recording the presence in a household of a ward, therefore, Joe's classification was "farm laborer (age) 16." His affectionate relationship with the James Henry Lobdell family was evidenced by later visits with them, personal correspondence to their young son, Will, born in 1875, and in Joe's later statements to the press. Joe explained his presence in the James Lobdell home years later during an interview with *Leslie's Illustrated Weekly Magazine.* Journalist John A. Sleicher stated that Joe "had found some things uncongenial in his home and was ready, at the age of nine years to accept the adoption of his neighbor."[25]

While living with the Lobdells, Joe was not a full-time servant or laborer. Because the couple was childless at the time, great affection was apparently lavished on him. He attended the District 7 one-room schoolhouse[26] where he was taught English, while retaining fluency in his first language, French. Rote learning was in fashion during Victorian times, and students were expected to memorize and be able to recite in front of the class lessons, such as all the bones in the body as well as long poems. Joe would have memorized Longfellow and Whittier, and verses such as:

I hear the tread of pioneers
Of nations yet to be
The first low wash of waves, where soon
Shall roll a human sea.

School often let out for the year as early as March 1 so that farm kids could help prepare the fields for spring planting.

Joe's spiritual life was also attended to. He had been baptized in St. Peter's Catholic Church, but, while living with the Lobdell's, he accompanied them on Sundays to the red brick Methodist Church in Schuyler Falls.[27] (The church is still standing.)

Next door to the Lobdell farm lived Charles and Martha Bates Mason. The Mason farm was home to three children: Melvin, Victor and, their youngest child, a daughter, Catharine, eight months, nicknamed "Kittie." According to the 1870 Census, the Masons owned real property valued at $5,000 and personal property valued at $1,600.[28]

Also appearing in the 1870 Census was the prominent Peter Weaver family, consisting of Weaver, 87, and his wife, Susan, 74, plus their adult children—Loren, 44, a potato starch manufacturer; Mary, 42; and Susan, 31.[29] Weaver was one of the wealthiest men in Schuyler Falls with real property valued at $18,000 and personal property at $6,000. His home was built of squared logs and, as he became more affluent, he enclosed the exterior with red brick, built an addition and erected a small barn. The house was equipped with the most modern convenience of the time, an indoor hand pump at the kitchen sink.[30]

Meanwhile, far away in Iowa, grief came to the Ladue household once more when Grandfather Gabriel died suddenly in 1871.[31] He had lived with his son's family intermittently for 20 years and family stories recalled him with great affection.[32] A handwritten entry in a family scrapbook records that Gabriel was buried in St. Mary's Spencer's Grove Cemetery in Urbana, but no stone marks the location of his grave.[33] Three months after Gabriel died, Francois and Philomen's only son, Charles, was born on September 10, 1871.[34] The older children attended public school while Mary, the child of Francois and Marie, attended a school for the hearing impaired where she learned sign language and established friendships with other children with similar needs.[35]

The ultimate tragedy for the Ladues came on December 17, 1874, when 44-year-old Francois died suddenly of a heart attack. Just before Christmas the bereaved family made their way again to the small cemetery on a wind-swept hill where Francois was buried beside his father.[36]

There is no surviving record that Francois and Philomen remained in contact with Almira and Joe in New York or with the families in whose care they had been placed. But word somehow reached Almira and Joe of their father's death, and they left for Center Point. Almira was a now a tall, strong young woman of 22. Joe, 20, was a quiet, compact young man, 5'6½" tall, with large brown eyes and a dark complexion. After four years of separation, the children of Francois and Marie were reunited. They remained for some time at Denison Bottoms with Philomen and the younger children to help with the demanding daily chores.

Many years later, in 1897, John Sleicher reported in *Leslie's Illustrated Weekly Magazine* that Joe decided to go west to "look after the small estate of his parent."[37] The truth of the matter is that Francois died intestate. When Philomen was subsequently appointed by the courts to administer the property, she promptly appointed her neighbor, Joseph Hunter, to carry out the task of administrator of the "Estate of Francis Ladue." Mr. Hunter's duties included disposing of the farm at public sale, paying the existing debts and distributing the remaining amount of $345.00 to Philomen. The total debts paid by the administrator were minor, amounting to $289.78; among other small sums, they included back taxes of $34.70 and $25.00 for Francois' coffin.[38]

After the farm was sold, Philomen and the children moved to Troy Mills, Iowa, where she was enumerated in the 1880 U.S. Census of Washington Township with the following members of her household: "Climina" (Clemence), 11; "Ida" (Mary Adele), 9; Charles, 8; "Marian" (Minnie), 5; and Joseph Laliberte, 19.[39] How Philomen supported the family is a mystery. In 1887 she returned to Plattsburgh with Clemence, Mary Adele, Charles and Marian, all issue of her marriage with Francois.[40]

Almira, Mary Catherine and young Philomen Laliberte remained in Iowa where they eventually married and raised children of their own. Andrew, too, returned to Iowa after his adventures in the West. Rose Delima Laliberte, known as "Delia," had returned earlier to Plattsburgh where she married in 1878.[41]

For some time following their father's death, Joe and Andrew worked together on the farm in Denison Bottoms. Like many other youth and adults, their imaginations were fired by articles and advertisements appearing in the newspapers from Cedar Rapids and Sioux City, Iowa. All touted the *Union Pacific Railroad* and opportunities available in the West. With their stepmother's anticipated move to Troy Mills and the endless flood of sometimes sensational newspaper reports of gold in the Black Hills of Dakota Territory, Joe and Andrew decided to "go West." It was agreed that Joe would go first and get established, while 17-year-old Andrew bided his time, waiting for news that work was available for him.[42] The Ladue brothers, like many ambitious men from the British Isles to Australia, saw gold as a way out of grinding poverty and the monotony of daily farm life.

The American West
The Black Hills: 1876-1880

The Black Hills today look much as they did when the Sioux set up vast encampments of teepees and freely rode their agile horses over the mountains—before the land was scarred by mining operations. The thud of the huge stamp mills no longer pierces the air and mining is no longer the main industry. The breathtaking high country flows with rushing creeks and the hills rustle with pines bearing such dark needles that, from a distance, they appear nearly black – dark as the spruce of the Yukon.

Here the Miniconjou, Oglala, Brule, Hunkpapa, Sans Arc, Two Kettle and Sihasapas Sioux chased seemingly endless herds of buffalo in their Yellowstone and Powder River hunting grounds. Sioux children played peacefully on the banks of cool rivers. It is a dramatic landscape where jutting stones, like great walls, emerge from the earth, and ancient granite peaks stand in majestic silence.

In 1868, the U.S. Government set aside a large area as a reservation for the Sioux in the Treaty of Fort Laramie. For years prior to the Black Hills gold rush, small parties of prospectors had furtively entered the region, spurred on by news that some of Col. George Armstrong Custer's troopers had found small placer deposits in a stream. News spread quickly of the discovery.[1] Newspapers across the eastern United States quickly picked up the news, exaggerated the modest find, and fanned the flames of hopeful anticipation that enough gold was in the area to fuel another great gold rush rivaling that of California in 1849.

In Sioux City, Iowa, John Gordon read one such report. He organized a prospecting party and headed for the Black Hills (today parts of South Dakota and Wyoming), arriving in December 1874. The U.S. army, learning of the party's illegal presence, located and removed them the following spring.[2] Not easily discouraged, Gordon assembled another party and made a second attempt. The army intervened once more but, with the newspapers following the action and giving the Black Hills publicity, other gold seekers from Iowa and neighboring eastern states attempted covertly to avoid the troops to gain access to the riches.[3]

The federal government, in an attempt to gain control of the potentially mineral-rich region, first tried to purchase the Black Hills from the Sioux. They refused. The government then tried to lease the land. This offer, too, was refused. The Sioux believed that the Great Spirit who lived in the Black Hills had given them the buffalo to use for food and raw materials. They were not about to encourage whites to enter and disturb this sacred territory.

So the decision was made to restrict their movement by confining them to a smaller reservation. This "solution" left much of the territory open to prospectors. Eventually the troops abandoned the area, conveniently leaving the Black Hills hunting grounds of the Sioux at the mercy of those stricken with gold fever.[4] This lack of resolution of control and ownership of the Black Hills would haunt the U.S. Government until the present day and created a tangled web of clouded land titles to be faced by the Sioux, prospectors, mining companies and settlers.

The towns en route to the Dakota Territory began frenetic promotional campaigns to capture trade as men passed through. Occasionally these campaigns tried humor. Deadwood's Board of Trade, for example, in 1881 boasted that it had "the prettiest women, the bravest men, the laziest dogs, the meekest hack-men, the homeliest newspaper reporters, and the toniest bar-tenders in the world."[5]

Accounts of fabulous riches to be found in the Black Hills appeared on the front pages of newspapers including the *Sioux City Times* and publications in the Dakota Territory communities of Yankton and Bismarck. Later, during the Klondike Gold Rush, some accounts would make it seem that nuggets lay on the ground like gravel, ready for easy gathering. The cities of Portland, Seattle, Edmonton and Vancouver—all departure points for the Yukon—would launch similar (and often misleading or inflated) advertising campaigns to capture the miners' trade. Magazines printed special issues, and many firsthand accounts of prospecting trips were published in hardcover editions. Some of this inflated promotion continued during the several Alaska rushes, as late as 1904.

By June 1876, more than a thousand miners were prospecting on Deadwood Creek where it joined Whitewood Creek in a deep canyon on the north edge of the Hills. As in many rushes, most of them came too late and were disappointed. Before the end of March

1876, every foot of ground in Deadwood and Whitewood gulches had been staked.[6]

Following the order typical of the California gold rush of 1849, the seasoned prospectors who arrived first on the scene, from necessity and lack of civil government or law enforcement, developed systems of dealing with disputes and established mining regulations. Miners' meetings determined the size of claims in each camp and meted out a haphazard vigilante justice. But, as boomtowns swelled, civil government soon arrived to provide "law and order" and began the job of establishing a well-governed hamlet they hoped would last and attract permanent residents.

Young men who had not been old enough to serve in the Civil War and veterans who had never gotten over its excitement reveled in this new opportunity for adventure.

The exact date of Joe's departure from Iowa is unknown, but in 1876 he would have boarded the *Union Pacific Railroad* to travel as far west as Fort Sidney, Nebraska. If his train arrived at Fort Sidney prior to September 25—the date the first stagecoach arrived in Deadwood[7]—he would have walked north to Deadwood for the final 200 miles of his journey in company with ox-drawn freight wagons. This casual partnership of prospectors on foot and freight in wagons not only offered the traveler an occasional respite by hitching a ride, but also afforded some degree of protection through safety in numbers.

After September 1876 Joe could have taken the Deadwood Stage,[8] but that presented hardships of its own. Early stagecoaches were suspended on leather straps and passengers felt every rock, branch and buffalo wallow in the rutted roads. Understandably, many suffered from motion sickness. Riding any distance required not only fortitude on the part of travelers, but "demanded a certain etiquette at the time." Passengers were admonished by posters nailed to the depot walls not to "discuss politics or religion" and "to spit on the leeward side."[9] Nine passengers rode inside the jolting coach, but the exterior could accommodate an astonishing seven to nine more, plus baggage. Stages were frequently subjected to holdups by road agents, adding another frisson of danger for the traveler.[10] During the arduous 200-mile journey from Fort Sidney to Deadwood, stops were few, about every 20 miles. Dirt roads were not graded and in warm weather clouds of dust added to the misery of weary travelers. Winter offered a different challenge as the heavily loaded coaches got stuck in snow. After a thaw, passengers were expected to disembark, wading through oceans of mud, to help turn the wheels out of the mire. In her book, *Old Deadwood Days*, Estelline Bennett wrote that the stages carried basic equipment for use in removing the "gumbo" and that "all the men passengers got down and scraped it off with spades...."[11]

Stagecoach drivers throughout the American West had total authority over what happened inside and outside the coach, and many became legends in their own time. They had to be fearless men of integrity, much like the captain of a ship, and took great pride in "getting the stage through." Although arriving on time would have been an additional point of pride, obstacles frequently deprived the drivers of attaining a perfect record. Obstacles included hailstones big enough to kill rabbits and rattlesnakes, and ambushes by, or running battles with, angry Sioux. Such ambushes and battles became grist for many Western films, most recently in *Dances with Wolves* where a pickled-egg-eating freight driver pleads with his ambushers not to hurt his mules, even as they fill him with arrows. The only respite from Indians was during the colder months, when they generally stayed close to home.

Joe Ladue arrived in the rough new camp of Deadwood where dry-land gulls screeched overhead and tortoises spent most of the day seeking shade under wagons. He felt ready for any challenge, with "about one hundred dollars in his pocket, full of grit, industry, honesty and determination."[12] He wanted to get the lay of this new land before trying his luck at prospecting. The first employment he found in the area in 1876 was not mining, but "as a contractor for moving houses and doing other public work, meanwhile keeping an eye out for a place in a quartz mine."[13] Deadwood, Central City and Lead (pronounced "leed," denoting a vein of ore containing gold), like other mining camps, were built near networks of shafts and tunnels. Cave-ins on the surface were common and buildings were frequently left hanging on the edges of gaping holes, creating a ready market for house movers. And, as in all mining camps, working the ground took precedence over buildings, so they had to be relocated, usually to areas that had been previously worked or were not considered valuable mining property. In order to create a new community, permanent or not, public works offered alternative employment for the large number of idle men finding neither ground to stake nor work in the mines of others.

Joe was lucky to have arrived in 1876, because the following year, the first big railroad strike in the U.S. occurred and many out-of-work railroaders headed for the Black Hills looking for employment.

Deadwood is located in a narrow valley, or gulch, where buildings clamber up the hillsides, joining the retail district below by steep wooden stairs. The town promptly became the trading center for all the small mining communities in the area, including Lead, Gayville, Central City and Rochford. Most boomtowns were built near the goldfields for obvious business reasons. Locating on low land near a requisite water supply made them prone to flooding and, if built in narrow canyons or valleys, created a natural wind tunnel to carry flames when fires swept through destroying the wooden buildings. To add to the fire danger, sawdust or thick layers of newsprint were used to insulate the walls of stores and homes as a defense against the bitter Dakota winters. But this pitiful attempt to provide one form of protection proved fatal when hours after fires had been extinguished the trapped embers smoldered and re-ignited. Because of omnipresent fire danger, volunteer fire or "hose" companies were among the first civic groups organized, and they held an undisputed position of importance.

The first accommodations in Deadwood were wickiups or lean-tos erected against rock faces. As in most frontier settlements and boomtowns, these were followed by canvas tents, which were supplanted by hastily constructed log buildings. If a camp lasted more than a year or two and showed potential for permanency, rather elaborate brick or quarried stone buildings were constructed.

Mining camps were, by their nature, temporary. The tents and basic log or frame buildings, heated by wood stoves and lighted by candles or kerosene lamps, were frequently destroyed by fire or flood, and the men who lived and worked in those buildings moved on to the next location as soon as rumors of a new discovery reached town. In gold camps the talk was always of the latest find, who made it, how much to the pan, how much was taken out in a season, who sold out, who bought it and where the previous owner had gone. In twenty-first century terminology, it's called "networking" and the men who moved from camp to camp frequently knew one another. Early newspapers from Deadwood, Tombstone and Dawson City repeat names hauntingly familiar—names of entrepreneurs, entertainers, restaurant owners, saloon keepers, prospectors and confidence men. Lawman Wyatt Earp, for example, had a hand in Tombstone and eventually kept a saloon in Nome.

Joe Ladue was an astute observer and hard worker from an early age, and these attributes served him well all his life. House moving gave him a modest income and security while he kept on the lookout for more exciting opportunities. On May 20, 1877, the Hidden Treasure Mine opened its 30-stamp mill in neighboring Central City[14] and advertised for an engineer. (A stamp mill is used to crush gold-bearing quartz that is then washed with water and treated with either mercury or cyanide to separate the gold which, in quartz rock, is typically very fine.) The position paid $4 a day. Joe had no formal training and "had never run a steam engine" but his motivation and mechanical aptitude got him the job, and he was hired on as engineer at the Hidden Treasure Mine. Riding on his natural ability, hard work and eagerness to learn, he held that position for 18 months. In 1878, Joe was promoted and advanced to the position of foreman of the night shift. His salary then rose to $5 a day[15] compared to teachers in neighboring Nebraska being paid $16 a month.

As foreman, he was now established sufficiently to offer his younger brother a job at the Hidden Treasure. Joe sent a message and Andrew soon "trecked (sic) across the prairies"[16] and joined Joe in Central City. Shortly after his brother's arrival, Joe received an offer from a larger, 60-stamp mill. He was hired as superintendent at the princely wage of $10 a day. He held this position for a year, absorbing valuable technical knowledge. Years later, reporter John Sleicher, of *Leslie's Illustrated Weekly Magazine* wrote that during his Central City days Joe "spent all his leisure time in studying the secrets of gold-mining."[17] Although in decades to come Joe would prospect in distant locations and conduct operations on his own placer claims, his confidence in hard-rock mining and stamp mills never wavered. The noisy Black Hills mills and the tough, independent men who labored in them served as his classroom and teachers, but the lure of gold would take him farther and farther away from his boyhood home in Schuyler Falls and the dusty towns of Dakota Territory.

During the period Joe and Andrew lived and worked in the Black Hills they witnessed events that would shape the American West. The Sioux had observed, with shock and loathing, the trespass of miners, cattle ranchers, buffalo hunters and soldiers into their sacred lands. The resulting Battle of the Little Bighorn—then known as the Custer Massacre—was one in which the Sioux won the battle but lost the war. On June 26, 1876, the clash of Custer's Seventh Cavalry with superior numbers of Cheyenne, Arapaho and Sioux on a desolate, windswept Montana hill tolled the death knell for the freedom and traditional way of life of the proud Sioux Nation. Thereafter, they helplessly observed from smaller reservations where eastern-appointed Indian agents doled out rations, as their lands were taken over by miners and settlers, "sod busters" who often turned fragile prairie to dust that could blow away.

The newcomers had little understanding of or sympathy for the Sioux desire to preserve their ancestral hills and grasslands. The resulting skirmishes between the angry Indians and the go west whites continued into 1881.

Complicated legal resolutions were achieved regarding land and mineral rights of non-Indians, but, even before that date, it was too late for the Hidden Treasure Mine, which had taught Joe so much. The constant battles over land titles, a lawsuit with adjacent mine owners and frequent flooding of tunnels all took their toll, and the mine was closed. Other stamp mills suffered similar fates.

Meanwhile, two predictable events occurred that effectively ended the sudden euphoria of prosperity in the Black Hills. Heavier than usual snow fell the winter and spring in 1877-1878. (The weather has changed little in 130 years. On May 11, 2002, weather forecasters predicted 8" to 11" of snow were expected in the mountains of the Black Hills). When it melted, a flood occurred obliterating everything in its path. The ever optimistic citizens of Deadwood rebuilt. But the new town was short-lived. Joe and Andrew were working in nearby Central City on September 26, 1879, when the boomtown of Deadwood burned to the ground. The fire started at night in a bakery and raced to other buildings.[18] The flames roared out of control. When the sun rose the next morning the awful reality was revealed. The business section lay in ashes. It was an all too familiar scene to the miners.[19] Deadwood had embodied the spirit of the Old West and had spawned legends in American folklore. Wild Bill Hickok and his old friends, the poet scout Jack Crawford, Calamity Jane, and famed Sheriff Seth Bullock, whom Theodore Roosevelt saw as a man who embodied all that was good in an American, walked its streets. Men and women sought and, in some cases, made fortunes. It had become legendary as a rough mining camp and its sometimes violent history was romanticized by reporters and dime novelists. Deadwood rebuilt, this time with red brick, and many of those buildings stand today. Miners continued to work their placer claims and when the gold ran out they went on to the next Eldorado, mourning the loss of the brotherhood and integrity that existed in the earliest days of the camp.

Joe, now a mature young man of 25, had been away from Schuyler Falls for nearly four years, having spent some time in Center Point following the death of his father and then moving on to the Black Hills. Stamp mills were closing, some hoping to reopen at a later date. Joe would not have easily abandoned his job of superintendent of a mill at his then-generous salary. It is a probability that this disruption in mill operations afforded Joe leisure to travel back to Schuyler Falls. He missed his surrogate family—James Henry Lobdell, his wife, Carrie, and their young son, Will. So he made the trip east in the winter of 1879–1880. He paid his stagecoach fare at the Sidney Stage and Express Office on the ground floor of Merchants Hotel in Deadwood,[20] then rode the stage south to Fort Sidney, where he boarded the eastbound train. Arriving in Schuyler Falls, he stayed with his old friends at the Lobdell farm.[21] Homecoming must have been bittersweet since both of his parents were dead, and none of his siblings were living in the area. Perhaps hardest to swallow, he returned without wealth or success after nearly four years of steady employment in the Black Hills.

The *Plattsburgh Republican* reported Joe's return:

> Mr. Arnold Lewis and Joseph Ladue returned to this place recently from Black Hills. Mr. Lewis has been absent 3 years and will remain but a few weeks. He will be leaving, as we learn, about March lst with his family to make his future home in Colorado. Mr. Ladue returns soon to the Black Hills.

Arnold Lewis was suffering from tuberculosis and moved to Colorado desperately seeking a cure. Although Lewis was headed to California in February 1876, when the *Republican* reported his departure, he may have stopped and stayed in the Black Hills.[22]

The brevity of the note in the *Republican* makes it seem that Joe was reluctant to be interviewed. Characteristically, he failed to include any details of his 1879-80 trip in the biographical information supplied 11 years later to the *Leslie's* interviewer. Clinton County historian Emily McMasters wrote, 85 years later, that Joe's letters from the Black Hills and the Yukon had been destroyed by a fire at the Lobdell farm.[23] Thus many of his activities, motivations and thoughts lie permanently in shadow.

As Joe prepared to return to Deadwood, he found himself in the embarrassing position of having to borrow $100 from the Lobdells to pay the train fare. Apparently, all the salary he had earned from his work in the Central City stamp mills had vanished. Emily McMaster's notes state that he had been "enticed into a game and lost all his money."[24] She provides no source, however. If this is true, the devout Methodist Lobdells would not have been sympathetic. There is no evidence, during his later years in the Yukon, that Joe gambled except Jack McQuesten's brief reference to "playing cards" as Joe and his party wiled away the long winter of 1882 at Fort Reliance.[25] However, the chief recreational activity in all the camps was gambling and this was true long before, and after, Deadwood. There were more saloons and gambling halls in boomtowns than any other form of business, and the pitfalls of victims and dangers of card games and spinning roulette wheels abound in Western and gold rush lore. (There was a small minority that amused itself with keeping diaries, hunting game for the pot, writing letters, home musicales, reciting poetry, and writing and reading aloud "papers" on subjects from taxidermy to South America. For most, however, the lure of dance halls, whiskey and games of chance was irresistible.)

It is possible that with Joe's absolute determination to make his fortune in minerals, he had been enticed into one of the speculating schemes rampant as the boom era in the Black Hills waned. Naïve miners often invested heavily in bogus corporations and were bilked of their hard-earned money. John W. Leonard, in *Gold Fields of the Klondike*, commented that Ladue "went to the Black Hills in search of gold. He met with considerable success at first, but afterwards lost every dollar in a speculation in Deadwood."[26]

If he succumbed to the temptation of the gaming tables, Deadwood conmen had another trick up their sleeves; those who lost at gambling could write orders on future wages to pay their debts.[27] Whatever the truth behind his empty pockets, Joe had nothing to show for the years he worked in Central City, and the kindness of the Lobdells came through for him again as they advanced the funds for his return West.

When Joe arrived in the Black Hills in February 1880, he resumed work for mining companies. Residents of Deadwood felt so isolated from the outside world that daily stagecoach arrivals and departures marked "high lights of the day."[28] The local paper published names of passengers traveling on the daily stagecoaches and Joe Ladue appears twice in 1880: The February 24, 1880, issue of the *Black Hills Daily Times* reported "Departures by the Sidney coach yesterday: Mr. Cordeiro, J. F. Graham, John Hanley, Joseph 'La Due'."

And, on April 20, 1880, the same newspaper reported "Departures by Custer coach yesterday morning: W. H. Dwyer, T. F. Metcalf, Pat McHugh, Frank Vanocker, R. D. Kelly, Joseph Ladue, A. Kello."

When the U.S. Census was taken June 1, 1880, it showed Joe Ladue living and working at Rochford, Dakota Territory, 20 miles south of Deadwood. His occupation was "Works In Quartz Mill," although his specific position was not indicated. Joe shared a residence with Abraham Calder, 35, a quartz miner from New York State.[29]

Andrew, now employed at the Stand By mine in Rochford, was listed in the same census as a "laborer," living in a residence with five other millworkers,[30] which suggests that it was probably a miners' boarding house.[31]

Joe remained in Rochford until September. The prosperous days in the Black Hills were over. Newspapers across the country had reported the demise of the golden days of Deadwood and, at the same time, carried enticing accounts of silver discoveries in Tombstone, Arizona Territory. He decided to leave the Black Hills, and on payday that month[32] he sold some personal property to J. S. Graham and instructed that payment be made directly to his brother, Andrew (J. S. Graham was probably the same man with whom

Joe was traveling on the Sidney stage in February.) The "obligation" read:

> September 26, 1880
> J. S. Graham. Please pay to Andrew Ladue for those shoes and for that stove, which amounts to $29.00, and oblige.
> (Signed) Joseph Ladue.[33]

He seems to have been penniless again because he cashed paychecks given to him by Andrew totaling $180. He then boarded the southbound stage. The Ladue brothers never saw each other again.

Did Andrew turn over these paychecks in repayment for his fare west? Were they a loan to Joe? No one knows.

New Mexico and Arizona: 1880-1881

Between September 1880 and spring 1882, Joe continued his search for mineral wealth. He stated in the *Leslie's* interview that he decided "to strike out to make a fortune." Because he had not accomplished that goal in Dakota Territory, his quest now took him through Colorado by rail and stage and into the territories of Arizona and New Mexico.[34] In the fall of 1880 he arrived in Tombstone, Arizona, the town founded in 1878 by Edward Schieffelin, a veteran prospector who had finally "struck it rich." Like so many other prospectors, Schieffelin had found a lode of silver ore but lacked the funds to develop it into a paying concern. To raise capital, he formed a consortium, which included his brother, Al, and an assayer, Richard Gird. As he prepared to file for the *Tombstone Mining District*, his friends at Fort Huachuca, aware of the dangers of Apache attacks, half-jokingly remarked to Ed after learning he was to prospect alone, that "the only thing you will find is your tombstone." He proved them wrong.

The town of Tombstone quickly grew, spreading out awkwardly in a shallow dip on the side of a hill. It was soon the center of enormous mining activity. Land speculators moved in, applied for an illegal patent, leased and sold lots on dirt streets laid out in a neat grid. Stamp mills soon were pulverizing the silver loose from tons of quartz, and fortunes filled the pockets of many miners who had followed boomtowns all over the American West.[35] Active mining lasted almost seven years before rising underground water forced suspension of operations, but millions in silver and gold were extracted.

One of the fortunate fellows to partake of those millions was Edward D. Gillespie, born in Ireland in 1854, and naturalized a U.S. citizen in California. From September 1879 to February 1881 he was involved in five separate deeds of mine transactions in the Tombstone Mining District.[36] Gillespie's mining interests in the Tombstone area overlapped with his establishing the *Gillespie District* in southwestern New Mexico, 150 miles to the east, an area served by both stagecoach and the *Southern Pacific Railroad*.

New Mexico's mining activities at that time were primarily in the mountainous regions of the southwest corner of the territory, an area known as the Bootheel. Mines near the boomtown of Silver City produced gold, silver and zinc. Tailing dumps along the Mogollon Mountains still attest to the quantity of ore dug during the boom.

Nevertheless, Silver City was a magnet for those seeking their fortunes. It was surrounded by small satellite communities populated by prospectors, miners, storekeepers, stable hands, stagecoach drivers, blacksmiths and prostitutes. The names given of the settlements resound with adventure: Pinos Altos (Tall Pines), Buckhorn, Shakespeare, Hachita (Little Hatchet), Soldier's Farewell and Apache Wells.

The Gillespie District was an active one located "on the northeast slopes of the Animas Mountains." The site was also called the "Red Hill District," and "the two principal mines were the Gillespie and the Red Hill, both producing lead, gold, silver and copper."[37] More specifically, it was 50 miles south of Lordsburg, 20 miles from the border with Mexico and 30 miles southwest of Hachita, New Mexico Territory. It was "close to the Mexican and Arizona border, making it a convenient hideout for the Curly Bill Brocius and Clanton gangs of Tombstone, Arizona, 150 miles to the west."[38]

Gillespie "sank several deep shafts and found silver chloride. No production records from the era have survived and silver chloride is rare in New Mexico today. The Red Hill Mine workings were extensive and last operated in 1950 when 836 tons of shipping-grade ore were recovered from the old mine dump. The property today is abandoned and considered worked out."[39]

Ed Gillespie formed a consortium of prospectors, among them, Joe Ladue. The precise terms of their agreements are unknown, but they staked out claims working in tandem. "Staking" is literally driving a stick, wooden stake or post into the ground as a boundary mark. All four corners of a claim were usually staked. The size of a claim was determined by the laws of the particular mining district. Portions of tree trunks were also used as stakes—the bark removed, and a date, dimensions and name carved into the wood.

Joe seemed to have a special role in the consortium since two of the claims it filed indicate a location near the "Gillespie and Ladue Camp," suggesting they had a partnership-like relationship. They labored from December 1880 through June 27, 1881, scaling the mountainsides of the Continental Divide. Since many of these slopes were treeless and wooden stakes unavailable, they placed stone monuments or cairns to designate boundaries for each claim. (In New Mexico Territory at that time, what is known as a "claim" today was referred to as a "mine" and a record sheet of transfers of ownership was not kept on each "mine." Rather, every time it changed hands it was simply re-recorded chronologically in large ledgers.)

On January 10, 1881, at 5:30 P.M. one of Ed Gillespie's associates appeared at the office of E. Stine, probate clerk in Grant County, Silver City, New Mexico and filed in the Patent Mining Book the following claims:

> IRON HORSE MINE, located December 4, 1880, "in compliance with the requirements of the Mining Act of Congress, approved May 10, 1872,...a claim on a course of lead lode 600 feet x 1500 feet situate in the Gillespie Mining District, County of Grant, New Mexico...This claim is situated in the range of mountains about twenty miles west of the Hatchet range of mountains and about thirty miles South of the S. P. (Southern Pacific) Rail Road and, about twenty miles East of the Stean (Stein) Peak range of mountains, and, about twenty miles North of the line of Mexico, and shall be known as the Iron Horse Mine. The locators filing this claim were Edward Gillespie and Joseph Ladue.

Gillespie's relations with Ladue allowed the latter to locate mines on his own, such as:

> ETA LOBDEL MINE, located December 14, 1880, "in compliance with the requirements of the Mining Act of Congress, approved May 10, 1872,...a claim on a course of lead lode 600 feet x 1500 feet situate in the Gillespie Mining District, County of Grant, New Mexico...This claim is situated in the Range of mountains about twenty miles west of the Hatchet Range of mountains and about thirty miles South of the S. P. Rail road and about twenty miles East of the Stean Peak Range of mountains and about twenty miles north of the line of Mexico, and shall be known as the Eta Lobdel Mine. Located
> December 14, 1880, Joseph Ladue.

Joe surely held high hopes for his individual mining claim when he named it in honor of a member of the New York family that had been his source of affection and support since childhood. Perhaps he dreamed of repaying that $100 loan many times over.

During the period from December 4, 1880 (when Joe's name first appears in the Grant County records), and June 27, 1881 (when his name last appears in the records), the following claims demonstrate Joe's energetic participation in the Gillespie District:

Sole Locator:
Eta Lobdell Mine, located December 14, 1880
Home Stake Mine, located December 4, 1880
Sun Shine Mine, located December 14, 1880

Co-Locator:
Iron Horse Mine, located December 4, 1880
Pride of the West Mine, located April 17, 1881
Maud L. Mine, located February 18, 1881
Merimack Mine, located February 28, 1881
Lion Mine, located March 2, 1881
Thomas Price Mine, located May 20, 1881

Witness to other Locators:
Hera Mine, located January 25, 1881
Connors Mine, located February 17, 1881
Flagstaff Mine, located February 17, 1881
New Mexico Mine, located February 17, 1881
Nevada Mine, located February 26, 1881
Orizaba Mine, located February 17, 1881
Sacramento Mine, located February 18, 1881
Senator Mine, located February 18, 1881
Washington Mine, located March 21, 1881
Buckeye Mine, located January 27, 1881
Keystone Mine, located January 31, 1881
Frankfort Mine, located February 15, 1881
Silver Cloud Mine, located May 4, 1881 (the locator of this claim was Thomas Fox and a strange clause in the description states "...one half mile from Gillespie camp and James Etta Labale (sic) on the west...") Obviously, the clerk made an error

> either in this entry or in recording Joe's mine earlier as the "Eta Lobdel" (sic). We can only guess at the correct name of this claim.
> Trust to Luck Mine, located April 26, 1881
> Silver Star Mine, located June 3, 1881 and filed of record June 27, 1881

Other names appearing repeatedly in the *Grant County* records in similar capacities were:

> J. F. Smith, David Mackey, Richard Connors, Edward Spangler, Richard Tremble, Patrick Fleming, Jna. (Jonathan) Dennison, Hew (sic) Griffin, Michael Law, Thomas Fitzpatrick, J. A. Scott, W. A. Freeze, R. R. McClowd (sic), Byron Scoville, Charles Peters, George W. Whitcher, Baker Brand, F. Weidenjoefer, H. Meinard (sic), Th. (Thomas) Cathey, Christ. (Christopher) Noll, Thomas Chaty (probably the same as Thomas Cathey), R. E. McCoy, O. L. McAvoy (sic) and Peter Doyle, James Courtney and Chas. Phesant (sic).[40]

The group remained in the area for some time moving between the Gillespie camp and Tombstone and, although their location was "about thirty miles south of the *Southern Pacific Railroad*," it was necessary to travel by horseback or stage north to the depot at Lordsburg. The train made its way west across the flat, desert plain where dust devils swirling in the distance looked like smoke rising from a dozen hostile campfires. Treeless mountains surrounded the great basin and the view was broken only by stunted yucca plants, their tall stems unwilling to surrender the clusters of seed pods from the previous year. The train ride ended at Benson, Arizona, where one of three stagelines[41] waited to transport passengers the final 20 miles south to Tombstone, "The Town Too Tough to Die."

The danger from indigenes confronting Joe and other whites in southwestern New Mexico Territory cannot be exaggerated. Long before the time of the first contact with western Europeans in 1540, when the Spanish explorer Francisco Vasquez de Coronado (1510-54?) marched north from Mexico City in search of the fabled Seven Cities of Gold, indigenous tribes had roamed the region in complete freedom. Under the rule of Spain, the traditional way of life had undergone drastic changes, not only from the new Christian religion inflicted on them by royal command, but also as the territory was gradually settled by colonists awarded land grants by the crown. The Spanish introduced horses, which later became central to the lives of many Indians. However, at first, the indigenes were forbidden to own the animals.

Little mineral development was allowed by the Spanish crown. After Mexico gained independence in 1821, the area was constantly being explored for minerals. Apache raids on prospectors, miners and settlers increased after the United States annexed the territories of New Mexico and Arizona following the Mexican War, 1846-1848, and the government instituted the cruel reservation system.

During his time in Dakota Territory, Joe and other prospectors had their own apprehensions regarding the Sioux, but those skirmishes paled by comparison to Apache raids in Grant and surrounding counties.

The Apaches knew how to live in this harsh, demanding environment and had honed their survival skills to a fine art. They lived in wickiups of leafy branches and grass arranged over a dome-shaped frame. They hunted deer and gathered berries in the forested mountain valleys, and agave, yucca and mesquite beans on more arid land. They consumed everything from the inner bark of yellow pine trees to tumbleweed roots and rattlesnake meat.

The Apaches rebelled against intruders by staging frequent raids on settlers, mining camps and hapless travelers. The cycle of violence continued as settlers, miners and U.S. Cavalry joined in retaliation while desperate Apache bands eluded their pursuers across New Mexico and Arizona and over the border into old Mexico. In the "Bootheel" of New Mexico this attack and chase activity was directed by strong leaders. Cochise led the Chiracahuas, and Mangas Coloradas, the Mimbrenos. Cochise and fewer than 200 warriors held the army at bay for more than ten years. When Cochise did make peace with the U.S., Geronimo (c. 1829-1909) refused to agree with it, and with a small band went into the mountains. He and his followers terrorized ranchers on both sides of the border for 14 years.[42] Nine years before Joe's arrival, John Bullard, a prominent citizen of Silver City, was killed during an Apache encounter. The early settlers "never forgave the Apaches for...his...untimely death."[43]

Dry-country miners or "desert rats" were particularly vulnerable to Indian attack or ambush. Men of the Gillespie District took to working in heavily armed groups as they searched for veins and lodes and piled up their stone cairns. There were other hazards as well. The stagecoach ride west to Benson, Arizona Territory was also fraught with danger. While travelers going west by rail could partially let down their guard, the $3 stage fare from the depot at Benson 25 miles south to Tombstone bought, instead of relaxation, an uninvited thrill when outlaw gangs held up the stages and took bank or mine cash boxes, as well as valuables belonging to the passengers.

By April 19, 1881, part of the Gillespie group was back in Tombstone, and Arizona's famous newspaper, the *Tombstone Epitaph*, ran the following feature article on the Gillespie District:

> About one week ago we gave the first account of this district that has been published. From Mr. E. D. Gillespie, the discoverer, who is now in Tombstone, we have learned some additional facts about it. Mr. Gillespie discovered the district about two years ago, but did not go back until last October where he has been ever since. There are thirty men now in the district all from Tombstone. Among them are James Courtney, Michael Connors, Joseph Ladue, M. Lane, and Al Frazer, all well-known here. Mr. Gillespie has four locations, all showing well. They are the Great Western, Sunrise, Bay State, and Southern New Mexico. On the Great Western he has a shaft down 120 feet with a vein 2 1/2 feet wide, showing rich ore with native silver...The district is 30 miles south from Lordsburg on the S. P. (Southern Pacific) Railroad. There is an abundance of wood, water and grass. The great want of the district is a store carrying a general stock of merchandise. Provisions can be obtained at Lordsburg and Galeyville but for mining supplies they have to come to Tombstone, a distance of 140 miles.[44]

The men listed in the article, and others whose names appear in the Grant County patent book, were associated with Gillespie and staked and filed claims on his behalf but also staked and filed claims of their own as part of their agreement with him. Gillespie was known well enough in the area to have had a mountain named for him. Gillespie Mountain, with an elevation of 7,300 feet, rises on New Mexico maps at the center of the Continental Divide, about 20 miles from the border between the United States and Mexico and approximately 12 miles from the location of the old Phelps Dodge Smelter. Stein's Mountain lies approximately three miles from the *Southern Pacific Railroad*, while Stean (Stein) Peak (used as a surveyor's marking point in the Gillespie and Ladue claims) is a stone's throw from the New Mexico/Arizona border.

Joe had filed individually on the "Eta Lobdel Mine," "Home Stake Mine" and "Sun Shine Mine." It is likely, as part of his agreement with Ed Gillespie, these three claims belonged solely to him. Later, in the September 16, 1897 interview with John Sleicher, Joe related that he "found several promising prospects, and for one of these,...which subsequently failed to meet his expectations, he, unfortunately for (himself), refused an offer of twenty-five thousand dollars."

Joe was probably aware of the *Miners' Ten Commandments*, written during the California gold rush by a miner and newspapermen. Many miners posted broadsides of these commandments on their cabin walls. Commandment VII reads:

> Thou shalt not grow discouraged, and think of going home before thou hast made thy 'pile,' because thou hast not 'struck a lead,' nor found 'a rich crevice,' nor Sunk a hole upon a 'pocket'; lest, in going home, thou shalt leave four dollars per day, and go to work, ashamed, at fifty cents, and serve thee right; for here, by staying, thou mightest strike a lead and fifty dollars a day, and thy manly self-respect, and then go home with enough to make thyself and others happy.[45]

Miners didn't give up easily. Tombstone, Arizona, the town named in reply to a joke about death, the Town too Tough to Die, became a mining center, in spite of the fact that it was not served by a railroad. By 1881 the population was between 7,000 and 10,000,[46] including nearby mining camps, and historians consider it one of the most colorful and violent towns of the Old West.

The ultimate example of its violence took place on October 26, 1881. On that date, the gunfight at the OK Corral livery stable[47] blazed its way into newspaper headlines, the popular imagination, pulp fiction and the history books when Wyatt Earp, his brothers and "Doc" Holliday shot dead Billy Clanton and Frank and Tom McLaury, adding violence to a feud that would last for years.

On the other hand, most of the population of Tombstone was drawn there not for duels in the sun, but in the hope of finding wealth in the silver mines. Ordinary citizens and miners in 1881 had a number of lawful ways to occupy their time. They could have dined at *Nellie Cashman's Russ House* hotel restaurant on the corner of Fifth and Toughnut Streets for the grand sum of four bits,[48] or posed for a portrait at *Charles O. Farciot's Photography Gallery* in nearby Charleston. Guns and ammunition were in plentiful supply at *Spangenberg's Gun Shop* on Fourth Street, a half a block away from what had become the most infamous livery stable in Western lore.

Later, Farciot joined Ed Schieffelin and his party in 1882 on a prospecting trip to Alaska, and Cashman would eventually follow the rush to the Klondike.

In fact, Cashman might be considered the feminine counterpart of Joe Ladue. A petite, pretty woman with jet black hair and dark eyes, she was gifted with a stamina and toughness denied most men.

Nellie Cashman was born in Queenstown, county Cork, Ireland, in 1850.[49] According to her long-time friend, John Clum,[50] editor and publisher of the *Tombstone Epitaph*, she arrived in the United States "soon after the Civil War," although other accounts give her arrival date as early 1855. Nellie, her older sister Fannie (Frances) and their widowed mother emigrated together from Ireland. They settled in Boston for a time. As a teenager, Nellie worked as an elevator operator in Washington, D.C. In 1869, the Cashman trio moved to San Francisco. By 1872, Fannie was married and Nellie was in Virginia City, Nevada, operating a short-order restaurant. In 1874 she joined the gold rush to Cassiar, British Columbia. There she prospected, ran a miners' boarding house on remote Telegraph Creek and earned a reputation as a soft touch.

In the fall she went to Victoria for the winter and to collect supplies. But while there she heard that many of the 200 miners at Telegraph Creek were sick with scurvy. She hired six men to return with her. It took them 77 days to reach camp. But they brought in lime juice and other supplies and cured the men, who gratefully nicknamed her "Angel of the Cassiar."

Although women did not stampede to gold rushes in such large numbers as men did, some were fully as adventurous and mobile—as Nellie's history proves.

In 1878 she left the Cassiar to visit her mother, sister, nieces and nephew in San Francisco. When she heard about a strike in Tucson in 1879, she headed there and opened the Delmonico Restaurant. But wanderlust won out again, and she moved to Tombstone, about 80 miles south. There she formed a partnership with Jennie Swift, and the two opened the Russ House—popularly known as the Nellie Cashman Hotel. When her sister's husband, Thomas Cunningham, died in 1880, Nellie brought Frances and her five children to Tombstone to live with her. When Frances died in 1883 of tuberculosis, Nellie raised her nieces and nephew with remarkable flexibility and understanding.

Nellie was a leading citizen who helped organize the city and county hospital as well as the first Catholic church. She established a boarding house in nearby Bisbee, too. She also opened restaurants or boarding houses in Harqua Halan, Jerome, Nogales, Prescott and Yuma. For a time, dressed in men's clothes but distinguished by her brogue, she prospected in Baja California.

When news of the Klondike strike reached her in 1897, Nellie couldn't resist. She put together a grubstake of $5,000 and headed for the Chilkoot Trail. In Dawson, she opened a store in the basement of the Hotel Donovan and another Delmonico, and handed out free meals to men down on their luck. She was known to give miners loans, spent time nursing the sick, and was a tireless fundraiser for St. Mary's Hospital. She was held in such high esteem that her entrance into a saloon or dance hall was the signal for every man in the place to rise to his feet.

She acquired No. 19 Below Discovery on Bonanza Creek and it proved a prudent investment. Nellie became wealthy, but gave most of it away as grubstakes and in civic-minded contributions. She lived in Dawson until 1904, when she followed yet another strike to Fairbanks and opened a grocery store. Ivan Lake, writing in the Alaska Sportsman, described her as "hard as flint, with endurance on the trail equal to that of any man, but with an inexhaustible fund of good humor and a cheery word and a helping hand for anyone in need."[51]

In her later years, while living in Alaska, she developed pneumonia and sought medical treatment from the Sisters of St. Ann in Victoria, British Columbia, where she died on January 4, 1925, and was buried in the Catholic cemetery there.[57]

In 2003 the Russ House building in Tombstone was operating as "The Nellie Cashman Restaurant," and one wall memorialized her as the "Angel of the Camps."

Nellie Cashman was honored with a 29-cent U.S. postage stamp issued October 18, 1994, in Laramie, Wyoming. The stamp was part of the set of 20 called Legends of the West.

Although Tombstone held attractions for Nellie for nearly ten years, Joe was not as spellbound by this hot, dusty town in the Arizona desert. By 1882 he had moved on to San Francisco. In later years, the town of Dawson City in the distant Yukon would present a distinct contrast to the roaring camps Joe Ladue had known in the American West.

The Yukon Years: 1882-1898
Wonderful Prospects in Newly Found Places

It's the great, big, broad land 'way up yonder,
It's the forests where silence has lease;
It's the beauty that fills me with wonder,
It's the stillness that fills me with peace.
"The Spell of the Yukon," by Robert Service

The region takes its name from the Loucheux word Yu-kun-ah, or "great river." It is the name of a 2,000-mile giant that begins in southern Yukon Territory, flows northwest, and then arcs southwest through the heart of Alaska and to the Bering Sea.

The Yukon was prehistorically and historically an important transportation route, summer and winter, in a region that still has few roads. Its banks abound with history and artifacts. It flows through open tundra, forested valleys, rock bluffs, muskeg and black spruce woods. Rainstorms can raise the water level downstream without warning. Some areas have to be portaged, especially at high water during spring runoff and where there are rapids. Williwaws—sudden violent winds—can spill over mountains onto the river, raising whitecaps and waves capable of capsizing canoes. And there are constantly shifting sandbars.

Much of the territory is mountainous and more than half is wooded with spruce, poplar and lodgepole pine. The short summers are warm and brilliant. The winters are often bone chilling.

Joe left Tombstone regretting the decision he had made in New Mexico that resulted in missing out on the very fortune he traveled west to find. In San Francisco, however, he met others who shared his passion for prospecting. Some had known him in Deadwood or Tombstone; all were speculating about where they should look next.

The Yukon calls men with fortitude, and it called Joe Ladue.

For decades, experienced American prospectors embraced a hunch that if they followed the mountain ranges north there was more gold to be found. They were aware of drifts and faults, always looking for the mother lode—the principal vein of rich ore in a district or region.

Some had read the writings of explorer and geologist Alexander von Humboldt who believed that "the greatest mineral deposits lay in and about the Arctic Circle."[1] And so they did, especially in the rocks not far from a future boomtown, Dawson City.

In 1857 placer gold (loose flakes or nuggets found in alluvial or glacial deposits) was discovered in British Columbia on the Fraser River. Then in 1871 and 1874 big strikes were made in Canada's Cassiar Mountains[2] just south of the 207-thousand-square-mile region known as the Yukon District. At that time, only three prospectors were known to have ventured into the district and little gold had been found.

As the diggings ran dry in the Cassiar, miners traced the Stikine River to its mouth, finding rich sandbars along the way. By 1880 they had moved northeasterly up the coast of Alaska. In the mountains behind present-day Juneau, Cassiar veterans Richard Harris and Joseph Juneau were taken by Auk Tlingit chief Kowee to a location that became known as the Silver Bow Basin. They found rocks and lumps of gold "like peas and beans." Neighboring Douglas Island also proved rich in hard-rock deposits.

The region around Juneau, still known as the Gold Belt, had some limited deposits of placer gold that could be seen with the naked eye and sometimes removed with low-tech methods like panning, rocking and sluicing. Hard work with a pan allows one miner to process about half a cubic yard of gravel a day. A Tom and Riffle box allows production to rocket to 30 cubic yards of placer material a day. However, most of the gold in the Belt was microscopic and had to be removed with hard-rock methods including blasting and crushing with stamps (descending pestles operated by water or steam power). Hundreds of stamps began to operate round-the-clock, 362 days a year in Juneau. Soon the world's largest quartz mill (gold is often found in quartz) was in operation, producing up to $500,000 a year in gold.[3]

Five years before Harris and Juneau made their way up Gold Creek to Silver Bow Basin, Joe heard the story about the daring adventures of George Holt, who in August of 1875,[4] with at least one other prospector, crossed over Chilkoot Pass[5] and traveled deep into the Yukon District of Canada's North West Territories.[6] Holt's party had paddled a canoe to Dyea, Alaska, at the north end of Lynn

Canal. (Sudden severe winds and waves on Lynn Canal can capsize small boats, and to this day there are uncharted rocks.) From Dyea, Holt somehow eluded the Tlingit Chilkats who had, for years, jealously guarded this trade route from sea level into the Interior and menaced anyone who wanted to enter the valuable territory they considered their exclusive domain.[7]

Holt made it over the pass without incident, but later said that on one of the lakes at the headwaters of the Yukon River he met a group of Takus who showed such signs of hostility that his party of prospectors was forced to "precipitately" retrace their steps. He described the encounter: "Yes, we struck it. We struck good color at our last camp, but things got too hot. We had to skip from them Takus."[8]

In the autumn of 1875, Holt described his venture to Lt. W. R. Quinan, quartermaster for Company "A" of the Fourth U.S. Artillery at Sitka. Quinan passed word along to Major Campbell, commander of the Alaska District. The news fired Campbell's imagination, and he planned an expedition to the interior the following summer. He instructed Lt. A. B. Dyer to "make a thorough examination and report of that wonderful country."[9]

The expedition never materialized. In the spring of 1876, the Fourth Artillery was transferred southeast to Fort Wrangel and Major Campbell received orders to begin the process of closing all the posts in Alaska.[10] Washington now believed the Sitka Tlingit to be quiescent, and the troops were needed elsewhere to fight in the Indian Wars. No further attempt to enter the Yukon was made from the south until May 1878 when Edmund Bean and three brothers named Rath were turned back by the Chilkats at the foot of the Chilkoot.[11] The frustration of the prospectors would drag on another two years before the U.S. military intervened to open the pass to the public.

In May, 1880, Captain L. A. Beardslee of the *U.S.S. Jamestown* received an invitation from Klotz-Kutch,[12] a Chilkat chief, in which he indicated he would welcome white men to "come and prospect" in the interior of Alaska. Captain Beardslee soon sent a message of confirmation that was read aloud to tribal leaders who did not read English:

U.S.S. *Jamestown,* Off Sitka, May 20, 1880

> To the Chiefs of the Chilkats, Klotz-Kutch and Elquesah,
> CHIEFS: You have sent me through Skeenga-Stocheen and Stickeesh, Indians in whom you and I place confidence, an invitation to the white men to come and prospect your country, and have promised to be their friends. The men who now come are those I have invited in your name. I feel sure from what I know of the bravery and honesty of the Chilkats that you will keep those promises; therefore I send them, and the Great Father at Washington will be greatly pleased to hear that they have gone, and more pleased to hear next fall that you have all remained friends.
> The officer who delivers this acts as my representative.
> L. A. Beardslee, Commander, U.S.N., and Senior Representative of the Government[13]

Finalizing this agreement with the Chilkats was a turning point in the history of the Yukon District. Explorers and prospectors were soon crossing over the Pass regularly. Explorers mapped and renamed rivers, lakes and mountains, disregarding the names given to them centuries before by the Indians of the coast and of the interior. Ironically, prospectors were frequently shown the location of gold deposits by Indians like Kowee. Surely neither Kowee nor the Indians of the interior had any idea of the dramatic upheaval about to forever reshape their territory and traditional subsistence lifestyle.

Edmund Bean led the first party of 19[14] miners into Chilkat country and they were accompanied by a military escort of 13 men commanded by Lt. E. P. McClellan.[15] The other members of the party were: Robert A. Duggan, George G. Langtry, Thomas Lineham, Dankert A. Peterson (Petersen), James Tallon, Patrick McGlinchey, William Zoble (Zable), M. A. (Hays), Antone Marks, Dennis Barrett, Thomas Keirnan (Kernan), George Hankrader (Harkrader, Harkrider), J. Newton Massen (J. N. Warren), Fred Cushman, P. Uontenman (Preston Cloudman), James McCloskey, John Lemon and Solomon B. Mathews.[16]

Lieutenant McClellan and his men turned back at Dyea at the end of Lynn Canal. From there Bean and his party walked ten miles, generally following the Dyea River, to the tree line spot that became known as Sheep Camp, then climbed six miles to the summit of

Chilkoot Pass. In the final four miles to the summit, the grade is 30 percent, increasing to 35 percent in the last half mile. On the other side of the pass, they descended 14 miles to the first of the mountain lakes that form the headwaters of the Yukon River. (They were still 500 miles from the moose pasture that would eventually become Dawson City.)

On the shore of Lake Lindeman they felled green spruce, whipsawed[17] planks and built crude boats. When the ice melted they crossed the chain of lakes and portaged between them until they entered the river. Later they portaged around a narrow canyon pulsing with tumultuous currents and a three-mile section of wildly undulating rapids below. Thirty miles farther downriver they came to Lake Lebarge and, at its northern outlet, again entered the river and floated 30 miles to its confluence with the Teslin. On this river they spent the remainder of the season prospecting the sand and gravel bars. By fall they had found little gold, and with provisions running low, made the arduous trip back up the Yukon, across the lakes and over Chilkoot Pass to the coast.[18]

The following spring George Langtry, Patrick McGlinchey and two other men, all of whom had been in the Bean party, again crossed the Chilkoot.[19] This time they followed the Yukon past the mouth of the Teslin to the Big Salmon, ascending it about 200 miles, and finding good pay on some of the bars. This was the first discovery of gold in significant quantities made in the Yukon District.[20] In the fall they, too, returned to the coast.

The story of this discovery quickly made its way by moccasin telegraph down the coast to Seattle and Portland, and eventually to San Francisco where Joe heard it. At the time, many Americans thought the Yukon was in Alaska. Even if they knew it lay in Canada, it was generally a blank spot on the map to the majority of them.

The parties of miners struggling over the Chilkoot in 1880 and 1881, however, were not the first whites traveling on the Yukon River or viewing the vast wilderness that became known as Canada's Yukon Territory many years later.

Since 1833 the Russian-American Company had traded with Inuit along the coast of Alaska from its post at St. Michael's Island on Norton Sound in the Bering Sea, about 80 miles from the Yukon River mouth. In 1835, Andre Glazunov, a company trader, traveled overland on the ancient "Anvig" trail to the Yukon and was the first white man to see what the Inuit called the "Great River." He traveled downriver to the Indian village of Ikogmiut (now Russian Mission), about 200 miles from the mouth of the Yukon. The next year the company established its first post on the Yukon at that site. In 1838, another post was established 300-350 miles farther upriver near a "Koyukon" Athabaskan village at a site they called Nulato.[21] This was to be the company's farthest inland trading post.[22] But beginning in the early 1860s they made an annual 240-mile journey upriver from Nulato to the mouth of the Tanana where they met with Hudson's Bay Company traders from Fort Yukon and Indians from throughout the region. This trade fair was held on neutral ground, at the mouth of the Tanana a tongue of land traditionally called Nuclerai, and generally known to white traders as Nuklukayet.[23] Naturalist William Dall, who traveled upriver with Russian traders in 1867, wrote that "Here no man might bring his quarrel, no tribe its feud."[24]

The Canadian Athabaskan people—the semi-nomadic Kutchin, Han and Tutchone—roamed over much of the upper Yukon River Valley. Their ancestors had been living there since at least 8000 B.C. Many efforts have been made to estimate the precontact number of Indians living in northwestern Canada. None of the studies, however, has extended beyond the Kutchin, many of whom lived in northern Yukon. In his 1978 analysis of these studies, noted anthropologist Dr. Shepard Krech III estimated the number of "Kutchin" to be 5,400 before the arrival of Europeans.[25] Data available on the Han and Tutchone is of more recent origin and does not speculate on precontact population numbers.

Petrof reported in the 1880 U.S. Census that there were 82 Indians at Fort Reliance (Nuklako) and 107 at Fort Yukon. In 1883, Schwatka reported 150 at Nuklako and 75-100 at Johnny's Village. Since the traditional Athabaskan lifestyle was a round of residences at various camps (muskrat camp, fish camp, berry camp) throughout the seasonal calendar of subsistence harvest, all these numbers may be unreliable. That is, the people counted at the stations may be those who were engaged in trade during the days Petrof or Schwatka was counting, while equal or greater numbers might have been hunting or gathering elsewhere.

There was good trade in marten, beaver and fox. But all the Russian-American Company's activities along the river came to an end in 1867 when Russia sold Alaska to the United States.[26]

In 1840, Robert Campbell, 32, an ambitious, God-fearing Scot employed as a fur trader by Hudson's Bay Company, traveled into the Yukon District from the south. In 1842 he established, on Frances Lake in southeastern Yukon, a trading post he named Glenlyon House. In 1846 he moved farther inland to the Pelly River where he established a post he named Pelly Banks. Two years later he traveled down the Pelly to its confluence with the Lewes. On June 2, 1848 he "fixed upon a place for the fort" on the left bank at the mouth of the Pelly and began construction. The site of Fort Selkirk had been, like the site of Nuklukayet, a traditional meeting place for various peoples before the whites arrived. Here Northern Tutchone met to trade with the Chilkats. The Pelly Banks post was closed in 1850; Frances Lake post was closed in 1851.

Fort Selkirk operated until August 1852 when an entire tribe of Chilkats from the Alaska coast pillaged the settlement. Thereafter, Hudson's Bay Company abandoned all efforts to trade in that part of the Yukon for many decades.[27] The coastal Tlingit, and the inland Tagish, Tutchone, Kaska, Han and Kutchin continued to trade among themselves. Trade goods included caribou skins, dried clams, oolichan oil or "grease," and seaweed.

In 1846, Alexander Hunter Murray, also an employee by Hudson's Bay Company, entered the Yukon District from the north via the Mackenzie River. Near its mouth he entered the Peel River, followed it to a portage over McDougal Pass and eventually went down the Porcupine River to its confluence with the Yukon. In the summer of 1847 three miles up the Yukon, on the right bank, Murray boldly constructed a trading post he named Fort Yukon, not unaware it was in Russian territory. The Hudson's Bay Company continued trading at that site until the summer of 1869 when it was then determined to be within the U.S. boundary. Taking into account the Alaska Purchase of 1867, the company then moved 12 miles up the Porcupine to a site believed to be within what was then known as the British Northwest Territories, and there constructed a new post, Rampart House.[28] Making the move with them were clergy of the Church of England whose first missionary,

William Kirkby, had arrived in the region in 1861.[29]

Neither the Russians, the Hudson's Bay Company, nor the missionaries were seeking gold. The traders wanted only to profit from furs and discouraged prospecting by their employees. The missionaries wanted only to save their "dusky flock" from some peril the Indians had never imagined.

Nevertheless, gold was inadvertently discovered by a missionary in 1863. On a creek no one would officially name for decades, Reverend Robert McDonald "saw so much gold...that he could have gathered it with a spoon."[30]

In the years 1868-1869 five American trading companies attempted "to establish themselves in this district,"[31] most at St. Michael's Island on Norton Sound.

Two years later, however, most of the trade was controlled by the Alaska Commercial Company.[32] The company established posts at several points along the river but, until 1874, did not venture beyond Fort Yukon[33] and the trader there, Moise Mercier was the only white man between that location and the coast of Alaska more than 1,000 miles southwest. There he traded with the local Kutcha-kutchin and the Han from upriver.[34] Later, a trader would write that Chief Cetsah, of the Han, who lived at the mouth of the Tr'on dik (Klondike River) had for some time been insisting that Mercier build "a station near his house."[35]

The Alaska Commercial Company understood that much of the area occupied by the Han clearly lay within the Yukon District. But that fact was not a sufficient deterrent to the company's San Francisco owners when they became aware of the potential of Leroy Napoleon "Jack" McQuesten who arrived at Fort Yukon August 15, 1873.[36] In McQuesten, a farmer's son from New England who had experienced the California gold rush, the company saw a man with temperament and skills well suited for trading with Indians. The resident priest, Monsignor Isidore Clut, who had known McQuesten when he was an employee of the Hudson's Bay Company, recommended him as "a very honest man and a good fur trader."[37] Good natured and generous, McQuesten would prove his worth and later earn the title "Father of the Yukon."

Other men also arrived at Fort Yukon that summer via the Mackenzie and Porcupine Rivers. They were Arthur Harper,

Frederick Harte, George Finch, Andrew Kensellar, George McNiff (or McNipp), and Alfred Henry Mayo. (Another man, Samuel Wilkinson (by some writers referred to as George Nickelson, may have also been among those who arrived.) Harper was born in County Antrim, Ireland, in 1835. He left for the United States when a teenager. During his youth he traveled west to California and made his way up the coast, arriving in the British Columbia goldfields in the late 1860s.[38] Al Mayo, a veteran of the American Civil War, was born in Brownville, Piscataquis County, Maine, in 1845.[39] When an Indian at Fort Yukon showed them some copper he had found on the White River Harper, Finch and Harte set out up the Yukon, "to try for it." They prospected briefly near the mouths of rivers later known as the Forty Mile, Sixty Mile and Stewart. They spent the winter at the mouth of the White River and ascended it the following spring[40] to look for copper.[41]

Harper and his party were the first prospectors in the Yukon Territory, having preceded even the daring George Holt. Kensellar was hired by the Alaska Commercial Company to work at its Nuklukayet post (often referred to as "Old Station")[42]. McQuesten, Mayo and McKniff spent the winter of 1873-74 near the mouth of Beaver Creek,[43] about 100 miles downstream from Fort Yukon. In the spring they moved back to Fort Yukon and, on May 16, started downriver by boat with Moise Mercier who was headed for St. Michael to deliver the furs for which he had traded over the winter. At "Nuklukayet Station,"[44] they met Arthur Harper and his companions who had recently arrived from upriver. Although no copper was located, they "had done considerable prospecting but they found nothing that would pay. They found gold in all of the streams, but they did most all their work on White River and there has never been anything found there since."[45] Finding no provisions at the post, both parties decided to continue on to St. Michael. There they met Moise's brother, Francois,[46] who was in charge of the Alaska District for the Alaska Commercial Company. He soon employed Harte and Mayo to work as traders at established posts along the lower river. Harper, Finch and Wilkinson decided to continue prospecting.[47] McQuesten and Frank Banfield (also known as Bonfield or Barnfield), a recent arrival at St. Michael, were employed to travel upriver to a site in the Yukon District well within Canadian territory and establish a trading post to be called Fort Reliance.[48]

In August 1874 Francois Mercier, Jack McQuesten and Frank Banfield left St. Michael and made their way 1,500 miles upstream aboard the company's little steamer *Yukon* making its first trip above Fort Yukon.[49] Accompanying McQuesten were a Trondek chief called Cetsah (or Cotsah) and ten of his men.[50] Cetsah would finally have a "station near his house." On August 20,1874, the party came to a site on a high bluff on the right bank of the river about six miles downstream from present-day Dawson City. After unloading trade goods, Mercier started back downriver for St. Michael. McQuesten and Banfield, with assistance of friendly Han from the village of Nuklako across the river,[51] immediately began construction of a house and store that comprised Fort Reliance,[52] the first American trading post in the Yukon District. (While the Alaska Commercial Company's sole purpose for establishing Fort Reliance was to exploit the fur trade, its location on the Yukon River just 600 miles from the southern coast of Alaska would, within a decade, greatly facilitate the ability of miners to prospect the country for gold.)

Here, in this remote, beautiful and lonely spot, McQuesten and Banfield spent the winter. There was no one else within hundreds of miles who spoke English, and communication with their Han neighbors was mainly through Chinook trading jargon and sign language. In years to come McQuesten would spend many more winters at Fort Reliance and other posts up and down the river. Banfield appears to have left the country the following summer. Eight years later Joe Ladue would spend his first winter in the Yukon at Fort Reliance with McQuesten.[53]

Fort Reliance was composed of six crude log buildings, shingled in birch bark. McQuesten hired the Han to carry logs for construction and fuel and to hunt and dry meat for the winter.

The approximately 150 residents of Nuklako were one of a number of small groups of the Han whose traditional territory extends to a point some miles south of the Klondike, east to the headwaters of the Klondike, Porcupine and Peel Rivers, north to a point about midway between Charley's Village and Circle City, and west to the headwaters of the Forty Mile and Charley Rivers in Alaska. The Han villages at the time of the American traders' arrival on the upper river were Nuklako, Johnny's Village (Klat-ol-klin to the Indians and referred to at times by traders as Fetutlin,[54] a mile upriver from present-day Eagle) and Charley Village (referred to by Schwatka as Charley's Village), 50 miles downriver. The Han also had a summer fish camp at the mouth of the Forty Mile.[55]

For many centuries before the arrival of white men, trade was brisk among the Indians of the upper Tanana country and the Han along the upper Yukon. One of the routes was from the Tanana overland to a tributary to the White River that they followed to the Yukon.[56]

Han dwellings in 1874 were constructed of caribou hides over a framework of saplings. A fire pit in the center of the tent provided heat, the smoke escaping through a hole at the top, the only opening other than the doorway. When they traveled, the hides were removed and taken with them, the poles left in place for their return.[57]

By the time Schwatka passed Nuklako on July 18, 1883, construction of dwellings had changed. What he saw were substantially built houses, "being of logs and brush piled up." He estimated there were "150 souls."[58]

When Schwatka passed Johnny's Village, on July 21 he saw "six houses and 75-100 souls." Francois Mercier, who was the Alaska Commercial trader at Belle Isle north of Johnny's Village told Schwatka that the Indians called the village Klat-ol-klin.[59]

On July 23 Schwatka passed the third and last of the Han settlements, Charley's Village, which he described as "an exact counterpart of the one called Johnny's Village, even to the number of houses (six) and side of the river (western) bank."[60]

In winter the Han wore a caribou hide parka that reached to the knees with a hood attached, and trousers, also of caribou hide. Moose hide moccasins and mittens completed the winter outfit. Summer clothing was similar, but the fur, which had been worn next to the skin for warmth in winter, was then turned to the outside. Many garments were decorated with porcupine quills dyed various colors derived from boiling cranberries or huckleberries.

Staple foods of the Han were, for hundreds of years, moose, caribou, bear, mountain sheep, mountain goats, ducks, geese, ptarmigan and a great variety of fish and berries. From huckleberries they made an alcoholic beverage that prospectors called hoochinoo, or hooch.[61] (The word hooch derives from the Hutsnuwu Indians of a particular southeast Alaska village, Kootznahoo.)

Anglican missionary, Reverend Vincent Sim, who visited Nuklako in 1883, reported that there were ten rather unsubstantial houses, each with at least four families. Some of the residents were, at times, visitors from upriver and from the Tanana River of Alaska. He wrote that the Indian houses of the Han farther down the river (Johnny's Village) were of better construction.[62]

In their earliest years as traders, before they acquired their own steam-powered craft, McQuesten, Harper and Mayo traveled downriver each spring with their furs in large Indian freighting canoes manned by a crew of ten skilled paddlers. When McQuesten arrived at Nuklukayet the end of May 1875 he met Harper who had continued his prospecting on the streams of the upper Yukon and "discovered gold...he thought would pay wages."[63] Based upon his faith in what he had found, Harper, McQuesten and Al Mayo formed a partnership to work for the Alaska Commerical Company handling all the fur trade between Nuklukayet and Fort Reliance, while continuing to prospect in various parts of the country. No formal agreement survives, but the partnership, generally known as McQuesten and Company, would last fourteen years.[64]

The partners agreed among themselves that McQuesten and Mayo would do most of the trading and that Arthur Harper would spend much of his time prospecting.[65] He continued to prospect on the Stewart, Sixty Mile, Forty Mile and White Rivers and, although he found only fine gold, his letters to miners in the Cassiar District of British Columbia encouraged them to travel to all these sites to do further prospecting.[66] But the Chilkats at Dyea blocked early movement into the country from the south until 1880. The only information McQuesten had about activities on the upper river was a report in the fall of 1880 that "there were white men on the head waters of the Yukon and traveling about with boats. I supposed it was prospectors looking for gold and it proved to be the case as Densmore (sic Dinsmore) and Slim Jim (Wynn) were in about that time."[67]

Trader/prospectors sometimes took on odd jobs collecting specimens of flora and fauna—when the pay was right. The greatest diversity of birds north of the 60th parallel is found in the southwest corner of the Yukon—more than 170 species in Kluane National Park alone. Birds range from grouse to swans, from bald eagles to the electric blue and black Steller's jay.

Sometime during the period 1874-77, McQuesten, Harper and Mayo were employed by Lucien M. Turner, chief signal officer of the U.S. Army to collect "many specimens of birds" from the interior.[68] Later, Joe Ladue, and others who traded for the Alaska Commercial Company also collected sepecimens. The Alaska Commercial Company had, on the second floor of its 310 Sansome Street Building in San Francisco, a museum containing "the most complete ethnological collection of that part of the world which existed anywhere." All the specimens were brought in by the company's employees and were "household as well as hunting, clothing and trinkets made and used by the native Eskimos, Aleuts and Indians in such districts where the company was active."[69]

The summer of 1877 McQuesten and Company saw the beginning of what would be five years of stiff competition when another American firm, the Western Fur and Trading Company, began trading with the Indians along the river from St. Michael to a site that is now present-day Eagle, Alaska.[70] The new company had substantial backing, entered the country with a large supply of trade goods, and was also able to lure Francois Mercier away from the Alaska Commercial Company.[71]

That same year McQuesten, who had been trading at Fort Yukon since 1875, returned to Fort Reliance. During the fall months he prospected on the Sixty Mile where he found "some places where a man could make $6.00 to $8.00 per day but not extensive enough to put on a string of sluices."[72] Throughout the winter months he traded with the Han and in the spring made his annual trip downriver to St. Michael to deliver the furs he had acquired, and to replenish his supply of trade goods. McQuesten, as did Harper and Mayo, focused on the fur trade but, in their free time, all three went prospecting. Had they made a big strike their lives and the history of the Yukon would have been quite different. It is clear, however, that from the beginning they decided to establish themselves as residents in the north. Not only did they sign on with the Alaska Commercial Company, they married Indian women. In 1874, 35-

year-old Arthur Harper married 14-year-old Seentahna (Jennie), an Athabaskan girl he met at Koyukuk Station on the lower river. Al Mayo, 29, married Jennie's cousin, 14-year-old Neehunilthonah (Margaret), daughter of the chief at Nuklukayet. Four years later 42-year-old Jack McQuesten married 18-year-old Satejdenalno (Katherine, or Kate), a Creole[73] he met at Kokerine's, a trading post on the lower river.[74] The three couples were married according to traditional Athabaskan custom and later in ceremonies conducted by Anglican missionaries.[75]

Kate, who had attended school at Ikogmiut on the lower river, could speak Russian as well as her Koyukon Athabaskan language.[76] After their marriage, Jack retained someone to teach her American cooking and English. Jennie, Kate and Margaret proved to be valuable partners as their husbands traded with Indians along the river. Each of the couples raised a large family. The Mayos had twelve children, the Harpers, eight, the McQuestens, eleven.[77] For more than twenty years the families moved up and down the river establishing small posts, initially for the fur trade, and later providing miners' supplies to men coming into the country to look for gold.[78]

The three Athabaskan women, while adapting to life with white men whose culture was totally different from their own, utilized their native skills, making parkas, mukluks and mittens for their families and for sale to miners. They gathered wild edibles and medicinal herbs their people had used for centuries. Over the years all three women earned the respect and admiration of the men who lived in the camps and traded at the posts.

It seems likely that Jack London, who spent a winter in the Yukon during the Klondike Gold Rush, based several of his characters on this trio of wives. In "An Odyssey of the North," prospector Alex Gunderson is a mighty seven-footer, weighing 300 pounds, a "king of Eldorado." After a hard day on the trail, Gunderson's wife, Unga, "rested against his great breast like a slender flower against a wall.... She could make a meal of sun-dried fish or a bed in the snow.... She knew the ways of the moose, the bear, and the little blue fox, and of the wild amphibians of the Northern seas; she was skilled in lore of the woods, and the streams, and the tale writ by man and bird and beast upon the delicate snow crust was to her an open book...."[79] Most of the early prospectors who entered the Yukon after the opening of the Chilkoot Pass in 1880 had the great disadvantages of the brief summer season and the fact that the only food and supplies available to them were those they could carry on their backs. Unless they took time out to hunt or fish, the best they could hope for was two or three summer months[80] of intense prospecting before they would be forced to begin the arduous trek to the coast. Fort Reliance was 600 miles from the coast of Alaska and accessible to the prospectors, but even if they had known of its existence, there was generally only enough food for the traders and their families, and no tools for mining. It would not be until the summer of 1884 that McQuesten and Company regularly stocked, or as McQuesten expressed it in his *Recollections*, "went...to being in" miners' supplies.[81]

By 1880, the Western Fur and Trading Company had become a formidable rival of the Alaska Commercial Company. Francois Mercier, described it as a "strong company...an aggressive firm..." and competition between the two was fierce. Each established posts up and down the Yukon, and each strived to gain the upper hand by offering the Indians more and better trade goods for fewer furs than the other. The effect on both companies was a slim margin of profit.[82]

The head count taken that year by Ivan Petrof for the U.S. Census Bureau shows that along the Yukon between St. Michael and Fort Reliance there were 15 to 20 trading posts. He indicated the following populations at the main trading stations

	White	Athabaskan	Creole	Eskimo
Fort Reliance	1	82	0	0
Fort Yukon	2	107	0	0
Nuklukayet	2	27	0	0
Nulato	2	0	2	163
Andreavsky	1	0	12	0
Anvik	1	0	94	0
St. Michael	4	0	5	100

The total population between St. Lawrence Island and Fort Reliance was 6,870: 18 whites, 19 Creoles, 2,557 Athabaskans and 4,276 Eskimos. Unfortunately, Petrof did not record the names of residents.

However, he did report the number of furs taken in by the traders during the winter of 1880: 32 wolf, 310 lynx, 3,781 beaver, 206 silver fox, 5,000 red fox, 1,791 white fox, 2,000 marten (sable), 7,774 mink, 152 bear, 2,000 muskrat, 310 land otter. The total was 24,129. The market value was estimated to be between $75,000 and $80,000.[83]

By the fall of 1881 the little steamer *Yukon* was in very poor condition. McQuesten wrote that it was a wonder to him that since he was "Captain and Engineer at the same time…we didn't blow her up or sink her as I didn't know anything about steam boating." When he reached Fort Yukon that fall he expected it to be the "last trip" for the *Yukon* and "laid up our steamer near the slough for the winter." When the river broke up the following spring the water was unusually high and the ice "gorged and backed up in a good many places and when we got to Fort Yukon we found that the ice had jammed into the slough where our steamer was lying and sank her. There was nothing to be seen, the ice had smashed her all up."[84]

Knowing the condition of the old steamer, the Alaska Commercial Company had ordered a new boat. Constructed in San Francisco, the new steamer was disassembled and brought to St. Michael aboard its ocean going steamer *St. Paul*. When McQuesten arrived at St. Michael in late July he and a number of other traders joined the three carpenters sent by the company and they all went to work:

> In four weeks had her launched and on the 20th August we left St. Michael.…When we launched her, Mrs. Lawrence (Lorenz) the Agent's wife, broke a bottle of wine over her bow and named her 'The Yukon' after the old steamer.…We made the trip to Fort Reliance all right and she made very good time coming up considering that everything was new.…Her dimensions were 75 feet length (by) 20 feet.…She looked very large to us at that time and we were very proud of her.[85]

During one of McQuesten and Harper's earlier trips to St. Michael with furs, they had shared with the officers of the Alaska Commercial Company's' steamer *St. Paul* the tantalizing clue that "a little gold was to be found almost everywhere" in the district.[86] When Langtry and McGlinchey's story of gold on the Big Salmon arrived on the coast the fall of 1881, the evidence was finally too great and too much for any miner to resist. As excitement rippled through the new town of Juneau and the streets of San Francisco, many prospectors began trying to work out some way to get to the Yukon. Among them was Joe Ladue.

In the spring of 1882 Joe and five other men—William Domingo Moore, John McGraw, John Rogers, Harold Harris Pitts[87] and Robert Adams—gathered outfits and left San Francisco aboard the steamer *State of California* headed north to Alaska to search for gold. They spent a week in Juneau, then sailed on to Dyea located near the trailhead for the 32-mile Chilkoot Trail, topped by a daunting 3,500-foot pass. The next three days were spent organizing their tons of supplies into manageable packs. They had enough food to last two years and it appears their plan was to spend the winter at Fort Reliance. So great was the quantity of their provisions they hired 82 Chilkats to carry them from Dyea over the pass to Lake Lindeman. Their outfit consisted of "80-pound sacks of flour, 1,000 pounds of beans, 1,000 pounds of bacon...canned fruit and other canned goods." In addition were the usual miners' kits: blankets, rockers, rocker iron, whipsaws, handsaws, gold pans, picks and nails.[88]

When the Chilkat packers left them at Lake Lindeman and returned to the coast, Ladue and his party cut trees, whipsawed logs and built two large scows. On July 12, 1882, they set off across the lakes leading for the Yukon River. They probably hoisted sails to take advantage of the frequent summer winds on the upper lakes.[89] Concerned about drowning or overturning, the men paid little attention to the deep purple lupines and wild pink roses blooming on the banks.

After crossing the series of headwater lakes, they entered the meandering, swift and beautiful green waters of the Yukon. They were explorers on a river about which few white men had any knowledge. Leaving the lakes, they floated for about 25 miles when they heard a distant whisper on the wind that soon rose to a murmur and eventually an intimidating roar. Quickly they worked their scows to shore and tied them securely while they reconnoitered ahead. What they saw startled and amazed them. Rising about 80 feet from the river's surface were the sheer walls of a canyon, later known as Miles Canyon.[90] Here the river, running full from the melting of mountain snows, narrowed, and the confined water surging between the rock walls had become a raging torrent, a huge, frothing crest at its center.

Below the canyon lay their next surprise, great rapids, half a mile long, with crashing waves rising in white crests so much resembling the flowing manes of giant steeds that, in years to come, it would be called *White Horse Rapids*.[91] The only way for Joe and his party to continue on safely was to portage around the two and three-quarter miles of the canyon and the rapids. One traveler on the river later estimated that the swift water of the canyon and rapids would have taken them through in about "2 minutes, 20 seconds."[92] The portage wasn't long, but the thousands of pounds of provisions that had been carried over the pass by Indian packers now had to be hoisted onto their own backs and relayed in multiple trips.

For nearly two months Ladue and his party floated down the Yukon toward Fort Reliance, stopping "from point to point along the route, prospecting and finding gold."[93]

Fall arrives early in the Yukon and already cold nights had brought out the yellow of the aspens and poplars that extended from the banks of the river to the rolling hills beyond. On September 5, as Joe and three of the men in his party floated through this golden corridor, they saw wood smoke rising from the chimneys at Fort Reliance. The first to see the scow approaching was probably a Han at the post or those at their village across the river. Typically, visitors were welcomed by the Indians with much shouting and gunfire,[94] so Jack McQuesten was soon standing on the high bank watching, astonished and delighted, as Joe, William D. Moore, John Rogers and John McGraw eased their scow to shore. Their arrival was a historic event. These men, who had traveled 600 miles from the southeast coast of Alaska over land and water, were the first prospectors to have ventured that far into the Yukon by that route and would be the first to remain throughout the winter.[95] McQuesten had been mostly alone in the country for eight years. On his annual expeditions to St. Michael he had brief encounters with other traders, but his was the only post in the Yukon District, so he had not expected to see a craft approaching from upriver with men on board who spoke English and brought news from the world he had left behind. When Joe explained that they planned to remain to work the streams the next season, McQuesten genially pointed to an area where they could build their cabins.

Three days later, on September 8, McQuesten took Joe and his party on a prospecting trip to the Sixty Mile River where Arthur Harper had "found gold...that he thought would pay."[96] (Fort Reliance was considered point zero on the Yukon River for determining distances. The Sixty Mile River was found to be about that distance from the Fort, thus, its name.) They found some nuggets worth about 25 to 30 cents.[97] McQuesten would later record that they "found very encouraging prospects about 15 miles below Miller Creek (a tributary of the Sixty Mile), Jo (sic) Ladue panned out several pieces that weighed 10 ct. "The ground was frozen and we had to thaw out the ground by fires. It took us 3 days to sink one hole ten feet deep and the water came in so we had to abandon it before we got to bedrock."[98] (The best quantities of gold are generally found at bedrock, but bedrock could lie conveniently near the surface—or as many as 100 feet below.)

By the time McQuesten, Joe, Rogers, Moore and McGraw returned to Fort Reliance, Harold Pitts and Robert Adams had arrived from upriver with the party's second loaded scow. Another group of prospectors arrived a few days later: Tom Kanals, James Carr, George Spangenberg, James Miller, Peter Scofield, Charley Powell, Jean Baptiste St. Louis and Joseph Paris.[99] All planned to stay the winter. Joe later stated, "We went into winter quarters about Sept. 25. The weather was lovely, with not a particle of snow. The wild geese and ducks were just starting back south, but snow came soon and we were shut in. It was very cold."[100] The cabins were built near the site of the post, but some distance north of the store.[101] Joe's party had brought plenty of food for the winter, but the others were "not so well supplied." McQuesten had "plenty of flour on hand," however, so there was enough for all and they "passed the winter and had plenty for the following summer."

The cabins built by Joe and the others averaged 12 by 14 feet.[102] The logs were eight or nine inches in diameter, the sides of the cabins about nine or ten logs high. The roof was nearly flat, a rise of two feet at the ridge being common. The roof extended four to six feet over the front (and only) door and the area was frequently partially enclosed as an Arctic entry and store room. The roof was made of poles covered with a layer of moss and a foot of mud. In summer, weeds and grass flourished, and some prospectors used the roof to plant a vegetable garden. There was only one window opening, usually covered with flour sacks. They may have used white ginger bottles if they were available. The bottles were about as long as the logs were thick and were set vertically.

Joe's cabin was constructed of green logs, i.e., they had been cut only a short time before being used in the construction. With the onset of the Yukon winter with temperatures dropping to a frigid 60 degrees below zero Fahrenheit, along with the considerable heat generated inside, the logs frequently made sounds like small explosions. One wonders how many nights Joe was awakened by these loud complaints from logs in distress. There were few stoves in the Yukon, so the cabins Joe and the others built at Fort Reliance were heated by a circle of rocks on the floor with a pit in the middle where a wood fire was kept burning. The chimney was a square hole in the roof.[103]

McQuesten's heat was probably provided by a Russian oven. It was described later by one of Joe's prospecting party as being "made of stone in the shape of a large box-stove, from three to four feet long inside, from 18-20 inches wide, and the same in depth, with an iron plate on top to cook on. The chimney is built of the same material."[104]

During the long, cold, dark winter McQuesten and his new neighbors spent congenial evenings at the "Station" playing cards and telling stories, and "the winter passed away very pleasantly....it was the first time with the exception of one year that anyone was living near that I could converse with."

The exception was 1874 when Frank Banfield spent the winter at Fort Reliance.

Throughout October, November and December 1882, the days grew shorter. As the nights grew longer the sweeping celestial curtains of red, white, yellow and green of the aurora borealis often brightened the skies. As Christmas approached, the McQuestens, their children and the prospectors decided to celebrate. There were plenty of spruce boughs handy to the post for making wreaths and garlands for decorating the cabins and store. They decided to hold a Christmas party, much of it outdoors during the brief light of midday on the twenty-fifth, and to invite the people of Nuklako. The festivities were not unlike the first Thanksgiving at Plymouth Plantation. The white men brought to the festivities a variety of dried and canned fruits and vegetables, carols in at least two languages and the Christmas story; the Indians brought moose and caribou meat and their own songs, games and dances. Throughout the day that place of deep silence was filled with laughter and songs and the beat of drums. The Indians took particular pleasure tossing the white men high into the air from a tautly stretched moose hide. The object of "the blanket toss" was for the tossee to land upright, a skill the newcomers had yet to acquire.[105]

This gathering of white men and Indians was the first of its kind in the Yukon district, another historic event. They were people from varied cultural and linguistic backgrounds, a microcosmic United Nations. London-born Harold Pitts spoke with a British accent. Joe and Jean St. Louis spoke French and English. Kate McQuesten was fluent in her native Koyukon-Athabaskan language, could speak Russian and some English. McQuesten spoke English with a Yankee accent and residents of Nuklako spoke their native Takudh. McQuesten's "Indian interpreter"[106] contributed to the linguistic melting pot; he was more or less fluent in English and a number of the Indian dialects spoken along the river.

That winter of 1882 the men at Fort Reliance convened the first miners' meeting in the Yukon District. McQuesten said that the purpose was to "make laws governing the size of placer claims and water rights so that everyone knew what he was entitled to in case anything was struck...."[107] The men were settled for the winter, but their minds were on the return of the sun and the prospect of gold to be found in this distant and different land of Yukon.

Sometime after the river froze, Joe and some of his party took provisions by hand sleigh and dogs to the upper reaches of the Sixty Mile River where they had found good prospects the previous fall. There they built a cache—a small, windowless, cabinlike structure that stood high above the ground on four vertical posts safe from bears. In it they stored supplies for use the following summer when they planned to return to continue prospecting.[108]

Early in the spring of 1883, Joe, Jean St. Louis, George Spangenberg and Peter Scofield left Fort Reliance and traveled 80 miles north over the river ice to the former trading post of the Western Fur and Trading Company at present-day Eagle, Alaska, to visit Francois Mercier who was in charge of a post for the Alaska Commercial Company.[109] The new post, which Mercier had named Belle Isle, was as remote and lonely a place as Fort Reliance. Mercier recorded that when the party arrived unexpectedly on April 9 he was "astonished and delighted" when he "perceived they were indeed whites, and the foremost gave me his hand, addressing me in French. It was Joseph Ladue, French-Canadian, native of the area of Platsburg (sic) N.Y."[110] These four were the first prospectors to travel that far down the Yukon from its headwaters.

Just prior to Joe's arrival at Belle Isle, an Athabaskan Indian from the Tanana region had brought Mercier a piece of "rich gold quartz" he had found on the headwaters of the Forty Mile River. Hearing this, Joe was eager to start out on a search for the Indian and the outcropping from which he had obtained the sample. Mercier, considering Joe "a very energetic man" provided him with a grubstake and guide.[111] Their agreement was that, if anything of value was found, the profits would be shared on a percentage basis. Spangenberg and Scofield returned to Fort Reliance while Joe started out for the upper reaches of the Forty Mile. Unfortunately, after several weeks of searching, he found neither the Indian nor the source of the quartz sample.[112]

At the headwaters of the Forty Mile, Joe was joined by several men from Fort Reliance and went overland to the cache on the Sixty Mile. As soon as the weather warmed and the ice melted, they began prospecting on Miller Creek. They stayed until fall and found good prospects, but having neither tools nor sufficient supplies "were not able to get much."[113]

Besides Joe's party, and those who later arrived at Fort Reliance, several other men had crossed the Chilkoot the summer of 1882. Among them were: Thomas Boswell, John Dougan (Duggan), Robert Robertson, D. Bertrand, Frank Dinsmore, John Riley, Preston Cloudman, Robert Fox, Thomas Curney (Kernan, Kiernan) and Levy Herod.[114] They traveled down the Yukon to the Pelly, ascended it for some distance, but found little gold and returned to the coast in the fall.[115]

Another party, headed by explorer and scientist, Dr. Arthur Krause of Germany, was on expedition for the Bremen Geographical Society. During May and June of 1882 they made explorations of the Chilkat and Chilkoot Passes, the sources of the Takhini and the Yukon Rivers, respectively, before returning to the coast. Because of Dr. Krause's explorations, the accuracy of his observations and the extent of his and his brother Aurel's collecting, Germany soon had more information about the southern Yukon and the coastal Tlingits than any other country.[116]

One prospector who had heard about the gold in the Alaska/Yukon District was Edward Lawrence Schieffelin whose name was familiar to Joe from his days in Arizona. Schieffelin had found rich deposits of silver and founded the town of Tombstone.[117] In the spring of 1882 Schieffelin was in San Francisco where he chartered the schooner *H. L. Tiernan*. On July 13, after gathering supplies to last for three years, he and his six companions set out for St. Michael, Alaska. Besides Schieffelin's brother, Effingham, the party consisted of "Old Charlie Farcoit" (Farciot),[118] Charles Sauerbrey, Jack Young, Johan Adrian Jacobsen, (a Norwegian ethnologist…of Germany), collecting information and specimens for the Royal Museum of Germany,[119] and Henry De Wolfe, who Schieffelin said "claimed to be a correspondent for the *New York Herald*," but that he "never saw any of his articles."[120] Lashed to the deck of the *Tiernan* was a small paddle wheeler, the *New Racket*,[121] which had been built on the West Coast and disassembled for transport.

Arriving at St. Michael on July 25, they reassembled the little steamer and on August 3, with Charlie Farciot at the wheel, they "got into the mouth of the river." They traveled several hundred miles upriver to Harper and Mayo's trading post at Nuklukayet where they established a camp and began prospecting the area. When the temperature dropped quickly in mid-September, they constructed cabins and settled in for the winter.

The next summer they resumed prospecting on the bars of the Tanana finding some promising colors. But Schieffelin decided they did not warrant his remaining: "I came to the conclusion that the prospects were too poor to justify my sojourn any longer and I abandoned the country."[122] Old-timer Gordon Bettles would later write that, "They were the first prospectors to locate in the central section of the Yukon River...."[123] When De Wolfe returned east the next fall he took with him McQuesten's news that there was "a little gold to be found everywhere" in the district, but apparently he never published information about his reconnaissance.

For McQuesten and Company, Schieffelin's decision to "abandon the country" came at a propitious moment. Since they had begun trading for the Alaska Commercial Company in 1874 they had worked on commission.[124] In 1883 the partners informed the company that either their commission had to be increased or other, more satisfactory, arrangements would need to be made. When their request was denied, the partners decided they would operate as independents in direct competition with the company. Their first move was to acquire the *New Racket* from Schieffelin "for a lower cost than it would have had in San Francisco."[125]

Surprised by this move, the company, understanding they would be hard pressed to replace these experienced veterans who had traded so successfully for them the past eight years, quickly offered better terms.[126] Beginning that season McQuesten and Company sold their furs to the Alaska Commercial Company at the current market price and purchased trade goods delivered to St. Michael at 25 percent above San Francisco wholesale. They also had to pay freight charges. The costs were high, but they had complete freedom to establish the value of the trade goods and the value of furs brought in by the Indians. This agreement allowed the traders to realize immense profits for many years.[127]

Another significant and welcome change for McQuesten and Company occurred that summer when the Alaska Commercial Company bought out the Western Fur and Trading Company. Included in the purchase price of $175,000 was the steamer *St. Michael* that had been on the river since 1879.[128] Francois Mercier, who had taken McQuesten to the site of Fort Reliance in 1874, had, since 1877, been a trader for the Western Fur and Trading Company. In 1880 he opened a post one mile downriver from the Han's Johnny Village[129] at the site of present-day Eagle, Alaska but closed it the following year. With the imminent departure of that company from the river, Mercier returned to the Alaska Commercial Company and began trading at the same site during the fall of 1882. These events had set the stage for the meeting between Joe and Mercier in the spring of 1883.[130]

The trading companies' business at that time was exclusively to exchange trade goods such as sugar and guns for furs. From the first days of British and American trading, beginning with the Hudson's Bay Company in 1842 at Frances Lake and the Alaska Commercial Company and others in 1868 at St. Michael, the toll taken on fur-bearing animals in the far north was devastating. Agents for the Russian-American Company had already decimated the sea otter. Now other animals were sought. During the 12-year period 1868-1880, the early trading companies, including the Alaska Commercial Company and the Western Fur and Trading Company took in 103,313 mink pelts, 105,920 marten and 68,230 muskrat, a number 600 percent greater than that taken in by the *Russian American Company* in the Alaska District during the previous 18 years.[131]

Regarding the summer of 1883, Joe stated several years later in an interview with the *New York World* that:

> ...we went back to the cache we had made the previous winter at the head of Sixty-Mile Creek, and we put in the balance of the summer prospecting in that locality. We stayed there until fall.

In the same interview, however, he stated:

> We intended to go into mining the next spring on some of the creeks we had already explored, but that summer the A. C. T. Company steamer *Yukon*, the only steamer on the river, broke one of her engines and could not get up the river. In consequence, we had to drop down to the mouth of the Tanana River, where we spent the second winter.[132]

While Joe's recollections of his whereabouts the summer of 1883 are confusing, Lt. Frederick Schwatka of the U.S. Cavalry recorded that he met Joe in July of that year at Charley's Village about halfway between present-day Eagle and Circle City, Alaska. Schwatka and his party of seven were traveling down the Yukon on a 15' x 40' raft, making a reconnaissance of the river from its headwaters to the mouth for the U.S. Army. Schwatka noted that Joe was traveling in a "fairly-made scow over twenty feet long, about half a dozen wide and three feet deep," one of the two he had built at Lake Lindeman the previous summer. Joe told Schwatka that he was on his way downriver to Nuklukayet where he intended to spend the winter with McQuesten, Harper and Mayo. Seeing that Schwatka's raft was in very poor condition, Joe offered his services to take him to St. Michael. Schwatka, however, decided the scow was too small and settled for reinforcing his raft.

It was from Schwatka's contact with Joe that he learned the proper pronunciation of the name of the great river, a pronunciation still in use that places the accent on the first syllable (Yú kon), rather than the second, as was typically heard in the United States at the time.

Joe told Schwatka that the Han living at the settlements of Charley Village and Johnny's Village were "the most friendly and best-natured Indians on this part of the river."[133]

At one point south of Fort Yukon, Joe took a shortcut at a bend in the river, into which Schwatka's ponderous raft could not enter. Joe said he would go ahead and find a good camping place for the night. He didn't appear again, however, until Schwatka had already made camp. He explained his delay was because he had been hunting ducks, and produced two or three ducks that Schwatka considered "in the very prime of their toughness as corroborative testimony." Schwatka, however, surmised the true story was that "all hands and the cook had gone to sleep, whereupon the scow had likewise rested on the soft bottom of some friendly sandspit." Schwatka felt his suspicions were confirmed when later "Jo did not like the pace we kept up, or rather that he did not relish being awakened whenever his scow sought the quiet of an island shore."[134]

By the time they reached Nuklukayet, the raft of Schwatka's party was again beginning to break up. There they met Arthur Harper who gave them a 12-ton "barka, a small-decked schooner" with flying jib, to complete their trip down to St. Michael.[135]

Joe's leisurely pace down the river had to do with prospecting on the bars along the way. At some point he met McQuesten coming upriver and traveled with him until the steamer broke down about ten miles below Belle Isle.[136] At that point Joe and Charley Powell "went on in a boat to...a quartz ledge and done some work and come back to Tanana (Nuklukayet) where we all wintered."[137]

It was not the call of gold but the call of souls that brought another man into the Yukon District during the summer of 1883—

Reverend Vincent C. Sim of the Episcopal Church Missionary Society of England.[138] In midsummer he visited the Han at Fort Reliance. There he found "a large number of Indians... the wildest" he had seen. The "state of morals is very bad," he wrote, "especially among the women...." The Han had never seen a Christian missionary before, and Sims apparently thought he had succeeded in delivering some of them from their supposed depravity, at least the 115 (mostly children) whom he baptized.[139] Another Anglican missionary, Rev. Thomas H. Canham wrote in 1898: "The Indians are very ignorant and superstitious. They are filled with fear by their medicine men...."[140]

Early that summer four men, Richard Poplin, Charles McCoskey, George Marks and Benjamin Beach hiked the 33-mile Chilkoot Trail and descended the Yukon to the Stewart. There "they found good prospects in the fall" on some of the bars, and at the end of the season went downriver to Harper and Mayo's post at Nuklukayet where they, too, spent the winter.[141] This was the first time that gold in significant quantity had been located on the Stewart.

Both McQuesten and William Ogilvie wrote that by the end of the 1883 season all the men who had arrived at Fort Reliance the previous fall had left the Yukon, except Joe and Charley Powell.[142] Some traveled downriver into Alaska; others, no doubt, left the North Country discouraged since they had not made a strike; many had simply run out of provisions and were ignorant of the skills necessary to live off the land.

Joe, Powell, Carr and Charles Farciot, formerly with the Schieffelin party, William D. Moore and John McGraw joined McQuesten, Harper and Mayo at Nuklukayet the winter of 1883-4.[143] Along with performing necessary chores of sawing and chopping wood, cooking, melting snow to do laundry and giving haircuts, they spent much of their time playing cards and checkers and telling stories, as had the men sequestered at Fort Reliance the previous year. Joe talked about his continuing hope that gold-bearing quartz would be found in the Yukon and of his days in the Black Hills of Dakota Territory where he had been Superintendent of the Hidden Treasure Mine, and later, a 60-stamp quartz mill, of his prospecting in New Mexico and the successful stamp mills in Tombstone. McQuesten recounted his brief career as a voyageur with the Hudson's Bay Company and how he gave it up when he realized that the 200-lb. packs, so easily carried by the French-Canadians, were too much for him. He, Harper and Mayo recounted their days on the headwaters of the Hay River, east of the Yukon District, where they trapped and traded with the Indians, of their prospecting on Peace River and, of particular interest to their winter companions, their search for gold on the tributaries of the Yukon since 1873. And everyone was eager to hear the tales Poplin, McCoskey, Beach and Marks had to tell of the prospects they had found on the bars of the Stewart River the previous summer.[144]

All the men had come into the country to search for gold and every story of prospecting done on a creek or bar whetted their appetites, tantalizing them with the hope that the next season they would find the treasure that eluded many of them in the camps of the Black Hills, Colorado, New Mexico, Arizona and the Cassiar District of British Columbia.

Most of the men at Nuklukayet were healthy that winter, except William D. Moore and John McGraw, both of whom were suffering the torments of scurvy, a disease caused by deficiency of ascorbic acid (vitamin C) in the body.

Early symptoms include pain during movement and irritability. After several months on a restricted diet such as dried meat, flour and beans, bleeding under the skin, under the fingernails and around the hair follicles may begin. Loose teeth, inflammation of gums and joint weakness are common symptoms.

Since vitamin C functions in bone and connective tissue growth and other repair, in advanced scurvy old bone breaks may even open up. Eating citrus fruits, tomatoes, potatoes, cabbage and green peppers prevents scurvy. Wild greens such as dandelions and lamb's-quarter are efficacious, as are spruce tip tea and very fresh meat. Joe figured they had gotten scurvy because their diet had consisted mainly of bacon and "rusty" ham and thought he and the others had avoided it by eating fresh rabbit meat.[145]

Since the steamer *Yukon* had broken down below Belle Isle the previous summer,[146] no supplies reached Fort Reliance and the post was closed for the first year since 1874. The people of Nuklako, as they had for centuries, traveled to their traditional winter hunting grounds in the uplands of the Blackstone River and the Tombstone

Mountains where they could find moose and caribou.

When the ice left the river in May 1884, all the miners left Nuklukayet and traveled upriver with McQuesten aboard the *New Racket*. Most were headed for the Stewart. Joe, Charley Powell and Mike Hess, a miner from the lower river, apparently not impressed with the stories of gold on the bars of the Stewart, disembarked at the Sixty Mile and proceeded to prospect on some of its tributaries for part of the summer. Finding little color, the trio tried the White River but met with the same dismal results.[147]

But Joe had been mistaken about the Stewart, and that summer significant quantities of fine gold, although in some instances the consistency of flour, were discovered by Thomas Boswell, Howard Franklin, Harry Madison and John Frazer.[148] Other miners on the Stewart that summer were Peter Wyborg, Frank Moffat, Jerry Bertrand and Richard Poplin. All of them took out at least enough gold for a grubstake to see them through the winter and the next season.[149] In the fall they all traveled down to Fort Reliance where they spent the winter.[150]

The Yukon prospector usually traveled alone, worked alone and typically was "broke," his worldly goods being what he was able to carry on his back. The earliest men, those in the country from 1873-1887, looked for "free gold" on the "bars" of the rivers and creeks. Not until 1887 did they experiment with digging shafts down to bedrock where a pay-streak might be found. The pay-streak could be near the surface, or 30 feet or more below it. If there was no pay-streak another shaft was sunk, and another until gold was struck, or the prospector gave up or simply ran out of food. If he found nothing, he was forced to return over Chilkoot Pass to the coast where he would work throughout the winter to get another grubstake for another season of prospecting. Some who found enough gold to get them through the winter remained at one of the trading posts and trusted McQuesten and Company to give them a grubstake for the following season. To many men, looking for gold was like an addiction and they did whatever was necessary to return to the wilds.[151]

McQuesten recorded that in the summer of 1884, "There was no clothing or boots suitable for men to work with and the indications were that there would be men coming into the country every year...." As a result, he decided to stock miners' supplies.[152] That fall he traveled down to St. Michael, boarded the oceangoing steamer *St. Paul* and went out to the Alaska Commercial Company's offices in San Francisco. He spent much of that winter trying to persuade the owners that it was time for them to expand beyond trade goods for the Indians and include supplies for miners.[153]

Most of the men in the country in the winter of 1884-85 were at Fort Reliance where Al Mayo was in charge. In the early weeks of the winter Joe and some of the men went moose hunting in the Klondike River Valley. He and his party hiked up Rabbit Creek (later known as Bonanza) to a small "pup" or tributary (later known as Eldorado) that entered on the left bank, where they made camp.[154] They had no idea that the gold they had sought high and low lay under their feet during the day and under their bedrolls at night.

When the ice went out of the river in May 1885, Joe and Howard Franklin left Fort Reliance and floated down toward St. Michael. Arriving at Nuklukayet in late June they met a U.S. Army reconnaissance party under the command of Lieutenant Henry T. Allen. He had arrived at the post June 25 having spent the previous months exploring the Copper and Tanana Rivers. Their journey over mountains and through the tundra had been long and difficult and they were near starvation. The trader at the post, Andrew Androvsky, had little to offer them but a few crackers, beans and salt. Fortunately for Allen, Ladue and Franklin had with them "about 75 pounds of flour, 50 of which they kindly let us have."[155]

Soon after Lieutenant Allen came ashore at Nuklukayet, Athabaskans began to arrive from Fort Yukon, the Tanana and the Koyukuk River regions on their annual "trading and pleasure expeditions." Whether or not they felt some patriotic allegiance to the United States, on the 4th of July they celebrated all day and all night. There were competitions in jumping and wrestling and a Indian ball game. They fired guns, shouted and danced for hours.[156] Harper and Mayo had left Fort Reliance on the *New Racket* in late May and planned their arrival at Nuklukayet to coincide with the celebration, as it presented the biggest trading opportunity of the year. Among the great quantities of furs offered for barter the traders found many of excellent quality. The Indians of the Tanana, in particular, were expert trappers who tendered the unblemished pelts of American sable, mink, beaver, otter, black bear and white, red, black and silver-grey foxes.[157] After several days of trade, Harper and Mayo proceeded downriver to St. Michael, their steamer now fully loaded with furs.

When Lieutenant Allen left Nuklukayet later that summer, Joe followed in a canoe. When they reached the Melozikakat River, the largest tributary entering from the north between the Tanana and Koyukuk Rivers, he left the party for a time to prospect the bars. He traveled up that river about 75 miles; finding nothing promising he returned to the Yukon and continued downriver.[158]

Harper and Mayo arrived at St. Michael in early August to deliver their furs, pick up trade goods and, for the first time, miners' supplies. McQuesten had returned earlier from San Francisco aboard the steamer *St. Paul.* Soon the river steamers and the barges they towed were loaded, the *Yukon* with trade goods for the Indians, the *New Racket* with 50 tons[159] of food, clothing and tools for the anticipated miners. When they reached the village of Kaltag, Joe was waiting and he boarded the *New Racket* for the trip upriver to Fort Reliance.[160]

Although by 1885 mining on the bars of the upper Yukon and the Stewart was increasing and McQuesten and Company was starting to carry miners' supplies, furs brought in by Indians in considerable numbers still formed the bulk of the company's business. From their three posts on the river that year,[161] Fort Reliance, Belle Isle and Nuklukayet, and from the annual trade gathering, it was estimated that 7,350 pelts were received by the Alaska Commercial Company: 1200-1500 beaver; 100 cross fox, 100 black fox, 300 red fox, 300 bear, 4,000 marten, 200 otter, 600 lynx, 150 wolverine, 100 wolf. The value of all the furs delivered to St. Michael that August was about $27,000.[162]

Accounts differ about who mined on the Stewart that summer, and how much gold was found. Two men, John Frazer and Thomas Boswell, who had mined the bars the previous summer, were among those who recovered significant amounts on what became known as Chapman's Bar, about 90 miles above the mouth of the Stewart, and Steamboat Bar, another seven miles farther upriver. McQuesten wrote that "they went to work and made $100 a day each."[163] One miner, Mike Hess, wrote to a friend that Peter Wyborg, John Frazer, Frank Moffat and George Matson joined him and, using rocker boxes, they took out $30,000.[164] This was the first time gold had been found in such quantity in the Yukon. Other men reported as having been on the Stewart that summer were Frank Dinsmore, John Hughes, John Powers, Steven Custer, Charley Powell, a man named Chapman and two brothers, Hugh and Al Day. There were more men, perhaps as many as 100.[165]

In late August Boswell came down to Fort Reliance for supplies and McQuesten and Joe soon arrived with the *New Racket*. Unfortunately for Joe and a number of other miners who had been prospecting downriver, Boswell declared that on the Stewart "they got nothing, and that they intended to trap furs that winter." This was a direct violation of the unwritten code among prospectors that everyone was to be told when a strike was made. Later McQuesten wrote that he thought Boswell was "very wrong in his not telling the other boys as there was only five of them and they were all prospectors."[166]

As soon as the 50 tons of miners' supplies were unloaded, McQuesten headed the *New Racket* upriver to trade for furs at Fort Selkirk, taking a number of prospectors and their supplies with him. Boswell disembarked at the mouth of the Stewart to wait until McQuesten returned from Fort Selkirk to then transport him and his supplies up the Stewart to his camp. McQuesten recorded that Joe, Thomas Williams and Mike Hess continued on to Fort Selkirk with him. There, the three men "built a boat and went up on the (Yukon) river to some bars that had been worked the summer before," one likely being Cassiar Bar, 70 miles below the mouth of the Teslin.[167] "They worked until late in the fall..." with little success and, when temperatures began their usual precipitous plunge, they floated downriver to Stewart where they spent the winter.[168]

Dominion Lands Surveyor R. G. McConnell, who made a survey of the Yukon River basin in 1888, reported that by the end of the 1885 mining season many gold-bearing bars had been located on the Stewart River and the yield of gold was valued at $100,000.[169] Although not all the men had found a great amount of gold, most had at least made enough to see them through the winter and another season of mining.

In the fall of 1885 Frank Dinsmore and John Hughes traveled back over Chilkoot Pass and down the coast to Juneau where they told of the significant quantities of gold being found on the Stewart

River. The news spread quickly and soon 300 men were laying plans to cross over the Chilkoot the following spring.[170]

Francois Mercier left Alaska the summer of 1885, never to return. He arrived in San Francisco on August 30 and traveled on to his home in Montreal.[171] His brother, Moise had left in 1874.[172]

Sixteen men wintered at Fort Reliance and Belle Isle that year. McQuesten wrote that "they were all expecting to strike it big: R. (Richard) Poplin, P. (Peter) Wyberg (Wyborg), F. (Frank) Moffatt, J. (John) Frazer, T. (Thomas) Boswell), Joe (Joseph) Macheal (Michael), Ike (Isaac) Powers, J. (John) Chapman, C. (Charles) Powell, A. (Al) Day, H. (Hugh) Day, Mike Hess, T. (Thomas) Williams, Steven Custer, (Howard) Franklin and his partner, Joe Ladue."[173]

In May 1886 Joe, Peter and John Nelson (Nielsen) and Dan Sprague formed a partnership for the purpose of prospecting on the Klondike River. Peter Nelson later wrote that traveling cross-country from Fort Reliance they "struck the Klondike about forty miles up." Finding "light prospects at the mouth of several creeks...we did not consider it worthwhile, as we could make all the way from fifty to one hundred dollars a day on Stewart River...."[174] McQuesten, Harper and Mayo had learned to follow the men who followed the gold, therefore, in the summer of 1886 they closed Fort Reliance, and Harper established a trading post at the mouth of the Stewart River.[175] It was named Fort Nelson after Edward William Nelson of the U.S. Army Signal Service. He was stationed at St. Michael from 1877-1881 and collected specimens of flora and fauna.[176] Fort Reliance was never again opened for trade and, by 1887, most of the buildings had been torn down, their timbers recycled as rafts or fuel for steamers.[177]

Joe mined on the Stewart the summer of 1886 and would later tell a reporter for the *Seattle Daily Times* that there he "did a little better, but did not begin to get much, so I went to Belleisle Station...and started trading for the Alaska Commercial Company" (i.e., McQuesten and Company).[178] Bar mining—panning or rocking sandbars in rivers and creeks—as the practice was along the Stewart—was considerably easier than bushwhacking for prospects or digging shafts to bedrock.

Ladue very likely learned his considerable trading skills by watching "Jack" McQuesten during his time at Fort Reliance. McQuesten was judged the best trader on the Yukon, a skill he had learned from his days with the Hudson's Bay Company. In 1883 Lt. Frederick Schwatka, on a reconnaissance of the Yukon River for the U.S. Army, observed McQuesten trading with the Loucheux at Fort Yukon:

> I was present at an afternoon parley with them, and was greatly impressed at the patience exhibited and required by traders among these savages; a patience such as not one shopman in a thousand possesses, according to my experience, however great a haggler he may be. McQuestion (sic) had learned the art of patience from his old employers (Hudson's Bay Company), probably the most successful bargainers with savages the world has ever seen.[179]

As trader for McQuesten and Company at Belle Isle, the trade goods Joe had to offer were shotguns, rifles, pocket knives, white or red flannel shirts, calico shirts, prints, heavy cloth, shawls, cotton drill, bullets (28 to the pound), #4 shot, butcher knives, tin pans of various sizes, tin cups, metal or pearl buttons, linen thread, silk handkerchiefs, French neckties, British belts, Canadian belts, gunpowder and wide or narrow ribbon.[180]

At Belle Isle that winter Joe traded with the Han from Nuklako, and from Johnny's Village about one mile upriver from the post. In an interview with *New York World* in August 1897 he amended his previous statement about the Stewart saying, "There on the Stewart River was our first mining camp. We found very good mining on the river bars. The bars paid all the way from $2 to $5 and as high as $100 a rocker."[181]

A rocker and shovel were the miner's tools on the Stewart and many other streams in the early days.[182] Joe described a rocker as:

> something similar to our baby cradles, with one end out. They have aprons in and a blanket in the bottom. They are set on an incline. The dirt is put into a hopper and discharged over an apron, then back down on the blanket and from there into the river again. The gold clings to the blanket and the dirt does not.[183]

The only exception to "rocking" during those years was in the fall of 1886 when four men arranged with McQuesten and Company to use the engine of their steamer, the *New Racket*, "to work pumps for sluicing with."[184] The steamer's original owner, Ed Schieffelin, had it constructed with the capability to carry on placer or quartz mining, which meant that her equipment could be used to pump water for sluicing or to crush ore.[185] Sluicing turned out to be very profitable. Each of the four men cleared $1,000 in a month, and "paid an equal amount to the owners of the boat as their share." Considerable gold was taken from the bars of the Stewart during the 1885 and 1886 seasons. Of the several dozen men mining those two seasons, some made at least $5,000 each. The largest amount taken out by an individual was reported to be about $6,000. Some men netted as much as $30 a day, and some instances of $100 per day "were spoken of."[186] Not all the men were as lucky, and even those who had found good gold on the bars of the Stewart (Steamboat, Low Water, Black Mike's, Dutch John's, Joe Jay and others) were disappointed when they all faded quickly after two seasons.[187] But, just as the miners were becoming discouraged with the Stewart, news reached them of a strike about 120 miles downriver.[188]

Since miners began entering the country in 1882, McQuesten had been a great friend of the prospectors, grubstaking many of them and encouraging them to try their luck on the major rivers and their tributaries. In the fall of 1886 he grubstaked Howard Franklin and five other men to prospect on the Forty Mile River.[274] According to Franklin, he, Andrew J. Maiden, Phil Brown, Jim McAdams, Tom (Mickey) O'Brien and Henry "Tuck" Lambert started up the river the first week of September. "As we poled up...we panned on the bars and got prospects on every one." Making use of the daylight on the evening of the seventh, Franklin left camp and walked upstream about two miles. Finding a place where the bedrock was exposed, he dug out a shovelful of dirt and saw in it several pieces of gold. Back at camp the dirt was panned and, when the gold was weighed, the entire party was startled and amazed. Not only did it weigh out at $8.50, it was coarse gold. The next day the excited miners started up the Forty Mile. Late in the day they "got good prospects" on a bar Franklin named "discovery bar," and on which he staked a claim. It would later be known as Franklin Bar. On September 12, Franklin and Phil Brown poled up the Yukon to

Fort Nelson.[190] The news they carried hit the discouraged miners like a bolt of lightning and soon it traveled to the men working the bars of the Yukon and the Stewart.

Although the Stewart River could still be depended upon to yield enough to see a man through another year and a living could be made on Cassiar Bar, the Pelly, Big Salmon and Teslin Rivers, there was only fine gold on all of them. This new discovery with its "nuggety" gold, the kind that rattled in the pan, was the first to be found in the Yukon and too much for most to resist. Soon the rush to the Forty Mile was on and for the next ten years most of the upper river was deserted.[191]

Cabins were quickly built at the mouth of the Forty Mile. By late fall there was a community[192] of 100 to 200 men at the new site impatiently awaiting the spring and the opportunity to try their luck on what promised to be the best diggings yet found in the Yukon. A number of men spent the winter in the few cabins that remained at Fort Reliance, or may have built new ones.[193] Some miners stayed at Belle Isle and about 25[194] elected to remain at Fort Nelson at the mouth of the Stewart. Some later reports indicated that before spring the men at Stewart camp were close to starvation. There were many cases of scurvy, thus much suffering, but Joe was adamant that "Every man was an experienced miner and had all the provisions and supplies he needed. There was not a death at Stewart that winter."[195] McQuesten wrote later that there were "200 men wintered at Fortymile and 20 men at Stewart. There were plenty of provisions of the staple kind for all."[196] The "staple kind" usually meant beans and biscuits, alternating with biscuits and beans. Scurvy does not necessarily kill if it is arrested in time. However, it is a painful, debilitating disease. Jack London suffered from it during his winter in the Yukon and blamed it for his ill health during the rest of his life.

Before the river froze in the fall of 1886, Jack McQuesten traveled upriver and over Chilkoot Pass to Dyea, where he caught one of the year's last steamers to San Francisco.[197] At the 310 Sansome St. offices of the Alaska Commercial Company he tried to persuade President Lewis Gerstle to send 40 or 50 tons of supplies to the Stewart River. Gerstle refused. Later, when word reached San Francisco that McQuesten was in Portland, Oregon, organizing a company of his own to bring goods into the Yukon Valley, the Alaska Commercial Company changed their minds and telegraphed McQuesten that they would be pleased to complete negotiations with regard to the shipment of the required amount of goods to the mouth of the Stewart River. The shipment was delivered the following summer to Forty Mile. Frank Buteau, who had been in the camp for the past year wrote later:

> They shipped the goods, and one could easily see from the brands and quality of goods received that they did not want any miners in the Yukon River Valley. The bacon was in slabs three feet long, all of which was yellow. We called it 'Yard Bacon'. The flour was moldy, the rice was lumpy, the fruit that was green and in the beans were plenty of rocks and gravel.... We did not receive better fare until 1893 when the N. A. T. Company came in, after which time the A. C. Company gave us better provisions.[198]

In contrast to Buteau's opinion about the company's attitude toward miners was a letter from Gerstle in May 1886 to Mr. Lorenz, the company's agent at St. Michael. The company, having learned that a large number of miners had already started for the Yukon and Stewart Rivers, informed the agent that additional supplies were being sent and that prices should not be increased, thereby avoiding any possible suffering that the large increase of population, insufficiently provided with articles of food, might occasion. Gerstle also directed Lorenz to sell only to consumers, and "in such quantities as will enable us to relieve the wants and necessities of each and every person that may have occasion to ask for it."

Gerstle also stated that any other traders in the employ of the company or who draw their supplies from the stores of the Company, doing business on their own account, must not be permitted to charge excessive profits; otherwise all business relations with such parties must cease, as the Company can not permit itself to be made the instrument of oppression toward anyone that they may come in contact with.

> It is useless to add that in case of absolute poverty and want the person or persons placed in that unfortunate position should be promptly furnished with the means of subsistence without

> pay, simply reporting such facts at your earliest convenience to the home office.[199]

It was the opinion of at least one Forty-Miler that:

> The liberal treatment accorded the Prospectors in the Yukon Valley by McQuesten & Mayo was given with the full concurance sic? of the Alaska Commercial Company It was that same splendid faith they had in the manhood & honesty of those early pioneers of the north that made it possible to discover and develop some of the greatest goldfields in the world's history....[200]

Since the discovery of gold on the Forty Mile occurred after McQuesten left for San Francisco in September, it was decided that word must be gotten out to him about the strike. He would need to increase his order to meet the needs of the many miners who were certain to arrive at the new diggings the following season. It was too late to send word by boat, so Thomas Williams offered to make the perilous trip over the Chilkoot. It was the first time any white man had attempted to leave the Yukon by that route during the winter. He took a quantity of coarse gold from Forty Mile with him.

When he and his companion, "Indian Bob," reached the summit of the pass in January 1887, they were caught in a blizzard that lasted several days and they were soon on the verge of starvation. Williams was so weak he was not able to continue, so Bob constructed a "snow hut" to provide some shelter for him, and traveled on alone to Dyea. There he met several men at "Healy's Store" who immediately set out to rescue Williams. They brought him back to the coast, but his condition continued to deteriorate. A few days later he died. Bob faithfully delivered the message, which allowed McQuesten to increase his order and thereby avoid a shortage of food at Forty Mile the following summer. This was another instance of a Yukon Indian providing an invaluable service to white men.[201]

Back in Forty Mile, on December 18, 1886, between eight and nine o'clock at night, the deep winter silence was broken by a visitor from the heavens. A meteor fell somewhere between there and Belle Isle. Frank Buteau said:

> When it struck we heard a report like a cannon fired at sea would make, and could feel a slight jar. Later we learned that Joe Ladue, who had a trading post at Eagle (Belle Isle), saw the meteor was south of him, and we saw it north of us, it must have fallen between Eagle and Forty Mile.[202]

While McQuesten was "Outside" ordering food and miners' supplies, Mayo and Harper remained at Fort Nelson to provide for the miners there and to take in furs from the Indians who trapped throughout the area. In June 1887, Harper journeyed to Forty Mile to oversee the construction of a new store that he and his partners would open in July.[203] Until the store was ready, business was conducted from a tent. The clerk at the tent and subsequently at the new store was Frederick Harte, who had come into the Yukon in 1873 with Arthur Harper.[204] Justifying his personal plea to Gerstle, McQuesten and Company did a booming business at Forty Mile. William Ogilvie, the Dominion land surveyor assigned to determine the U.S./Canadian boundary, was in the area in 1887 and estimated that they sold about $60,000 in food and miners' supplies that year.[205]

Before the spring thaw of 1887, Joe and his partners, John Nelson, Thomas O'Brien and Skiffington "Skiff" Mitchell, made their way over the ice on the Forty Mile River, and in May began working with rockers on Franklin Bar.[206] Later, when melt water was running high in the river they built sluice boxes and a water wheel to facilitate their task.[207] Of the new camp, Joe would later say:

> We had some good diggings at Forty Mile. That was really the first of the Klondike camps.[208] The diggings consisted of bar diggings and bench diggings. Bar diggings are those where the gold has been thrown up on the bars by the action of the water. It is drift gold. Where the point was just right the eddies would whirl the gold around and throw it upon the bars. The bench diggings were in deposits (in terraces along the banks, often marking former shorelines) made by large flows of gravel in which the gold was carried along.[209]

Estimates of the amount of gold taken out during the 1887 season ranged from $65,000 to $150,000.[210]

About 100 to150 men came in over the Chilkoot that spring, making a total of 200 to 300 miners in the district, most of them on the Forty Mile.[211] The trip over Chilkoot was arduous, no matter what the season. Frederick Schwatka described his journey there in June 1883 in his 1885 book, *Along Alaska's Great River*:

> …by seven o'clock (in the morning) all my long pack train was strung up the precipitous pass, making one of the prettiest Alpine sights that I have ever witnessed, and as seen from a distance strangely resembling a row of bowlders (sic) projecting from the snow. Up banks almost perpendicular they scrambled on their hands and knees, helping themselves by every projecting rock and clump of juniper and dwarf spruce, not even refusing to use their teeth on them at the worst places. Along the steep snow banks and the icy fronts of glaciers steps were cut with knives, while rough alpenstocks from the valley helped them to maintain their footing. In some such places the incline was so steep that those having boxes on their backs cut scratches in the icy crust with the corners as they passed along, and often times it was possible to steady one's self by the open palm of the hand resting against the snow. In some of these places a single mis-step, or the caving in of a foot-hold would have sent the unfortunate traveler many hundred feet headlong to certain destruction.[212]

McQuesten and Harper ran the only store at Forty Mile, and the prices of miners' supplies were very high, a fact that made it difficult for many of the miners to remain in the country unless they found gold in good quantity. Mayo continued to operate the post at Stewart, mainly for the fur trade.[213]

Joe knew everyone in the Forty Mile area in 1887 and likely met "Dutch Kate" Wilson, the first white woman to cross over the Chilkoot. She had with her a ton of provisions, expecting to remain for some time. It does not appear that she was prospecting for gold but, not finding any way to provide for herself, she left for St. Michael the following summer.[214]

Forty Mile was the first mining camp of significant size on the Yukon. Crime and violence have historically been an inherent aspect of such frontier communities, but the Forty Mile camp did not meet those expectations. The reason may have been that, once in the vast and remote wilderness of the Yukon, it soon became apparent that one could not survive without his fellow man.

Everyone in Forty Mile, with the exception of the traders and Indians, was a transient. They were there to get rich and return home safely. Yet they understood they were in a demanding environment that required they nurture their relationships with one another.

Disagreements among traveling companions or mining partners were often resolved simply by a parting of ways; violence was not an option. In Forty Mile camaraderie took precedence over competition, cooperation over personal interest.

Journalist Tappan Adney was dispatched to the Yukon in 1897 to write a reliable first-hand account of stampeders' experiences for the *London Chronicle* and *Harper's Weekly*. Adney found that the Yukon's early miners were generally a peaceable and a generous lot:

> Beyond a few quarrels that would be laughed off by the others, there was no trouble among them. One custom in particular that shows this feeling was that when the 1st of August came, and there were any who had failed to locate a bar, they were given permission to go upon the claims of such as had struck it and to take out enough for the next season's outfit. This peaceable condition has, in general, characterized the Yukon.[215]

Founded in 1857, *Harper's Weekly* was one of the most influential publications of its day. It simultaneously reported on, influenced and made history during its 60-year career. For example, it reported on the American West, covering topics such as railroads, life on the plains, the Navajo people, specifically (1890) and Indian territory in general. It kept its audience well informed about exploration and settlement in the West—and, as settlement moved north—in Alaska and the Klondike. At a time when topics like immigrant and ethnic Americans were far from mainstream, it even reported on issues relating to Black Americans (1857-1874).

It is notable, then, that *Harper's* assigned Adney to make his way over the Chilkoot and downriver to Dawson City. During the hectic first months of the rush, there was heated competition among magazines for on-the-spot coverage. *Leslie's Weekly* sent correspondent John Bonner to write about the Klondike Gold Rush in 1897. He reported from Skagway, "the Gate of the Klondike," in the September 30 issue.

One old-timer, arriving at Sitka after three years in the Yukon, made the comment:

> We are out of the reach of the protecting arm of the law, but we have a sort of common law which is ample to protect the life and property of any honest man; but a slippery scoundrel would find it binding on him uncomfortably. A committee settles all disputes according to exact justice.[216]

There were no chosen leaders among the early miners. Men looked up to included McQuesten, Harper, Mayo and Ladue and the small, experienced coterie who had been in the country for several years. Traders had provisions vital to survival; "old-timers" or sourdoughs had knowledge of the geology, the terrain, the weather, the Indians and mining methods that were essential to success in prospecting. Joe Ladue could supply all.

In the early days of Forty Mile when justice was needed, it was found in the "miners' meeting" that was simply an assembly of all those in the area who chose to participate. Anyone could call a meeting to have his or her grievance heard. Private disputes could be aired and settled, crimes prosecuted and justice meted out. Mining regulations were established and bylaws were developed whenever it was decided they would benefit the camp. After an issue had been argued, the decision was made by a simple majority vote. Decisions were final; there was no system for appeals.[217] Two factors that facilitated the effectiveness of miners' meetings were the reliability of the miners' dealings with one another and the concern for integrity. It was imperative for survival of the whole that erratic behavior by individuals be controlled and, if not by one's personal code of ethics, then by the judgment of the community as represented by the miners' meetings. Without a formal code, it was understood by the vast majority that whether one was prospecting, traveling, or simply in need of directions or information, cooperation and support were paramount. Violators of standards of common decency were seen as a threat to the survival of all. As one writer put it, "Whoever struck the first blow had the consensus of opinion of the camp against him."[218]

Miners' meetings "did not dispense a highly formal, 'impersonal' justice, but 'justice' as much from reputation of the parties as from the facts." They were not so much concerned with punishing a man for what he had done, rather, with ensuring there was justice available for all and that the guilty would not pose a future threat to the community. Among men of good will, which most were, it was possible to identify any problems that arose and decide on remedies that were understood and accepted by all.[219]

The availability of miners' meetings, coupled with the possibility of banishment from the country, worked to dampen the potential for extreme violence that might have resulted from serious conflicts. For example, Frank Leslie attempted to poison and then shoot his partners on the Stewart River in the winter of 1886-87. His partners, rather than retaliating with violence, took him to Forty Mile where they called a miners' meeting. Leslie was banished from the country.[220] Banishment meant that the miscreant would be given "a handful of beans, or a little rice and told...to get" downriver with the admonishment that he was never to return.[221]

From the 1880s until 1892, when many men came in to mine the good gold of Miller Creek, the unwritten miners' code of mutual trust continued to guide the behavior of traders and miners alike. Another example of this occurred when Harper and Ladue received a shipment of goods at their trading post on Sixty Mile Island. John Sidney Webb wrote in the March 1898 issue, of *New Century Illustrated Monthly Magazine* that there were so many men waiting in line to replenish their outfits, Harper told them to:

> sail in, and help themselves, and keep an account of what they took, and hand it to him. Present the list to him. There was a discrepancy of only six cans of condensed milk between the sum total of the taking individuals and the entire amount of provisions called for by the manifest of the boat, and this might have been a mistake made by a shipping clerk.[222]

Herbert Heller wrote in *Sourdough Sagas*: "Strange as it seems, the Golden Rule provided the Sourdough with guidance in most of their relationships with their fellow men in this land of gold."[223] Mrs. Eli Gage of Boston agreed. Her husband was an auditor for a trading company. When the couple moved to the Klondike, Mrs. Gage found life there rough and tumble, but she thought the miners themselves "the kindest, most considerate and most practically honest people that I ever met," and she doubted she could find these qualities to the same degree in "Chicago or other civilized places."[224]

The character of the Indians, in some respects, resembled that of the kind and considerate miners, although few references to that fact are found in the recorded history of the Yukon. One observer, while apparently as racially prejudiced as the majority at the time, wrote:

> The savage, when you find him without the cussedness taught by the white man, makes a pretty good citizen. He may be lazy, but he is honest; and perhaps his laziness is only due to the fact that he has always had a "squaw" to do chores around, and has never been trained to the white man's ways of working; but let any fellow try following an Indian on snow-shoes for a couple of days, and his ideas soon change...He is A1 on the trail. Another thing about the Indian is that when one has grub they all have grub. This is the way of the Stick Indians inside, and you can cache your grub in their country or leave things lying around, and they won't touch them....[225]

William Dall, Director of the Scientific Corps assigned by the *Smithsonian Institution* to the Western Union Telegraph expedition to Alaska from 1865-1867, wrote later of the Indians he met along the Yukon:

> The Men of the Yukon had, like other men, their careers, affections, tragedies and triumphs. The valley whose rim enclosed their world, since they knew none other, was as wide for them as our world is for us. It is certain that for their world they had worked out problems, which we are still facing with puzzled trepidation in ours. No man went hungry in a Yukon village. The trail might be lined with temporary caches, yet no man put out his hand to steal. Men were valued by their achievements and their liberality. Any man might rise to eminence and leadership by showing his fitness in his community. The stranger was welcomed without inquisitiveness, sheltered and fed without ostentation, and sent on his way without fee or reward. The

> dead were protected and remembered; their deeds of prowess handed down as examples for the young. Their religion was vague and their politics mostly a minus quantity; but in practice they knew what was just and good, and in the main made it their rule of life.[226]

William D. Moore had come into the Yukon with Joe in 1882, and had regular contact with the Indians along the river for many years. He described them as "a most peaceable and orderly race. They welcome the presence of white settlers and are only too anxious to become friendly whenever any disposition is shown by the newcomer."[227]

Several years later Joe was asked about law and order in the Yukon during the early days:

> "Were there no thieves?" "Not one." "No cut-throats?" "None." "Gamblers?" "Plenty. Everybody gambles, especially in the long winter nights." "Don't they cheat?" "No." "Why not?" "The saloon-keep ers won't have it." "How can they prevent it? Are there no professional gamblers in the camps?" "Yes, but they put up a straight game. And, there are men, too, who have been pretty bad before; I have heard that some of them were ex-convicts and fellows who had run away to escape prison and hanging. But none of them try anything on in there." "But, why don't they?" "I don't know." "What are they afraid of? Has anyone ever been punished?" "Not that I remember." "Well, why don't thieves steal...?" "I guess they dasent."(dare not)[228]

Unfortunately, as the number of miners increased and, with the arrival of saloons, character and justice mattered less. In a lecture given in Victoria, B.C., in 1897, William Ogilvie stated:

> Cliques formed, and if a miner was not on the "inside," he had little chance of getting a fair hearing, and certainly could not expect justice. One instance of this occurred in Forty Mile. When a man called for a miners' meeting he was told that he had to pay a $20 fine for calling the meeting. Obviously the victim in this case was an outsider and had no friends on the inside.[229]

In 1897, when asked his opinion on later-day miners' meetings, Joe agreed with Ogilvie:

> The miners on the Yukon are shrewd, experienced men, and sometimes they are tricky. I do not like the kind of government they set up for themselves, except in the very first stages. It is all by miners' meetings. They begin by being fair, but after a while cliques are formed which run things to suit the men who are in them, or, which is just as bad, they turn the sessions into fun. Nobody can get justice from a miners' meeting when the women are on one side.
>
> Sometimes in winter, when there is plenty of time, a dispute that is left to the miners' meeting grows into a regular trial, with lawyers (there are several among the miners) engaged for a fee, a committee in place of the judge, and a regular jury. Witnesses are examined, the lawyers make speeches, and the trial lasts till nobody who listens to it at all knows what to think. I never liked it. The best way, according to my experience, for two men who can't agree to have a settlement is to choose their own committee, each side picking a representative and both selecting a third. Then the committee is fair, and generally the decision is satisfactory.[230]

In at least one instance, miners' justice was carried out beyond the camp's limits—in fact, beyond the country's limits. In the fall of 1887, miner John Bremner was murdered by Indians on the Dolby River, a tributary of the Koyukuk in Alaska.[231] The following summer Joe joined 15 other miners and set out to administer justice.[232] The vigilantes vowed they would "make it their business that summer to seek every Indian murderer and hang him." Arriving at the mouth of the Koyukuk, they borrowed the Alaska Commercial Company steamer *Pioneer*,[233] and made their way upriver to the location where Bremner had met his end. At a nearby Indian camp they learned that an old medicine man and his 18-year-old nephew[234] had been the culprits. After confronting them, the younger man confessed that it was he who had actually committed the murder.[235] He was loaded into the miners' boat and taken to an island at the mouth of the Koyukuk where he was hanged from a cottonwood tree. To ensure their job was complete, the miners fired several shots into the body.[236]

That same fall saw the first thawing of the ground with fire to get at the gold locked inside. Over the years miners had not only been looking for gold, but also looking for some way to move beyond the sandy bars to the frozen ground on the banks of the rivers. Thawing the ground with fire had been conceived of, but the idea had never been put to practical use. (McQuesten and Ladue unsuccessfully attempted it on the Sixty Mile in the fall of 1882.) At Franklin Gulch in 1887, Fred Hutchinson had to stop work when the pay-streak he was following extended beneath the water of the stream.

That winter, however, after the ice had formed, he chopped down several inches making sure he did not break through to the water below. As the water froze deeper, Hutchinson would chop down another few inches. What he created was an ice shaft to the ground. Then he began building fires, thawing down a few inches a day until he was able to take out a little "pay dirt." His neighbors observed this innovative technique and thought it was hilarious. But the following year two of them tried it themselves, apparently without particular success. In a few years, however, "burning down," albeit slow, advancing about one foot per day, would be the miners' primary method of reaching bedrock where the pay-streak was found. Soon they were excavating horizontal tunnels which followed the pay-streak, a procedure called "drifting."[237]

One of the difficulties of early Yukon mining was the shortage, not only of food, but also of tools. Shovel and pick handles broke, as did the points of picks. If a miner had poor tools, or no tools, when the season opened in the spring, his operations would be essentially stalled until the arrival of one of the steamers from St. Michael later in the summer. If he could not wash out at least enough to purchase food for the winter and the next season he would be forced to leave the country in the fall. At Forty Mile during the winter of 1887-88 John Nelson and Frank Buteau saw the opportunity to remedy this situation and decided to start a small business repairing miners' picks. Joe made a trip upriver to Fort Nelson to get steel and borax from Al Mayo who had apprenticed as a blacksmith and, with ingenuity typical of the early men in the Yukon, they established a going concern. Buteau described their blacksmithing operation:

We had to fashion tools out of the crude materials on hand as

> we had no blacksmith equipment of any kind. We made a bellows out of moose skin that had been tanned by the Indians only to find that it was porous and allowed the air to escape through the skin. We then melted moose tallow and coated the inside of the skin with it after which the bellows worked satisfactorily for our purposes. We used a boulder for an anvil and a pole ax for a sledge. We made charcoal and used it for blacksmithing as there was no coal available.[238]

That winter, as usual, the men at Forty Mile played cards and checkers, drank whiskey, told stories, chopped wood, kept their sourdough starter warm and waited impatiently for winter to release its grip on the waters of the Forty Mile. Some couldn't wait, and by late April loaded their sleighs with provisions, a gold pan, shovel and a rocker box and started out. Finally, in mid-May 1888, those who had remained in camp heard the ice of the Yukon begin to groan as cracks appeared, and soon great blocks of ice, some ten feet thick, began to move downriver tumbling and crashing against one another, creating a sound that likely terrified those who heard it for the first time. Soon the ice of the Forty Mile joined the turmoil. And when it was over, everybody headed for the creeks to see what luck they would have in the new season.

Those who returned to bars they had located the previous summer shoveled the gravel into their boxes and "rocked" as fast as they could, stopping periodically to wash out the riffles and pad to see how much gold had accumulated. Others prospected from bar to bar, hoping always that the next one would prove a bonanza.

By the end of the season, however, it was clear that none of the miners in the Forty Mile district had struck it rich, including Joe. Frank Buteau wrote that getting "$500 to $1,500 was considered a good year's work. Three thousand dollars is the most I know of that anybody made during a year."[239] The nuggety gold that "rattled in the pan" had been an exciting change from the "flour" gold of the bars on the upper Yukon and the Stewart, but few, in fact, found nuggets in quantities sufficient to keep them in the inhospitable Yukon. "No important strike was made anywhere in this (Forty Mile) district in 1888." It was estimated that the total amount of gold taken was worth only $15,000.[240] At the end of the 1888 mining season, not only did winter stop all the activity, but most of the miners who had worked the "bars" of the Forty Mile that summer left the district for good. They felt there were not enough good prospects to encourage them to return. They expressed themselves as "glad to get away from the country," and as having "no ardent belief that gold exists in the Yukon Valley to such an extent as to warrant any great hazard to search for it or to attempt to develop anything of the kind."[241]

By the time the heavy hand of winter's cold turned off the flow of the water of the Forty Mile bringing mining to a halt, a disappointed Joe, too, had given up on the Forty Mile. He had "mined for two whole summers...and then went over the boundary about 300 miles where I began ranching at Fort Selkirk."[242] He had been mining on Franklin Gulch and nearby Troublesome Bar, both on the U.S. side of the boundary. His route "over the boundary" took him over a ridge of land to the headwaters of the Sixty Mile, down that river to the Yukon, and then upriver about 115 miles to Fort Selkirk.

Joe spent that winter and the following summer at Fort Selkirk with Arthur Harper and his family. He devoted most of his time to what he termed "ranching—cultivating potatoes, turnips, radishes and cabbages. But the growing season was short, as usual; frost was early, and "nipped almost everything." That was to be his last attempt at "ranching" in the far North.[243]

Meanwhile, the summer of 1889, the Alaska Commercial Company had brought to St. Michael a new steamer for the river. It was called the *Arctic*, with dimensions unheard of on the Yukon: 28 feet wide by 140 feet long by 6 feet deep.[244] Its captain was William D. Moore. Unfortunately, on its maiden voyage, loaded with 200 tons of food for the traders along the river, it "struck a rock or snag and sank, completely destroying all the provisions."[245] The company sent Indian men upriver with the message that there would be no deliveries of food that season, advising the miners to make their way to St. Michael where there was ample food for all for the winter. When that word reached Joe at Fort Selkirk, he, Arthur Harper, Jennie and their children left downriver on the steamer *New Racket* (now owned by Harper and christened by him, "*Little Pelley*"). About 200 men were living at Forty Mile, 80 of whom had insufficient food for the winter. According to one miner who was there, all 80 crowded aboard Harper's little steamer and headed for St. Michael.[246] For years to come, that winter was known among sourdoughs and veteran miners as the "year of the famine" or "starvation winter" because all along the river there was so little food.[247]

Sometime during the summer of 1889 Harper had decided to leave his old partners, McQuesten and Mayo, to operate as an independent trader.[248] That winter Harper and Joe stayed about 30 miles above Nulato[249] and spent much time discussing the possibility of forming a partnership for the purpose of trading on the upper Yukon.[250] The country was wide open to them. There were furs to be had, numerous creeks to be prospected and many miners needing supplies. And, there was no competition. They decided to operate a "joint business" independent of the Alaska Commercial Company but in a relationship that, as was the case with McQuesten and Mayo, effectively made them agents of the company[251].

In the fall of 1890, the Harpers and Joe traveled together up the Yukon on *Little Pelley* to an island at the mouth of the Sixty Mile where Joe disembarked to construct a trading post and living quarters.[252] Harper and his family continued upriver and established themselves at Fort Selkirk where the only remnant of the Hudson's Bay Company post, destroyed in 1852, was a stone chimney.[253] Joe stated later that he immediately "went into the mercantile business." Harper stated in his June 30, 1896, application for 160 acres of land at Fort Selkirk that he "occupied it in 1891...."

Although it was reported later by Tappan Adney that Harper and Ladue operated a "joint business," their business relationship until 1895 is uncertain. What is known is that in January 1894 Harper placed an advertisement for his Fort Selkirk operations in the Yukon Press:

A. HARPER,
FORT SELKIRK.
GENERAL
MERCHANDISE.

Miners operating on the Lewis or Hootalinka rivers, will find it to their advantage to obtain their outfits at this establishment. We carry a large stock of

Groceries and Provisions, Clothing,
Boots, Shoes, etc., etc.,

All our goods are of First-class Quality,
carefully selected, which we will sell or
trade on reasonable terms.

HIGHEST PRICES PAID FOR FURS
TERMS CASH.

In 1895 the partnership was advertised in Juneau as "*A. Harper and Company.*"[254] Both men, in addition to trading, raised large gardens, Joe more successfully because the alluvial soils of Sixty Mile Island did not hold permafrost. Harper, in an attempt to defeat the cold ground and early frosts and extend the growing season, purchased "an immense awning made of heavy cotton which he lowered...every clear night when frost threatened."[255] Much farther north, at Nuklukayet, McQuesten had been successful some years in growing potatoes and onions of good quality, and turnips weighing up to six and a half pounds each.[256] In 1889, the McQuesten garden at Forty Mile, tended by Kate, produced "10 tons of turnips, some of the largest weighed 7 pounds."[257] Turnips, one of the cultivated vegetables introduced to Alaska by the Russians, were a commodity that kept well for months in root cellars, packed in layers of dry sand.

Every spring for the next six years the partners transported to St. Michael the furs they took in from the Indians and brought back trade goods and miners' supplies on *Little Pelley*, whose engineer was old-timer, Alex McDonald (not to be confused with the "Big Alex" McDonald, "King of the Klondike"). Profit in furs was a sure thing. But as for the gold potential of the Sixty Mile, its tributaries (Glacier, Miller, Bedrock, Little Gold and others) and nearby Indian River and its tributaries, it was more a matter of faith and speculation. Considerable prospecting had been done on many of those creeks, particularly by Harper, but little gold had been found. Joe knew, from his own prospecting in 1886 with the Nelson brothers and Dan Sprague, that there was gold in the Klondike Valley but he neither returned there nor does it appear that he particularly encouraged other prospectors to do so. It is curious, therefore, that he stated in an interview with *New York World* in 1897 that several men at the Sixty Mile Post "had faith in that country—which I did myself—in the vicinity of the Thron diuck (Klondike) river."[258]

While Harper's focus was mainly on the fur trade at Fort Selkirk, Sixty Mile Post was centrally located in relation to all the creeks on which Joe and Harper pinned their hopes. Their plan was to encourage prospectors to work the creeks and provide them with grubstakes.[259] The post became a gathering place with at least 100 miners remaining there for the winter of 1890-91.[260] Many came as a result of Harper's enthusiastic letters to his acquaintances in the Cassiar District of British Columbia where he had mined before coming to the Yukon.[261] Business was very good for the partners, but Joe was to suffer accusations that he was telling lies about the potential of Indian River and was "almost driven from Forty Mile by the irate miners"[262] on one of his visits there.

By the summer of 1891, however, Joe's faith in the country began to pay off. Gold was discovered on Miller Creek[263] and in 1892 on nearby Glacier Creek.[264] Claims sold for as much as $2,000 on Glacier,[265] and, on Miller, were "the first rich diggings of the Klondike country."[266] Until the big strike by Skookum Jim and friends in the Klondike Valley in 1896, Miller Creek was mined successfully, yielding about $300,000 in 1894[267] and $400,000 in 1895.[268]

No record has been located to indicate whether Harper and Ladue had grubstaked any of the lucky prospectors on Glacier and Miller. If they had, the partners would have profited considerably since the terms of a grubstake meant they would receive an agreed-upon percentage of the profits of any strike that was found.

Harper and Ladue's trade with the indigenous people was extremely profitable. In June 1892 the partners arrived at Forty Mile with several bales of furs they had taken in the previous season. Henry Davis, was there and later recorded:

> Included were a lot of tanned moose skins...also nine thousand martens and lots of fox and lynx in ten big bales. They got their fur cheap, for if an Indian wanted a rifle, they stood it on the floor and the Indians stacked their skins to the top of the rifle.

> A sack of flour came the same way, flat ways on top of each other. Robbers I say they were.[269]

Some prospectors used bottles or vials of patent medicine as improvised thermometers. When mercury solidified, they knew it was minus 28 degrees Fahrenheit, a temperature at which chopping wood or dog sledding was still feasible. When unadulterated whiskey froze, it was minus 55 degrees Fahrenheit—usually too cold to travel.

At some time during his years at Sixty Mile Post, Joe purchased a circular metallic thermometer, the only one in the area. It worked on the principle of expansion and contraction of steel according to the temperature. However, it was unreliable because its accuracy depended in great part upon its being properly adjusted—very difficult to accomplish. Miners greeted the invention with enthusiasm, and for a time during the winter consulted it before beginning a journey of any length on foot. It was known up and down the river as "Ladue's Wheel."

One example of the "wheel's" inaccuracy occurred when some men came to the post to buy food. Before starting the return trip to their camp, they checked "Ladue's Wheel," which registered 83 degrees below, too cold for even the shortest journey. Every day for a week, the wheel continued to indicate extreme cold. The impatient men decided they could delay no longer. They set off, and on their way stopped at a camp where the miner had "an accurate instrument." It registered 32 below. When the word got out to the camps and back to the trading post, "Ladue's Wheel" became notorious, and the butt of many a joke.[270] But Joe in these days was full of optimism and could take a good joke, even one at his own expense. Ogilvie described him as "ever-smiling."[271]

In 1893 the post at Sixty Mile was renamed "Ogilvie" by Harper and Ladue for Dominion Lands Surveyor, William Ogilvie, pursuant to an agreement Harper and McQuesten had made in 1887 "to name any future posts they might establish in Canadian territory after Canadian officials...."[272]

In midsummer Joe had a visitor who had come over the Chilkoot Pass and down the river. He was English explorer and sportsman, Warburton Pike. Joe was in disbelief when Pike informed him he was "not mining, and only running down the Yukon as the shortest way out of the country." Pike would later write that Joe finally came to the conclusion "we were either Government officials or gamblers—apparently the only professions left open to the traveler on the Yukon who is neither miner, trader nor missionary."[273]

Following Pike's visit Joe had another visitor, one who would indirectly play a significant role in his life a few years later. When Captain Henry Henderson and his partner, Donald Robertson, arrived at Ogilvie they "gathered around Joe Leduc (sic) to get the news of the country and to find where was the best place to look for gold." He recommended Miller Creek and the next morning they started out. After several weeks of prospecting Henderson and his partner were running low on food and returned to Ogilvie. Just as they arrived, the Alaska Commercial Company's steamer *Arctic* was docking, carrying the Yukon's first sawmill to A. Harper and Company After helping unload the sawmill, Robertson, an experienced sawyer, was hired by Joe to run the mill at $10 a day; Henderson was hired to travel up the Stewart River to bring the *Little Pelley* down from the "McQuestron(sic)" River and to "make trips to Forty Mile for supplies, paying me $10.00 per day to take charge of her and I agreed to go." While on the Stewart, Henderson used the pumps of the *Little Pelley* for sluicing. Leaving the Yukon that fall, Henderson traveled to Aspen, Colorado, where he visited his brother, Robert, whom he hadn't seen in six years. When he described to his brother "the fine gold on the bars of the rivers and the coarse gold at Forty Mile," Robert's response was, "That is a rich country. I'm going there and nothing will stop me this time." (Fourteen years earlier he had asked Henry to go to the Yukon with him.)[274]

Meanwhile at Forty Mile camp, McQuesten and Company continued brisk trade in furs and mining supplies. Miners were working on Franklin Gulch and Miller, Glacier, Dome, Nugget, Poker and Davis Creeks. McQuesten and Company had also established a post downriver at Circle City near the new discoveries on Birch Creek.[275] But business for McQuesten and Company was about to change significantly. The total control of the Alaska Commercial Company since 1883 had resulted in prices well beyond what many considered justified or fair, and another entrepreneur was about to challenge the monopoly.[276]

In 1892, John Healy,[277] the most outspoken critic of the high prices, got the backing from several wealthy Chicago men, primarily the owners of the Cudahy Meat Packing Company, to establish the North American Trading and Transportation Company. By 1893 it had a new boat on the river, the *Portus B. Weare*, named for the president of the company, and opened a post across the mouth of the Forty Mile River, which they named Fort Cudahy. Miners referred to it as "Healy's Company."[278] North American Trading and Transportation Company opened a second store at Circle City. With this increased competition, prices of goods at both places immediately plummeted.[279]

By 1893 Forty Mile, as well as Ogilvie, was the scene of much activity. Population numbers were impossible to determine as miners moved constantly between the camp and their claims. Among those numbers were several women, wives of traders and some miners' wives. There was the greatly respected Kate McQuesten. She cared for her five children and, every summer while maintaining a large vegetable garden, Kate found time to serve as interpreter for her husband. Other resident females included Margaret Mayo, Isabella Healy, wife of the manager of the North American Trading and Transportation Company, Selina Bompas, wife of the Anglican missionary in charge of the St. John's Buxton Mission, and Bridget Mannion, Healy's maid, whose later marriage to miner, Frank Allwood, would be the first in Forty Mile.[280]

Circle City camp sprang up following the discovery of gold on Birch Creek by two Creole brothers-in-law, Pitka Pavaloff and Sergei Gologoff Cherosky. McQuesten had grubstaked them[281] and wrote, "In the spring of 1893 I gave Pitka and Soniciska (sic), two Indians, provisions to go prospecting on Birch Creek."[282] Unfortunately, because of their lack of knowledge of how properly to stake claims, and the devious activities of several white men, Pavaloff and Cherosky lost their ground, even though McQuesten interceded on their behalf.[283] Cherosky and his wife Irinia were long-time interpreters for McQuesten and, for some period before 1874, provided the same services for trader Moise Mercier at Fort Yukon.[284]

In 1893 Circle City was the first mining camp to be established along the Yukon River on the American side of the boundary. Because of floodwaters the following spring, McQuesten's store, along with the whole town, was moved to its present site on higher ground.[285] By the winter of 1894-95 the new McQuesten and Company store was open for business.

There, too, was the North American Trading and Transportation Company with a new trading post of its own. Within a year the population swelled to over 1,000 and Circle City became the largest log settlement in the world—often referred to as "McQuesten's town." With most of the best gold claims in the Sixty Mile and Forty Mile regions already staked, miners coming into the country headed for Circle City from which they could follow the ten-mile trail to the new Birch Creek diggings. The majority of the hundreds of men who poured into the country were Americans and, on Birch Creek and its tributaries, many found the good gold they had traveled so far to find. Circle City was the largest mining camp on the Yukon up to that date, and would remain so until January 1897. There were miners' meetings for settling disputes, but the camaraderie that had bound men to one another and the code of conduct that guided their relationships were things of the past. Still, although there were several saloons, dance halls and gambling halls, it was not a particularly lawless town. In fact, it was "the most peaceable of mining camps," in which a single U.S. marshal was able to handle law and order with little difficulty.[286] Among the log buildings rose three restaurants, a number of bakeries and several laundries, a tinsmith's shop, a barber shop and bathhouse, two theaters, three blacksmith shops, churches, a hospital, and Jack McQuesten's library brought from Forty Mile. On the shelves were two "bibles"—one, the Holy Bible; the other, equally revered by miners, a volume written by geologist Alexander von Humboldt.

In 1895 the community, by an unusual series of events, acquired its first public library. The *Dawson Daily News* reported in its February 5, 1907 issue that the *Fairbanks News* had carried the story as given to them by Peter L. Trout, a miner at Circle City from 1895-97. Trout reported that the library would not have come into existence if it had not been for a can of butter. A "luxury-loving" miner on Deadwood Creek "ordered a can of butter from civilization for his own delight." The *News* continued:

> One day a messenger came hurriedly down the creek, calling to every man he passed that the can of butter had been stolen and a miners' meeting was called in town at once.

Every man threw down pick and shovel on the instant. The news passed quickly from claim to claim and in a very short time everyone was headed for town. That was a sober looking lot of men. Everyone seemed to feel the gravity of the crime and the stain it put upon the good name of the community.

On a motion a committee of six was appointed to examine every tent and cabin on the creek. In less than ten minutes the committee returned to the meeting with the can of butter.

The second cabin searched had discovered the butter. Additional evidence of the owner's guilt was found in the partially devoured slices of buttered bread found upon his table.

There were varying opinions as to what to do with the man. Some suggested hanging. This seemed, to the majority, too severe a penalty, and banishment was finally settled upon.

The butter thief was supplied with "a little money and a boat" and warned never to return. All his property—cabin, claim and other possessions—went on the auction block and "fetched about $1,600." These were the first public funds Circle had ever had and since there were no public expenses, no one, for some time, knew what to do with them. Trout said, "Finally, we hit upon the idea of the public library. That $1,600 brought into the public treasury by one small tin of butter, gave Circle its public library, and it was a very good one, too."

George Carmack, a prospector[287] who had come into the country in 1885, was at Ogilvie in the fall of 1894. Carmack was the son of a forty-niner. With Harper's encouragement he had prospected on the Sixty Mile River and Quartz Creek, a tributary to the Indian River. He found little gold and returned to Ogilvie where he spent that winter. He remained at Ogilvie part of the next summer and worked at Harper and Ladue's sawmill.[288]

Carmack had earlier established, for John Healy, a small store known as "McCormick's Post" or "Stick George's" Post on the Yukon River about 20 miles above Five Finger Rapids.[289] Although the store was never very active, it was Healy's intention that trade would be carried on with the Indians at Tagish and those living along the rivers in the interior. Carmack left a note at the post in the summer of 1894 saying that he had "Gone to Forty Mile for grub." Little did he suspect the incredible events that would surround him in the years ahead. When gold seekers stopped by in 1897 on their way to the Klondike the note was still pinned to the door but Carmack had not returned.[290]

A Trip East

By 1894 Joe had accumulated "maybe $7,000 or $8,000" from mining, mainly on the Stewart and from his joint business with Arthur Harper so, for the first time since 1879, he had planned a trip back to his hometown of Schuyler Falls, New York. In early February he and George Baker, an employee of McQuesten and Company at Forty Mile, started out overland from Ogilvie to deliver their reports to the Alaska Commercial Company offices in San Francisco.[291] They had two sleighs loaded with provisions and dog food, and a team of seven dogs to pull each sleigh. They knew it would take at least three weeks to travel the nearly 600 miles to the coast where they could board a steamer from Juneau. Winter travel in the Yukon during those years was always a risky venture, full of hazards and sometimes fatal, even to experienced men properly dressed. Joe and Baker expected the exhausting work of breaking trail much of the way and temperatures that would hover between 50 and 60 below zero. They also knew that in Yukon winters there would likely be no wind, the air would be dry and, therefore, the cold more tolerable.[292]

But, during the first day of their journey, the highly unusual happened—a strong wind rushed at them from the north blowing the snow into high drifts and creating a wind-chill of 100 below zero. These conditions continued for 300 miles. The relentless wind howled day and night. Where the snow was particularly deep it was impossible for the dogs to pull the sleighs through. It would take Joe and Baker a full and exhausting day to break trail, packing down the snow with snowshoes for as few as ten miles before returning to where they had left their sleighs. The following day the dogs pulled their sleighs over the ten miles of newly broken trail. The next day this arduous process was repeated.

When the men made camp at the end of each day, both they and their dogs were exhausted. They cleared an area in the woods, fed their dogs chunks of dried salmon, built a fire to thaw their precooked beans,[293] melted snow for drinking water, put up a windbreak and chopped enough wood to last until morning. Some nights they may have built two fires and slept between them, a common practice among winter travelers. In the mornings they awakened under huge drifts of snow and to the sound of the relentless roaring wind.[294] They thought their ordeal would never end. Even seasoned miners would have marveled at how they survived, escaping without even serious frostbite; some, in years to come, were not to be so lucky. Baker and Joe arrived in San Francisco on April 10, 1894, and after delivering their reports to the company, Joe continued his journey home by railroad.

Two months after Joe and Baker's journey out of the Yukon, Jack Tremblay, his bride, nee Emilie Fortin, and three Indian packers were on their way in, heading for Jack's claim on Miller Creek, a tributary of the Sixty Mile. Their route for much of the way was nearly identical to that of Joe's, but the weather had warmed considerably. They crossed over Chilkoot Pass and packed their provisions on sleighs from Lake Lindeman to Lake Bennett. There they cut logs, whipsawed planks and built two boats. Their food supply was supplemented by grayling which, in the spring, could always be caught in large numbers in the streams, and by ptarmigan, grouse, bear and porcupine meat. When the ice went out in mid-May, the party started out across Lake Bennett and on to Windy Arm, Tagish and Marsh Lakes. Of them, Emilie Tremblay would later write: "The clear and blue waters of those lakes were beautiful and sparkling under springtime sun. Those lakes are natural reservoirs fed by numerous ravines and valleys, creeks and rivers coming down from the mountains whose crests were still white with snow."

When the Tremblays arrived at Forty Mile they found it populated by "about 20 miners; among them, Jack McQuesten, Henry Rivers, John and Peter Nelson, Joe Roy, Napoleon Huot, Napoleon Picotte, Tom O'Brien and Howard Hamilton Hart." After a couple weeks they started poling their boats up the Forty Mile River, headed for Miller Creek. Within a few days they were at the mouth of Moose Creek. They made their way along that creek for about 30 miles, "up and down the mountains, through swamps and overburns and surrounded continually with mosquitoes." Crossing over a low ridge of land, they entered the upper reaches of the Sixty Mile and soon came to Miller Creek and Jack's claims. Miller Creek was the most productive of all the streams in the area and the scene of most of the mining activity in the Yukon in 1894.

The Tremblays became well known and admired greatly throughout the territory in 1894, and for many years to come in the Klondike. From 1898 to 1913, Jack prospected "up and down the mountains and the valleys" of the Klondike and worked as a mine foreman on 17 Eldorado. When mining was no longer profitable for the Tremblays, they bought a little house in town at the corner of Third and King Streets where Emilie opened a dry goods store. There they lived until Jack's death in 1935; Emilie continued to live there until 1940. Jack was buried in St. Mary's Catholic Cemetery in Dawson. Still readable on his white metal grave marker are the words "At Rest, The Body of Nolasque Tremblay, Better Known as 'The Grand Old Man' Jack. Born in Chicoutimi, Que., January 30, 1868. God Bless The One Everyone Loved."

The building with its sign, "Madame Tremblay's Store," remains in Dawson City, now the property of Parks Canada and one of only a few such remnants surviving from that period.[295]

While Joe was Outside during the winter of 1894-95, the miners at Forty Mile formed the Yukon Order of Pioneers, a fraternal organization with the Golden-Rule-like motto, "Do As You Would Be Done By." The founding of the organization was discussed during the summer of 1894 and, on December 1, a constitution was written, adopted and the order formally organized. The purposes of the organization were: the advancement of the great Yukon Valley, the mutual protection and benefit of its members, to unite the members by the strong tie of Brotherhood, and to prove to the outside world that the Yukon Order of Pioneers are men of Truth, Honor and Integrity.

Only a man who had entered the country by 1888 and, was indeed, "a man of Truth, Honor and Integrity" was qualified to apply for membership. In 1895, membership privileges were extended to all those who had come into the watershed of the Yukon by 1889. In later years the required date of arrival for membership was moved ahead several times. It was also decided, at the organizational meeting, that the Order would have "a pin with a square and compass and Y.O.O.P. in the center."[296] One charter member, Henry Davis, said they gave the contract for the pins to jeweler George Bemis, who "can make the pins when he is sober."[297]

It seems odd that Joe, one of the earliest of Yukon pioneers, was never a member of an organization whose purposes reflected his own beliefs and the way of life he had followed since 1882. During an interview in 1897 he told Lincoln Steffens of *McClure's Magazine* that he knew little about the order.

> It is something like the California Pioneers of '49. They have a gold badge in the shape of a triangle with Y.P. on it and the date '89. To be a member you must have come into the country before 1889. But the time limit used to be earlier, and it may be later now, for they have shoved it on up several times since I have noticed. The Society does some good. When a man gets sick and caves in it raises money to send him out. Now and then it gives a ball, and there are plans on foot to have more pleasures of that sort next winter and after that.[298]

While in New York, Joe stayed with the family of James Lobdell in Schuyler Falls where he had lived as a boy from about 1870 until 1874. During this visit he became reacquainted with Catharine "Kittie" Mason whom he remembered as the little girl who lived next door to the Lobdells. She did not remember him, since she was only four years old when he had left about 20 years earlier for Center Point, Iowa, following the death of his father, Francois.

It was apparently love at first sight for Joe, for Kittie would state later that Joe "wanted me to marry him then and go to Alaska. My father did not want me to go, so I decided to wait for him here."[299]

On several occasions, Joe took his friend, Willie Lobdell, the son of James and Carrie, and other young people to the Plattsburgh Theatre to see plays. One of them, *Uncle Tom's Cabin*, was based on the 1852 anti-slavery novel of the same name by Harriet Beecher Stowe. Mrs. Kate Hobbs Honsinger, who was still living in the 1960s, recalled being one of that group. She described Joe to Emily McMasters of Plattsburgh as "a thin, dark complexioned man of medium height, very quiet and unassuming." Joe and Kittie apparently kept their romance a secret as Mrs. Honsinger also stated that none of Joe's friends "knew anything of Kittie Mason."[300]

When Joe left on his return journey to the Yukon, March 12, 1895, he had as companions two adventurous young men from Clinton County—Ellis Turner, 22, and Willis Lamay, 32. A local newspaper carried a note that "A large number attended the 'Goodbye' party for Ellis Turner last Friday evening. He leaves with

Jos. Ladue for Alaska next week."[301] They traveled on the Union Pacific Railroad across the country through Chicago to Cheyenne, Wyoming,[302] and from there left for San Francisco on the Southern Pacific arriving March 17th. While in San Francisco they stayed at the Palace Hotel. On the 19th Joe took them "around ...the city." Ellis Turner ran out of words when he wrote to his sisters, Ruby and Anna: "I wish you could see what I have seen. I can't tell you much about what I have seen. A person has no idea of the world or a city 'till they have seen sum of it."[303] Ellis did have a chance to show his family many of the sites he saw on his trip and during his stay in Alaska and the Yukon, as he carried a camera in his pack.

On March 20, the trio visited Chinatown, a community of 60,000 people, and apparently such a dangerous area that they had to have a "police detective" accompany them.[304]

On the same day, Joe and his party bought part of their "out fit for the youcon." Ellis Turner received a letter from home that day and wrote back to his family that he "never felt better than I do now." He was very excited about his journey north, writing that he was "in a hurry to get started."[305] Before leaving San Francisco around the 23rd of March, Joe purchased a "steam bot (sic) engine" for the *Little Pelley*.[306]

The ocean voyage from San Francisco turned out to be very rough, which was not unusual. When they docked at Port Townsend, Washington, on March 25, Joe wrote briefly from the Central Hotel to Willie Lobdell in Schuyler Falls:

> Dear Friend Willie,
>
> We arrived here this morning, 4 A.M. and will sale (sic) 6 P.M. to Juneau. I was quite sea sick I tell you. Ellis was terrible sick, and Will about as I was. We had terrible weather but from here & up we have the [more sheltered waters of Alaska's] inside passage, so it will be all right! I am almost worn out had so much to do in San Francisco and the hard trip up has almost knocked me out. the fair (sic) from San Francisco to Juneau is only $20 first class so you see we will get up quite cheap. I remain yours truly,
>
> Jos Ladue.[307]

Ellis Turner's letter to his family following that leg of the trip was upbeat, typical of those he would write throughout his stay in the north. As sick as he had been, he wrote that he was "enjoying (his) ride."[308]

At Port Townsend, Joe and his companions boarded the steamer *Topeka* bound for Juneau. Passengers included about 100 men headed for the Yukon. Turner wrote home that one stop along the way was the Haida Indian village of Metlakatla where there were "only three four (sic) whites. They have a fine church, school, stores and a sawmill." A 16-piece band trained by missionaries performed for the travelers, "so we had some fine music while we were there."[309]

Arriving in Juneau on March 29, they bought more of their outfit "for the youcon...seed, stove, tent and provisions." They found prices at Juneau to be "not much higher here than they would be in Plattsburgh—best flour $1.25 per sack."[310] Here they gained a traveling companion, 45-year-old Mrs. J. T. Wills of Tacoma, Washington, who would become the first woman to travel over the Chilkoot for the sole purpose of searching for gold in the Yukon.[311]

That spring of 1895, hundreds of men were making their way over Chilkoot pass, heading for the tributaries of the Sixty Mile and Forty Mile Rivers, but mainly for Birch Creek. Joe and his party arrived on March 31 at the small coastal community of Dyea, Alaska. Edgar Wilson, at the Healy and Wilson trading post, told them that about 400 men had already gone ahead of them. As they began their trek, each pulling a sled full of provisions weighing 400 pounds, Joe knew the terrain that lay ahead of them; Turner and Lamay were still so excited about their great adventure they gave little thought to anything beyond the challenges of the day. After a few days, however, even Turner would say in a letter to his parents that the trip on April 2 through the canyon leading to the Pass was "hard, hard traveling."[312] How much harder must it have been a little farther on for Mrs. Wills whose sled weighed 250 pounds. Mrs. Wills pulled her 250-pound sled by herself from Lake Lindeman over the icy trail to Lake Lebarge, a distance exceeding 150 miles.[312]

By April 4 the four travelers had muscled their entire outfit to the top of Chilkoot Pass except "bed and grub box." For all of April 5-8 it "snowed and blowed hard," said Turner, and their cache at the summit was buried under 15 feet of snow. Joe did not feel well on the seventh, but on the eighth, even though the bad weather continued, they started down the mountain to Lake Lindeman. Joe had acquired dogs earlier in their trip north, but until now they had simply trailed behind, getting used to the climate and changing altitude. Now, while Turner and Lamay pulled their sleds to Lindeman on the ninth, "Joe broke his dogs to draw."

On April 10 they were traveling down the lake, and with "Joe and his dogs in the lead" they made 15 miles in five hours "over the ice." On the eleventh they "went 18 miles, very easy." The twelfth they went 10 miles; the thirteenth, 15 miles, saw their first flock of migrating geese, and went hunting, shooting two rabbits. On the fifteenth they arrived at the lower end of Marsh Lake, having traveled a total of 104 miles since leaving Lake Lindeman; 135 miles since leaving Dyea. The sixteenth was a day of "good sleighing" down the river, making camp at the head of Miles Canyon. The next day they portaged their outfits in relays around the hazardous Canyon and the even more dangerous White Horse Rapids just below.

By the eighteenth the party was at the upper end of Lake Lebarge, traveling quickly, passing 23 outfits that day. On the nineteenth they crossed most of Lake Lebarge, passing 42 more outfits. After a slow day of travel through a storm on the twentieth they made it to the lower end of Lake Lebarge where they found about 70 men building boats. At this point their 285-mile journey from the coast, pulling the heavily laden sleighs, ended. The remainder of the trip would be spent floating down the Yukon.

April 21 and 22, Joe and Turner cut logs; on the twenty-third they whipsawed 200 feet of planks and, after allowing them to dry for a few days, started building their boat on the twenty-seventh. On the 29th Ellis "picked gum" (congealed spruce sap) to seal the seams of their green lumber boat, and on April 30 it was launched.

On May 2, the party set sail down the Thirty Mile section of the Yukon. The river was not completely clear of ice, but they had a safe and uneventful trip the remaining 300 miles to Harper and Ladue's post at Ogilvie, where they arrived May 19. Turner wrote home to his mother saying that the greatest sight he had seen since leaving home was "the ice jam in the Yukon. I saw ice ten ft. thick piled up."[314]

Turner also noted that "Joe's man has got his gardin all in. He has a very plesent (sic) place and a very good house." "Joe's man" was probably Ladue's Creole friend and interpreter, Alexy[315]. Another person who was likely at the post at the time was Susie Lamar, the wife of a miner, who may have been Joe's housekeeper.[316] Turner noted too, that "Mr. Harper," Joe's partner, had "nearly sold out all his goods, and his share of the lumber which was cut last winter is worth about $8,000, and he has a large room filled with nice fur which is worth about $10,000."[317] (If an equal partner, Joe's share would have been $9,000.)

Soon after their arrival, Joe informed Turner that he would not have work for him at Ogilvie that summer, but mentioned the possibility of making $10 per day working in the mines on Miller Creek. So, Turner and Willis Lamay started for Forty Mile, one hundred miles down the river. When they arrived they learned that if they wanted to work on Miller Creek they would either have to haul all their provisions for the season 60 miles to the mines or pay very high prices for food while they were there. Turner chose not to go to the creek. Instead he took a job loading wood on steamers a few miles down the Yukon at $4.50 per day, plus board. When that work was finished he was hired by the North American Trading and Transportation Company to work in their sawmill at Fort Cudahy on the same terms. At that point he and Lamay built a cabin which they shared. Their monthly expenses were $25.[318]

A month later, when Arthur Harper arrived at Forty Mile on June 16, it was a sizable community of about 500. On the steamer *Little Pelley* he brought with him the furs taken in the previous winter at Fort Selkirk and Ogilvie. Meeting Willis Lamay, and sizing him up as reliable, Harper asked him to go aboard the Alaska Commercial Company steamer *Arctic* when it arrived and go back up to Ogilvie to skid logs for the sawmill and to later cut hay, which he did.[319]

In the late summer of 1895 Turner's family received the disturbing and worrisome news from Ellis that "there has been eleven men drowned coming in this summer...." Up to that time none of his letters had mentioned the ever-present danger the Yukon River proffered to everyone who traveled it.[320]

There was also much concern that summer about the delay in the arrival of the North American Trading and Transportation Company's steamer *Weare* bringing supplies for the winter. If it failed to arrive, the majority of the men in the area might have to leave the country for lack of food.

Although gold had been found in significant quantities on many creeks in the Forty Mile and Birch Creek areas, Joe was concerned that people "outside" were getting an incomplete picture of life in the north and ignoring the certainty that not everyone who entered the country in search of gold would find it. He was also keenly aware that emotional strain would be an important issue with some of the would-be adventurers. In a letter to the editor of the Plattsburgh Sentinel, dated Ogilvie, North West Territories, July 22, 1895, Joe stated that while he had no doubt that Alaska and the North West Territories "are rich in minerals and will eventually show up some of the richest mines ever discovered it remains to be proven." He also found "on a trip through the mining fields last week, miners doing well and as many more homesick and discouraged." He pointed out that one of the greatest hazards of the North was the lack of provisions, but added that it appeared there would be plenty of food for the coming winter.

He concluded in a lighter vein that "Mr. E. Turner and Wallace (Willis) Lamay wish to be remembered to their many friends in Clinton County. They are well satisfied with the country. At present Mr. Lamay is working at his old business, making hay with the 'old Armstrong machine.' Mr. Turner is at Forty Mile Creek, working at the Carpenter's trade with success. He says what he misses most is his horse and buggy and the good feather bed at home."[321]

Since 1892, the Reverend William Bompas, Bishop of the Anglican Church's Selkirk District, had been corresponding with the lieutenant governor of British Columbia regarding the "importance or necessity" that the province "obtain immediate Governmental control of the district which is practically in a state of Anarchy."[322] Bompas complained that the local Indians were brewing moonshine and that Indian women were being debauched and prostituted. It was not until 1895, however, that the Canadian government took heed and established a North West Mounted Police post at Forty Mile.

In the spring of 1894, two officers of the North West Mounted Police, Inspector Charles Constantine and Sergeant Charles Brown, arrived at Forty Mile to "inquire into the conditions then existing in the district which is now known as the Yukon Territory."[323]

Constantine and Brown requested reinforcements. The following summer, on July 24, a party of 20 police arrived at Forty Mile aboard the steamer *P. B. Weare*.[324] Among them were: Inspector Charles Constantine, second in command D. A. E. Strickland, Assistant Surgeon A. E. Wills, Staff Sergeants Murray H. E. Hayne and Charles Brown, Corporals E. Newbrook and P. C. Angel, Constables F. Webster, E. Telford, J. Thornton, E. J. Ward, M. R. Gowler, A. Pinkerton, D. Sinclair, A. P. McKellar, S. R. Churchill, J. Murray and two brothers, L. and E. W. Jenkins. Six of the seven officers brought their wives.[325]

After surveying the swampy land on which they would build their fort, the Mounties divided into two work parties. One set about the task of digging drainage ditches; the other went upriver to the mouth of the Twelve Mile River to cut logs. Tying the 400 logs into four huge rafts, they floated them down the river to the new site. The North American Trading and Transportation Company sawmill was rented to cut the logs into planks for the fort, barracks and residences. Fort Constantine was constructed between the North American Trading and Transportation Company's Fort Cudahy and the Forty Mile, facing that river. In six weeks the police erected eight separate buildings: guard room, hospital, officers' quarters, quartermaster's store and offices, bath and washroom, barracks room, mess room and kitchen. The next summer when a reading room and a recreation room were constructed the logs were cut from "the exact spot" where Dawson City would be founded by Joe in August.[326]

The duties of Inspector Constantine, as officer of the fort, were to "represent...all the departments of government having interests in this region." More particularly, he was authorized to "perform the duties of Dominion lands agent, collector of customs, collector of Inland Revenue"[327] and mining recorder. Joe expressed his concern that not only did miners now have to pay royalties on the gold they were taking out, but they also had to bear the 25 percent customs charge on all American goods brought into the territory by the traders. Before the end of 1895 the North West Mounted Police had collected $15,000.[328] For miners not working rich claims, these duties made it impossible for them to remain in the country.[329]

The make up of the mining camp had changed considerably from the early days when character, camaraderie and miners' meetings kept harmony. Sergeant Hayne would later write that the police were sent to the Yukon "because of reports of arbitrary, and often indefensible decisions on points of law and equity arrived at and enforced by the miners' meetings."[330] Surveyor William Ogilvie wrote that "miners' meetings as a means of adjudication became unsatisfactory and often unjust." One Forty Mile miner told him, "I'll never attend another miners' meeting as long as I live."[331] Although there was little serious crime at Forty Mile or on the creeks, the North West Mounted Police were welcomed and were soon accepted as a positive presence throughout the area.[332]

In July 1895 Joe penned another letter to the editor of the *Plattsburgh Sentinel*, mainly complaining about the intrusive presence of the police. Ladue felt there was no need for them. He had been in the country "for nearly twenty years" and had "never seen a more orderly, peaceable camp." He said that from 1884 up until 1895 there had never been a "shooting scrape, and only one robbery...." The two men involved in that incident had been "sent out of the country in 1885, and that settled petty larceny up to date."

Hoping to encourage more prospectors to head north, he described the summer of '95 as a "lovely one," and added pointedly that "discoveries are being made daily."[333] That August, Ellis Turner left for Circle City with the North American Trading and Transportation Company head carpenter, John, to build a warehouse and several cabins.[334] Later he would write, "We did not get as many built as we intended to before Jack Frost stepped around too lively for us to work at carpentering."[335]

As the summer of 1895 drew to an end, the men who planned to winter at Ogilvie, Forty Mile, Fort Cudahy, Fort Constantine and Circle City were busy gathering wood for the cold weather that could descend just about anytime after the end of August. Logs were usually cut upriver, assembled into rafts and floated to the camps. Felling trees was accomplished with a crosscut saw, either the one- or two-man type. Blocking the logs, (i.e., cutting them into chunks to be split) was also done by crosscut, but occasionally with a buzz saw. A buzz saw had a movable platform on which logs could be laid and pushed along in front of the blade so blocks could be cut to length to fit the fireboxes of the metal "Yukon" stoves that were in use at the time. Such a saw would have been powered by an engine that was smaller, but similar to, those used in the sawmills in Harper and Ladue's sawmill at Ogilvie, and the mill owned by the North American Trading and Transportation Company at Fort Cudahy.

However firewood was prepared, there had to be plenty. Most miner's cabins were dark and small, about 12 by 14 feet, and low-roofed, but the cold of a Yukon winter had a way of penetrating even the nine-inch logs of which they were constructed. Winter wood-piles were prominent near any cabin, and dominated the view in all the camps during the late fall and winter months. Winter quarters could, with considerable effort, be kept reasonably warm, but tended to be more claustrophobic than cozy.

By that winter Fort Cudahy's population had grown to about 300.[336] The structures included all the buildings of the North American Trading and Transportation Company, its sawmill, and "many fine cabins," most of which served as living quarters for its employees.[337] The compound was connected to Fort Constantine by a boardwalk. Turner thought it looked strange for a while "to see a British flag afloat." The only entertainment Turner could find on Christmas night was a "Native dance" at Forty Mile that was, in fact, very popular among the men.[338] The women attending, particularly Kate McQuesten, were in great demand as dance partners. There were so few women at frontier camps that men sometimes wrapped scarves around their upper arms and acted the part of women dance partners.

In 1895, Forty Mile was considerably larger than Fort Cudahy, comprised of 80 or 90 log cabins. And, in addition to McQuesten and Company's two-story, 30 by 60 foot store that dominated the shoreline, there were two blacksmith shops, a tin shop and hardware store, two restaurants, a dress shop, a watch repair shop, two bakeries and the offices of two doctors. The town also had six saloons. Popular piano tunes drifting from their open doors competed with a 24-hour chorus from the community's "about three hundred dogs."[339]

The North American Trading and Transportation Company, in spite of the unpopularity of the gruff John Healy, provided the Alaska Commercial Company with stiff competition at Forty Mile and Circle City throughout that winter. But McQuesten was the most respected and well-liked man the length of the Yukon River. His honesty, fairness,[340] kindly manner and policy of providing grub-stakes as well as supplies on credit gave him a distinct advantage over his competition.

Irinia Pavaloff Cherosky Callahan, who traveled upriver on board the steamer *Yukon* with McQuesten one spring in the 1880s, later wrote that:

> On the way up everywhere we stopped at the villages the Indians were so glad to see Jack McQuesten, they shot off guns and carried him off the boat, took new white English blankets and spread them on the floor of their tents and sat him down on the blankets and gave him a big feast. The way the Indians treated him, wherever we stopped, I knew they loved him like a father.[341]

During the winter of 1895-96 neither the traders nor the miners could have guessed that, within a year, both Forty Mile and Circle City would be replaced by another mining camp in the richest gold district ever to be discovered in the Yukon. Indeed, some of the individual claims would be the richest discovered anywhere in the world.[342]

Joe's optimism that provisions would be in good supply that winter proved only partially correct when the steamer *Weare* froze in the ice 100 miles below Forty Mile and everything had to be brought up on sleighs. There were no horses in the camp that year, so dogs and men pulled the sleighs. Before spring there was little food left at Ogilvie and many went hungry.[343] Sergeant Murray Hayne described a man he met who was coming down the river from Ogilvie the next spring as:

> a pitiable sight. We gave him as good a meal as we could muster, and his eyes looked as though they would start from his head at the sight of such a luxury as sugar. They had not tasted sugar or salt at Sixty Mile all the winter, and they were simply existing—how, it is impossible to say—until a steamer should come up with provisions.[344]

From October through most of December temperatures were mild, for the Yukon. Turner wrote to his family "we are not having a very hard winter."[345] In January 1896, however, temperatures plunged to 72 degrees below zero, and the stories Turner had heard the previous summer about the earth's being frozen down 30 feet began to seem more believable. The only factor that made temperatures of –35 and lower attractive was that there was typically no wind.[346] Turner's observations about the long nights that persisted throughout December and January were typical of his attitude toward all his experiences in the north. He merely pointed out that after about four hours of twilight, "the rest is northern lights and starlight."[347] Turner preferred the winter because "the cold doesn't bite as bad now as the mosquitoes did last summer."[348] Mosquitoes were known to drive strong men to tears.

By late March 1896 claim holders on Birch Creek and the tributaries of the Forty Mile and Sixty Mile Rivers were preparing to start another season. The two friends from Schuyler Falls, Willis Lamay and Ellis Turner, thought they might work on Miller Creek. Lamay went up in mid-March, decided not to remain, and returned in early April bringing with him some newspapers from, of all places, Plattsburgh, New York. In early June he traveled upriver to Ogilvie to "settle up with Joe." After that he planned to return home "on the first boat."[349] Turner worked briefly in the mines that summer but, upon his return to Fort Cudahy, found no work at the North American Trading and Transportation Company. His disappointed family in Schuyler Falls received word that: "I cannot say that I will cum home (sic) this fall now."[350]

Joe and Harper departed on January 26, 1896, for San Francisco. The temperature hovered around 60 below during much of their winter journey to the coast, but they were experienced frontiersmen and undaunted. At Dyea they went aboard the steamer *Rustler* and arrived at San Francisco about March 1.[351] The sea voyage was difficult, as usual. Joe wrote to his friend, Willie Lobdell, in Schuyler Falls from near Juneau that he could write only a brief note because "the boat is pitching so badly I will have to close."[352] The purpose of the trip was to purchase machinery for a new sawmill and to negotiate with the Alaska Commercial Company about putting another boat on the river to run downstream from the upper lakes. The company refused, saying it would cost too much,[353] a decision they likely regretted. Within a few years the White Pass and Yukon

Route railway brought in several boats and gained control of all the enormous amount of commercial traffic on that portion of the river. Before leaving San Francisco, Harper purchased a small steamer he named the *Beaver*, with which he hoped to gain the capability to deliver supplies to miners if new discoveries occurred on the upper river.[354]

On March 10, Joe, the new sawmill, a large quantity of trade goods and about 1,000 pounds of food left San Francisco on the Alaska Commercial Company's steamer *St. Paul*. He would later say that he bought so much food, probably reflecting on his ranching days, because "nothing grows there." Arriving at St. Michael, Joe's freight was transferred to the company's riverboat *Alice*. It traveled upriver to Ogilvie, arriving June 24.[355]

It's a typical for a 22-year-old man to possess a temperament suited to childcare, but Ellis Turner's letters home demonstrate his tender side and his genuine feelings for his younger siblings. He put this tenderness to good use during the first few days of June 1896 when he cared for twin boys at his cabin in Forty Mile. They were the 16-month-old sons of Hugh and Mary Day. The Days and Hugh's brother Al, had been mining on Miller Creek near Jack and Emilie Tremblay, the children's godparents, when Mary became ill. The family came to Forty Mile at the end of May to find treatment for Mrs. Day, but doctors were not able to help her and she died June 13 of pneumonia, at age 38, and was buried in the Forty Mile cemetery.[356]

Since there was no work in Forty Mile for Ellis Turner, in June of 1896 he traveled down to Circle City, writing to his family that if he stayed in the country the following winter it would be there. Although later that summer Turner was again offered work by the North American Trading and Transportation Company at the store or sawmill, he decided instead to "ship on the *Weare*." He traveled downriver to St. Michael where he accepted a job with the Alaska Commercial Company "unloading the ships, then packing lumber in the shipyard, then to helping the carpenters." While employed by the Alaska Commercial Company, Turner learned how to operate the engines of the river steamers and was offered a job as oiler on the *Bella*.[357] He was paid $45 per month during the season, and the same to remain with the boat during the winter, with promise of a position as engineer for the following summer. Apparently pleased with his new opportunity, he wrote in a September 8 letter that, he was "not cumming (sic) out this fall."[358]

A devoted correspondent, Ellis wrote to his family from Fort Yukon, in a letter dated October 20, 1896, relating his first negative experience in the north. Turner mentioned that the captain of the *Bella* refused to pay him his wages until he said he would "call a meeting on him." Had the captain not paid, that miners' meeting might have been one of the last ever held on the river.[359]

Joe understood that men coming into the country needed to be optimistic to sustain themselves through the rigors, physical and mental, that faced them on every hand. He did his part, as William Ogilvie said, by encouraging them with "tales of wonderful prospects at newly found places."[360]

One of those who came was a Canadian, Robert Henderson, whose brother, Henry, had been at Ogilvie in 1893. Henderson grew up on Big Island, Pictou County, Nova Scotia, and had been trained as a carriage builder. In the spring of 1894 he crossed the Chilkoot and, for most of the summer, prospected on the Teslin and Pelly Rivers with scant success.[361] In the fall he arrived at Ogilvie with two partners, Kendrick and Snider.[362] The following summer when Joe returned from Schuyler Falls, Robert Henderson is reported to have said to him, "I am a determined man. I won't starve. Let me prospect for you. If it's good for me, it's good for you."[363] Convinced of the man's honesty and grit, Joe "stayed with him" and recommended Henderson try the Indian River country.

Henderson prospected along the Indian River and on Quartz Creek, one of its tributaries. Near the head of that creek he climbed to the top of a ridge.[364] From that magnificent viewpoint he saw on his right the dark seam of a creek in a deep valley trailing off to the northeast, a creek flowing, he believed, to the Klondike River. This was the creek he chose to prospect. He apparently paid little attention to two other small streams in the distance on his left. They would soon be known as Bonanza and Eldorado. Robert Henderson, the dauntless, persistent prospector, had been that close to the treasure he was seeking and would never find.

By the spring of 1896 Henderson had taken out of his new diggings "$800 in gold," the first significant quantity to be taken out of the Klondike Valley.[365] His ground was yielding only eight cents to the pan,[366] but on June 20, 1896, he wrote to his brother, Henry:

> Dear Brother—I am well and have struck it right at last. I called the Creek Gold Bottom. It runs into the Klondike. If it rains this summer will get some gold out; if not, will do big work in the spring. From your brother—Bob.[367]

Joe later described his contact with when he returned to Ogilvie to send that letter and pick up supplies:

> After making the discovery he came back and told me about it, as I had been putting up for him for three years—I mean I had 'grub-staked' him—and he wanted me to move my sawmill and everything down to the mouth of the Thron-Diuck (Klondike), where Dawson now stands, and to take up a townsite as it was going to be a big camp.[368]

Henderson purchased supplies and sent them overland on Joe's two packhorses to the promising new site.[369] He then floated down the Yukon to the Klondike, which was the shortest route back to his Gold Bottom claim. Joe soon followed.[370]

When Henderson arrived at the mouth of the Klondike, he found George Carmack at his fish camp with his Tagish wife, Kate (Shaaw Tlaa), their daughter Graphie Grace, Kate's brother, the well-known packer, Skookum Jim (Keish), and her nephews, Dawson Charlie (Kaa Goox) and 17-year-old Patsy (Koolseen).[371]

Since that meeting, there has been much discussion about how the conversation that mid-August day in 1896 between Henderson and Carmack may have shaped the history that followed. The story typically told has been that Carmack, upon hearing about Henderson's discovery on Gold Bottom, asked if there was any chance he too could "locate" on that creek. Henderson's response was, "Well, there's a chance for you, George, but I don't want any damn Siwashes (referring to Carmack's family) staking on that creek."[372]

Robert Henderson's version of the encounter, as reported some years later by his brother Henry, was that Robert told Carmack to "go over and stake a claim, I think all those creeks are good. If you find anything better than mine let me know." This, he said, was what "Cormack promised to do." There was no mention of an ethnic slur referring to Jim and Charlie or Kate.[373] In a letter dated December 19, 1898, Robert Henderson told Tappan Adney, a correspondent for *Harper's Weekly*. "Joe Ladue is the best man to decide about who Discovered the diggins in the Clondick(sic). Write to him and see what he has got to say about it."

Joe's understanding of what transpired between the two men was that:

> At the mouth of the Thron diuck he (Henderson) met this man McCormack [Carmack], who was fishing for salmon, and coaxed him to go up with him and make a location, telling him what he had discovered there. McCormack did not want to go at first, but finally went and made his location, he and two Chilkoot Indians. The names of these Indians were Skookum Jack (Jim) and Dark East (Dawson) Charlie. Coming back they crossed over from Gold Bottom Creek, that being a cut-off. On their way back they struck this Bonanza Creek and found gold there in paying quantities. They went to scratching round, and made the discovery out of which they got four claims—Nos. 1 and 2 below the discovery claim, and No. 1 above.[374]

The gold discovered on Bonanza Creek that day, August 16, 1896, would lead to one of the greatest gold rushes the world had ever seen. George Carmack later wrote that the next day:

> Taking my hand ax, I went out into the center of the flat to a small spruce tree and blazed it on the up and down stream sides. With a pencil, I wrote on the up-stream side, this notice:
> TO WHOM IT MAY CONCERN: I do this day, locate and claim, by right of discovery, five hundred feet, running up stream from this notice. Located this 17th day of August 1896.
> G.W. Carmack.

Carmack also measured out a second claim for himself "by right of location" (i.e., the right of the discoverer), and a claim each for Charlie and Jim. After measuring out the claims, he went to a tall birch tree and wrote on it: "I name this creek 'Bonanza', George Carmack."[375]

For over a century there has been considerable debate about who actually discovered the first gold in the Klondike Valley and on

Bonanza Creek. Many assumed that Carmack was simply "the" discoverer, apparently of both. In later years, Henderson was accepted as the first to discover gold in the Klondike; Skookum Jim, the discoverer of Bonanza. Neville Armstrong, who spent many years mining in the Klondike, wrote that Carmack told him it was Kate who actually made the discovery.[376] But, in 1898, others also claimed the honor.

One claimant was David Brackett. Soon after news of the Bonanza discovery reached the coast, Brackett stated that he had traveled to the interior of Alaska (Canada) for many years in pursuit of fur trade with the Indians. He stated that "It was while on one of these journeys in 1879 that I found the nugget." He claimed he had "camped on the ledges above what I am sure is now called Bonanza Creek...I went up the Yukon in 1881 and tried to locate my creek again, but failed."[377] If Brackett's story is true, he was fortunate to have eluded the Chilkats on the coast of Alaska who had not yet agreed to allow white men to cross the Chilkoot.

In late July 1897, W. J. Arkell, owner of *Leslie's Illustrated Weekly Magazine*, reported to the *Seattle Daily Times* that he claimed "the gold fields in the Klondyke regions by right of discovery for the estate of E. J. Glave." Glave headed an expedition to Alaska in 1891. However, neither Glave's written description of that expedition nor its accompanying maps indicate that he traveled to the Klondike region.[378]

Robert Henderson never claimed to be the discoverer of the gold on Bonanza Creek, but for many years he did "claim right of discovery" in the Klondike Valley. He eventually lost his original claim on Gold Bottom and, although he continued to prospect the streams of the Yukon for many years, he never did find the "good gold" he had spent a lifetime seeking. By 1903 he had petitioned the Canadian government to give him "the amount of ground or its equivalent in money I was entitled to as discoverer...." (The government eventually awarded him a pension of $200 per month.)[379]

In more recent years, it has been recognized that the first discoverers of gold in the Klondike Valley were Joseph Ladue, Dan Sprague and John and Peter Nelson. But Carmack's staking the discovery claim on the creek he named Bonanza was the climax of a series of western North American gold rushes, which began in California in 1849.

Among the papers of George Snow, historian for the Yukon Order of Pioneers, is a declaration written by Peter Nelson describing his partnership with Joe Ladue to prospect on the Klondike:

> On the 22nd of May, 1886, John Nelson, Dan Sprague, Joe Ladue and myself formed a partnership for the purpose of prospecting the Klondike River. We took one Indian with us. When we got to Fort Reliance we packed from there across to the Klondike, a distance of about thirty-five miles. The weather was very hot and water scarce. We struck the Klondike about forty miles up.
>
> Our first day's travel up the Klondike, we stopped on a bar on the left-hand side of the River, late in the afternoon. The bar had a heavy growth of willows, and was composed of coarse wash. We went to prospecting it and found it would go from twenty-five to thirty cents to the pan for about three inches from the surface. We did not consider it would pay us to stop, as it was a small bar. We found light prospects at the mouth of several creeks coming down, but we did not consider it worth while, as we could make all the way from fifty to one hundred dollars a day on Stewart River, if we caught low water.[380]

While it is true that Joe found good gold on the bars of the Stewart later that summer, it is curious that he did not follow up on the prospects he and his partners found on the Klondike and did not encourage other prospectors to try their luck. Certainly they must have told every man they saw. And why, too, was it that many old-timers, even after hearing of the discovery in 1896, continued to believe that the Klondike Valley was only "moose pasture"[381] and not worth investigating? To them the valley was too wide; the geologic formation was not right; the indications were too good on the surface.[382] For all their excellent qualities, many of the old-timers were intransigent in their beliefs. They "knew" that gold in good quantity was found only on the west side of the Yukon River and, with the exception of the Stewart River, that had been the case. But Joe knew there was gold in the Klondike Valley and, when Robert Henderson told him of his success, he made plans to go there himself.[383]

The first men to hear of the strike on Bonanza were Dan

McGillivary, David Edwards, Harry Waugh and David McKay, a party of disheartened prospectors Carmack met poling up the Klondike when he was on his way to Forty Mile to register his discovery claim. He also told two French Canadians, Alphonse Lapierre and his partner, George Remillard. Next were men who were fishing at the mouth of the Klondike: Joe Cooper, Fritz Kloke and Dan Monahan.[384] The first stakers on Bonanza, however, according to William Ogilvie, were Edward Monahan and Greg Stewart on 28 and 29 Below Discovery on August 19. The following day Dave Edwards, John Moffat, Daniel Robertson and Charles Kimball staked numbers 16, 17, 18 and 19 Below Discovery. The mining records at the Klondike History Library in the Dawson City Museum show that on that date Harry Waugh and David McKay also filed on 15 and 3 Below Discovery. On August 22, Fritz Kloke filed on 9 Above Discovery. Dan McGillivary, who was among the first on the scene, did not register his claim on 16 Below Discovery until October 23, 1896.[385]

A little later other men came along who refused to believe Carmack's story. An example is two men who came down from Indian River. One partner asked the other, "Should we go up and stake?" Replied the other, "Why I wouldn't go across the river on that old Siwash's word (meaning Carmack)." Another party argued for three hours about whether they should stake, but finally decided to go on to Circle City.[386] One man said later that on Eldorado he

> couldn't find a colour in the creek; but what I could see was a sign stuck up reading, 'This creek is reserved for Swedes and Moose.' Now, I weren't a Swede, and I sure weren't a Moose! So I passes her up. What happens? Why, a lot of fools take her up and she's the richest ground in the country. Nice, ain't it!—and me working for wages?[387]

On the twentieth of August, Carmack, Charlie and Patsy traveled downriver to Forty Mile. Before registering their claims on the 24th with the mining recorder, Inspector Constantine,[388] Carmack went to a saloon to tell his story to the miners who had come down from their claims on Miller, Glacier and Davis Creeks to get supplies. At first they laughed at the very idea of a "bonanza" in the Klondike

Valley. "Strike! Hell," said a miner at a nearby table. "That ain't no news. That's just a scheme of Ladue and Harper to start a stampede up the river."

Carmack responded, "That's where you're off, you big rabbit-eating malamute. Neither Ladue nor Harper knows anything about this." When Carmack emptied his Bonanza gold from a cartridge shell for all to see, the mood quickly changed. The miners stood staring in silence at the shiny metal. Gold on each creek has a unique appearance and this was not like any gold they had seen before. One by one, they slipped out the door and within 24 hours Forty Mile looked as if it had "seen its best days." The rush—a mere local trickle compared to the flood was to come—was on. Many Forty Milers would soon be counted among the Klondike Kings.[389] Some still doubted, but no prospector could resist a rush once it starts. Everyone left; some who were drunk were thrown into boats by their friends.[390] When Carmack "went down to Forty Mile and reported," Joe said, "the people began to come there like wildfire. There was no stopping them."[391]

Unknown to Carmack, Joe was among the first to hear of the big strike on Bonanza when he arrived at the mouth of the Klondike on August 24. He had followed Henderson downriver and the next year he would state that:

> Strangely enough, and as if by some great good fortune, I had come down the river about the same time McCormack (Carmack) left Gold Bottom, and had picked out a town site where Dawson City now stands, a little more than a mile from the Bonanza Creek claims. In this respect I was very fortunate, as it now stands in the midst of what is called Bonanza Gold Mining District, and all claims are so recorded. As a matter of fact there is no other place for a town site, and I consider myself lucky in getting hold of it.[392]

Joe immediately set out the perimeters of a 160-acre town site and on July 27, 1896, his application was delivered by a man named McLean to Inspector Constantine at Forty Mile with fees of $10 per acre plus a $50 survey fee.[393]

Joe had started for Forty Mile himself, but met a man near the mouth of the Klondike who wanted to purchase 1,000 board feet of lumber. Joe couldn't resist a bird in the hand. Entrusting his application to McLean, he returned to Ogilvie for nails and lumber. When he arrived back in Dawson he, with the help of three other men, D. A. Robinson, S. S. Ayres and John Whitney, "commenced erecting the first house in that region on September 1st, 1896." In four days they had the 12 by 14 foot one-story log cabin completed. This first house in Dawson had one room, a door, two windows and faced the Yukon River. As it turned out, the cabin had been built in the middle of what would become First Avenue (present-day Front St.).[394]

Soon after the roof was on, Joe returned to Ogilvie to get a load of lumber and the sawmill he and Arthur Harper had purchased in San Francisco the previous spring. He also brought down goods to be sold in the store he would set up in the newly constructed cabin. The sawmill, he described as consisting of "a 125 horsepower engine and one 48-inch circular saw and one 52-inch, a carriage, planer and matcher, which is a saw-mill complete." Within six days the mill was set up and running.[395] (The original mill, delivered to Ogilvie in 1893, may have been owned by the Alaska Commercial Company, and was apparently left at Ogilvie. The new one was the property of Harper and Ladue.) Shortly after getting the sawmill operational Joe constructed a 22 by 40 foot warehouse on First Avenue.[396] The first lumber he sold was for sluice boxes on the Bonanza claim of Robert Lowrie at $130 per 1,000 board feet. The logs were cut from along the Thron-Diuck (Klondike) River and floated down to Dawson.[397]

McGillivary, Waugh, McKay and Edwards were the first men on the new "diggings" to make a cleanup. When they took their gold to Dawson, Joe weighed it at his store and announced to a crowd of men assembled outside: "How's that for two and a half days' shoveling in: $4,008!"[398]

The sawmill, which was owned by *Harper and Company*, was referred to for some time in Dawson as "Harper's Sawmill." The mill cut lumber for several other cabins constructed that fall, all with about the same dimensions as Joe's. The first was built by Daniel Robinson, the second by Robert Lowrie, an old-timer from Forty Mile, the third by Theodore Anderson, the fourth by John Moffatt, the fifth by Charles Kimball, the sixth by A. J. Ferguson, (whose wife and Isabella Healy, wife of the manager of North American Trading and Transportation Company, were the only women in town) and the seventh by Charles Olsen. All were built on Second Avenue behind the stores of the Alaska Commercial Company and the North American Trading and Transportation Company, both of which were built on First Avenue facing the river where the steamboats landed. Until the extreme cold weather of the Yukon winter set in, building continued. By the spring of 1897, there was a total of about 30 houses, all constructed of lumber from the Harper and Company sawmill. Some of the owners were Winfield Oler, Ed Parks, Dave Richards and "Big Alex" McDonald.[399] By the first of October 1896 the population of the new mining camp had grown to about 500.[400]

Following his interview with Joe in August 1897 John Sleicher of *Leslie's Illustrated Weekly Magazine*, reported: "Having secured this greatest prize (the town site), he (Joe) looked over the gold country and carefully selected and quickly purchased some of the richest claims that could be found."[401] No official record was located to indicate he purchased a claim in 1896, but he did stake a claim, 39 Eldorado, which was "located 1896, 28 Nov." and recorded "1896, 14 Dec. Number of Instrument 319."[402]

Leslie's Illustrated Weekly (1855-1922) was one of the most popular tabloid-form magazines of its day. It was aimed at the average American reader and emphasized images over text—in the manner of *Time Magazine*. Thomas Nast was one of its famous reporter/illustrators. During the Civil War, when many of its correspondents were sent out to sketch battles and other maneuvers, *Leslie's* had a circulation of over 150,000. *Harper's* was its main rival. *Leslie's* was known for scenic vistas such as Niagara Falls and for writing about remote landscapes. For example, in the spring of 1877, Mrs. Leslie had penned a series "From Gotham to the Golden Gate," with descriptions of frontier landscapes and western towns. Therefore, writing about Joe and the Klondike was typical of the kind of story *Leslie's* favored.

Life in Dawson and on the creeks that winter remained much as it had been in Forty Mile. Joe stated, "The temperature ran down to 54 below which was the coldest we had. It probably averaged about 20. We had to dress warm in flannels and furs. I cannot say the people suffered." He also stated that the character of the town was "good....Everyone attended to his business. There was no lawlessness. Men were on their claims working."[403] But Inspector Constantine anticipated that the following summer thousands of gold seekers, people of every description and intent, would be descending upon the new camp. In preparation, he planned to move the Mounted Police headquarters from Fort Constantine to Dawson the summer of 1897 and construct a post at the south end of town on the 40-acre government reserve.

During the winter of 1896-97 there was one saloon in Dawson. Commenting on it to the *New York World* in August 1897, Joe said that its bartender, George Westbrook, sold "whiskey, beer, ale and about everything that is in other saloons....Everything was 50 cents a drink, no mixed drinks, and no water for a chaser. The saloon kept open all the time, night and day. I guess it did pretty well."[404] William Ogilvie, who was in Dawson at the time, wrote that Joe had a saloon and that the following summer it was called the "Pioneer."[405]

By the first of June 1897 two more saloons opened for business, the White Elephant and the Blue Elephant, named for the colors of the tents that housed them. One writer who was on-site described "Ladue's Pioneer saloon" as "a comparatively imposing structure of clapboard, while the other two were fashioned of canvas over a board framework."[406] Another wrote that in 1896 Ladue "built a cabin in the middle of town and opened his first barrel of whiskey."[407] William Ogilvie, too, wrote that there were three saloons in town, one "a log saloon, Joe Ladue's."[408] Joe would have done well in the summer of 1897 when the price of a drink went to a dollar![409]

Joe neither stated nor implied that he owned a saloon in Dawson, something that his staunch Methodist friends, the Lobdells in Schuyler Falls, would certainly have frowned upon. Joe's name does not appear on alcohol import records during those years, and documents show that in the summer of 1898 the Pioneer was owned by three old-timers, Frank Dinsmore, Bill McPhee and Harry Spencer. All of the saloons by that time were also gambling houses operating roulette wheels and games of faro and poker around the clock.[410] When big cleanups were made on the creeks the summer of 1897, much of the gold made its way into the coffers of those establishments.[411] July1, Dominion Day (today called Canada Day), and July 4 were occasions in particular when alcohol consumption soared. American prospectors celebrated Dominion Day with Canadians, and the Canadians returned the favor three days later because 80 percent of the prospectors around Dawson City were Americans. Sometimes, the occasions blurred one into the other—to the consternation of sober residents and Mounties alike.

There was no restaurant in town until the summer of 1897 because "there were no supplies in the country to run it,"[412] and it would have had few customers anyway, since most of the miners spent the winter on their claims burning down to bedrock, drifting along pay-streaks and bringing up the thawed dirt bucket by bucket to be piled in a "dump" until it could be sluiced the following spring. As the smoke curled skyward from the tents, cabins and mine shafts, the air up and down the valleys of Bonanza and Eldorado crackled with excitement. It was not a question of whether there was gold in the dumps, but rather, how much!

Two women on the creeks that winter were Mrs. Ethel Berry and Mrs. Salome Lippy. Joe stated to reporters that he "saw them often" and that they spent their time keeping house. They gathered nuggets from their husbands' claims to pay for daily expenses, but they did not cook for other miners nor did they take in their sewing and laundry, as some reports later indicated.[413] A third woman on the mostly male scene was Mrs. J. T. Wills who had come over the Chilkoot with Ladue, Turner and Lamay in 1895.

Joe's town site was situated on the north side of the Klondike, a short distance from its mouth. It was about 46 miles south of Forty Mile and six miles upriver from the site of Fort Reliance. On January 9, 1897, the official survey was begun by Dominion Lands Surveyor, William Ogilvie as "Lot 3 in Group 2- 160 acres."[414] Ogilvie recorded in his field notebook that on January 11 "Joseph Ladue showed me where he had marked the SW corner of his land."[415] The boundary was established beginning at a point midway between present-day Princess and Harper Streets, north along First Avenue (now Front Street) to Sixth Street (now Albert Street), east to Tenth Avenue, south to a point mid-way between Princess and Harper Streets and west to the point of beginning.[416] About 110 acres were on the flat; 50 acres on the incline. The town site was laid out with avenues running north and south; streets running east and west. In general, all avenues were 66 feet in width; streets were 50 feet in width. Ogilvie stated that it was necessary "to make (streets) this width to obviate the removal of nearly every cabin which had been erected in the town at that time."[417]

It was at the time of the survey that Joe named the new community, Dawson City in honor of George Mercer Dawson,[418] director of the Geological and Natural History Survey of Canada. Joe stated, in an interview with the *Seattle Daily Times* in the summer of 1897, that Dawson "was a very sociable man, and I named the town site as a little compliment to him."[419] This would have been in keeping with the agreement made with William Ogilvie in 1887 regarding naming new communities.[420] At about the time of the survey Joe was appointed postmaster but, said he "had too much other work to do and had to give up being a public official."[421]

William Ogilvie, who would later become commissioner of the Yukon, reported that while he was surveying the town site he was involved in a practical joke played on Joe:

> Harry Ash, a 'Cheechako' from Juneau, had brought with him some very fine specimens of gold-bearing quartz. Now, Joe's satisfaction with the results of the past winter's work in the Klondike was almost perfect; the only thing required to round it out to absolute perfection was the discovery of a big vein of gold-bearing rock; but Joe had remarked in a tone of conviction, 'She's comin,' boys; she's comin!' One of Joe's associates in business thought it would be a pity to disappoint him, and arranged with Harry Ash to put up a job on him. Ash then began to show, in strict confidence, some of his specimens of quartz, with mysterious hints that their source was not very far away. Among the favoured few was, of course, Joe's partner, who, beaming with joy, took him into the secret, with strict injunctions not to mention the matter to a soul, as Ash was not ready for proclamation yet, having first to stake, and so fix his record as to make himself absolutely safe. As evidence of what was communicated, specimens of the gold-bearing quartz was shown. This was more than flesh and blood could stand; he called on Ash, and by many winks and nods let him know that

he was 'wise' to some things supposed to be profound secrets. Ash, of course affected great chagrin that his secret was revealed, and 'wanted to know who talked.' Joe would not tell, but vowed eternal silence if he were let in. Ash told him he could not yet proclaim the find, as was the custom, but would let him (Joe) in just as soon as he had seen Mr. Ogilvie and learned all about how to locate and record a quartz claim. Joe, being on very good terms with me, undertook to see me and hurry the matter along. Ash and he called on me, and by diagram I fully explained to them the way to locate, mark and record a quartz claim. I asked no questions, but after the meeting Joe came to me in the strictest confidence—of course—told me all he knew, and as proof of what he said showed me a small bit of the rock, which certainly looked good.

Ash was to stake that day, and then Joe would be given the tip. He would go out, find the place, then signal me by fires, and I was to go out with my instruments, trace the lode as far as possible beyond Ash's location, when Joe would stake on the continuation, to be followed by myself if I wished, then Joe's partner, and we would all be rich. 'Everlastingly rich! Have barrels of money!' Soon after Joe left his partner saw me, put me 'wise,' as he termed it, to the whole ploy, and told me that six others with Joe were to be victimized; all the seven being selected on account of their supposed superior knowledge of mining—quartz mining particularly. At the appointed time all seven were separately given the tip, each being led to believe that he was the only one.

They started very secretly from seven different points. Arrived at the scene of action, it was not long before each began to see that others were in the woods, and as secrecy had been absolutely required of them, and was necessary to success, for each, like Joe, had friends to follow, they spent the whole day dodging each other. When they returned, tired and hungry, in the evening the chaffing and greetings accorded them can best be left to the imagination.[422]

Another story involving Joe's activities in the early spring of 1897 was apparently seen as humorous at the time. C. S. Hamlin wrote:

> An old Indian tells Joe La Due, 'Me heap sick. No eatum.' Joe goes and gets a cup partially filled with Worcestershire sauce and in Chinook tells him to drink it all. In one gulp it is gone. This is a new one on him. His mouth and throat seem on fire. One whoop, then for the river goes that Indian. Soon he comes back. 'How do you feel now?' As he rubs his hands from his lips to his stomach he says, 'All same'.[423]

Since Joe appears to have had considerable respect for Indians, perhaps at the time, Worcestershire sauce was considered an appropriate treatment for stomach complaints of Indians and whites alike.

Joe's town site was ideally located for the mining area of the Klondike (known at the time as the Bonanza Gold Mining District) but in 1896 much of it was essentially a swamp.[424] In winter it froze solid; in the warmer months it was soggy and mosquito infested. The streets were a sea of mud and there was "a most foul odor."[425] Its great advantage was the large eddy that had formed from near the mouth of the Klondike and extended to the north end of the town site, which made it a good docking site for riverboats. Joe stated in an interview with the *New York World* in August 1897, that he had sold town site lots for as little as $5.00 in 1896, and one for $5,000.[426]

A constant din throughout the town late into the fall was produced by the operations of the Harper and Company Sawmill, at the north end of First Avenue.[427] Day and night it ran, supplying the mines with sluice-box lumber, and the town and vicinity with building material. In an interview the following summer Joe recalled, "The men stand behind one another waiting to obtain their lumber and it was all I could do to supply the demand."[428] Joe employed 15 men to operate the mill. Sawyers and engineers were paid $15 a day; common laborers, $10 a day. There were always plenty of men available to work but Joe complained that "they changed every day. As soon as a man gets a little money he wants to quit and go prospecting, and we have to break in new men about every day."[429] No sawing and little building could be done during the winter because of the cold, which often hovered around 50 below. But timber could still be felled, to wait until May when the ice went out, and floated down to the mill.[430] Aside from the several cabins built in the town the previous fall and winter, Dawson was a small tent town strung along the riverfront, a town running on the adrenalin of anticipation.

One of the persistent threats to those who remained in the Yukon after "freeze-up" was lack of food. Joe and many of the other old-timers still remembered the winters of 1887 and 1890 (the "year of the famine"), and 1895 when, particularly at Ogilvie, there was little food and the men there had simply "existed."[431] Fortunately, as William Ogilvie recorded, the Alaska Commercial Company steamer *Arctic* arrived at the new camp on October 14, 1898, "with... many tons of much-needed supplies." Many were often hungry before the arrival of the first boat the next spring, but no one starved. Still, as one man wrote, "A sack of beans made a well filled sack of gold dust look like rubbish."[432]

Certainly many of these men on short rations suffered from scurvy. Jack London describes this disease in his story *In a Far Country*:

> In the absence of fresh vegetables and exercise, the blood became impoverished, and a loathsome, purplish rash crept over their bodies. Yet they refused to heed the warning. Next, their muscles and joints began to swell, the flesh turning black, while their mouths, gums, and lips took on the color of rich cream.

The languor caused by scurvy had its psychological effects. London continues:

> Instead of being drawn together by their misery, each (of the two partners sharing the cabin) gloated over the other's symptoms as the scurvy took its course. They lost all regard for personal appearance, and for that matter, common decency. The cabin became a pigpen....The hair of their heads and faces grew long and shaggy, while their garments would have disguised a ragpicker. But they did not care. They were sick, and there was no one to see; besides, it was very painful to move about.[433]

No record has been found of a formal partnership agreement between Joe and Arthur Harper prior to 1896. Their "joint business" under the name of "*A. Harper & Company*" had flourished at Fort Selkirk and Ogilvie since 1891 but it appears that Ladue was not an equal partner during that time. Harper was the sole owner of the

Fort Selkirk post and his business was almost exclusively fur trading with the Indians of the Pelly River drainage. At Ogilvie where they traded for furs, sold mining supplies and provisions to prospectors and, from 1893, ran the sawmill. Their business paid them well and they had great faith that gold in significant quantities would sooner or later be found on the upper river. They were true entrepreneurs, anticipating a big strike and patiently waiting. To that end they encouraged, sold outfits to, and, in many cases, generously grubstaked the men who were in the country to prospect for gold. The post at Ogilvie, particularly, became a center for outfitting and Joe always tried to have enough provisions on hand so miners could remain in the country during the winter months. With the discovery on Bonanza Creek in the Klondike Valley their long wait was over; business opportunities were everywhere and the pioneering lives of Harper, who had been prospector and trader along the Yukon for 23 years, and Joe, who had been similarly engaged for 14 years, were about to change forever.

In November 1896, because of the phenomenal expansion of their business, Joe and Harper entered into a formal partnership agreement, its purpose being "to trade and conduct business generally within the...Yukon District." The partnership was initially to be in force for a period of six months, but could be extended. Contributed to the partnership were the "real estate and interests" of both parties, except Harper's general merchandise business at Fort Selkirk, which included his steamers the *Beaver* and the *Little Pelley*.[434] Ladue's contributions to the partnership were the "Townsite" of Dawson City, "the joint business in the mercantile line conducted by the said firm at Ogilvie...and his interest in the sawmill...." All interests and property subsequently acquired by either of the partners would become joint property of the partnership. Neither man had staked gold claims up to that time, but both soon did, and those claims became partnership assets.[435] Thus were the *Harper and Ladue Townsite and Development Company* and the *Harper and Ladue Sawmill Company* officially established. Thomas W. Kirkpatrick joined them that winter in the operation of the *Townsite Company*.[436]

November 3, 1896, was a day of particular importance in the Klondike. On that day, "rich ground was opened up on 21 Above

Discovery on Bonanza." As the owner of the claim "burned" down he sampled the newly thawed gravels below the muck and started to find $3.35 per pan, this at a time when eight cents to the pan was considered good pay. Finally, any uncertainty about Bonanza Creek was put to rest; "the doubters converted," everyone electrified. On the fourteenth, miners on Eldorado were taking out pans as high as $18.[437] Still later in the month "a big strike was made on 6 Eldorado took out as high as $22.00 to the pan!" But this yield was peanuts compared to the $100 pans that were later taken out on both Bonanza and Eldorado. One pan washed out on Eldorado was $800. More gold would be taken out of those two creeks in 1897 than had been taken from Sixty Mile and Forty Mile claims combined in any one season. Sergeant Hayne of the North West Mounted Police would later write that:

> The gold was so abundant that when a miner went down into his prospecting hole with a lighted candle, the bystanders could see the gold glittering in the gravel as the feeble rays fell upon it. The oldest Californian "boys" were speechless with amazement, and affirmed it was the richest strike they had ever known by a very long way. It was so regular and continuous and covered such a large unbroken area of country that men were afraid to speak of it in its full richness. It seemed too marvelous to be true.[438]

William Ogilvie, in a lecture given in Victoria, British Columbia in 1897, stated his belief that Bonanza and Eldorado creeks would eventually "turn out from $60,000,000–$75,000,000."[439] He was also quoted in the *London Times* as stating that "about 100 claims...on Bonanza Creek...will yield from $250,000 to $500,000 each."[440]

On November 17, 1896, Arthur Harper filed an application for "any vacant ground not already covered by other applications filed up to this date in the vicinity of the mouth of Klondike River on the easterly bank of the Yukon River."[441] Harper included a sketch showing that he was applying for the 18 acres of land between the exciting Harper and Ladue town site and the 40-acre government reserve on which the North West Mounted Police would construct Fort Herchmer the following summer. This land was contributed by Harper to the partnership and would eventually be known as the

Harper Addition to the Harper and Ladue town site.

Other parcels of land adjacent to either the original Ladue town site or the Harper Addition were eventually acquired and were known as the Menzies, Smith and Day Additions. These "additions" were each purchased from the Crown jointly by Stewart Menzies, A. H. Day and Jack Smith and the *Ladue Townsite Company* for $10.00 per acre.[442]

In November 1896 Joe submitted an application to Inspector Constantine at Forty Mile for 480 acres of land at Fort Selkirk. In it he stated that he wanted the land "for the purpose of raising horse feed, believing there will be important developments in that part of the country and horses will be much required." The plot was surveyed on November 24, 1896, and an application fee of $50 was paid.[443] No definitive action on Joe's application was taken and it was canceled in December 1901.[444]

At the same time, Harper submitted two applications for parcels of land at Fort Selkirk, one for 160 acres, and another for 480 acres adjacent to it on the north and bordering Joe's. Both were surveyed on November 24, 1896, and application fees of $50 each were paid. Harper described the 480 acres he was applying for as that "on the westerly bank of the Yukon River north of the gravel flat on which the old Selkirk trading post was situated...."[445]

In his application for the 160 acres, Harper described them as "the site of my present trading post. This piece of ground comprises that on which the Hudson's Bay Company*'s* fort called Selkirk stood nearly 50 years ago. I occupied it in 1891."[446]

Although Harper declared he had "occupied" the 160-acre parcel of land since 1891, he also stated in the same application that "In the summer of 1890 I occupied and built on the 'gravel flat' situated on the westerly bank of the Yukon River...on which the Hudson's Bay Company*'s* fort named Selkirk stood for some time nearly fifty years ago." It was on this site that he had established his trading post. From 1890 until 1896 he built quite a remarkable community consisting of a residence, 18 by 24 feet, a storehouse "for the proper prosecution of my business as a trader," a warehouse "for the reception of any goods, 30 by 26 feet,...and three cabbins (sic) for the accommodation of the Indians who trade with me and white men traveling up and down the river." He also kept several horses at Selkirk, which he fed from grasses cut from ponds. But, the grass was of such poor quality for fodder that the horses, although able to survive the winter, were generally unfit for work.[447]

In 1892 when a representative of the Anglican Church arrived to establish a mission at Fort Selkirk, Harper had allowed him to build a "dwelling house" (30 by 26 feet) and a schoolhouse (25 by18 feet). But in 1896, when the Anglicans made an application for about five acres of land, which was part of what Harper considered to be his, he executed a sworn statement as the original settler of the site saying that, if granted title to the acreage he had applied for, he would "convey to the mission a sufficient area of ground to properly prosecute their mission work, but deny them the right as original holders to any part of it." The statement, written and executed at Fort Cudahy June 30, 1896, was recorded July 1 by William Ogilvie, Dominion Lands surveyor. One of the witnesses to the signing of that statement was Willis Lamay of Schuyler Falls.[448]

Meanwhile, in the late fall of 1896, the 1,500 men[449] at Circle City heard of the strike on the Klondike from an Indian who arrived at the North American Trading and Transportation Company store.[450] Most dismissed the man's story; a few started out. When freighter Sam Bartlett[451] arrived he told the men that the Klondike stories were a "bilk," that Ladue was only trying to attract men to his new town site.[452] In mid-November the good news of Bonanza reached Oscar Ashby, a saloonkeeper. Again, the men had a laugh. But, in mid-December when Frank Dinsmore and Harry Spencer read a letter to them from a friend with a claim on Bonanza, the crowd took it more seriously. Dinsmore immediately fitted out a dog team and traveled to the Klondike to see for himself what truth there might be to the story. When Spencer received a letter from Dinsmore in late December and read aloud to everyone the opinion that Klondike was "immensely rich" and that Dinsmore had "never seen anything like it," the stampede was on.[453] Every able-bodied person began assembling an outfit. Many left good claims; some left caches full of provisions. Finally, many were believers and, once the stampede got underway, nothing deterred even the skeptical. Sergeant Hayne would later write that "Everyone who could beg, borrow or steal a dog team started to make the difficult journey. From the New Year to the end of winter there was a continuous procession along the ice of Americans heading towards the mouth of the Klondyke."[454]

Within a short time Circle City, previously the most active mining camp on the river, was a ghost town with the new sobriquet, "silent city," its former inhabitants now in the Klondike, most likely regretting they had delayed so long getting there.[455] Bonanza and Eldorado had been completely staked[456] within the first few weeks of discovery, the latecomers had to settle either for claims on the side gulches or try to buy shares, which many did. Many of the early stakers were offered enormous prices for their Bonanza and Eldorado claims and many of the men from Circle City had plenty of money; the cleanups on nearby Birch Creek the previous season had totaled about $900,000. The selling and buying of claims, or partial interests in claims, accelerated when the Circle City miners arrived in the Klondike and continued for many months to come.[457]

Ellis Turner was in Circle City in the fall of 1896 when an Indian delivered the news of the strike on Bonanza. In October he wrote to his family that "there has been several new cricks struck this summer, sum of the best diggings ever."[458]

But Ellis, too, chose to ignore the report of the strike. Instead he went in the opposite direction to Fort Yukon, spending much of the winter looking after the steamer *Bella* for the Alaska Commercial Company. By March 1897 he had changed his mind. That month he set out over the ice for the Klondike, pulling a sleigh loaded with 200 lbs. of provisions. He took neither tent nor stove because that "would add fifty pounds to my load." He made the 80-mile trip to Circle in six days, breaking trail all the way. The next morning he left with an additional 100 pounds of supplies. Soon, however, an uncommonly high wind and snowstorm struck and he "was obliged to lay off for eight days." On April 1 he arrived in Forty Mile, having traveled 200 miles from Circle. Two days later he was in Dawson. Hearing that "every claim was taken clear to the summit of the mountain, I hired to Mr. Ladue for $10 per day. I am now working at the mill and intend to stay here until my turn comes at mining."[459]

By June 1897, Dawson was the premier mining camp in the north. Everybody was in the Klondike; even Juneau was deserted.[460]

The population jumped to 4,000.[461] Among them were 40 white families and 200 Indians. Many men on Bonanza and Eldorado were already wealthy. Some Forty Milers and others, however, who had spent years searching up and down the Yukon and its tributaries, ended up with little or nothing. They had simply not been able to believe that there could be anything of real value in the Klondike Valley. Many who did stake claims didn't bother to mine them and sold them for almost nothing compared to the riches realized by the new owners.[462] One old-timer, Leo Dietrick, was the original staker of No. 16 Eldorado but sold it because he thought Eldorado "too far back in the hills to be any good at washup time…In those days we thought no more of a claim on Eldorado than we do of a glass of beer today…." Later, when No. 16's new owner was taking out a fortune in gold Dietrick said, "There is nothing like it...I may make a trip into the hills and again try my luck."[463]

The potential of the Indian River and its tributaries, in which Joe had so much faith, was still unknown in the spring of 1897 because everyone's attention was focused, riveted, on the Klondike. Surprisingly, William Ogilvie, who had been in the territory off and on since 1887, believed that the Stewart, which Joe and many others had given up on in 1886, "would prove, if not equal in richness to Bonanza and Eldorado Creeks in gold deposits, of vastly greater extent."[464] Early in the summer of 1897 there was even a stampede to the Stewart but it turned out to be a great disappointment.[465]

Hunker and Gold Bottom had not been thoroughly prospected, but Ogilvie speculated that they and their tributaries would eventually "give us two or three hundred more claims, a great many of which will over top $100,000 each."

A little work had been done on Too Much Gold, a tributary to the Klondike 35 or 40 miles from its mouth, with poor results.[466] The greater extent of the Klondike goldfields was yet to be prospected.

There were also "fair indications of quartz" found in the Gold Bottom Valley. In years to come there would be much prospecting and speculation related to the quantity and value of quartz in the Klondike District. And, while Joe and his associates would eventually locate over one hundred quartz claims in nearby Moosehide District, large-scale hard-rock mining was never developed in the

Klondike.[467]

The first mail from miners to relatives and friends arrived Outside in January 1897; the next month some started for the Klondike.[468] In addition to these were about 1,000 others who came into the southern Yukon earlier in the winter and knew nothing about the Klondike strike; they were heading for Circle City and nearby Birch Creek. They must have been amazed that spring when they rounded the bend in the river and saw the tent cities on the Klondike and Yukon river banks. One of the first things they saw, however, was a large sign erected by saloon keepers at Lousetown across the mouth of the Klondike above Dawson: "Danger Below: Keep to the Right." In other words, "Stop here! This is the best and safest place to land your boat." The sign implied that, if they continued on to Dawson, they were certain to encounter unspecified evils. The evil to Joe was that people coming into the country would not land at his town site. William Ogilvie came up with a solution to Joe's problem; he suggested that he tie down the steam whistle on his sawmill to attract the newcomers. It seemed to work, for soon Joe's town, Dawson City, was the hub of activity for the Klondike region.[469]

Strangely, that spring there were only 1,500 men in Juneau waiting to start for the goldfields.[470] Strange, since many letters sent Outside the previous winter described so specifically what had been found. One miner, Fred Brewster Fay, wrote home to a friend: "The stories told are not exaggerated. One hundred dollars to the pan is very common. One can hardly believe it, but it is true." Casey Moran wrote: "Friend George: Don't pay any attention to what any one says, but come in at your earliest opportunity. My God! It is appalling to hear the truth, but nevertheless the world has never produced its equal before. Well, come. That's all."[471]

Joe stated in August 1897 that "Reports of the richness of the gold diggings were going out all winter, but people did not believe them. Every mail carrier that went out took these reports with him, but people thought it was a fake or at least greatly exaggerated."[472]

The decisions argonauts would have to make if they were to start out on such a venture were significant. In most instances everything they possessed would be at risk and, although they didn't know it, even their lives. They needed more evidence that such riches actually existed, giving some assurance that the trip would be worth the sacrifices as well as the investments in time and money. Many delayed or didn't go at all. Those who did decide to make the trip, while they didn't know they would be too late to stake on Bonanza and Eldorado where the biggest strikes had been made, were to be among the lucky ones compared to the tens of thousands who would follow in 1898 because there were numerous creeks throughout the Klondike Valley that had not yet been prospected—creeks on which many would find their fortunes.[473]

"From January to April, 1897, about $4,000,000 were taken out of the few placer claims then being worked."[474] Sluicing began in April 1897 and soon there were "cleanups"—cleanups like no one in the Yukon had ever seen. Shouts of amazement and delight echoed up and down the little valleys as the incredulous men found 100, 200, 500 and 800 ounces lining the riffles and mats of their sluice boxes. On Number 16 Eldorado two cleanups were made in one day yielding a total of 1,350 ounces of gold. The cash value at $17 per ounce was $22,950.

One of the successful miners on Bonanza was the energetic Mrs. J. T. Wills,[475] who had spent the winter of 1895-96 at Circle City baking bread and operating a laundry. She heard of the new strike early and was among the lucky individuals who acquired a claim, possibly from an old-timer who didn't know what he had, and sold it for whatever he was offered. Over the winter her claim was worked and when she left in the summer of 1897 it was valued at $250,000.[476] Her concerns about supporting her ailing husband vanished.

The weather during the winter of 1896-97 was typical, with lows plunging to about minus 54 degrees Fahrenheit, and an average of 20 below.[477] Partially because of the cold, which reduced the chance of typhoid fever, there were no deaths that winter, either in town or on the creeks. Joe reported that the first burial in Dawson was in May 1897. Bert Stickney had drowned on the upper river and his body was brought to Dawson. Perhaps concerned that he would be blamed for the death, his partner, Hogan, who brought Stickney's body downriver, did not want to come to shore. Joe, Arthur Harper's son, Fred, Philip Kelly, and some others paddled a boat out to retrieve the body.

The second death was Clinton G. Felcht, from Oregon, who had just sold his claim in the spring for $12,340. In early June 1897 he was found dead in his cabin built on a lot in Dawson that he had purchased from Joe the previous October.[478] The effects of Stickney and Felcht were put into safekeeping by the gold commissioner, who, at that time, before there was a police presence in town, was responsible for forwarding valuables and personal items to relatives.[479] Coffins for both men were made from lumber provided by the Harper and Ladue Sawmill and they were buried on a steep, rock-filled hill at the north end of Dawson. The following year it became known locally as the "Typhoid"[480] or "Father Judge's Cemetery," and, even later, as the Third Avenue Cemetery.[481] Stickney's wooden marker remains today and, surprisingly, the inscription is readable: BERT STICKNEY, DIED May 16, 1897, 26 YEARS."

For all the golden harvest that spring on Bonanza and Eldorado, many men would have gladly traded considerable amounts of it for "grub." There was some relief when, on June 2, the first steamer to make it upriver, arrived from Fort Yukon where it had wintered. It was the Alaska Commercial Company's *Bella* loaded with 400 tons of much-needed food as well as supplies and 225 passengers. The Company immediately opened for business in Joe's original cabin, taking in about "$6,000 in sales as a result of the first day's sales."[482] But, the 400 tons weren't nearly enough to feed everyone in Dawson and on the neighboring creeks, and many were eagerly awaiting the arrival of the North American Trading and Transportation Company's steamer the *Weare* that had wintered at Circle City.

On June 8 the *Weare* arrived carrying 300 tons of freight and 25 passengers. Among them was Eli Weare, the president of the company. The company's manager, John Healy, had specifically ordered from headquarters the previous fall a full load of food and other essential goods but, when he found that most of the freight was whiskey, his reaction was swift and alarming. Orin Jackson, Healy's son-in-law, later stated that Healy "lunged at Weare in a blind fury, grasped him by the throat and shook him like a rat, demanding to know why his orders...had been disobeyed." Jackson intervened and saved Weare from Healy's rage.[483]

By the end of June 1897 "several hundred buildings had been erected, including stores, supply stations, hotels, restaurants, saloons and residences."[484] But on the creeks and in town most people were still living in insubstantial, flapping canvas tents. Entrepreneurs and all the trappings of a mining camp were arriving daily. By the end of the summer the population of the district passed 6,000, and there were additional stores, saloons, dance halls, a North West Mounted Police detachment and the churches of Anglican, Presbyterian, Baptist, Methodist and Roman Catholic denominations.[485] As in Skagway, conditions in the town were extremely unsanitary, and "the most villainous odour prevailed."[486] By the summer of the following year conditions had not improved and typhoid took the lives of many.

In the latter part of July the North American Trading and Transportation Company brought its sawmill up from Fort Cudahy and soon had it in operation on an island in the mouth of the Klondike River. It and the Harper and Ladue Sawmill ran day and night, and by October 1 there were more than 500 houses in the town, "many of them very large and expensive." Most of these were located between First Avenue and the mountain behind the business section. Still Ladue and Harper had made no attempt to drain any portion of the town site and it was covered with stagnant water to a depth of a foot in many places.[487]

During that first summer of Dawson's existence and beyond, there were constant complaints that government officials were corrupt. The most corrupt, or perhaps inept, of all was the Gold Commissioner's Office headed by Thomas Fawcett who had been appointed land agent May 21, 1897. Miners complained that when they had staked a claim, their application for registering it was frequently held up at the commissioner's office while staff members, friends or those willing to pay under the table, were given a "side door" tip which allowed them to go the claim, stake it for themselves and register it before the original staker's claim was processed. Timber berths, too, were to be had at a price by those willing to put out the cash to officials. Even post office officials lined their pockets—by distributing mail for a fee at a side or back door to those weary of waiting in the long lines.[488]

Throughout the spring and summer of 1897 "crowds of small

boats were pouring into Dawson from the upper river...bringing women, supplies, horses and mules; the forerunners of the rush of the coming summer."[489] With the influx of so many newcomers, the character of life in the Yukon shifted, continuing the change that had begun with the rush to Miller and Glacier Creeks in 1891 and 1892. The sense of brotherhood, trust and fair play that had been the foundation of a way of life was quickly fading. Inspector Constantine reported, "The majority of newcomers are from the United States, many of them could well be spared in any community. The rush has brought in toughs, gamblers, fast women, and criminals of almost every type, from the petty thief to the murderer."[490] The unsavory element, however, soon found that for those who violated the rules (apparently with the exception of government officials) there was hard labor on the barracks' woodpile. For murderers, the gallows was a certainty, followed by unceremonious burial behind the police barracks cemetery at the east end of the jail.[491] Confidence men like Soapy Smith and his larcenous gang thrived in Skagway because the Mounties wielded no sway in that American town.

Mary Kellogg Sullivan, who was in Dawson the summer of 1899, wrote:

> While walking down the street in Dawson one morning about nine o'clock I passed a group of men all wearing sober faces. 'They're done now,' said a rough miner, glancing in the direction of the Barracks, where a black flag was fluttering at the top of a staff.
>
> How so?" asked another, just come up to the group.
>
> Three men hung over there, an hour ago. They're goin' to bury 'em now" and the speaker twitched his thumbs toward the Barracks, then farther east, where a rough stretch of ground lay unused. Here could be seen policemen and soldiers, evidently in the midst of some performance not on their daily routine.[492]

Two of the men were the so-called "Indian murderers," the Nantuck brothers, Jim and Dawson who had murdered William Meehan. The third was a white man, Edward Henderson, who had murdered his partner, Thornburg Peterson.[493]

Treatment of felons was harsh from the beginning. The way in which the police disposed of a convict's body in 1908 was typical of how they handled such things.

The *Dawson Daily News* of October 7, 1908, details how the body of Ned Elfors, convicted of murdering one David Bergman near Fort Selkirk, was done away with in the most ignominious manner. Elfors had been hanged October 6:

> In the still hours of the night, when the shades were deep and when slumber dreams had bound the good people of Dawson, a squad of men from the Dawson barracks carried the rough board coffin containing the body of the foul murderer, Ned Elfors, to the brink of the black slough running through the police yards, and buried it eight feet deep in the earth.
>
> There amid the muck what little substance is left of Ned Elfors will be until absorbed by the breast of nature. The exact spot where the murderer lies is so obscured that it can not be discerned by inquisitive eyes.
>
> Should ghouls go after the remains of Elfors, they would find little for their troubles. The coffin was literally filled with quick lime, and over this was thrown enough water to set the mass seething. While the turbulent mass was sending up pungent fumes, the lid was nailed on, and the coffin covered, and the flesh and bone of the dead murderer and thief left to be cooked and consumed.

Sometime during that heady summer of 1897, Ellis Turner prospected on some of the creeks in the district and, in October when he arrived back in Schuyler Falls, he told a reporter for the *Plattsburgh Republican* that he had "located a gold claim on one of the tributaries to the Klondike" and that he "intended to return to his claim the next spring." He never did.[494] Ellis married and worked as a carpenter the remainder of his life. Many homes he built still exist in Plattsburgh.

What finally triggered the Klondike Gold Rush proper was the arrival on the west coast of miners from Bonanza and Eldorado mid-July 1897 aboard the Pacific Steam Whaling Company's steamer *Excelsior* and the North American Trading and Transportation Company's steamer *Portland*, which had boarded these passengers at

St. Michael. Huge crowds watched in awe as the men from the goldfields came down the gangplanks carrying bags and boxes of gold dust and nuggets.[495] The *Seattle Daily Times* printed an extra on July 18, headlines blaring in an enormous typeface:

THE *STEAMER PORTLAND* HERE!
BROUGHT DOWN HALF A TON OF GOLD!
RICHES OF THE FAR-FAMED MONTE CRISTO
OUTDONE![496]

Among the miners on the two steamers, William Staley had $112,000, Clarence Berry, $100,000, Henry Anderson, $65,000, Inspector Strickland of the North West Mounted Police had at least $44,000, and possibly as much as $130,000! One man had with him 1,300 pounds of gold worth about a quarter million dollars! What temptation for outsiders in the midst of an economic depression. The North American Trading and Transportation Company, apparently concerned about the possibility of piracy or mutiny enroute to Seattle, mounted a *Maxim* gun, a single-barreled machine gun, on the *Portland*."[497]

In San Francisco, when the *Excelsior* arrived July 15,[498] many became believers in the stories of the Klondike strike when Thomas Lippy carried on his back into the *Selvey and Company Smelter* a 150-pound sack of gold. Joe estimated its value at about $28,000.[499]

The stories in the Seattle and San Francisco papers were picked up by news services and quickly circled the globe. The reaction was unprecedented.

Another Trip East

Joe had spent the winter of 1896 and the spring of '97 in the Klondike working with his partner, Arthur Harper, managing the sawmill, and, with the assistance of Thomas W. Kirkpatrick, supervising their town site company. With rare exception, the 50 by 150 foot lots had been selling for up to $500 each; the following summer many of those same lots would sell for $10,000—to a successor.[1]

But once more, the ties that bind summoned Joe back to New York. When he left Dawson on June 23, 1897 aboard the *Alice*, the sawmill was operating at full capacity around the clock and the Alaska Commercial Company wanted every board and beam for the construction of their 40 by 80 foot, two-story store, a 30 by 190 foot warehouse, three other large warehouses and a two-story log house to be used by employees as living quarters.[2]

Just before his departure, Joe made two major decisions. He purchased claim No. 23 Below on Hunker Creek from Joseph Desroches[3] and gave lawyer, S. O. Morford[4] power of attorney[5] to "conduct all my business in the Yukon District, N.W.T." For the next 14 months Morford would be Joe's "resident agent," and "legal advisor."[6]

On July 15, 1897, Joe arrived in San Francisco aboard the Pacific Steam Whaling Company's steamer *Excelsior.* Estimates of how much gold he had with him have ranged from $5,000 to $50,000, but he reported that he brought out $5,000.[7] While he did not bring out much gold, he had with him a collection of nuggets, "one almost as large as a duck's egg and nearly pure gold."[8] He "reckoned" he was worth $75,000.[9] When his partner, Arthur Harper, arrived in San Francisco on September 15 he carried $60,000 in gold. Jack McQuesten, who was on the same boat, had $30,000. Frank Dinsmore, another sourdough who traveled out with McQuesten and Harper, had also struck it rich. He too, had $30,000.[10]

When Joe was interviewed in San Francisco by the *Seattle Daily Times*, the reporter saw him as no one had seen him before, writing:

> nor did he think it necessary to stop at a felt hat and tan shoes, for on his finger glistened a diamond ring, across his waistcoat

> there hung a double-breasted chain and on one end of the chain was a new watch of the best American make. His scarfpin was a small nugget of native gold and nuggets that had been fashioned into sleeve links for the adornment of his cuffs.[11]

Inspired by his own success and surrounded by others who had found their fortunes in the Klondike, Joe apparently decided to celebrate as never before. However, this showy jewelry did not seem to have lasting importance for him, because when he returned to Schuyler Falls the ring, scarfpin and sleeve links were placed in a box, where they remained.

As soon as Joe set foot in San Francisco, men and women wanting to know about Klondike gold besieged him:

> "Where was it, exactly? How much was there? How could it be picked up? When should we go?" These were some of the questions he patiently tried to answer. He told them that no one knew how much gold there was in the Klondike, but not to start out without a year's supply of provisions, and then not until "the fifteenth of March on..." He said he felt that the all-river route was best but, that if a man decided to go in by land, the Chilkoot Pass route "isn't so bad." However, he also pointed out that he would "not advise anybody to go there. That I will not do."[12]

After fifteen years in the north country, Joe knew well its hardships. He knew that horses for the White Pass Trail were now selling for $150 in Skagway, at a time when 25 cents bought a three-course meal. He knew 40 round trips would be required to transport 2,000 pounds of supplies over the Chilkoot—a trail too steep for horses. Other hardships of the north were eloquently described by William Ogilvie:

> Every dollar found there, it might be said, is the product of physical pain and misery. In summer there are mosquitoes innumerable, swamps, too, to be traversed, and mountains to climb. Now while those infernal flies and mosquitoes are biting, sometimes life itself is thought to be a curse. This I know from actual personal experience. I have seen strong men shed tears of impotent rage at these innumerable and almost invisible enemies.[13]

Statements of realities like these held little sway as large Dawson trading companies further whetted the appetites of would-be argonauts with newspaper advertisements, such as the following, in the *Seattle Daily Times*:

> Now is the time to go to the KLONDYKE country where, according to last reports, gold is as plentiful as sawdust, and miners receive $15.00 per day. We now offer the last chance of reaching this wonderful country from Seattle direct to the mines on large and elegant passenger steamers.
>
> THE NORTH AMERICAN TRANSPORTATION & TRADING COMPANY'S STR. PORTLAND
>
> Leaves Seattle July 20 connecting at St. Michael's with elegant river steamers direct for the mines. For rates and further information apply at the Company's office 618 First Avenue, Seattle.[14]

Advertisements and articles whipped the populace into a frenzy. When Joe's eastbound train pulled into Chicago, crowds again surrounded him, hungry for first-hand details. Hundreds, thousands, wanted to hear from Joe Ladue, the man who owned City in the Klondike. When one man asked if he had really seen gold taken out of the Klondike, he responded:

> Have I really seen gold taken out of this Klondyke district? Well, I guess I have. I panned gold on my own dump last spring. I took out nine pans on claim No. 23 Hunker Creek 3 (English) pounds 8s (shillings) in nugget gold. I saw two pans panned out by a fellow named Mercier and his partner which paid 114 pounds. I guess I got my share.[15]

At some point on his journey back to New York, Joe gave interviews to a number of newspapers and talked about the value of his interests in the Klondike. He said he had been offered $100,000 for them, "just as they stand, but I would not sell for three times that amount. The offer has been made to me in coin, but I declined because I know what I have got there and I know how to hold on to it." He planned to return to Dawson in March 1898 when he would probably sell out "perhaps for $300,000, perhaps for

$500,000."[16] In the years that followed he must have deeply regretted he had not accepted the offer of "coin."

When Joe arrived at the Lobdell's home in Schuyler Falls at the end of July, he was relieved to be free of the crowds.[17] Inquisitive strangers were fewer, but still curious locals came, by foot, bicycle and horse and buggy down the narrow, dusty roads and across the fields. County historian Emily McMasters recorded in 1965 that "Every man who lived within a radius of 10 miles and who had a horse and buggy drove to Schuyler Falls to shake his hand. It was like a County fair."[18]

Shortly after Joe's arrival, Lincoln Steffens, a reporter for *McClure's Magazine*, knocked at his door and requested an interview. Joe agreed, probably hoping that if his story were printed, the public would be satisfied and he would be left in peace. That Steffens was given this assignment shows how important a "catch" *McClure's* considered a piece about Joe. Educated in Europe, Steffens (1866-1936) later became associated with the leading liberal and radical movements of his day. He got his start on the editorial staff of *McClure's*, becoming its managing editor from 1902-06.

McClure's was an illustrated magazine founded in 1893 by Samuel McClure, and known for covering controversial topics such as labor disputes, working conditions in mines, the Rockefellers and the Molly McGuires. It sold for 15 cents and published authors like Stephen Crane, Rudyard Kipling, Jack London and Arthur Conan Doyle. Of course, it wanted to cover the phenomenon of the Klondike Rush through the experiences of Joe.

Asked by Steffens what was needed for the trip to the Klondike, Joe described the outfit he knew so well:

> Here is what ought to be put in an outfit: a camp stove, frying pan, kettle, coffee pot, knives and forks and spoons, and a drill or canvas tent; an ax, a hatchet, a whipsaw, a two-inch auger, a pick and shovel, and ten pounds of nails. For wear, heavy woolen clothes are best—not furs—and the stoutest overshoes you can get, with arctic socks. Then there is "sleigh" as we call it, really a sled, six or eight feet long and sixteen inches in the run. It is safest to buy this in Juneau, for those you pick up in other places won't track. I don't take a canoe unless I am late going in, but they make the lightest and strongest in Victoria, at about 160-

> 200 pounds weight. The simplest thing to go down the river on is a raft, but to make that or a boat you need, besides nails and tools I named, two pounds of oakum and five pounds of pitch. A year's supply of grub, which can be bought as cheaply in Juneau as anywhere, I think, is: 100 pounds of flour, 150 pounds of sugar, 100 pounds of bacon, thirty pounds of coffee, ten pounds of tea, 100 pounds of beans, fifty pounds of oatmeal, 100 pounds of mixed fruits, twenty-five pounds of salt, about ten dollars' worth of spices and knicknacks, and some quinine to break up colds. The total cost of this outfit is about $200, but no man should start with less than $500, and twice that is ten times as good.

Steffens described Joe as:

> the weariest-looking man I ever saw. I have known bankers and business men, editors and soldiers and literary men who had the same look out of the eyes that this pioneer of the northwest country has; they were men who had made money or a name, earned by hard labor that which others envied them. The disappointments that ran before the final triumph limped in had spoiled the taste for it. None of the them showed the truth so plainly as the founder of Dawson, the city of the Klondike.

Throughout the interview, Joe's answers were "simple, plain, colorless, almost lifeless." What he exhibited, however, does not appear to have been either indifference or bored patience. His answers were clear and complete, if brief and lacking drama or animation. He was tired from business, from traveling, from the constant demands of inquisitive people, and perhaps, even then, suffering from tuberculosis. When asked how much he had in the Klondike, he responded wearily, "Enough." Seeing his exhaustion, Steffens asked him why he was planning to return.

> "I have to," he answered. "I've got so many interests to look after. There is the sawmill and the logging and Dawson and a couple of claims staked out (39 Eldorado staked; 23 Above Hunker, acquired) that have to be worked. You've got to attend to things, you know.

As Steffens continued to probe for more information, Joe finally said he was "willing to tell all" he could as long as it was understood that he was "not advising anybody to go there.... It goes pretty hard for some of the men that go in. Lots of them never come out, and not half of those who do ever make a strike." He was also concerned that with the great number of people rushing to the Klondike, there would be starvation the coming winter.

Joe again recommended that those who did decide to go to the Klondike, take the all-water route to St. Michael by steamer, and from there by riverboat up the Yukon to Dawson. But, for those who wanted to go by land, he said:

> The Chilkoot Pass is the best. You start from Juneau and go by steamer to Chilkat, then to Dyea, eight miles, where you hire Indians to help you to the summit of this Pass. From Dyea you walk ten miles through snow to Sheep camp, which is the last timber. From there it is a climb of six miles to the summit, 4,100 feet high, and very often you or the Indians have to make two or three trips up and down to bring up the outfit. Leaving the Indians there, you go down, coasting part way fourteen miles to Lake Lindeman. That is five miles long, with a bad piece of rapids at the lower end. But if it is early in the season, you sled it on the lake and take the mile of rapids in a portage to Lake Bennett, which is a twenty-eight mile tramp. It is four miles' walk to Caribou Crossing, then a short ride or tramp to Takoon (Taku) Lake where, if the ice is breaking, you can go by boat or raft, or if it is still hard, you must sled it twenty-one miles, to the Tagish River and Lake, four miles long. Take the left bank of the river again, and you walk four miles to Marsh Lake, where you may have to build a raft or boat to cover its twenty-four miles of length. If not, then you must at the bottom, for there begins the Lynx River, which is usually the head of navigation, for unless the season is very late or the start very early, the rest of the way is almost all by water.
>
> Thirty miles down the Lynx River you come suddenly upon Miles Canyon, which is considered the worst place on the trip. I don't think it is dangerous, but no man ought to shoot the rapids there without taking a look at them from the shore. The miners have put up a sign on a rock to the left just before you get to it, so you have warning and can go ashore and walk along

> the edge on the ice. It is sixty feet wide and seven-eighths of a mile long, and the water humps up in the middle, it goes so fast. But very few have been caught there, though they were killed, of course. Below the canyon there are three miles of bad river to White Horse Rapids, which are rocky and swift, with falls, but taking chances is unnecessary, and I consider it pretty good dropping. After the rapids it is thirty miles down to Lake Labarge, the last of the lakes, which is thirty-one miles to row, sail, or tramp, according to the condition of the water. From there a short portage brings you to the head of the Lewis River, really the Yukon, though we do not call it that till, after drifting, poling, or rowing two hundred miles, the Pelly river flows in and makes one big, wide stream. I must warn men who are going in to watch out for Five Fingers Rapids, about 141 miles down the Lewis, where they must take the right-hand channel. That practically ends the journey, for, though it is 180 miles from the junction of the Pelly and Lewis, it is simply a matter of drifting.

Joe's final comment to Steffens was not surprising, and probably was repeated by many another old-timer from the Yukon: "All I have doubt about is the character of some of the men who are rushing in to get rich by just picking up the gold." As Steffens was leaving, he saw a number of Joe's neighbors approaching across a field. Joe "dropped the bagful of nuggets for them to pass around and finger, and stare at...and went off to the barn and hid."[19]

At about the same time, Joe was interviewed by John A. Sleicher of *Leslie's Illustrated Weekly Magazine*, *McClure's* competitor. Sleicher described Joe:

> He is about five feet eight inches in height, weighing about one hundred and sixty pounds, with a square strong face indicative of his origin, heavy black eyebrows, thick black hair, and a dark mustache. His eyes are brown, and his complexion, darkened by exposure, is almost that of an Indian.... He is reticent and retiring, and a man of steady habits. Sudden wealth and the prospect that he may become one of the richest men of our times have not changed him in the least. He has a well-poised head, reaches a decision quickly, and adheres to it firmly. Many of the wealthy financial men of New York who have met him since his

> recent arrival in this city have been surprised at the ease and freedom with which this mining prospector, fresh from a wild and adventurous life, carries himself. He dresses plainly, displays no jewelry, speaks with deliberation and great care, but never of himself when he can avoid it.[20]

A reporter for the *New York World*, who interviewed Joe in August 1897, wrote:

> Ladue is not an educated man in the school-book sense. He is simple and homely in his speech. He is not imaginative, he does not exaggerate.…In his pocket to-day he had sixty nuggets ranging in size from a pea to a silver dollar and worth in the aggregate probably $2,700, and he declared, with a substantial "damn," that he never had any girl and doesn't want to marry any of them. But he didn't explain the reason.[21]

Two years earlier Josiah Spurr of the United States Geological Survey met Joe at Ogilvie Post on the Yukon River, and later wrote that "he shook hands shyly and silently, a man whom years had made more accustomed to the Indian than to the white man."[22]

What neither Steffens nor Sleicher could know of Joe was that in the Yukon he stood tall among those sourdoughs who were most respected, or that he was often referred to as "Smiling Joe." He was so well thought of by the Indians, that when he was in his store, they would conduct their business with no one else.[23]

In late July 1897 Joe gave an interview to a reporter of the *Plattsburgh Republican.* The reporter prefaced his article:

> There is probably no man alive who is better posted on Alaska than Mr. Joseph Ladue. He is a typical pioneer: strong, hardy and resolute—a man of iron.
>
> Mr. Ladue has not only worked his muscles to good advantage to himself, with the result of abundance of this world's goods, but has evidently all this time been closely observing the conditions of that strange country—the Yukon valley—which has so suddenly become one of the great centers upon which human interest throughout the world is focused.

The interview continued:

> Republican: "How can people live in such a cold climate?"

Ladue: "You will suffer more from cold in Clinton County than there. I have chopped wood in shirt sleeves in front of my door when the thermometer was 70 below zero and suffered no great discomfort. The air is very dry. We usually have about three feet of snow and it is dry as sand. The winter days are very short. At Dawson it is only about 2 hours from sunrise to sunset. It rises and sets away in the south. But there is no pitch darkness. The twilight lasts all night. The northern lights are common all through that region. Then in summer it is the other way. The day there now is about 20 hours long, the sun rising and setting in the north."

Republican: "How can you work comfortably in winter?"

Ladue: "Nearly as well as summer. The mining is done largely in shafts which are sunk to bedrock, and then by drifting or tunneling. The ground is always frozen solid below a depth of 2 feet, except on the islands, and there is no need of shoring as there is no danger of its caving. The gravel is chopped out and picked out in a frozen condition and thrown up on the dump. And, when the warm weather comes it thaws and is washed and the gold separated."

Republican: "How about game?"

Ladue: "There are many fur-bearing animals—black fox, bear, otter, mink, etc. The fur of the black fox is very valuable. When in the fur business I have sold these skins as high as $250."

Republican: "Have any quartz veins been located in the Klondike region?"

Ladue: "I think not. Am not sure."

Republican: "Do you think that any localities in Alaska will be found that are as rich in gold as this (Klondike)?"

Ladue: "I doubt it. The indications are that the richest deposits are east of the Alaskan line."[24]

Shortly after his arrival in Schuyler Falls in early August, letters began arriving asking for money, wanting him to try a particular product or make an endorsement. One product he did endorse was Royal Baking Powder. The advertisement in a Plattsburgh newspaper read: "I have always used the Royal Baking Powder in Alaska and Northwest Territory as no other gave equal satisfaction in that harsh climate. I also found my customers always insisted on having that brand."[25] In 1902 the *Royal Baking Powder Company* published Camp Cookery, for "all out-door cooking." In it they wrote: "Joseph Ladue, of Dawson City fame, says that in Alaska and in the Northwest Territory he never used any other brand than Royal Baking Powder, as no other can stand that harsh climate. Mr. L. N. McQuesten, the 'Father of Alaska,' writes in the same way."[26]

Letters arrived by the hundreds and Joe hired two assistants to help him read and answer them. One was from a woman who wanted to open a boarding house in Dawson; another was from a "capitalist" who wanted to purchase his claims. When a letter arrived from a "refined and educated" widow he put it in his pocket.[27]

A letter of another kind, from Elvira L'More, was a long and dramatic "begging" letter. She wrote to Joe from Boston asking him to help her:

> get a claim and it would make me richer and very happy if I could get gold enough to make me comfortable. I would feel rich so you see it would not take but a few dollars to make me rich and happy in this world....I think you can't blame me for trying to get something in the gold region and hope you will forgive me for asking this favour of you....I have been better off than I am now but failures and losses have made me poor. My husband died very much in debt and our farm was sold and I paid his debts and a very little left....

Mrs. L'More went on to describe in great detail many more difficulties she had experienced and her current state of need.[28] It is not known whether Joe responded to her letter.

Most of the letters Joe received asked the same questions he heard everywhere he went. Finally, he decided to stop the avalanche of requests by writing a book. It was titled *Klondyke Nuggets: A Brief Description of the Great Gold Regions in the Northwest Territories and Alaska*. As proof of its value, the cover bore an image of an impressive gold nugget provided by the author. Joe was described as "Founder of Dawson City, N.W.T., Explorer, Miner and Prospector." It sold for ten cents.

After making the decision to write this book, he published an announcement in the August 13, 1897 issue of the *Plattsburgh*

Previous Page: Joseph Francis Ladue, "Founder of Dawson City" (from Klondyke Facts, *Joseph Ladue)*

Top: Joe's childhood home in Schuyler Falls, NY (Joseph Francis Ladue III Collection)

Above Left: Andrew Ladue followed Joe to Deadwood. (Keith LaDue Collection)

Above Right: Catherine Marie (Mary) Ladue Hendryx whose scrapbook provided many answers. (Ronald Scott Hendryx Collcetion)

Above: Deadwood was the wild, open town in the Dakota Territories where Joe learned the "secrets of gold mining." (Nebraska State Historical Society)

Opposite: Apache leader, Geronimo and his troops conducted fierce raids on miners and stage travelers near Tombstone, Arizona. (Arizona Historical Society, Tucson, Arizona, AHS #20602)

Above: Joe's 50 lb. bag of flour saved members of a U.S. military reconnaissance from starvation. L-R: Lt. Fred Fickett, Lt. Henry Allen, Robinson. (Fred Fickett Collection, Consortium Library, University of Alaska, Anchorage)

Opposite Top: Arthur Harper, Joe's business partner, Harper's second wife, Irena (L) and her sister, Martha Walker c.1897 (Margaret Ogilvie Collection, Yukon Archives, Print #77/7, PHO 77)

Opposite Bottom: Trader Al Mayo's family. L-R: Catharine, Florence Margaret, grandson Sullivan, Al, Antoinette, Annette. (Antoinette Roberts Woods Collection, courtesy of Barbara Nelson)

Above: Jack and Kate McQuesten, loved and respected by early pioneers and natives of the Yukon, at their home in Berkely, California in 1905. (copied with permission of Crystal McQuesten Morgan, ca 1970)

Above: The Chilkoot Pass during the Klondike Gold Rush was one of several difficult routes to the gold fields. All supplies, including the canoe in this photo were carried on the backs of early stampeders. (Museum of New Mexico, Palace of the Governors History Library Collection, Photo #106398 by B.L. Singley).

Above: Dawson was first a "Tent Town." (Vancouver Public Library Collection, Yukon Archives #2011)

Above: In the goldfield miners worked frantically with shovels and wheelbarrows as rocker boxes have an insatiable appetite for gravel. Vancouver Public Library Collection.

Above: Ellis Turner, the gentle young man from Plattsburgh was seasick on the sea voyage from Port Townsend to Juneau, as Joe reported in his 1895 note to Will Lobdell. (Ellis Turner Family Collection, Courtesy of Velma Newton; Copy of Joe's note Collection of Joseph Francis Ladue III)

Above: Ladue-Yukon Transportation Co. steamer, Gold Star *at Dawson City, 1900 with the* Bailey *and* Yukoner *(National Archives of Canada)*

Opposite Top: First Dawson Townsite and Harper & Ladue Mill Co. office. Thomas Kirkpatrick, standing left in doorway and S.O. Morford, standing third from right. (MacBride Museum Collection, Yukon Archives #3770)

Opposite Bottom: Harper & Ladue Sawmill and employees, Dawson City, 1898. (Dawson City Museum/Klondike History Library)

OFFICE
DAWSON TOWN SITE CO.
AND
Harper & Ladue Mill Co.
401

Joseph LADUE Gold Mining
& Development Co of Yukon

LADUE - YUKON
TRANSPORTATION CO'S
STEAMERS
"GOLD PICK" LINE
JOHNSON - LOCKE MERCANTILE CO.
GENERAL AGENTS
SAN FRANCISCO AND SEATTLE

MORGAN CITY
OF
NEW YORK
No 497
Seattle April 26
Wilse Photo

Opposite Top: An elaborate brochure promoted Joe's transportation company's accommodations from San Francisco to Dawson City. (Courtesy Candy Waugaman)

Opposite Bottom: Ocean steamer Morgan City, *flagship of the Ladue-Yukon Transportation Company's Gold Pick line at Seattle, April 26, 1898. (University of Washington Special Collections Division, # Wiln 497)*

Above: Joe, Kitty and Francis Ladue. Neighbors said Francis lived "like a little prince." (Ed and Star Jones Collection)

Top: Joe's home in Schuyler Falls was his largest investment. Joe, Kitty and Francis enjoyed it together for a brief three years. It remains today. (Ed and Star Jones Collection)

Bottom: Workers prepare for fall harvest on the Ladue apple farm in Peru, NY (Joseph Francis Ladue III Collection)

Sentinel informing all past and potential correspondents that their questions would be answered in this inexpensive form:

> I duly received your letters asking for information regarding the gold regions. As you must know the number of these letters is very large. I have arranged, therefore, to furnish the American Technical Book Company, 45 Vesey Street, New York City with a book of all the facts relating to the discoveries in the great northwest.[29]
>
> They will be pleased to send you "*Klondike Nuggets*," giving a brief description of the Gold Regions, postpaid, on receipt of ten cents, but my larger work, "*Klondike Facts*" will include interesting illustrations and a map. It will be a book of 224 pages (when published, it was 205 pages) and will be sent, postpaid for 50 cents in paper covers and one dollar in cloth. Write to the publishers for it. The information will be the staking out of mining claims, the best route, cost and advice to people going into the country.
>
> My mail has been so exceptionally large that I regret it is impossible for me to write you personally as my movements are very uncertain.[30]

From the handsome, dark green cloth cover of *Klondyke Facts* gleamed the same nugget in bright gold, while on the title page Joe was described both as "author of '*Klondyke Nuggets*,' and founder of Dawson City, N.W.T."

Klondyke Nuggets was a paperback booklet of 92 pages. It contained primarily quotes from the writings of William Ogilvie, apparently used by the publisher without his permission. This infuriated Ogilvie and caused a permanent breach between him and Joe.[31] At one point, Joe disclaimed any connection with the book and requested that his name be removed from future copies printed. When *Klondyke Facts* was published it contained several quotes from Ogilvie for which he was given credit.

All That Glitters
The Joseph Ladue Gold Mining and Development Company of Yukon

Among the hundreds of letters Joe received in Schuyler Falls proposing all kinds of ways he might want to invest his newly acquired wealth were some from prominent businessmen and financiers.[1] It may have been from those letters that he was enticed with a prom ise of great rewards if he formed a new corporation separate from his already successful partnership with Arthur Harper. There were plenty of potential financial backers for a company whose purpose was to exploit the riches that most people believed were ready for the taking in the new goldfields. Around the world, the word "Klondike" was electrifying! Hundred dollar pans of gold were being found; Bonanza and Eldorado claims were "world beaters."[2] It was just what investors would want to hear. The supposed possibilities were too great for Joe to resist.

In early August 1897, Joe retained the services of Plattsburgh attorney, Elmer F. Botsford of the firm of Beckwith and Botsford.[3] On the tenth they were in New York City, registered at the Murray Hill Hotel.[4] They made their headquarters at 100 Broadway where they met[5] with the Wall Street law firm of Brown and Wells to draw up articles of incorporation for The Joseph Ladue Gold Mining and Development Company of Yukon. These were filed with the Secretary of State in Trenton, New Jersey, August 27, 1897, and filing fees of $1,000 were paid.[6] The company was capitalized at $5,000,000, divided into 500,000 shares (100,000 preferred; 4,000,000 common) to sell at $10 each. The original plan was for the stock to be placed for sale on the New York and London Stock Exchanges, but it was only sold "on the curb," which means simply that it was not sold on the exchanges, but through brokers and advertised in newspapers and/or other media.[7]

As of September 1897, one broker of Ladue company shares was H. W. Coffin with offices in the Washington Loan and Trust Building, Washington, D.C. Coffin held 250,000 shares offered for sale at "$10 each, fully paid and non-assessable."[8]

It could be said that Joe, like so many others, had been carried along by what seemed to be the unlimited potential to make a fortune in the Klondike. He risked most of what he had acquired during his 15 years in the Yukon and, in his own way, joined the stampede he was cautioning others against. Into the corporation he placed his half share of the Harper and Ladue partnership, which included 50 percent of the trading post at Ogilvie, the Dawson town site, the sawmill, extensive timber berths and two rich placer claims, 39 Eldorado and 23 Below Hunker, believed to be two of the richest placer claims in the Klondike. In return, the newly-created corporation paid him $16,024.15 in cash and issued in his name 24,700 shares valued on paper at $2,470,100, making him the principal stockholder. Any profits Joe would ever realize beyond this initial cash payment would be dependent solely upon sale of the shares and/or payment of dividends. Arthur Harper "ratified" the transfer of Ladue's partnership share and purchased a large block of shares in the new company. Arthur Harper's estate continued to receive profits realized from his 50 percent share of the Harper and Ladue partnership into the first part of the 20th century.[9]

In late 1897 John Sleicher interviewed Portus B. Weare, the chairman of the Executive Committee of the North American Trading and Transportation Company. Weare made several comments about Joe and the company he had formed:

> When he entered Alaska five years ago, "Joe" Ladue already ranked next in importance and influence to the A.C. Company. I consider Ladue a very able and smart man. He was smart enough to make our Company pay him four thousand eight hundred dollars for a part of a lot at Dawson City upon which to build a warehouse.

Weare was less enthusiastic about Joe's involvement in forming The Joseph Ladue Gold Mining and Development Company of Yukon.

> I have heard that Mr. Ladue is putting his property into a Company with a capital of five million dollars. For what he has to turn in I consider this very low. I have no interest in this Company. Your smart financiers in New York have simply found Mr. Ladue as they find many other prizes and got all the benefit of his labors for fifteen years.[10]

Many companies were formed to do business in the Yukon following the strike in the Klondike. *The Ladue Company* was definitely a huge corporation, being one of seven capitalized at $5,000,000. By far, the largest trading companies in Dawson, however, were the Alaska Commercial Company and the North American Trading and Transportation Company, both capitalized at $25,000,000. Given the ephemeral nature of gold rush communities and the presence of such large and firmly established corporations, it was a courageous act for considerably smaller companies to attempt to compete with them.

The Ladue Company Board of Directors, in addition to Joe, was composed of some of the wealthiest men of the time:

Chauncey M. Depew, president of the New York Central and Hudson River Railroad Company.

Charles H. MacIntosh, lieutenant governor of the Northwest Territories.

Thomas L. James, ex-postmaster general of the United States and president of the Lincoln National Bank.

A. W. Emery

L. J. Needham

Eli A. Gage, secretary of the North American Trading and TransportationCompany of Yukon.

H. Walter Webb, third vice president of the New York Central and Hudson River Railroad Company

William J. Arkell, owner of Judge and *Leslie's Illustrated Weekly Magazine*.

Smith M. Weed,[11] president of the Chateaugay Railroad Company

J. Nesbitt Kirchoffer, senator for the province of Manitoba.

John Carstensen, comptroller of the New York Central and Hudson River Railroad Company

Irwin C. Stump, ex-director of the Anaconda Mining Company

Edwin G. Maturin, secretary of the Corporation Trust Company of New Jersey.

Elmer F. Botsford, director of the First National Bank of Plattsburgh, N.Y.

Thomas W. Kirkpatrick, resident superintendent of The Ladue Company, in Dawson City.

The company had five officers: Joseph F. Ladue, president and general manager; Smith M. Weed, first vice president; Charles H. MacIntosh, second vice president; Elmer F. Botsford, secretary/treasurer; Samuel C. Conkling, assistant secretary; general counsel was J. S. L'Amoreaux, New York, N.Y.; attorneys for the company were Brown and Wells, 36 Wall St., New York, and Beckwith and Botsford of Plattsburgh. Judge S. O. Morford was the company's attorney in Dawson City.

General offices of the company were at 20 Nassau St., in the Wall Street. district of New York City[12]. The *Seattle Daily Times* reported in late August 1897 that the Ladue Company had its "headquarters...and capital" in Seattle.[13] No other sources were located to corroborate that statement, which may have been part of the Seattle campaign to convince the world that it was the primary West Coast port where outfits could be purchased and transportation obtained for the Klondike.

After completing their business in New York that August, Joe and Elmer Botsford returned to Plattsburgh and then traveled to Ottawa, Ontario, seeking to secure title to the Dawson town site. Joe had received assurances that patents would be issued, but they had not yet been received. In Dawson, The Harper and Ladue Townsite and Development Company was advertising lots for sale:

> Desirable Lots for Residence and Business Locations. For Sale By Harper & Ladue Townsite Co. Office Corner Second Street and Fourth Avenue.

Placing this advertisement was a simple matter of walking to the back of their own building where The *Klondike Nugget* had rented space for its offices.[14]

On the same day the articles of incorporation were filed The Joseph Ladue Gold Mining and Development Company of Yukon published a prospectus issued to attract investors, shares to be available for sale at 10:00 A.M. on August 28. Potential shareholders were enticed by a description of the company's properties that were of "great value."

> A well-known and wonderfully rich gold placer property, located in the heart of the Gold Bottom Mining District of the Klondyke. This Gold Placer property embraces a zone 1,000 feet in length (two claims), 4 feet in thickness, with a known

> width of 200 feet, which further development is almost certain to expand to 400 feet. The yield of this property shows a result of $12 per cubic foot in coarse nugget gold. Mr. Ladue estimates that ten men, with proper machinery, can wash and extract an average of $30,000 per week from this property, basing his estimate upon the results of the work already done...A conservative estimate of the value of the gold contained in this pay streak of gravel would give the sum of $9,600,000. And, even this amount is reasonably certain to be doubled.

In addition there was "A gold-bearing quartz property 1,500 feet in lenth by 600 feet in width...This is the mother lode from which the millions of treasure of the Gold Bottom Mining District have been drawn." Incredibly, the ore was stated to show an average return of $300 per ton. It was stated that "Arrangements are already being perfected for the erection of a stamp mill on this property," and "the property will become productive in the immediate future." (By early 1898 the company had plans to purchase a "splendid stamp mill of a new kind," that would "be operated by steam and contain two sets of tools, with power for 20 stamps."[15] It would not be delivered until 1901.

The prospectus went on to emphasize that "Since the departure of Mr. Ladue from Dawson City, Mr. T. W. Kirkpatrick...has been instructed to acquire other placer properties for his benefit. Those which are acquired and in process of acquirement will have a total length of one mile." Although these new claims were acquired in Joe's name, his half-interest would be assigned to the corporation, while Arthur Harper retained his half-interest.

The prospectus claimed that the Canadian government had also given Joe "the franchise of the exclusive right to cut timber...the importance of this grant can hardly be exaggerated, since it covers timber lands along both sides of the river for a distance of 15 miles from Dawson, and which in conjunction with the saw mill hereinafter referred to, confers a practical monopoly of the lumber trade of the City of Dawson...." In fact, many other companies and individuals were also issued timber berths along the Yukon River and its tributaries.

There was also "A LARGE SAWMILL BUILT BY MR. LADUE

NEAR DAWSON CITY" that was earning a profit of $1,350 per day. The demand for lumber for building purposes, for boats, fuel, flumes and sluices boxes could not be met, thus "this cannot fail in itself alone to earn a moderate dividend on the capital stock of the Company."

Another important item in the company's prospectus was "A CHOICE PARCEL OF 80 SELECTED LOTS, each of 25 feet frontage, to be located in the center of the business portion of the City of Dawson." It was the intent of the company to sell many of the lots and to develop others to be used as rental properties.

Also considered important to potential investors was the fact that the company had set aside "the sum of one million dollars of its cash capital for the development of the quartz property and 'new claims,'" and to allow the company to pursue business interests that might become available.

The final statement of this exaggerated and seductive prospectus read:

> This Company having acquired extensive holdings of productive Klondyke property capable of earning large dividends on its stock, offers to investors advantages not possessed by any other existing Company. The Company desires to add that it also contemplates the undertaking of transportation and other industrial enterprises under its Canadian charter which promise to be enormously profitable.

The transportation company was pursued immediately, a decision that would have a significant impact on the Ladue Company for several years to come.[16]

Shortly after the company was registered, it acquired the Golden Wedge Mining Company of Rossland, British Columbia.[17] At the time the Golden Wedge property was purchased, however, it had not been shown to be productive, and its future would be no better.

A fact not included in the prospectus was that the Ladue Company had branches at St. Michael and on the Dall River in Alaska.[18] The Dall River enters the Yukon from the north about 146 miles downriver from Fort Yukon. A store may have been opened at that location to trade with the Indians of nearby Stephen's Village.

After concluding formation of the corporation, Joe returned by train to Plattsburgh. On September 17, 1897, a telegram arrived for Joe at the company's Nassau Street office in New York City from Samuel Breck of the U.S. Adjutant General's Office in Washington D.C.:

> The Secretary of War desires to confer with you in regard to the upper Yukon Country and the practicability of relieving distress for food if it should occur during the closed season. Of course your expenses will be paid. Please reply paid here.
> Samuel Breck, Adjutant General[19]

The first reply to the adjutant general was a telegram:

> New York, Sept. 17/97. Your telegram forwarded to Joseph Ladue at Plattsburg(sic).
> The Joseph Ladue Gold Mining and Development Company of Yukon[20]

Three days later, a second reply was sent from the company offices:

> To Paul Breck, Adjutant General, Washington. Mr. Ladue was in the Adirondacks when telegram was received. Left for Washington last night and will arrive there at hotel Arlington 8:30 tonight.
> The Joseph Ladue Gold Mining and Development Company of Yukon

On September 21, 1897, Joe met with the distinguished looking Secretary of War, Russell A. Alger, to discuss methods by which food could be transported to the Klondike for the ensuing winter months. Later the same day he "called on President McKinley who appeared deeply interested in his suggestions for the relief of the Klondikers."[21] One method the U.S. government was considering was the use of "ice engines" that would pull large sleighs loaded with provisions. Joe told the president he thought the idea "impracticable, owing to the fact that when the river freezes the ice in the center is forced up, forming great hillocks." He also believed that dog teams pulling sleighs loaded with supplies were not practical since they could generally haul only as much food as was needed just for the dogs. Joe advised that a courier be sent immediately from the coast of Alaska across the Chilkoot Pass to urge all who could to "embark on the last outgoing steamer." He also recommended that "all who have not provisions and who can return to St. Michaels before the river freezes...."[22]

However, Secretary Alger did not send a courier immediately, deciding instead to wait for a report from Army Captain P. H. Ray, at Fort Yukon, to determine just how severe the food shortage problem actually was. In the end the government was not able to launch a successful effort to get food to the Klondike. Only one steamer succeeded in getting to Dawson that fall and many were hungry before spring.

In the fall of 1897, before his meeting with President McKinley and Secretary Alger, Joe had been approached by the Klondike Snow and Ice Transportation Company to use his name as its president. His understanding had been that the company had built a machine, "The Snow Conqueror,"[23] that was able to travel over the ice and snow pulling large sleighs, and was solely for the purpose of implementing a government relief effort to get food to the Klondike, a concept that at the time he apparently endorsed but would later advise against. It appears, however, that he decided not to recommend the snow machine. When he learned that the company had abandoned its original plans and discovered they were advertising that they would be carrying paying passengers, Joe informed them that he "would have nothing to do with such a scheme." For some time, however, Joe was under suspicion when the Klondike Snow and Ice Company took money from its would-be customers, but provided no passenger service. Officials of that company were eventually apprehended and the courts clarified that Joe had no part in such activities.[24]

Toward the end of November Joe received the sad but not unexpected news that his friend and business partner, Arthur Harper, 62, had died of tuberculosis in Arizona. James M. Wilson, a merchant of Dawson and executor of his estate, along with Harper's heirs, chose to continue with the Harper and Ladue partnership agreement, which they did for many years. Until Joe sold his half interest to the Joseph Ladue Gold Mining and Development Company of Yukon, the profits from his partnership with Arthur Harper were divided evenly between them. Beginning August 27, 1897, what would have been Joe's share of profits went to the new company. At the time of Harper's death, the partnership "owed large sums of money," and for a considerable time much of its profits were used to pay off that indebtedness.[25] The Ladue Company accepted responsibility for what would have been Joe's partnership share of that indebtedness.

When news of the establishment of the Ladue Company reached Dawson, a short-lived newspaper, the Dawson City Glacier (which appears to have been a spoof, lampooning many individuals of the Klondike) published the disparaging statement that "'Promising' Joe Ladeau, who promises everything that comes into his head, is at his old tricks in the states. The New York papers have a good deal to say about him. Joe is a smooth worker even if he comes from the country."[26] The truth of the matter is that $10 million was taken out of the Klondike in 1898. There is no evidence that any of Joe's business activities in the Yukon or Outside were ever questionable. The truth of the matter is that $10 million was taken out of the Klondike in 1898.[27]

The Ladue-Yukon Transportation Company

On April 1,1898, the Ladue Company announced a new stock issue "for the purpose of creating additional working capital for the transportation business which the company has now entered into, having its fine steamship, '*Morgan City*' already on the Pacific coast." The issue was preferred stock to which holders were "entitled to receive in each year out of the earnings of the company a fixed cumulative dividend of 6 percent before any dividend shall be paid upon, or set apart for, the common stock."[28]

An advertisement in the March 19, 1898, *Plattsburgh Daily Press* attempted to attract additional investors:

> Wealth of the Klondike
> Shrewd Investors Are Sure Winners
>
> The Joseph Ladue Gold Mining and Development Company of Yukon,Finding opportunity for the extremely profitable use of additional working capital in connection with its transportation business, the company now offers for investment a limited amount of its new six percent preferred stock.
> Pro Rata division of all surplus earnings
> Joseph Ladue was the pioneer of the Klondike [and] was the founder of Dawson City.
> Obtained a monopoly of the adjacent timber lands.
> Purchased the original quartz discovery in The Klondike, thought to be the "Mother Lode."
> Established the only saw-mill in the Klondike district.
> Controls the Canadian patent on Dawson City.
>
> Mr. Ladue came east with this basic wealth and interested the most successful and highest class of financiers, forming one of the strongest and most powerful Companies yet organized. His Klondike placer claims of 500 feet each,"Mother Lode," Quartz property on Gold Bottom Creek, saw-mill plant, lumber rights, and some of the best lots in Dawson City have been turned over to the above company.

> The above company has since purchased the Fine passenger S.S. "*Morgan City*"800 feet long, 2,500 tons burden, and carrying capacity for 700 passengers, which will operate between San Francisco or Seattle and Skaguay up to about the 1st of June when she will be put in commission to St. Michael's in connection with four riverboats and four more freight scows on the Yukon River.
>
> All the valuable assets of the company are behind this stock and investors are assured of ample protection.
>
> Price of preferred stock $10.00 per share, payable 50 per cent on application and balance on allotment of shares. (Right reserved to withdraw stock without notice.) Subscription for the stock should be sent to
> E. F. Botsford, Treasurer, 20 Nassau Street, New York.

Joe said he was "forced into the (transportation and freighting) business because the big companies were not making preparation to handle the freight they should. We could not get freight room and had to put our steamers on to carry our freight."[29] That was a correct assessment at the time, which was probably late in December 1897. The Alaska Commercial Company had announced that they would not be carrying "a pound of freight to the diggings" because they required "every foot of their space to convey their own goods to their own stores in Alaska." The North American Trading and Transportation Company adopted a similar rule. The only other transportation available was the small fleet of steamers and riverboats of the newly formed Alaska Exploration Company. What Joe may not have been aware of was that "fleets of tramp steamers" were making their way from eastern ports to the West Coast.[30] Another likely reason Joe decided to venture into the transportation business was his belief that new diggings would be opened up on the American side (Alaska) that would be "even be richer than they have found already."[31] By the end of January 1898 the Ladue-Yukon Transportation Company had been established, "the largest and best...which has undertaken this business." The company's plans were big, as were its oceangoing and river fleets, and its investment.

The Johnson-Locke Shipping and Mercantile Company, the

largest commission house in San Francisco, was agent for the Ladue Company's Gold Pick Line. The ocean steamers advertised were the *Morgan City*, *Cutch*, *Tillamook*, *Grace Dollar* and "four others." All were "first class steamers."[32] Like other shipping lines, the Ladue-Yukon Transportation Company flew distinctive banners on its steamers and riverboats, proudly declaring, "L. T. Co." In addition, symbolizing the company's purpose of transporting passengers and freight to the land of gold, each vessel displayed the long, flowing Gold Pick Line flag. The dark blue banner bore a gold circle on which was centered the image of a miner's pick. On the *Morgan City* the gold circle and pick also appeared in another form, painted on the smokestack.

The *Morgan City*, the flagship of the line, was built by Harlan & Hollingsworth at Wilmington, Delaware, in 1876.[33] It was purchased by The Ladue Company from Collis P. Huntington, one of four Sacramento merchants who became a captain of industry as one of the "Central Pacific Railroad's Big Four...."[34] On January 31, 1898, the ship was issued a certificate of registry. The purchase price was about $120,000; the cost of alterations the company made was $31,363. Among ocean liners of the day it was of considerable size at 38 by 281 feet[35] and had a depth of 20 feet (depth referring to the number of feet of the ship that was in the water) and had two decks. Its gross tonnage was 2,303 tons and was described as an "iron screw steamship" with a "round stern" and 1,000-horsepower engines.[36]

The *Cutch*, built in 1884 in Hull, England, was bought and rebuilt by the Ladue Company in 1898. It measured 23 by 180 feet, a "schooner-rigged propeller [craft] of 324 tons...licensed to carry 150 passengers." When it was rebuilt its gross tonnage was increased to 676, more than double its original capacity,[37] and it was registered at Vancouver, British Columbia.[38]

Neville Armstrong, who mined for several years on Russell Creek, a tributary to the MacMillan River, related in his book *Yukon Yesterdays* his misadventure aboard the *Cutch* in 1898 (presumably prior to its expansion):

> The coldest, the most miserable and uncomfortable voyage I ever made between Vancouver and Skagway was in the small steamer *Cutch*. In size she was little better than an average tug-boat; there were a few deck cabins and she rolled and pitched

> gloriously at the slightest pretence of a sea. On this particular journey we encountered a succession of gales, finally ending up in a blizzard. The snow froze hard as it settled on everything and the rigging was soon treble its normal size.
> The ship's anchor assumed huge proportions. Axes and hot water had to be used to clear the doors of the cabins (which opened on to the deck), also steps, hatches, etc. Those of the passengers who owned fur coats were very fortunate, as the temperature in the cabins was close on zero. But we eventually arrived safely at Skagway and were a very much photographed ship.[39]

The *Tillamook*, 32 by 126 feet, was built about 1887 in San Francisco, had a gross weight of 265 tons, and a draft of 9.9 feet. It was "enrolled" rather than registered at San Francisco, given the official number 145448 and signal letters K. D. R. H.[40] The Ladue Company purchased it for approximately $30,000.[41] The *Grace Dollar* was a "newly-built" steamer. All four steamers were scheduled to sail for St. Michael where passengers and freight would be transferred to the Ladue-Yukon Transportation Company's riverboats.[42] No further mention was made of the "four others."

The Yukon River fleet was advertised as consisting of nine "first class steamers": *Clan McDonald, Gold Star, Rideout* (named for Walter R. Rideout, president of the California Yukon Trading Company of California), *Alviso, City of Dawson, Gamecock, Staghound, Pinafore* and *Powell.*

Information could not be located on the *Pinafore* and *Powell.* The seven others were described as follows:

Clan McDonald: built in Aberdeen, Washington, 1891, 25 by 92 feet, gross weight: 230 tons, 100 horsepower engine.

Gold Star: built at St. Michael, Alaska, for the Ladue-Yukon Transportation Company in 1898, 22 by 94 feet, Gross weight: 160 tons, draft: 3.8 feet.

Rideout: built in Stockton, California, for the Ladue-Yukon Transportation Company in 1898, 32 by 149 feet, gross weight: 278 tons, draft: 3.5 feet.

Alviso: built in Sausalito, California, in 1895, 23 by 115 feet, gross weight: 197 tons, 40 horsepower steam-driven engine, draft: 6 feet.

City of Dawson: built in San Francisco, California, in 1898 (probably for the Ladue-Yukon Transportation Company), 26 by 114 feet, gross weight: 230 tons, draft: 5.5 feet.

Gamecock: built in Portland, Oregon, in 1898 by the Joseph Supple Company for the Ladue-Yukon Transportation Company, 38 by 178 feet, gross weight: 772 tons, draft: 7.9 feet.

Staghound: built in Portland, Oregon, in 1898 by the Joseph Supple Company for the Ladue-Yukon Transportation Company, 38 by 178 feet, gross weight: 772 tons, draft: 7.9 feet.[43]

An 1898 magazine article described the Ladue-Yukon Transportation Company in glowing terms:

> The Ladue-Yukon Transportation Company is not a small affair, got ten up on the spur of the moment to meet a temporary need. It is backed by unlimited capital, officers, and men of well-known reputation and financial standing, and its service handled by the best men that money can obtain...men of tried experience in looking after the comfort and safety of its passengers.[44]

The Johnson-Locke Shipping and Mercantile Company, in its role as agent for Ladue, published an extensive, multi-color brochure. The brochure publicized some of the endorsements Joe had agreed to, for products useful to miners. Those products included California "Drifted Snow" Flour, Germea (a cereal with "73 percent nutriment"), Baker's Cocoa and Chocolate, Royal Baking Powder and Eagle Brand Milk. "It is only the ignorant miner who allows any other brand to be foisted upon him," says the text describing the latter. "An experienced miner possibly may have a cheap brand palmed of (sic) on him, only to find when he reaches Alaska—and 80 degrees below zero, that there it is worthless."

In addition, the brochure included pictures of men climbing the Chilkoot Trail, prospectors in their boats, and plowing with a dog team. The text, promoting the company's Gold Pick Line, continued:

> Our steamers which will cover the ocean service from San Francisco and Seattle to St. Michael will be the finest and best

> fitted vessels on this coast.... They have large passenger accommodations, which have been newly-fitted and equipped, and will be as convenient as those on any first-class ocean steamer plying the Pacific Ocean. The steamers are manned by the most efficient and capable officers. Their table will be furnished with an abundance of every staple article of food, together with all such delicacies as may be practicable to supply for an ocean voyage.
>
> These vessels are handsomely fitted, lighted by electricity, steam-heated, have comfortable smoking rooms, and [a] ladies' social hall. From St. Michael to Dawson City or points on the Yukon River service will be covered by as fine, if not the finest and best equipped stern wheel riverboats that will be on the river the ensuing season.

The front of the elaborate, multi-page brochure reads:

> Ladue-Yukon Transportation Co.
> GOLD PICK LINE
>
> Johnson-Locke Mercantile Co., General Agents
> San Francisco and Seattle
> 204 Front St., San Francisco
> Steamship Department. (Ticket and Freight Office Address)
> 609 Market St. San Francisco, California
> or 112 Yesler Way, Seattle, Wash.
>
> Joseph Ladue, President
> Smith M. Weed, Vice-President
> E.F. Botsford, Secretary Treasurer
> Elmer F. Botsford, General Traffic Manager
> Operating The Ladue Yukon Transportation Company
> 20 Nassau St., New York

Sailing dates were scheduled from San Francisco on June 1, July 1 and August 1; and from Seattle June 5, July 5 and August 5. Distances were given as: Ocean distance, 2,420 miles; river distance, 1,722 miles, for a total of 4,142 miles.

To further capture the interest of potential passengers, the brochure contains a lengthy description of the wonders of a trip to Alaska and the Yukon goldfields on the Ladue-Yukon Transportation Company's ocean and river steamers:

> Now, that the first rush of the unthinking mass of greedy fortune hunters is over, wiser men are beginning to look to the more natural inlet to the great Yukon River Valley. From now on the "All Water Route" will be the only one considered.
>
> Let us anticipate a little, and take an imaginary trip a month or two in advance of the real one which we together with many other admirers of nature, lovers of adventure and tired, overworked mortals will enjoy in company with the miner, expecting to dig out his fortune, the capitalist seeking to invest his, and the merchant, the mechanic and the laborer determined to "make or break."
>
> Before we sail from San Francisco...let us inspect the floating palace which is to be our home for nearly two weeks, the S.S. "*Morgan City*."
>
> A promenade up her 300 feet of deck discloses, in passing, the comfortable fitted up state rooms. Her spacious and handsomely furnished cabins are suggestive of the finest private drawing rooms, and her kitchen is most complete in all its appurtenances. Her table is unsurpassed by any ocean liner.
>
> Comfortably located, amid all the conveniences that the ingenuity of experienced men can devise, or money procure, we sail quietly out of the Golden Gate with good company—music, books, cards and other amusements—we scarcely realize, when we touch Unalaska, that we have been on the ocean eight days. Sailing up Behring Sea, we pass the Pribilof Islands, which have furnished the world with sealskins and caused so much International discussion. Occasionally a whale is "sighted" and schools of porpoises play around the ship.
>
> Reaching St. Michael, we divide our time, while the ship's cargo is being unloaded, between hunting, fishing and studying a new type of humanity—the Esquimo. After a day or two of rest we are transferred to one of the finest riverboats afloat.
>
> As we ascend the grandest river on this continent and next to the largest one on earth, we are delighted with the ever changing

> scenery which passes in panoramic beauty and grandeur before us.
>
> At Nulato, the mouth of the Kayukuk, we drop a small party who are to prospect that great river, which is said to be rich in gold.
>
> On reaching Rampart City, we find a village of log houses and 1,500 people, all contented and happy, some having made big strikes on the Minook creek.
>
> A little farther up stream we pass the mouth of the Tanana River, through which is expected to pass, within a year or two, millions of gold. Four Hundred miles of riding through what is known as the "Flats" brings us to Circle City, the former centre of mining interests. Between here and Dawson on the American river the latest big "finds"' have been made.
>
> Dawson City—that place with which all the world is familiar, yet to which few have gone—is finally reached, and we are fresh and vigorous, ready for the work before us. A vote of thanks is extended to the obliging corps of officers who have done so much to make our journey a long-to-be-remembered pleasure trip.

Johnson-Locke added a warning that people should "Have nothing to do with the fake companies. Remember, a vast number of unreliable steamers, second-class boats and all sorts of make shift vessels have been employed in this traffic the last year."

The brochure, in a section titled: "Work at High Wages," pointed out that there were also, in the Klondike:

> great opportunities for those who do not care to mine. Physicians, dentists, blacksmiths, machinists and artisans; lumbermen, barbers, butchers, bakers and laboring men will earn wages and fees which would seem fabulous to them today. There is a Klondike right [here] in Dawson City for boarding-house keepers and tradesmen. Grocers will thrive as they have never done before. Carpenters and builders will find more work than they can do, with wages beyond their fondest hopes.[45]

All this promotion coupled with improved transportation paid off. By the end of the summer of 1898, Dawson boasted scores of saloons and dance halls, two hospitals, three churches, schools, banks and theaters, with a population estimated at 25,000. It attracted writers like Rex Beach and Jack London, who in turn, would attract others through tales of their northern experiences.

By the spring of 1899, all the creeks in the area were staked. Between 1896 and 1905, Klondike creeks yielded more than $100 million in gold.[46] However, during the late spring of 1899, rumors of a discovery of gold on Anvil Creek near Nome, Alaska reached Dawson, and within one week during August that summer 8,000 miners left for this new strike.

Although Joe's dreams and plans for the Ladue-Yukon Transportation Company and the advertising of Johnson-Locke were on a grand scale, and they may have had no doubt that they would all come to fruition, there remains little evidence that the number of planned ocean steamers ever went into service, or that most of the riverboats ever plied the waters of the Yukon. The only oceangoing ships known to have been operated by the company were the *Cutch* and the *Morgan City*. The others were gradually disposed of. Among the riverboats, the company retained the *Rideout* at least through the summer of 1898. That summer the *Tillamook* towed it to St. Michael. By the summer of 1899 it was owned by the California Yukon Trading Company.[47] In September 1904 its name was changed from *Rideout* to *Ida May*.[48]

The *Gold Star* was sold in early 1898 at St. Michael (where it had been built) to the Gold Star Transportation Company and was owned for some period by an old-time, Forty Mile miner Chris Sonnikson, who operated a freighting business until just prior to his untimely death on May 30, 1901. The *Gold Star* was in service on the Yukon River until June 1902 when she was "broken up," her machinery installed in a new riverboat, the *Thistle*.[49]

The *Staghound* and her sister ship the *Gamecock* were both wrecked on the treacherous Columbia River bar on their way to St. Michael.[50] The remains of the Staghound were purchased by Daniel Kern and converted to a towboat named *Hercules* for use on the Columbia River. The *Gamecock* was converted to a stern-wheeler tugboat by the Willamette and Columbia River Company.[51] The *Clan McDonald*, *Alviso* and *City of Dawson* never left the West Coast. The *Clan McDonald* was cut down for use as a tugboat in 1899 to work on Washington state's Skagit River. In December 1902 it was destroyed by fire. The *Alviso* was used on the Columbia River for a number of years, then taken to California for passenger service between San Jose, Los Gatos and Santa Cruz. On December 15, 1921, it, too, was destroyed by fire. *The City of Dawson* was out of service by 1911.[52] The fates of the *Pinafore* and the *Powell* are unknown.

Another factor thwarting the plans of the transportation company was, just as service was about to begin, it became evident that freight could be shipped more cheaply on the ships of the North American Trading and Transportation Company (which had reversed its policy of carrying only its own freight), or Alaska Exploration Company (which had acquired several more oceangoing and river steamers). This fact, along with the loss of the *Staghound* and the *Gamecock*, may have caused the company to sell the vessels not already delivered and to cancel orders still incomplete. The steamer *Morgan City*, the schooner, *Cutch*, and riverboats *Gold Star* and the *Rideout*, however, had apparently already been purchased.

When the *Morgan City* was acquired in New York City, it was on her last stop on trips she had been making between Galveston and New York for a number of years. She was refurbished and was ready to set sail for St. Michael around Cape Horn in late January 1898 with up to 600 passengers, for a scheduled arrival at San Francisco about April 10. The Ladue Yukon-Transportation Company had made traveling on the *Morgan City* even more attractive by offering each passenger for the Klondike a year's supply of provisions to be delivered upon arrival in Dawson.[53]

In the spring of 1898 the Plattsburgh Daily Press, in an effort to increase its circulation and get a step ahead of its prime competitor, the *Plattsburgh Republican*, decided to sponsor a "Klondike Contest," the winner of which would receive a free trip to the Klondike aboard Ladue's *Morgan City* and one of its riverboats. The winner would also be awarded a free year's supply of provisions—and met at Dawson City by famous pioneer and company owner, Joseph Ladue. On February 5, the Press ran two columns inviting readers to "hit the trail to Dawson City."

The contest, which began February. 17, would be won with "votes." That is, if a reader clipped and sent in the daily coupon, he received one vote. If a reader signed up a new subscriber and sent in a completed subscription form, he received 312 votes. When the contest ended April 23, F. L. Kemp of Ausable Forks had signed up the most new subscribers, for a total of 112,883 votes. In second place was Mrs. T. N. Spaulding of Saranac Lake with 110,638 votes; third place went to William Delano of Ticonderoga with 70,121 votes. Mr. Kemp, however, decided he had no great desire to go to the Klondike, having a very good position with J and J Rogers Company, which he thought it would be unwise to give up for the uncertainties of the goldfield. This could have meant a public relations disaster for the Press, but the newspaper bought out Kemp's first prize and awarded it to Mrs. Spaulding, then gave the second prize, a trip from Plattsburgh to the West Coast, to William Delano.

Kemp was given a medal in recognition of his hard work that had considerably benefited the Press. What the press did when Mrs. Spaulding, whose husband was already in the Klondike, also declined the prize, is not known.[54]

The winner of the Klondike contest, had he decided to accept the first prize, would have traveled across the country by rail to San Francisco where he would have met the *Morgan City* and its captain, John G. Dillon.[55]

At this point, however, fate intervened in the form of wartime necessity. In support of the war with Spain, the U.S. Army needed ships to charter for transporting troops and war materiel to the Philippines. On June 7 the *Morgan City* was chartered (perhaps commandeered) for $660 per day. The company made some "necessary repairs" needed to prepare it for military service, and was reimbursed, $2,519 by the government. Between June 7 and November 3, 1898, the *Morgan City* was part of the Third Philippine Expedition. On June 26 when the ship departed San Francisco, it had on board the First Idaho Volunteer Infantry and the First Nebraska Volunteer Infantry headed for Manila, not St. Michael.[56] After completing a number of trips to Manila the charter was terminated November 3 of that year.[57]

On January 4,1899, the adjutant general's office in Washington, D.C. sent a telegram to the commanding general, Department of California, authorizing him to again "charter the *Morgan City* under the best terms obtainable, and in addition to the freight which she is to take to Manila, she will be put in order to carry such officers and their families and men of the Twentieth Infantry as will equal her accommodations...." The next day, January 5, a new charter was made negotiating with the Ladue Company for a lower rate, $500 per day. Having inspected the *Morgan City* prior to its new mission, on January 7 the commanding officer of the California Department sent a telegram to the adjutant general in Washington, D.C., indicating that the *Morgan City* "can not be ready for sea till January 25; work is progressing day and night."

Refitting complete, on the evening of January 25, the *Morgan City* sailed from San Francisco headed for Manila with freight and "thirty-two officers, 4 officers attached, 1,253 men, 1 surgeon, 3 acting assistant surgeons, 4 hospital stewards, 11 privates Hospital Corps...and five hundred thousand rounds small-arms ammunition, caliber .30." By early May the *Morgan City* had returned to San Francisco. Taking on a new load of military personnel and equipment, it departed again for Manila where it arrived May 26 reporting there were "no casualties." On June 24 she set sail on a return voyage to San Francisco with "464 sick." By August 8, 1899, she again set sail from San Francisco for Manila.

On September 1 disaster struck. The adjutant general's office received a telegram telling that the transport, *Morgan City*:

> under guidance (of an) experienced pilot, struck reef in Inland Sea, 8 miles from Onomichi (Japan) 250 miles from Nagasaki, about 4 a.m. September 1; backed off at daylight, vessel filled very rapidly, was beached, and all saved; officers and crew did splendid work; have telegraphed to Kobe for food; am sending wrecking crew, vessel, food from here; cargo almost all lost. Can you send me transport from Manila? Castner, Quartermaster.

The next day, the *Morgan City* was "in hands of owners and crew" and the Japanese government had provided quarters for the troops. On September 5, 1899, the transport Ohio sailed for Nagasaki, Japan "to receive '*Morgan City*' troops."[58]

The wreck of the *Morgan City* occurred because of negligence on the part of the pilot. Oscar Schutt, an employee of the U.S. Postal Service, wrote in a letter to the Postal Record that they had made a "delightful passage across the Pacific." However, at Kobe, Japan they took on a new pilot who had just brought the steamer *Valencia* through the same area of the "Japan Inland Sea." He had been "up for thirty-six hours and was not in a condition to pilot our ship through." The "watch" had called out a number of times, "land ahead," and the second officer had reminded the pilot that there was land and that they should slow down. The pilot and the second officer argued, but the pilot insisted he had plenty of time to turn. Fortunately, the second officer rang the gong to signal the engineers to reduce speed. On Saturday at 3:40 A.M. the ship struck a rocky point of land. Said Schutt, "It felt as though the ship was crumbling to pieces.... There were 768 souls on board."

After several hours, the captain succeeded in backing her off the rock, but soon it became apparent that she was holed and filling with water. The decision was made to head for shore about two miles away where he could run her onto the beach. Most of the passengers and some of the freight were safely on the beach in very short order. Soon, however, the ship began to sink. Those still aboard were just able to escape by jumping overboard as she slipped out of sight. Signal fires were maintained throughout the following night, but to no avail. A Japanese steamer eventually picked up passengers and crew, taking them to Nagasaki where they met the U.S. steamer *Ohio* that took them on to Manila. Mr. Schutt concluded his letter with, "If she had struck running at full speed, I am afraid few of us would have escaped."[59]

It was reported by the *Yukon World* in its February 11, 1905 issue that "The general impression at the time was that there was an 'incipient mutiny' on the *Morgan City* and that in the process a murder was attempted on board, and the would-be murderer was put in chains."[60]

Two of the other three oceangoing vessels planned for use by the Ladue-Yukon Transportation Company suffered fates similar to that of the *Morgan City*. The *Tillamook* was owned by Swayne and Hoyt of Alameda, California, when it was wrecked November 29, 1900, at the north end of Wood Island Reef off Kodiak Island, enroute from Unalaska to Seattle, due to a "miscalculation."[61]

The U.S. Steamship Company owned the schooner, *Cutch*, when it was wrecked August 24, 1900, enroute from Ketchikan to Skagway, Alaska due to "carelessness of Officer in Chg." It was carrying 35 passengers and 29 crew members, all of whom were rescued. Part of the cargo it carried belonged to the Ladue Company.[62] In 1904 the *Grace Dollar*, which may have never sailed for the Ladue Company, was nearly wrecked at sea during a storm south of the Columbia River.[63]

Meanwhile, in Dawson City, town site lots were selling, and the sawmill was earning $1,350 per day. The placer claims, however, needed "to be worked." It had been decided by the company that government royalties (then at 10 percent) and the high cost of labor ($10 per man per day) made working their claims unprofitable, although they were among the richest in the district. Thomas W. Kirkpatrick had continued as resident superintendent and had proven to be an excellent manager of the company's affairs.[64]

Joe spent considerable time during the fall of 1897 working with Elmer Botsford to secure title to the Dawson town site and to establish the Ladue-Yukon Transportation Company. By mid-December he finally had time to take care of his personal life. Three years before he had met a pretty, vivacious young woman he had previously known as the little girl who lived next door to the Lobdell farm. She was Catharine Marie "Kittie" Mason, the daughter of a retired farmer, and "one of the best-known and respected young ladies of Schuyler Falls,"[65] then 24 years of age. Joe was 42, and apparently it was love at first sight for both. She told a reporter for a New York City newspaper in 1897:

> We have been sweethearts for three years, but Mr. Ladue has known me longer than that, nearly all my life—twenty years of it. When he was a young man just starting for the West to make his fortune, I was five years old. He remembers me a little girl in pinafores who lived on the next farm, but I have no recollection of him then. He lived with the Lobdell's, our nearest neighbors. There was little (time for) romance in our courtship.[66]

Their renewed courtship was brief, from September until December. On December 15, 1897, at 7:00 P.M. they were married at the Mason family home in Schuyler Falls by Reverend H. C. Petty, pastor of nearby Lorne Methodist Church. Joe gave his bride $1,000 in gold and the Reverend Petty a $100 gold piece.[67]

Immediately following the wedding the couple left by horse and buggy for the railroad station in Plattsburgh where they boarded a train for New York City and arrived the following morning. Joe was a significant public figure, significant enough that a New York newspaper made the effort to write about his honeymoon. The article describes their secluded quarters:

> An unpretentious third-story front room at No. 79 West Forty-fifth Street...Their little nest is cozy and comfortable; it shows none of the obtrusive luxuries that are to be found in the modern hotel, but it has an atmosphere of romance about it and evidences of a lover's attention; his remembrance of things his sweetheart was fond of: flowers, bonbons, books and sofa cushions. A bunch of fragrant violets like they gathered in their walks around Schuyler Falls in the days of their courtship were placed near her rocking chair at the window yesterday afternoon where she waited for her husband, who had gone downtown, and on a table within reach were a lot of magazines and two big plates, one covered with little fancy cakes in coats of pink, white and chocolate icing, the other with candies. Nearby stood the photograph of her husband, the man who worked three years in Alaska to bring home enough gold to marry her. They intended to remain in New York for about a week, and then make a hurried visit to Boston and get home in time for Christmas.[68]

Their honeymoon was interrupted in less than a week when Joe received a telegram summoning him back to Plattsburgh. Upon his return, he and Elmer Botsford immediately left for Ottawa, Ontario, to meet with government officials regarding the Dawson City town site application.[69]

On January 15, 1898, the newly married Ladues purchased the Benjamin Weaver house in Schuyler Falls from his heirs for $2,500. The deed was in Kittie's name.[70] They undertook major renovations and moved in soon after April 1 when the work was completed. The two-story house had been built of squared logs and, at some time, had been modified by enclosing the logs with red bricks. The architectural style was Greek Revival, popular in upstate New York in the eighteenth and nineteenth centuries. The first floor consisted of an entryway, living room, dining room and kitchen. Although the kitchen was modernized, the hand pump in the sink was retained and would not be removed until 1999. An off-set hallway with open stairs led up to a large, second floor landing, master bedroom, guest room and two small rooms at the back used as servants' quarters. A modern bath was installed with a claw-footed tub set in an alcove. The woodwork was changed, using the popular bulls-eye pattern at window and door corners; the walls papered in bold patterns. Carpets covered the wide floorboards. They chose dark, heavy and substantial Victorian furnishings. Later, an oil painting of Joe's oceangoing ship, *Morgan City*, graced the living room wall.

A porte-cochere was added at the right side of the house over the driveway allowing guests to drive carriages through and disembark under its wide roof, protecting them from inclement weather. A small barn at the end of the driveway served as a carriage house for the buggy and a stable for the Ladues' two bay horses. It was a handsome, well-furnished home, perhaps not quite the grand mansion expected of a "Klondike millionaire," but represented Joe's substantial degree of success.[71]

On February 7, 1898, while Kittie busied herself with details of the renovations, Joe was attending the first annual meeting of his company. Directors and shareholders of the *Joseph Ladue Gold Mining and Development Company* met at its Jersey City offices on the corner of Greene and Grand Streets. Three new board members were elected: James A. Roberts, James Grant and Willard Brown. At that meeting Joe relinquished his title as general manager and Samuel T. Conkling, who had been assistant secretary of the company, was appointed to that position. Walter H. Lyon became his assistant. S. O. Morford, who was Joe's legal advisor and agent in Dawson, became the company's attorney, replacing the firms of Beckwith and Botsford and Brown and Wells. Thomas W. Kirkpatrick continued as resident superintendent at Dawson City. Joe retained his position as president.[72]

A short while after the annual meeting Joe and Kittie left Plattsburgh by train for San Francisco. Many years later Kittie described the trip to Emily McMasters as a "nightmare," because of the crowds of men who rushed on the train at every stop, "all fallen prey to gold fever....There was no privacy on the train and it was sometimes delayed for two hours." While in San Francisco they were the guests of Mrs. Henry R. DeLaplain and visited Charles and Harriet Day, all former residents of Clinton County.

But, when Joe and Kittie returned home March 4, 1898, he was in very poor health and placed under the care of Dr. Barnes of Plattsburgh. To help with housework they employed a maid; for outside work they hired John Hosford as chore boy. The company's business was always on Joe's mind and he hoped to recover sufficient energy to return to Dawson City in the summer to oversee the opening of a general merchandise store.[73]

In spite of the weariness that plagued him, Joe accompanied Smith Weed, a member of the Ladue Company Board of Directors, to New York City on business. They traveled by train from Plattsburgh on March 11. After returning to Schuyler Falls from the city, a local newspaper reported: "Joseph Ladue continues to improve in health and expects to be able to visit Plattsburgh in a few days."[74]

On March 19, 1898, Joe purchased a 320-acre farm in Peru, New York, in Kittie's name, from the "heirs of Wm. E. Bentley," Lillian M. Stearns and Nettie J. Everett, for $8,800. This property was known locally as "The Merchant Farm."[75] To its existing apple orchard Joe added 250 trees, making it one of the largest of its kind in the area. Edward Donah who was "thrifty & intelligent" worked the farm on shares.[76] Joe equipped the farm with horses, wagons and machinery for planting and harvesting.

The Ladues were immediately accepted as solid members of the community and opened their home for charitable events. Kittie, who was active in the Women's Christian Temperance Union, sponsored a fund-raising "hash dinner" on May 12 for the organization at a cost of 10 cents per person.[77] Whether she was aware of rumors that Joe once owned a saloon in Dawson is unknown.

In each of the small communities in the area, the Plattsburgh newspapers had a correspondent who reported local news for the personal columns. There was little respect for privacy, and whatever happened was, in tabloid fashion, grist for news. In its May 27 edition the *Plattsburgh Sentinel* reported that "Joseph Ladue, Esq. of Schuyler Falls is confined to his home by sickness and may not be able to take the trip to Dawson City with Mr. Botsford as he expected to."[78]

It had become apparent to Joe and Kittie that his health was continuing to deteriorate. Their spirits were lifted in June when they were invited to call on President William McKinley and his wife, Ida, at the imposing Hotel Champlain nearby. Lake Champlain was one the President's favorite summer retreats and, during his brief presidency, he and his wife visited as his schedule allowed.[79] At their meeting Kittie received a bouquet of red roses, some of which were pressed and kept for many years in a family Bible.[80]

Later that month Kittie entertained at home with an evening musicale. The "local contact" for one of the newspapers reported:

> We were permitted by special invitation from Mrs. Joseph Ladue to meet about 20 of her friends and neighbors, at her residence and listened to a musical entertainment rendered by Prof. Leslie Weston, of Morrisonville, on Tuesday evening. We congratulate Mr. Weston on his success as a musician. He is master of his profession.[81]

Back in Dawson, the residents and the miners on the creeks complained bitterly about the high cost of living. Nothing had changed since 1896. The Alaska Commercial Company and the North American Trading and Transportation Company had moved their operations from Forty Mile to the new district almost as quickly as the rush there began. Both companies were huge, as was the new Alaska Exploration Company. They all sold only retail, set prices as they liked and made competition from smaller businesses nearly impossible. When news arrived in April that the Ladue Company would open a general merchandise store in the fall, it was welcomed by all and their feelings were expressed in the April 1, 1898, first edition of the *Klondike News*:

> This powerful corporation will do much to break the iron rule of the old companies, and its advent into the commercial world of Dawson will be hailed with delight by those who have so long felt the despotism from no competition.[82]

Joe's popularity was expressed at home, too, when the *Plattsburgh Daily Press* hailed him as the "Hero of the Klondike," and the "King of the Klondike" and his endorsements were much sought after.[83]

Samuel Conkling was general manager of the Ladue Company

from the February 7 annual meeting until the end of August, but was in Dawson only once and for a short period. He arrived on June 28 from Ottawa with a letter from the Assistant Secretary of the Interior that reiterated what had been indicated on several earlier occasions, that a patent for the Ladue town site would be issued, assuring the company's legal right to transfer titles to the lots they sold. Conkling left Dawson at the end of the first week of July aboard the steamer, *Willie Irving*, hoping that the government's promise would soon be fulfilled.[84]

Four days prior to Conkling's arrival in Dawson, Superintendent Charles Constantine, who had been commander of the North West Mounted Police since they were stationed at Forty Mile in 1895, left for a new assignment Outside. Since his arrival three years earlier he had earned the respect and affection of many, including the members of the Yukon Order of Pioneers. Later, Andrew Baird, a past president of the Pioneers, wrote that when Constantine was about to leave the territory the lodge called a public meeting to wish him Godspeed. When he entered the hall he was accorded a standing ovation. He was presented with a sack of gold donated by a hundred miners and an address commending his administration and paying tribute to Mrs. Constantine:

> That you may not go away without a reward for your good work in this country, if the gratitude and esteem of all those who have battled on this frontier with you in the upbuilding of a new empire may be counted as such.
>
> Your sterling integrity, your fairness in the administration of the District, your wise counsel and friendly advice in private, and the many unostentatious acts of helpful kindness to those in need when such acts often and nearly always meant self-sacrifice on your part; all these things have commanded our respect and endeared you to us. To Mrs. Constantine, a most worthy helpmate in your work, our rough words cannot express fittingly all we feel.
>
> The Yukon Order of Pioneers[85]

Joe was eager to return to Dawson City to open the new store and review the status of the company's many activities in town and on the creeks. By mid-June his health had improved and he traveled by train to the West Coast. On June 26, 1898, he and Elmer Botsford, secretary/treasurer of the Ladue Company, and now also general traffic manager of the Ladue-Yukon Transportation Company, left Seattle aboard the steamer *Umatilla* headed for St. Michael.[86] In early August, Botsford arrived in Dawson from St. Michael aboard the Alaska Commercial Company's steamer, *Susie*.[87] Joe remained at St. Michael awaiting a shipment of goods for the new store. He arrived at Dawson on Saturday, August 27, aboard the Ladue Company's only remaining riverboat, *Rideout*.[88] With him he brought 150 tons of freight and said that another larger shipment was enroute.

During this visit he made several personnel changes differing from those approved at the February 7 meeting by the Board of Directors. Walter Lyon, Botsford's brother-in-law, became overall superintendent, replacing Thomas W. Kirkpatrick. Lyon also assumed the responsibilities of general manager from S. T. Conkling.[89] Thomas Whyte, who had been foreman of the sawmill, was promoted to mill manager. Dr. T. Bates Cooke, who had overseen construction of the new store, was given the post of store manager, while W. J. Tormey was put in charge of the warehouse. Lyon and Cooke were both from Clinton County.[90]

In addition to personnel changes, Joe also made public in an interview with a Dawson newspaper, several other business activities the company had planned for the coming months: the size of the warehouse would be increased and the store extended back to 2nd Avenue, the company's placer holdings would be developed, additional placer mines would be acquired and a quartz mill was enroute. (It would not arrive until the summer of 1901.) He also commented that he was much pleased with the growth and stability now manifest in Dawson. (The population was about 15,000; thousands more were on the creeks.)[91] The changes which had taken place during the past year, he said, "are very marked, but are only what (he) had anticipated from the outlook last year."[92] It is likely, too, that he visited Johnson-Locke, agents for the Ladue-Yukon Transportation Company, at their offices in Dawson that summer.[93]

As news of Joe's arrival circulated through the town and out to the creeks, many old-timers came by the store to see him. Among them were several of his old Tr'ondek Hwech'in Han friends. Another who came to see him was Mary Hitchcock, one of two wealthy women who were perhaps Dawson's first tourists. She would later write, "The great man was behind the counter of his little shop, in his shirt-sleeves, waiting on an Indian who was trying to drive a sharp bargain over some cups and saucers."[94] One miner wrote later about Joe and some of his long-time comrades in the Yukon, referring to them as the "big four... McQuesten, Harper, Ladue and Battles (Gordon Bettles). We envy them this grand life of the open spaces of the Yukon....Later at Dawson when they met it did one good to see them greet each other."[95] It was to be the last time Joe would see any of them, or Dawson City.

Having given S. O. Morford power of attorney the previous year, to act on his behalf in all the legal affairs of the Harper and Ladue partnership and as attorney for the Ladue Company in Dawson, Joe had anticipated that a clear and comprehensive record of transactions would be available for his review. Apparently that was not the case and Joe was concerned about what he saw—or couldn't see. Two days after his arrival in Dawson he revoked Morford's power of attorney and filed in the territorial court a notice of Lis Pendens in which Joe and James M. Wilson, executor of the estate of Arthur Harper were plaintiffs, and S. O. Morford was the defendant. The action demanded that "said defendant be ordered and directed to convey to these plaintiffs in equal interest the title to said property, and to render to plaintiffs an accounting of all his transactions connected with the business of said plaintiffs...."The property in question consisted of 20 of the richest placer claims in the Klondike Valley in which the Harper and Ladue partnership held an interest. A review of mining records on these claims discloses S. O. Morford's signature appearing numerous times with no indication, however, that he was acting as attorney-in-fact for Ladue, Harper, or the Ladue Company.[96]

The Ladue Company that summer of 1898, had, in addition to the 20 claims on which Joe demanded an accounting, many claims or interest in claims on several creeks. On Bonanza they held title to Nos. 3 and 30 Above Discovery, Nos. 47 and 97A Below Discovery. On Hunker Creek Nos. 16, 23 and 25 Below Discovery and No. 30 Above. On Eldorado No. 15 Adams Gulch. And on Bear Creek "several claims," and on Gold Bottom "Extensive interests."[97]

The company's enormous mining interests, its sawmill and town site and the new store that was opened with Joe's arrival, all had potential for creating significant profit. Its Golden Wedge Mining Company in Rossland, British Columbia, however, was never productive. Not even its purchase price was recovered.

Within a few days of opening the new store on First Avenue in September, Joe placed the following advertisement in the September 9 and 28 issues of the *Klondike Nugget*:

> THE JOSEPH LADUE GOLD MINING AND DEVELOPMENT COMPANY OF YUKON
>
> Beg to announce to the citizens of Dawson and vicinity that they have opened a GENERAL SUPPLY STORE and are prepared to outfit miners with the usual supplies of all kinds at reasonable prices. None but the best quality of goods have been purchased by us and all have been specifically prepared and adapted for Klondike use. Come examine our flour, hams, bacon, sugar, eggs, teas, coffees, spices, canned fruits, dried fruits, tobacco, candles, clothing, underclothing, boots, shoes, stationery, etc.
>
> The Company mill also furnishes all kinds of matched, dressed and plain lumber at current prices.
>
> JOSEPH LADUE, PRESIDENT

Earlier that summer the Ladue Company became aware it would have to make an effort to drain the swampy town site. In some sections, water stood a foot deep. The soggy, low-lying muskeg or swamp was huge, extending from the river to Seventh Avenue. Twelve men were put to work digging ditches and laying pipe. Soon the water was out of the town site. However, citizens then complained that the drainage ditches made it difficult to travel across town, so they were filled in, while the water continued to be drained through the buried pipes. When the deep cold of winter arrived it froze the water in the pipes, water that remained frozen the following summer preventing drainage, and the surface water was back.[98]

On September 6, just before leaving Dawson aboard the steamer *Columbian*,[99] Joe gave power of attorney to J. E. Hansen of Dawson that empowered him to:

> transact any and all business and affairs with relation to the mercantile business conducted and carried on within the said Yukon

> Territory by me, or by the firm of Harper and Ladue..., to manage and control and dispose of any and all real property...,to enable the said Hansen to work, manage, control and dispose of any and all mining property of every kind or nature, that either I or the said firm of Harper and Ladue own within the Yukon Territory.

Ladue also directed that "all moneys, gold or gold dust" was to be deposited by Hansen with the Alaska Commercial Company at Dawson "to the credit of the firm of Harper and Ladue." In the event Hansen were to become unable to carry out these specific duties, Walter Lyon and William M. Heron were "to act jointly, and to have all the powers...granted to the said Hansen."[100]

Although Joe had placed his half of the Harper and Ladue Partnership assets with the Joseph Ladue Gold Mining and Development Company of Yukon, he still was responsible for maintaining the integrity of the terms of the partnership agreement he had signed with his old friend, Arthur Harper. J. E. Hansen would now be Joe's representative for partnership matters and was on-site to work closely with Wilson to honor the terms of that agreement. It is apparent by the broad-sweeping terms of the power of attorney that Joe, Hansen and Wilson anticipated continuing legal action related to the Notice of Lis Pendens filed with the court against S. O. Morford.[101]

One of the chief brokers of Ladue Company stock in 1898, was W. H. Spooner of Providence, Rhode Island. While Joe was in Dawson, Spooner placed the following overstated advertisement in the August 29 issue of the *Plattsburgh Sentinel*:

> FIRST ON THE KLONDIKE
>
> The Joseph Ladue Gold Mining and Development Company of Yukon.
>
> PRICE OF SHARES TO BE ADVANCED AUGUST 31, 1898.
>
> Mr. Joseph Ladue, the pioneer of the Klondike, and founder of Dawson City, aided by some of the most conservative and successful financiers of New York, is operating the strongest company yet formed for mining and trading in the Yukon gold fields.
>
> To this Company he has transferred placer claims on Hunker

and Gold Bottom Creeks, the "Marguerite" Quartz Mine, his Saw Mill, his Timber lease, that virtually monopolizes the saw timber on the Klondike, and large holdings of Choice Town Lots in Dawson City. The Company also owns the S.S. "Morgan City" now earning $20,000 per month, and has shipped up the Yukon several hundred tons of merchandise, for trade, upon which very large profit is assured.

The U.S. Government reports certify that the saw mill produces about two million feet of lumber in the open season, sales price of which is from $140 to $240 per 1,000 feet according to class.

CAPITAL OF THE COMPANY

Preferred Stock, 6% cumulative.	$1,000,000
Common Stock.	$4,000,000
Total Capital, per value $10 per share	$5,000,000

The preferred stock has a first lien on earnings for its dividend, and on the assets of the Company for its par value, and after all the stock of the Company has received 6 per cent, the surplus earnings are shared pro rata by the preferred and common stock.

Thus the preferred stock practically offers the safeguards and advantages of a first mortgage bond, coupled with an earning capacity as great as that of the common stock.

The undersigned has obtained a short option on a block of this preferred stock which he now offers at par, $10.00 per share. This option terminates August 31st, 1898, after which the price of the preferred stock will be advanced by the Company to $12.50 per share.

This is the last opportunity to get the preferred stock at par, and in time to participate in the autumn dividend. Shares will be allotted in the order subscriptions are received.

Send for map of Dawson, and data respecting Klondike.

W.H. SPOONER, 141 Westminster St., Providence, R.I.

Since Joe had last seen his town site in June 1897, huge changes had occurred. Stephen Smyth recorded in *The Yukon's Constitutional*

Foundations: The Yukon's Chronology that by "Royal Assent" on June 13, 1898, the Yukon District had become officially the Yukon Territory. What Joe had known as the Bonanza Gold Mining District[102] had been renamed the Klondike District. It measured "about 36 miles long by a little over 20 wide," encompassing about 800 square miles. In addition to all the claims on Bonanza and Eldorado, which had been completely staked within the first few weeks following the discovery, there were thousands more on the tributaries and gulches. It was projected by surveyor William Ogilvie that, by the end of the mining season of 1897, the total amount of gold taken out of the Klondike Valley would be at least $2,000,000; that in the next year and, for several years to come, "double that figure."[103] This estimate turned out to be far below actual production. One writer estimated that by July 1, 1898, 10,000 placer claims had been recorded in the Klondike District.[104]

Businessmen had poured into Dawson throughout the summer of 1897. Many bought building lots from the Harper and Ladue Townsite and Development Company. By the winter of 1897-98 there were several restaurants and saloons, an opera house, a barbershop, freighting companies, woodcutters, two blacksmiths, two watchmakers, a tin shop that made Yukon stoves, five or six physicians, and stores run by two large trading companies, The Alaska Commercial Company, and the North American Trading and Transportation Company. The Ladue Company had not operated a store from when supplies (that Joe brought from Ogilvie) were depleted in 1896 until his return in August 1898.[105]

One investor showing an interest in the Klondike during the summer of 1897 was Daniel Guggenheim of Guggenheim and Sons, a firm with large smelting interests in other parts of the world. In an interview with the *Seattle Daily Times* in July 1897 he stated that the new fields would yield:

> far in excess of even the present roseate conditions. For some time my firm has had expert mining engineers at work in Alaska, and their report says the Yukon gold fields will prove the richest in the world. My opinion is that as soon as the country has opened up and shipping facilities furnished, the output of gold will simply be enormous.[106]

In years to come the Guggenheims would buy up most of the claims on many creeks and carry on dredging operations yielding millions of dollars.

While Joe had been Outside establishing his companies during the winter of 1897-98, the news of the Klondike had spread across the continent and around the world. The great stampede that would last through the summer of 1898 was underway. Men and women everywhere, young and old, from every vocation and profession, were trying to figure out how to get to the Klondike. They left spouses and children, sold or mortgaged their farms or homes, closed businesses, quit their jobs and invested their life savings.[107] In many instances families and friends pooled their resources to send one representative to the goldfields. Little did they know that for most of them all the money and time they invested and all the toil and the great dangers that lay ahead would lead to nothing. They would leave that great country broke—disappointed and discouraged, if they left at all. As one writer expressed it: "These men made their way home, as best they could, out of the wreckage of the...Klondike rush."[108] No one knows exactly what went through the minds of those argonauts of '98. Perhaps they believed that all would be well forever if they could just get to the Klondike. Perhaps they didn't think at all, once struck by gold fever. One ninety-eighter expressed coarsely, but perhaps accurately, that "The main object was plunder."[109]

Seattle, Portland and other cities began to trumpet the advantages of putting together outfits within their borders. In October 1897 a Seattle newspaper printed a special Klondike edition with eight pages that was sent to every postmaster and public library in the United States. Victoria, Vancouver and Montreal followed suit.

The *Montreal Star's* "Klondike Number," published Feb. 12, 1898, offered maps and descriptions, do's and don'ts for the would-be prospector and concluded with this two-pronged bit of advice: "The *Star* would not encourage anyone to leave a comfortable home upon the mere chance of making a fortune, nor would it discourage hardy, adventurous spirits from trying the quick road to wealth." Promotional material like this inspired between 1,600 and 2,000 men from Edmonton alone to head for the Klondike.

Many stampeders from the United States saw the Klondike as a possible way out of the economic conditions that began in 1893 and were only slowly beginning to improve by the end 1896. With seven-eighths of the wealth controlled by one-eighth of the people, the vast majority were essentially living in poverty.[110]

The City of Seattle won the battle of the cities for the Klondike trade by advertising in such national periodicals as *Leslie's Illustrated Weekly Magazine*, *Munsey's*, *McClure's*, *Cosmopolitan*, *Harper's Weekly* and *Scribner's*.[111] All of the state of Illinois' 480 newspapers carried Seattle advertisements in March 1898.[112]

The Klondike hype, promulgated by every outfitter and port city in North America[113] and other parts of the world, created an atmosphere in which it was difficult to resist the call of great expectations to that far-away land. Few of those planning to start out for the Klondike knew of old-timer William D. Moore's 1892 admonition to anyone considering entering the Yukon: "The difficulties experienced in reaching it are very great, and none but those eminently fitted to undergo hardships and rough travel should venture in there."[114]

The majority of would-be miners were from the United States and Canada. Many traveled by train from eastern states and provinces to San Francisco and Seattle. There they crowded on boats of every description and every stage of sea-worthiness. They were off to the Klondike to scoop up the gold.

The trails leading to the Klondike were many: Chilkoot Pass (which Joe recommended), White Pass at the head of Lynn Canal, the Stikine or Teslin Route, the Taku Route, the St. Michael's all-water route (which Joe also recommended) and the Dalton Trail at the head of Pyramid Harbor. All the routes were dangerous, particularly the All-Canadian Route advertised by Edmonton and the All-American Route over the glaciers near Valdez, Alaska.

In late August 1897 *New York World*, hearing of the hazards on the Chilkoot and White Passes, directed one of its reporters, Sylvester Scoville, to establish another trail from Skagway to the lakes. He was given a check for $25,000 to purchase "giant powder" and to hire men to blast through mountains. It would be known as "The World Trail" and be four miles shorter and "more than 1,000 feet lower than the "White Trail" (White Pass). It never got beyond the planning stage.[115]

The Edmonton Route was so long and difficult that some who started over it didn't arrive at Dawson until 1900. Kristian Falconberg and his companion, John, left Edmonton with eight dogs they had purchased from Robert Lincoln, son of the assassinated American president, and when they finally arrived in Dawson they had been on the trail almost two years. Along the way they had suffered frostbite and illness, lost all their clothing and supplies and come close to starvation.[116]

Two thousand five hundred men and a few women started from Valdez, Alaska, in 1898. On the Valdez glacier they were bludgeoned unmercifully by howling blizzards that raged for days. Some died in avalanches that roared down the mountains, burying them as they struggled over the trail during the day or as they slept in their tents at night. Some who succeeded in crossing the glacier were drowned in the numerous lakes or the Copper River beyond. There was little firewood, so they were constantly cold; their food frozen. Most of the survivors gave up and turned back when they reached Mentasta Pass and saw ahead of them nothing but the vast wilderness of the upper Tanana. All endured great suffering, many died; few ever made it to the Klondike.[117]

Most of the stampeders, however, traveled over the Chilkoot and White Passes and, when the ice broke up on Lake Bennett and Lake Lindeman in the spring of 1898, 28,000 gold-seekers launched 7,000 boats and scows of every imaginable design.

One of those who traveled over Chilkoot Pass and downriver during the first influx of argonauts in 1897 was writer and poet Joaquin Miller of California. Miller set out from San Francisco with a flute and very little other equipment, intending to write about his adventures on his return home.

He wrote of his experience passing through Miles Canyon and White Horse Rapids:

> Boom! Bang! We were literally loaded into cannon, shot in and down and out as through and out of a gun into Byron's hell of waters; and then the shouts that went up with the tossing arms and waving hats! It was a hearty, heart-felt, human—as if the men were almost choking with solicitude; a wild, wild, Western shout from great strong men. Yet a shout with tears in it. But the regiment of unbridled white horses still plunged and leapt and

> charged in our wreck-scattered way. Ten thousand gleaming horses. These must be ridden down in one desperate dash. There was no old guard to follow, if our first brave charge failed. We must ride them down this instant, or be ridden down.... They smote us right in the breast until the water plunged ten feet into the air and drenched even the captain away back at the helm. The oarsmen were knocked down, but again they grasped their oars and again we plunged on, and again they were knocked down and the boat went reeling to the right. And then from our rear the rushing cataract came and spun us almost like a top, drifting and tossing us from one white horse to another as a toy. The captain now guided his boat from the bow.[118]

Miller remained in the Yukon the following winter and returned home the summer of 1898 minus a finger, an ear and part of a toe lost to frostbite, and suffered for many years from snow blindness.

Building boats that could steer a straight course and handle rapids was another challenge. In its November 1, 1899, Anniversary Number, The *Klondike Nugget* wrote:

> But few of the builders had ever seen a boat put together before, and many of the boats were miracles of construction. They were triangular, square, oblong, flat, oblate, spheroidal and rectangular...Some were pointed at both ends, and many had no point at all and traveled as well sideways as in any other fashion. In one particular they were all alike—all had masts and a great expanse of sail, and were manned by men who knew not fear, or else securely concealed it from mortal men.

The article went on to say:

> Many unknown bodies were picked up at various points in the river until freeze up in the fall, while the known deaths exceeded two hundred. No correct tally was attempted of the numerous wrecks at the various points of danger, yet some 350 were known of and remembered, one or two of them being steamers which were built on the lakes and had attempted the passage of the rapids.

In July the survivors arrived at Dawson, a great wave of humanity, soon to discover that there was nothing at the end of the rainbow they had followed through months of struggle against the elements and the land. Most didn't bother to travel to the creeks, but walked up and down First Avenue in and out of the saloons as if they were looking for someone to assure them their sacrifices and efforts had not been in vain—that there really was gold to be had—somewhere. Russell Bankson, author ofThe *Klondike Nugget*, a story of the early Dawson newspaper of the same name, wrote that the stampeders "...had fought death almost every step of the way over that 600-mile trail..." to reach the gold. But, there were no gold mines awaiting them and few of those who looked for work found it. Many had no choice but to put their outfits up for sale at a loss and to continue down the river and home—home to their mortgaged farms, home where their jobs had been filled by others, where they would have to face family and friends who had invested money and hope in them Bankson continued,." "the cold, hard facts seemed to have left them stunned and helpless...." The sad truth was, they were at least a year late.[119]

But, not all those who rushed to the Klondike experienced heartache and disappointment. Confidence men, card sharps and grifters from London to New York, and from Denver to Port Townsend, contrived to filch the money of the naive and the greedy. They ballyhooed phony companies or sold shares in non-existent mines. There were many sound companies formed that did go to the Klondike and rewarded their investors with dividends. But many existed only on paper and the sole profits realized were by the crooks who "mined the miners"—shifting money from the pockets of their victims to their own.[120]

Dawson in 1898

At the time Joe returned to Dawson in August 1898, The *Klondike Nugget* estimated the population at about 16,000[121] and there was little to remind him of the town he had left a year earlier. At the southern end of the city was Fort Herchmer, the 40-acre compound of the North West Mounted Police, which had been under the command of Superintendent Constantine until his departure on June 24, 1898. He had moved police headquarters to Dawson from Fort Constantine at the mouth of the Forty Mile River. Three small buildings were brought up from Fort Constantine. Six additional buildings were constructed but, "not having a sawmill (of their own and to save costs) the logs were all hewn on three sides, entailing a great amount of time and labour."[122] Having been hastily built using freshly cut logs, as the summer progressed, the buildings were covered with green, leafy sprouts, "giving promise of picturesque quarters after a while."[123] Adjacent was the 18-acre Harper Addition applied for (by Joe's now dead partner) in November 1896. Then came the 160-acre Harper and Ladue town site, with hotels and other businesses on First Avenue and hundreds of cabins and tents stretching east up the hill and sprawling toward the south end of town. (Just prior to his arrival, Joe's cabin had been removed from the middle of First Avenue where it had impeded traffic.)[124] One full block was taken up by the Alaska Commercial Company store and its warehouses, followed by another block of similar buildings owned by the North American Trading and Transportation Company. Beyond that block stood the Harper and Ladue Sawmill and the new Ladue Company Store, then more cabins. At the north end, "half a mile from the stores," was Father William Judge's new Catholic Church, the entire $25,000 cost of which had been donated by "Big Alex" McDonald. On the hill above was St. Mary's Hospital, recently expanded, and staffed by the newly arrived Sisters of St. Ann.[125]

Across the Klondike River from Dawson, "Louse Town," now respectably renamed Klondike City, had become a town in its own right. Across the Yukon River from Dawson was a sizable community known as West Dawson. In both communities most of the cabins were built on sloping land and sanitary conditions were far superior to those in Dawson.[126] Dawson was "the most unsanitary place imaginable"[127] and the unsolved drainage problems and lack of water and sewage systems proved fatal to many. Tappan Adney wrote: "There was no drainage, and, except by giving a warning about cesspools, the government did nothing but provide two conveniences, entirely inadequate for a town of nearly 20,000."

By August 1898 a typhoid epidemic had struck. The more fortunate cases received care at St. Mary's or Good Samaritan Hospitals. Father Judge recorded: "We have 135 patients at present, mostly typhoid fever, which has been very bad here since summer...."[128] One observer wrote that "The latter part of the summer typhoid began to rage and there were often eight or ten deaths a day."[129]

With the arrival of thousands of men and women that summer of 1898, one of the changes Joe had feared became reality. Along with the naïve and gullible, the honest and courageous adventurer, came those inevitably attracted to all gold camps, "the parasitic class." They were gamblers, prostitutes and small-time speculators looking for unsuspecting victims—and they fleeced many a stampeder.[130] Gone forever was the world of Jack McQuesten, Joe Ladue, Arthur Harper, Alfred Mayo and the men of Forty Mile who wrote the Constitution of the Yukon Order of Pioneers.

Another change was the presence of the "nouveaux riche,"[131] known in Dawson as the "Eldorado Kings," among them: Frank Phiscator, Antone Stander, Clarence Berry, Charles Lamb and the king of the kings, "Big Alex" McDonald, who owned wholly or in part, 62 claims on Eldorado, Bonanza, Dominion, Sulphur, Hunker, Gold Bottom, Bear, All Gold and Baker Creeks plus a number of bench claims.[132] McDonald's wealth would eventually be estimated at $8,000,000. All gained far more from the Klondike than Joe Ladue, but most lost every dollar of their great fortunes. Clarence Berry was among the exceptions, whose wisely invested Klondike gold brought him the good life in California.

One thing that had not changed was the corrupt operation of the Gold Commissioner's Office. The month before Joe arrived there was a huge scandal related to the opening of the benchlands for staking on Dominion Creek. Commissioner Fawcett had posted a notice that the opening date would be July 11, 1898. But, without further public announcement, the date was changed to July 9. A number of men, whether friends of Fawcett or his staff, or prospectors or speculators who had paid for the advance information, staked on the ninth—two days ahead of those who were waiting for July 11.[133]

Major James M. Walsh, who had been appointed chief executive officer of the government of the Yukon Territory in August 1897,[134] had little or no control over the Gold Commissioner's Office. Walsh said at one point that, "The administration of affairs on Dominion Creek has been a mess from start to finish and I am sick and tired of the whole business."[135]

One government official who was incorruptible was William Ogilvie who had been appointed commissioner of the Yukon on July 4, 1898.[136] Of him, his daughter Margaret said, "I don't think he did anything for money; he did it for the love of the job itself."[137]

Erena Harper, the second wife of Joe's deceased partner, Arthur Harper, with two of his sons, Frederick and Alfred, also came to town during July 1898. Erena needed to look after her extensive interests, i.e., her one-third of the assets of the Harper estate she had inherited. She also planned to travel to Fort Selkirk to occupy the property where Jennie and Arthur had lived.[138]

In December 1898, The Joseph Ladue Gold Mining and Development Company of Yukon was placed in receivership. While none of the legal documents related to this event has been located, *The Klondike Nugget* reported that James W. Wilson brought the action, as representative of the Estate of Arthur Harper against the Ladue Company. Although the wording of the suit appeared harsh, even strident, there was "no particular dissension" between the parties. The action was apparently taken only to ensure that the plaintiff would not suffer "loss in depreciation of value" of properties.[139] It is likely that this was a move to protect the Harper and Ladue Partnership properties that might be involved in the legal action taken against S. O. Morford.

Joe continued to be bedeviled by two town site problems that had persisted since 1896: The lack of a timely response to the application for a Dominion Patent, and the presence of "squatters" on town site lots.

In October of 1896 William Ogilvie had cautioned Joe about the sale of town site lots before a proper survey had been made. Much to his regret for years to come, many lots were sold before Ogilvie completed the survey in January 1897[140] and continued to be sold, even after it became clear that such sales were only contributing to the delay in the issuing of a patent. The government did not award Joe a patent on any lots in his town site until several years later because they required complete information on lot ownership: the name of the buyer, his address, place of residence, occupation, a description of the lot and the purchase price paid. Sufficient information was not, or perhaps could not, be gathered from owners of some lots, either by the company or the commissioner.[141] In some cases the owners were mining on distant creeks, and in others there was more than one owner, one or more of whom had left the country.

As commissioner, Ogilvie tried to partially remedy the situation by posting a public notice:

> PUBLIC NOTICE
>
> Patents to Town Lots in the Harper and Ladue Dawson Townsite
>
> All persons entitled to patent for town lots in the above mentioned townsite through purchase from the said Harper and Ladue or their legal agents are notified to call at the office of Raoul Rinfret, Esq. in the Registrar's Office to arrange for the issue of such patent.
>
> This notice applies only to lots purchased on or before the 24th day of December 1897, and only such of those as have not already been arranged for with Alexander McLeod, Esq. during the months of August and September 1899.

A number of letters went from the company to the commissioner's office and to the Department of the Interior inquiring when a patent would be issued.[142] In August, 1899, when the Department sent Alex McLeod to Dawson to "attend to all matters in connection with the issuing of Patents in the Yukon Territory," Joe must have thought that finally there would be a resolution to his dilemma.[143] But, by the end of 1899, the bureaucratic machinery continued to work in its mystifying way and the patent issue was still not settled, nor was it to be completely settled until 1902.

In an interview with The *Klondike Nugget* published January 17, 1900, Commissioner Ogilvie appeared to have the matter of the town site patents well in hand. Said Ogilvie:

> The original patents for real estate in Dawson may arrive from Ottawa with any mail. When they do, those who have purchased from the applicants (Harper and Ladue), or their grantees, and who have filed their claim of title with the registrar, will receive a certificate of title from the government. Those who have squatted on land will be ejected. There need be no apprehension on the part of property owners regarding the titles to land. The patents will issue, and as soon as possible, thereafter, the records will be straightened.[144]

It was not until July 1901, after Joe's death, that the Crown had apparently received all the information required to issue title on at least some of the Harper and Ladue Townsite lots. The patents (titles) were issued as a "Dominion Lands Grant to Joseph Ladue and James M. Wilson" (as executor of Harper's Estate). The lots to which they were given title were lots 1-13 in Block U and lots 1, 2 and 3 in Block V[145]

By January 1902 the Department of the Interior, too, was so frustrated over this long and drawn-out affair, its legal advisor, H. W. Newlands wrote to J. N. E. Brown, Territorial Secretary, saying that "the Registrar...should be instructed to register the (patents) and issue a certificate of title to the patentees free of any expense." This, the department had decided, was "the best way of closing up the Ladue Estate."[146]

Regardless of the instructions issued by Mr. Newlands, however, it was not until June 23, 1902, a year after Joe's death, that the next and apparently final issuance of remaining lot titles arrived in Dawson in the form of five separate "Dominion Lands Grants."[147]

"Squatters" on Townsite lots were a continuing problem for at least three years after Ladue's original application. While Ogilvie's survey in January 1897 had marked the perimeter of the town site, the only lots measured out were those on First Avenue (now Front St.) where businesses were locating and those just behind them on Second Avenue. When representatives of the Harper and Ladue estate approached Commissioner Ogilvie regarding the squatters on town site land, he "instructed them to try to come to some amicable arrangement." They were unable to do so and soon the squatters were declaring to Ogilvie that "they were presuming on the fact that they were on government ground or that Ladue would not get his ground...and [they] would stay indefinitely and pay the Government just such a price as they pleased for the ground occupied." Some of the squatters tried to place the blame on Inspector Constantine, saying he had told them "all the ground back of 7th Avenue was open." Ogilvie's opinion of that story was that "They are trying to play a game of bluff." He had told Constantine "more than once both orally and in writing that Ladue's application consisted of about 110 acres of flat and 50 acres of hillside.... He must have known that 7th Avenue barely reached to the foot of the hill...." It was his position that, "There is no reason why these squatters should have ignorantly settled on any part of the Ladue 160 acres. Ladue's representative was here all the time from June 1897 until the present time, and if they wanted to learn just where they squatted it was the easiest matter in the world for them to do so by applying to him. Their statement is simply a story to cover up an act which does not reflect very creditably on the actors...."[148]

Elmer F. Botsford, the manager and treasurer of the Joseph Ladue Gold Mining and Development Company of Yukon, wrote to Commissioner Ogilvie August 2, 1899, insisting that he "immediately furnish the Dept. (Interior) with the required report." This was a reference to the required list of buyers along with specific details on the purchased property—the Crown would not issue a patent to the Ladue Company until the commissioner filed that report. Botsford further made his case, saying purchasers refused to make payments as agreed upon and "squatters we are unable to deal with upon any terms and...we are in consequence obliged to suffer a considerable loss."[149]

Commissioner Ogilvie finally received official permission from the Department of the Interior to eject the "squatters."[150] He advised, encouraged and finally threatened physical ejection, but then didn't follow through. The "squatters" complained bitterly when asked to vacate and most apparently stayed put. And they were not without support. One F. W. Clements wrote to the Department of the Interior in 1899 stating that the "squatters" should not be compelled "to buy lots at outrageous prices" or should they "be thrown out of their homes. It would be an outrage." Perhaps Clements was one of the "squatters" himself.[151]

An example of the type of problem that arose because of "squatters," is when Harper and Ladue sold Lot #7 in Block L. T. to J. A. Hathaway for $200. For the next two months Hathaway "repeatedly tried to enter upon and occupy the plot in question, but has been prevented by certain squatters living on the ground."

Like summer's mosquitoes, squatters were a constant irritant. In or around May 1897, another "squatter," J. A. Williams, occupied Lot No. 4 of Block H. B. in the Harper Addition. "Upon being requested by the agent of Mr. Harper to pay for or vacate the property, the occupant, Williams, became defiant and refused to either vacate or purchase."[152] No record was located to indicate whether these cases or any of the many others similar to it were ever resolved satisfactorily for the company and Harper's Estate or those to whom they sold lots.

In early 1899 S. M. Graff was agent for the Harper and Ladue Townsite Company. By May that year the real estate brokerage firm of Stauf and Zilly was in charge of rental properties and the sale of lots.[153]

In February and March of 1899, Walter Lyon, the company's general manager, was in New York on business. He met with Elmer Botsford at the company's new offices in the Empire Building at 71 Broadway[154] and visited Joe several times at his Schuyler Falls home. Joe had been in poor health for some time, which had shortened his visit to Dawson in August and September of 1898 to ten days. When Lyon saw him, Joe was still very ill with the "nervous prostration which took him so suddenly last year." His doctors, however, thought he "was on the road to recovery." They had still not diagnosed his condition as tuberculosis from which he appears to have suffered for some time. Joe told Lyon he was intending to return to the Yukon the summer of 1899—a trip to which Kittie was vehemently opposed[155]—and which would prove impossible.

Joe was encouraged, however, when he and Lyon reviewed the company's very positive financial statement covering earnings from August 1897 to January 1, 1899. The report read as follows:

Earnings to January 1, 1899	
Earnings at Dawson, etc.	$186,284.06
Earnings on transportation	$54,224.92
Total Earnings	$240,508.98
Disposition of Earnings	
Mdse. at various Yukon points at cost	$40,928.68
Mining machinery	$6,600.00
Warehouse and other House construction	$35,650.00
Real estate bought (cost)	$36,000.00
Saw mill equipment bought	$1,932.00
Lumber and logs in stock at cost	$49,401.00
Due from leases	$3,400.00
Expense, account coal lands	$600.00
Cash paid account freight	$2,000.00
Accounts receivable	$35,700.00
Cash on hand in New York and Dawson	$27,797.30
	$240,508.98
Less	
Accounts and bills payable on account of above	$22,565.36
Taxes, insurance, rents, advertising, salaries and general expenses paid	$6,514.45
	$79,079.81
Net Profit to Date	$161,409.17

"A dividend of 6 per cent on preferred stock is recommended by the treasurer."[156]

Based upon this report it appears that the company still had conducted no mining operations on its several very rich placer claims, a fact Joe must have found distressing.

The actual dividends paid for the period August 1897 to January 1, 1899, were two payments of 3 percent each,[157] and were the only dividends the company ever paid to its shareholders including Joe, who held the majority of the stock. Based upon the number of shares the company had issued to Joe (24,700), as partial payment for his Yukon properties, his dividend should have totaled $14,820, assuming the value of shares remained at $10.

In February 1899, Joe purchased the ten-acre lot next door to his home in Schuyler Falls from James M. Coffy. Perhaps his years in the sparsely populated Yukon left him feeling crowded in the small village where backyards joined. On February 6 the deed was issued in his name after payment of $500 had been made.[158]

It was fashionable in the late nineteenth century for people of substantial income to purchase or build a vacation home on the shores of one of lakes in the Adirondack Mountains. Nearby Saranac Lake and Lake George were two of the most popular choices. The Ladues followed the fashion and purchased, for $1,500, a cottage with approximately two acres of land on Lake George from Nathaniel Holmes Bishop. The deed, dated September 27, 1899, granted ownership to "Catharine M. Ladue, wife of Joseph Ladue" and was recorded with the clerk of Warren County on October 20, 1899.[159] The Ladues considered purchasing a home in California, but never did.[160]

Joe had an interesting opportunity for public service in Schuyler Falls that year when the Democratic Party nominated him for highway commissioner,[161] which nomination he respectfully declined.

Energized by the company's dazzling report, Walter Lyon returned to Dawson with grand plans for the sawmill. Although the population of Dawson had dwindled to 4,236 by the summer of 1899,[162] in order to compete with the five other operating mills, Lyon installed modern machinery in the company sawmill and its capacity was increased to just over 1,000 board feet per hour. The upgraded mill had a wide range of machinery that allowed it to do planing, edging and cutting to length. Soon they would have the ability to make a variety of molding profiles. The combined capacity of all the mills in Dawson was 100,000 board feet of lumber per day. Their average output, however, was limited to about 60,000 due to the lack of logs of sufficient diameter.[163] Since 1896, the sawmills and riverboats had devoured hundreds of thousands of trees along the rivers and from the hills beyond. The demand for lumber was primarily from miners who were building sluices and for flumes to carry water from distant creeks to their claims.

All of Dawson's sawmills had "timber berths," each of which was one square mile in size, leased from the government for $250 per year through the Crown Timber and Land Agent in Dawson who was, for many years, attorney Francis Xavier Gosselin. In 1898 the Harper and Ladue Sawmill had one berth (one square mile) on the Yukon; in 1899 it had two square miles on the Stewart River. Gosslin was a member of the Yukon Order of Pioneers and is buried in St. Mary's Cemetery in Dawson.

Beginning in 1899 there was much speculation regarding the feasibility of quartz, or hard-rock mining.[164] Joe knew a great deal about quartz mining from his days in Deadwood and Tombstone and since his arrival in the Yukon he had always looked for gold-bearing quartz deposits. One of his primary properties in the Klondike was the "Marguerite," a quartz claim on Gold Bottom, where he had found what appeared to be an extensive vein of such rock and the company was continually trying to "prove up" on it. But that was not to be. One man who had a special interest in quartz mining in 1899 was Charles Carver, a veteran quartz miner from Montana. The *Klondike Nugget* stated that when it came to hard-rock mining Carver was "a wise one in mining matters, and when he says the Klondike will some day prove to be a good quartz field it carries more weight than from the ordinary observer." William Ogilvie declared in 1897 that he sampled specimens of quartz from nearby Bear Creek that tested out at $1,000 per ton. For all the speculation that season, significant deposits were not found to warrant the investment required to extract the gold.[165]

DR. B. F. Whiting, who visited Dawson in July 1900, described it as "a very neat and substantially built little city of perhaps 4,000 people, the streets filled with lazy dogs and idle men wandering aimlessly up and down with no apparent object...The arrival of a boat creates some little stir, as nearly everybody goes to see who comes and get the news of the outside world."[166]

The Ladue store, office and warehouses that summer were located at 223-225 First Avenue and 124 Third Avenue near the Clark and Ryan grocery store. In October the office was moved to Second Avenue. The store carried just about everything for the homemaker, farmer and miner:

> "fine and fancy" groceries, "self-dumping" ore cars, mining equipment, steam fittings, wagons, galvanized iron, building paper and builder's hardware (including windows, doors and hinges), haying tools, nails, mixed paints and oils, work clothing,

> bar glassware, bed springs, wool mattresses, kitchen chairs, household furnishings, floor matting, chocolate and fancy cream candies, marble oil cloth, Strauss overalls, rubber boots and shoes, high-top miner's shoes, ledgers, journals, Stetson hats, hard candy and stationery. The store offered delivery in town and to the creeks. The store also traded in furs. One advertisement read: "Trappers and Hunters... We pay the highest cash price for all kinds of RAW FURS."[167]

In early September, after spending the summer of 1900 in Dawson, Elmer Botsford left on the riverboat Sybil, taking with him "the best and most complete collection of Indian curios that ever left the Yukon."[168]

Meanwhile, in New York, May 8, 1900, proved a very special day for Joe and Kittie Ladue. They appeared at the Clinton County Court House and became the adoptive parents of the five-month-old son of Joe's friend, Willis Lamay. Cecil William Lamay was born December 16, 1899, and had been cared for by the Ladues in their home since his birth. His mother, Mary Jane Wells, had died January 6, 1900.[169] Willis and Joe had been friends since at least the spring of 1895 when they traveled by train to San Francisco and over Chilkoot Pass with Ellis Turner.

For much of his time in the Yukon, Lamay had worked skidding logs for the Harper and Company sawmill at Ogilvie and cutting hay. After Mary Jane's untimely death, Willis apparently felt he would not be able to properly care for his infant son and asked the Ladues to adopt him. Joe and Kittie realized they might not have children of their own and happily agreed to the adoption. The name appearing in the court record is "Cecil William Ladue." To family and friends he was "Francis."[170]

Dimming the joy of the new parents, however, was Joe's declining health that had persisted since late 1897. It apparently began with what doctors diagnosed as a severe "cold," a "cold" that did not improve and worsened to the point that the truth could no longer be skirted. His illness was identified as a "pulmonary condition"— in other words, tuberculosis. By November 1900 Joe's doctor recommended that he travel to Colorado Springs.[171] The elevation and climate there were considered beneficial for people suffering from respiratory disease. During this time Botsford and Lyon kept the company's president informed of its many activities and Joe may have been able to sustain some level of involvement in decision-making. How difficult it must have been for him to not be on-site in Dawson to oversee the large and diverse investment of his company.

Four months earlier, on June 4, 1900, a U.S. Census taker called at the Ladue home in Schuyler Falls and recorded the following: Joseph Ladue, head of household, b. July 1854, "Kitty," wife b. March 1870, married two years. Son, Cecil, b. December 1899. "Yes" to the questions do you read, write and speak English? Their home was listed as "Owned free." In the same household were Evalina Jock, age 17, and Arthur Bartlett, 21, as "servants who could read, write and speak English." It must have been a poignant moment when Joe told the census taker that he "had not been employed for eight months." When asked his occupation, the president of the Joseph Ladue Gold Mining and Development Company of Yukon simply responded "farmer."

On February 4, 1901, Elmer F. Botsford, secretary/treasurer of the Joseph Ladue Gold Mining and Development Company of Yukon, presented an annual report to the Board of Directors[172] covering the period January 1899 through September 1, 1900.

During that time, the company had done well overall. The wreck of the steamer *Morgan City* was reported as a loss to the company, although it appears there was, in fact, a significant net gain. When the schooner, *Cutch*, no longer owned by the company, was wrecked in August 1900 along the coast of Alaska, it was carrying some amount of freight for the Ladue Company that was insured for $5,023.75, a sum which was recovered.[173]

Before the opening of navigation in 1899, it had become evident to the company that the "all-water route" for transporting its freight from San Francisco up the coast of Alaska to St. Michael and then upriver to Dawson, had become "impracticable." The first passenger train on the White Pass and Yukon Railway crossed the summit of White Pass on February 20, 1899. At that point, the Ladue-Yukon Transportation Company abandoned the plan to use its own ocean steamers and sternwheelers for delivering goods to Dawson. The "all-water route" was soon also abandoned by all other navigation companies when the White Pass and Yukon Railway opened for freight and passenger business between Skagway and Whitehorse on July 29, 1900. For several years the Ladue Company shipped its freight via Alaska Commercial Company ocean steamers to Skagway where it was transferred to the *White Pass and Yukon* freight cars headed for Whitehorse, and then loaded onto the riverboats of the Canadian Development Company for the final 460 miles downriver to Dawson.[174]

Since the fall of 1898 the Ladue Company had operated as clearly differentiated departments: Mercantile, Placer Mines, Sawmill, Dawson City Real Estate, Coal Mines and the Marguerite Quartz Mine. The annual reports reflected the activities of each.

Dr. T. Bates Cooke of Plattsburgh had managed the Mercantile Department, which included the store and warehouses, since September 1898. Business had been good. Although it had dropped significantly since the boom days of '98, Cooke had proven to be an excellent manager. In the summer of 1900, the company undertook the upgrading and expansion of the Mercantile Department. First a new 40 by 50 foot corrugated metal warehouse was built on the waterfront across the street from the store. In it were stored bulk items such as flour and sugar. The store was then "refitted" with new shelves, counters and a new front. Shortly after the work was completed, however, it was decided that the store was too small to accommodate the volume of business, so it was moved to the vacant lot behind it, remodeled and made into a mess hall for employees. A new store, two stories tall was erected in its place. One portion of the building was 50'x160'. Following Jack McQuesten's earlier example, the entire building was sheathed in corrugated metal siding to protect it from a fate similar to the devastation fire had inflicted on Dawson's business district in the winters of 1898 and 1899. Most of the storefront consisted of four large plate glass windows. A striking display placed in a window one Christmas was "a massive piece of beautiful burned leather work showing an Indian's head and a winter scene."[175] With the larger store, the hardware section was expanded considerably. The total value of goods in the store warehouses on September 1, 1900, was $150,000; but, because of an insurance rate of eight percent on value and because of the care given to fire protection, the company decided to purchase coverage of only $60,000, a decision later deeply regretted.[176]

Elmer Botsford had supervised construction of the new store the previous summer. When asked about his predictions for the company's business, he commented as he pointed out the improvements being made:

> Don't look as if we were much troubled about the business outlook, does it? So far as present business is concerned, it is as good now as it generally is at this time of the year, in fact, we have no complaint whatever to make on that score, as the arrival of new goods has given a stimulus to business and we find the store doing a good steady business. The sawmill is running to its full capacity. We are living in hopes that the government will take the royalty off, or at least reduce it, so as to leave some of the gold in the country.[177]

The Sawmill Department had continued to be the company's "gold mine," its business increasing every season since it began operation in the fall of 1896. The *Klondike Nugget* wrote that the Harper and Ladue Sawmill was expected to continue operations throughout the 1900 season "without interruption...with enough logs within easy distance of the mill to keep the machinery in full blast from now on." Walter Lyon who, among his other duties for the company, was the mill manager, stated that it had about "30,000 feet of logs about 20 miles up the Yukon River that were ready to be floated to Dawson as soon as all the ice was out of the river."[178]

During the period covered by the annual report, the number of timber berths had increased from two square miles to eight[179] and an addition had been made to the mill to accommodate a new "cut-off saw, edger and other new machinery." A new two-story "dry-shed" had been erected for storing dressed green lumber. The net profit of the sawmill for the twenty-month period was $43,000.[180]

The selling price of town site lots had plummeted along with Dawson's population. So, the Dawson City Real Estate Department began to place more emphasis on the construction and rental of buildings on its lots in various parts of town rather than sales. A contributing factor to that department's loss of revenue was the ongoing difficulty with purchasers of lots defaulting on payments, since the company was still awaiting its patents and was unable to provide clear titles to buyers.[181] Its rented buildings housed the company's mercantile store and warehouse, Ladue Mill, mill sheds and additions, Mill Store (rented from the Townsite Company), a gymnasium, Dawson Private Hospital, the Guild Building, *Dawson Daily News*, Gold City Hotel, a Third Avenue tenement, a store, a residence and a "House (on the) Government Reserve." The department also owned a warehouse building 1,700 miles downriver at St. Michael.[182] The cost of constructing the buildings in Dawson was $29,378. Annual rents collected on the properties amounted to $13,920. The total assessed value of the real estate for taxation purposes was $288,350.[183]

The remaining departments were in trouble. While the potential for sale of coal was high, Botsford and Lyon thought the cost of mining it would have been prohibitive. Botsford estimated it would cost $50,000 to open a mine and extract the coal—but that it would not sell for much more than that amount. The Coal Department never became active.

Of all the operations, it was not expected by hopeful shareholders, and certainly not by Joe, that so little profit would be derived from the Placer Mines Department. The company had acquired many claims on Bonanza, Eldorado and other creeks since Joe placed his 39 Eldorado and 23 Below Hunker properties in the company. At the time of the 1901 annual report the company's interests included:

> 1/4 of 16 below Hunker; one bench claim opposite No. 5 below on Hunker; 1/4 bench claim opposite No. 42 Hydraulic Reserve, Hunker; 1 bench claim opposite 35 below on Hunker; 1/4 interest in bench claim opposite No. 6 discovery Last Chance; 1 bench claim opposite No. 2 above mouth Last Chance; one bench claim opposite No. 3 below discovery Last Chance; 1/4 bench claim No. 27 above on Little Blanche; and creek claims 105, 106, 107, 108, 109 and 110 below on Sulphur.

Botsford stated in the report that "Prospecting work was done on our Sulphur Creek Claims and also on bench claims and Last Chance, but it has not been deemed advisable to work these or any of our mines to any great extent at the present high prices for labor and royalty....In some instances, 65% of the gross output" was swallowed up in labor costs and the 10 percent royalty charged by the government. In its November 2, 1899, Anniversary Number, The *Klondike Nugget* commented:

> The imposition of the exorbitant, and in many cases prohibitive royalty caused many of (the) heavy producers to be closed down this season, the owners hoping that within a reasonable time the "powers that be" would come to a sensible understanding of the situation and either materially reduce or altogether abolish this "source of revenue" which is having the opposite effect to that which it was expected to produce by those who are responsible for it.

Inspector Starnes of the North West Mounted Police stated in his annual report for 1900 that government royalties collected on Bonanza and Eldorado and their tributaries that year totaled $515,385.29.

It may have been of some comfort to board members and shareholders when Botsford stated, regarding the Sulphur Creek claims: "With the pay streak located and the steam thawers at work...we hope to largely increase our income from the mines. No money is being spent in unwarranted prospecting or work, but all efforts are being directed towards the ultimate success with the least danger of a loss."[184]

However, Botsford continued to believe that the cost of operating a mine in the Klondike was prohibitively expensive on all but the richest claims.[185] Later reports did not indicate how much work was ultimately done on the Sulphur Creek claims or how productive they may have been. Concerning the Gold Bottom placer claims, he said they had "not proven as satisfactory" as had been anticipated, but provided no details.

Included in the holdings in that same report was No. 23 Below on Hunker, which, in the winter of 1898-99, was mined on a "lay." A lay was an arrangement made with another party (or "layman") to work a claim on a percentage basis. The lay on 23 Below Hunker was referred to at the time as a 50-cent (or 50 percent) lay.[186] The cleanup in the spring of 1899 was $6,400. Half, or $3,200, belonged to the miner who worked the lay. The remaining $3,200 was divided equally between the Ladue Company and the estate of Arthur

Harper. In the winter of 1899-1900 the company "put on a steam thawer" and mined the same property itself. The result was a gross earning of between $8,000 and $9,000. Subtracting labor, equipment costs and the royalty, the company felt the net profit was too low to justify continued work on the claim.[187]

Given the fact that some of the full claims owned by the company since 1897 were among the richest in the district, it is curious that they were not worked. The earnings, whether the properties were worked on a lay or by the company, while perhaps not being outstanding, would have been considerable. The manager of mining operations for the company was, for many years, Samuel Lansing.[188] Whether he, Botsford or Lyon made the decisions about how the claims should be managed, it appears the company consistently missed opportunities to add significant profit to its Placer Mines Department. It seems likely that, had Joe been able to supervise operations in Dawson, more of the placer claims would have been developed.

Another disappointment, particularly to Joe, was the Marguerite quartz property on Gold Bottom. After "not showing a sufficient and satisfactory vein in the development work done, work was temporarily suspended." Quartz mining had not been pursued because the "cost for labor and fuel" were still considered to be too high to warrant the development of any mines that had been located. By September 1901, however, there would be renewed interest in quartz mining in the Klondike.[189]

When shareholders attending the 1901 annual meeting expressed concern that no dividend had been paid for the 20-month period covered by the report, Botsford pointed out again that, given the loss of the steamer *Morgan City* and the decline of Dawson's population, he had chosen to reinvest earnings, upgrading properties and constructing buildings to create annually anticipated rental income.[190]

The Board of Directors apparently found Botsford's explanation of the company's "shrinkage in assets" unacceptable and appointed a committee to investigate. The stockholders appointed a committee of their own to work in conjunction with that appointed by the board.

The committees addressed all aspects of the company's operations reflected in the report. Of particular concern to the directors and shareholders were the details of earnings and expenses of the *Morgan City*. They may have been surprised by what they found, but apparently did not consider the discrepancies to be a major concern. At a May 6 meeting when the report of the committee appointed by the stockholders was made, the board accepted its findings and also approved Botsford's annual report as originally presented.[191]

The stockholders' meticulous investigation related to the *Morgan City* revealed:

Earnings:	
Johnson-Locke	$48,203.94
Barneson & Chilkott Company charter	$78,503.82
"Sale of Yacht *Yale*[192] and Chronometer" (Sic)	$850.00
Insurance collected	$88,328.09
Total Earnings:	$215,885.85
Expenses:	
Purchase price and cost of alterations	$151,363.81
Commissions for obtaining a charter	$13,396.85
Voyage from New York City to San Francisco	$17,319.93
Total Expenses:	-$182,080.59
Net Gain:	$33,805.26

Still in litigation, regarding the loss of the *Morgan City*, were the following claims: one against the Johnson-Locke Company for $12,732.27; another against the U.S. government for $9,420; and a third against the *Frankfort Insurance Company* for $18,888.88. If the courts decided in favor of the company for the full amounts of these claims, the final net gain on the *Morgan City* would be $74,846.41.

The report included the fact that Joe had, since the initial issue of shares to him in August 1897, been given an additional 53,354 shares with a "par value" of $533,540. It also indicated the total "balance due Mr. Ladue...$3,999,000."[193] On paper Joe continued to be a very wealthy man.

At the time the annual meeting was taking place at the company's New York City offices in the Empire Building, its president was still in Colorado Springs attempting to recover from tuberculosis.

In Dawson the Mercantile and Sawmill Departments of the Ladue

Company continued to operate at a profit in spite of their many competitors, taxes, customs duties and other charges the Canadian government levied on businesses. The Mercantile Department was hard-pressed to show a profit by competition from many other stores selling similar goods. The chief competitors were the North American Trading and Transportation Company and the giant new Northern Commercial Company, formed by the merger of the Alaska Commercial Company with the International Mercantile Marine Company and Alaska Goldfields, Ltd. Northern Commercial was one of two corporations organized by that merger. Its purpose was to conduct all mercantile activities in Dawson, on the creeks and at stores along the river. The second corporation, Northern Navigation Company, was exclusively a transportation company, operating stern-wheelers, mainly between Whitehorse and Dawson.[194] Smaller competitors of the Ladue Company store were Dawson Hardware, Schindler's Hardware, McLennan and McFeeley Hardware, Thomas Mahoney Trading Company, Holmes Hardware, Sargent and Pinska, McDonald Iron Works, Ames Mercantile and others. The two largest companies often took out full-page advertisements in local newspapers. The Ladue store continued to battle the new behemoths, placing its own, smaller, but bold advertisements in *The Klondike Nugget* beginning April 18,1901:

> LOOK OUT FOR US THIS SEASON!
> We will import more goods than ever before.
> The combination (merger) doesn't frighten us.
> Big bargains await you in carefully selected commodities.
> THE LADUE CO...IF YOU BUY IT OF LADUE CO., IT'S GOOD.[195]

The last line of the advertisement had been the company's motto since 1898.

By 1901 the depletion of old-growth timber along the rivers meant that finding logs of sufficient size posed a serious problem for the Ladue Company Sawmill. So serious was the shortage that, in early June 1901, Dawson City's mill superintendents hired 30 or 40 men to go up the Stewart River to fell timber. The logs were then floated down the Yukon to be divided among the town's six sawmills. In addition, throughout the summer, the Ladue Mill continued to cut from its eleven timber berths on the Yukon, Stewart and Pelly Rivers.[196] By this time, their profit was declining due to competition from the other mills, one of which, the Canadian-Yukon Lumber Company, was operated by the ambitious Martha Munger a mile away on the left bank of the Klondike.[197] A small fire at the Ladue Sawmill office in early July did little damage.[198]

All of Dawson's mills had to have access to the waterfront for receiving their logs. The annual government fee on such property was $7.50 per linear foot. The Ladue Sawmill had an impressive waterfront access of 150 feet for which they paid $1,125.00 per year. In 1901 the sawmill owners submitted a formal request to the Crown Timber and Land Agent to reduce the rental fee to $5.00 per linear foot, citing "the present dull condition of business."[199]

Elmer Botsford continued to consider placer mining unprofitable. The Placer Mines Department, therefore, remained essentially inactive the summer of 1901. One of its claims, however, No. 11 Below Bonanza, was worked on a lay by the company's general manager, Walter H. Lyon.

After six months in Colorado Springs, Joe was little improved. He and Kittie returned in May 1901 to their home in Schuyler Falls and were welcomed by their housekeeper, Mrs. Sibley.[200] The joy they shared upon their homecoming was shattered on the 27th of June when Joe died at home 8:30 in the evening.[201]

When Elmer Botsford received the sad news by telegram in far-off Dawson City, he stated that he could "hardly believe" Joe had passed away since he was not "seriously ill" at the time of Botsford's departure from New York. He went on to say:

> I have never met in all my life a more lovable and honorable man than Joe Ladue. I have known him ever since I can remember and in all that time I never knew him to lie or even exaggerate a fact. I feel his loss keenly, for the world does not hold many like him.[202]

Funeral services were held at three o'clock, July 1, in the parlor of the Ladue home. Mr. Clough, a family friend, made all arrangements. Ladue's gentle ways and many kindnesses had won him many devoted friends, and they came in large numbers to show their respect.

The ceremonies were jointly conducted by Reverend C. A. Bradford, minister of the Schuyler Falls Methodist Church, and Reverend Henry C. Petty, former pastor of the church who was, at that time, serving in Champlain, New York. Petty found it hard to accept that it had been only three and a half years since he had conducted Joe and Kittie's wedding. Numerous ornate floral arrangements flanked the casket and filled the room. Most poignant of all, perhaps, was the one sent by employees of the Ladue Company from Joe's town, Dawson City, displaying the words: "Our President."[203]

The long, horse-drawn funeral cortege left from beneath the porte-cochere, eased down the driveway and made its way slowly just a mile to the New Schuyler Falls Cemetery near the diminutive house where Joe Ladue was born. Buggies lined the wide central lane in the cemetery and overflowed onto the dusty road beyond as burial took place in the Mason family plot. A substantial pipe fence with an ornate wrought iron gate enclosed it. The first marker, placed flat on the sod, was a small granite stone on which is simply carved "JOSEPH LADUE 1855-1901."[204]

Kittie ordered a large imposing monument that was installed in 1903 near the center of the plot. The Hulihan brothers of Rutland sculpted it from "Barre granite" (from Barre, Vermont). The monument was made in three sections. The base or pediment is five feet six inches by three feet eleven inches, and one and a quarter inches thick. On top of the base is a section measuring four feet four inches by two feet nine inches, and twelve inches thick. The top section measures three feet six inches by three feet two inches, and twelve inches thick.[205] The top section, known as the "die," has curved corners and bears the simple inscription, "LADUE."

Reverend Petty wrote a personal recollection of Joe:

> The Honorable Joseph Ladue was born in year 1853, & died at his home in Schuyler Falls N.Y., June 27, 1901, aged 48 yrs. Mr. Ladue was left an orphan at an early age & soon after entered the home of Mr. Jas. Henry Lobdell, where he passed most of his time during schooling period, until he went forth into life for himself. While in the home & under the care of Mr. Lobdell he rec'd the influence of a Christian community as well as of a Christian home. When he became a man he left home & he tra-

versed the Far West & Southwest & passed various degrees of fortune & adversity. After some years spent in this kind of life he bot his passage for far off Alaska, then a wilderness unknown. He reached his destination & at once began to lay plans for success in business. His first undertaking was a lumber business which increased with time, & was a large & paying for the company at the time of Mr. Ladue's death.

About this time of our war with Spain, Mr. Ladue came out to the States with the joyful news that gold had been discovered in paying quantities in the region of Dawson, which he has founded. At once thousands made preparation to go to those new fields, & the little place which he had founded became a city of many thousands. Many seeing value in lands in the region, & taking Mr. Ladue at his word, were at once anxious to form a Company for the development of these regions, so the "Ladue Mining Company" was formed with Mr. Ladue as its pres. & this company have spared no pains to make a success of this undertaking & are today doing good work. Mr. Ladue made sev. trips to Dawson after the company was formed until disease began to undermine his hitherto rugged constitution. Mr. E. F. Botsford has also made annual tours to the Klondike & is now en route to that place, when ill health took hold of Mr. Ladue, he at once began the fight for life. Symptoms of consumption appeared & by doctors advice he traveled here & there, hoping that change of climate would be beneficial. but the disease gained on him & last fall he went to Colorado Spgs. bad.

This did not seem to relieve his sufferings. In May he retd, & grad. fell worse, until the end came on June 27th. Mr. Ladue and Miss Kittie Mason of Schuyler Falls (were married) on Dec. 15, 1897. Their quiet home in Schuyler Falls was always a cheerful home, & many found here a welcome.

The writer, who became acquainted with the subject of this imperfect sketch during his pastorate in Schuyler Falls, found him a man of kind heart & disposition, & a man who was truly a helper of the poor, & who performed many kind acts that will not soon be forgotten. He made many friends, & when he became your friend you could not help but learn that fact....

> Mr. Ladue is surv. by his wife & adopted son Francis. The community is in mourning for all feel that they lost a good man & citizen & one who was a friend to one & all. by Henry C Petty, former pastor & now pastor at Champlain N.Y.[206]

Although Reverend Petty put his age at 48 and the grave marker placed by Kittie gives an incorrect year of birth, Joe was actually 46 when he died.[207] He had been keenly aware of the seriousness of his condition. Tuberculosis was no stranger to men who had lived in the North and was the scourge of the nineteenth century. Just prior to departing for Colorado Springs, Joe executed his Will:

> I, Joseph Ladue of Schuyler Falls, Clinton County, New York, 46 years, do make, ordain, publish and declare this to be my last Will and Testament, that is to say, After all my lawful debts are paid, I give and bequeath to My beloved wife, Kittie Mason Ladue of Schuyler Falls, Clinton County, New York all my Estate both real and personal wherever situated of which I may be possessed, own or have an interest in at the time of my decease. I make, constitute and appoint Victor C. Mason, and James Henry Lobdell, both of Schuyler Falls, New York to be Executors of this my last Will and testament, hereby revoking all former Wills made by me....
> Joseph Ladue
> Signed and sworn to before me, this 28 day of November 1900.
> Elmer A. Kiet
> Notary Public[208]

His executors were his childhood guardian, James H. Lobdell, and Kittie's brother, Victor C. Mason.

The previous year Joe had transferred to Kittie, by "absolute deed and absolute bill of sale," his real and personal property in Dawson City. The real property consisted of a number of lots in Dawson and his "undivided" interest in a number of mines in the Klondike. All were transferred to Kittie for the purpose of paying Joe's share of outstanding debts of the Harper and Ladue partnership. The personal property was worth a scant $600, being a half interest in "a stock of goods owned by Harper and Ladue."[209]

The will was admitted for probate November 25, 1901.[210] The required appraisal was made and the cash value of Joe's assets was estimated at $6,499.87. The appraisal included several small mortgages and notes made to Silas and Sarah Trombly, Theron W. Day, Victor C. Mason, Jerome J. Bromley, Napoleon Jock, J. D. Everest and John W. Clay. The total value of the mortgages and loans was $1,151.55. Two horses had been received "in payment of debt," and sold in a "private sale" for $350. "Unsold property" was listed as "one roan colt, one mortgage, 4 notes."[211] Real estate, bank accounts and cash were not included in the estate appraisal.

Other assets were shown as 3,750 shares of preferred stock in The Joseph Ladue Gold Mining and Development Company of Yukon, valued at $3,750 and 10,687 shares of common stock valued at $1,068.[212] However, an affidavit prepared by Botsford in April 1902 noted that "The appraisal value of this stock is more than it could have been sold for at decedent's death."[213] In fact, there were no buyers for the stock.

The only unpaid account presented for settlement to the executors was a claim by Joe's brother, Andrew. Andrew filed a petition in September 1902 in Linn County, Iowa, against the Ladue Estate, alleging that on September 15, 1880, Andrew gave Joe three checks dated: July 15, for $45, August 15, for $60 and September 15, for $75. The petition goes on to say that Joe cashed the checks "but refused to make any accounting" to Andrew. Joe left Dakota Territory shortly thereafter for Arizona, New Mexico, and finally "Alaska" and had, over the next 21 years, not made an effort to repay the cashed payroll checks. The cashed checks amounted to $180, to which Andrew added six percent interest amounting to $230, for a total of $410.

J. S. Graham's obligation to Andrew in the Black Hills apparently had not been paid. Andrew included in his petition the old unpaid obligation from J. S. Graham when Joe left the Black Hills. He claimed the $29 debt plus six percent interest, increasing the amount to $75.

The total amount of Andrew's claim against Joe's estate was $515.78, which included the cost of filing the petition. The final payment ordered by the court was $481.[214] Ladue descendants do not know the exact circumstances regarding the origin of Andrew's claim. Nevertheless, there was a permanent estrangement between the brothers. Perhaps Joe had advanced train fare to Andrew when he went to the Black Hills and may have supported his younger brother until he was established and believed that the checks represented fair payment. Andrew may have interpreted any agreement differently. The facts will remain a mystery. Joe was highly regarded by all who knew him in the Yukon and New York and this event seems contrary to other references to his character.

The final settlement of the estate of Joseph Ladue was filed and approved by Judge John H. Booth on January 26, 1903. Kittie, Joe's sole heir, was to receive $8,514.44. This amount included the severely depreciated stock of the Ladue Company that was later purchased from Kittie by Elmer F. Botsford. Since the majority of their New York real estate was originally recorded solely in Kittie's name, it did not become an asset of Joe's estate.[215] Bank accounts were not included in estate settlements at the time, so there may have been a considerable balance of cash available to Kittie.

Dawson and the Ladue Company after Joe's Death

In 1901, the summer of Joe's death, there was renewed interest in the potential of quartz mining in the Klondike.[1] Elmer Botsford had no mining experience, but had heard much about hard-rock mining from Joe, and the so-called experts on the scene believed that the Klondike was full of gold-bearing quartz. He had come to believe that it would eventually replace placer mining as the leading gold producer of the Klondike District. The company's Marguerite quartz claim, which the prospectus of 1897 described in such glowing terms, had been a disappointment. But Botsford and many others continued to be optimistic that significant deposits would eventually be located.

The "richest quartz find" was made in mid-September 1901 by Thomas Keenan on Ophir Creek, a tributary of the Yukon River, about 12 miles above Dawson. A sample of the ore assayed at $26 per ton. Experts who examined the site said it "resembled the cropping of the famous copper mines of Montana." Keenan also discovered and staked an area lying between King Solomon Dome and the head of Gold Bottom Creek. The "Maid of Erin" ledge of quartz he found was considered as "destined to rank as one of the future big gold producers of the Klondike."[2]

All that summer and fall many men, including those of the Ladue Company, diligently prospected for gold-bearing quartz. Of special interest to the company was its ground near 26 Eldorado and what appeared to be large outcroppings on Lepine Creek, about 15 miles from Dawson. By fall, hopes were high and by the end of September there were two stamp mills established in town, one of them owned by the Ladue Company. Both mills were relatively small and, as it turned out, were used primarily for assaying purposes. The first mill, a two-stamp Tremaine Prospecting Mill brought in by George Munger and his sister, Martha, was erected near the mouth of the Klondike River. But Munger soon became discouraged with the prospects for quartz mining and closed his mill in December. Within a few months the Yukon Government leased the property, expanded its capacity and began offering assay services at a fee considered "affordable" to all miners.[3]

The Ladue Company Quartz Mill was conveniently constructed next to the sawmill on the corner of today's Albert and Front Streets and soon ore samples brought in by miners from various locations were waiting to be tested. The purchase of the stamp mill was a major investment for the company; it cost thousands of dollars just to ship and install it at Dawson. The building was two-stories high, had an unusually deep foundation and was heavily timbered to withstand the jarring of the stamps. A 25-horsepower "Climax" engine and boiler supplied the power for the mill. The four stamps, each weighing 850 pounds, were alternately raised six inches and dropped on the ore about 90 times per minute. In this manner, each stamp could crush four tons in 24 hours. The company assayer was G. E. Beraud who had been for many years, chief chemist and assistant superintendent of the Electrolytic Copper Refinery of the Anaconda Copper Company of Montana.[4] That fall, the concussion of the stamp mills rumbled across the town, joined with the piercing whine of six sawmills and the howls of hundreds of huskies, creating a cacophony that continually serenaded Dawson's population.

The sawmill continued to be the company's most profitable operation. During that season, logs were cut from 13 square miles of leased forestland located on the Yukon, Stewart and White Rivers and Ballarat Creek.[5]

Notwithstanding the success of the sawmill and store, at a March 1902 meeting of stockholders and directors, "Expert accountants" reported "a decrease in assets" for the second year in a row.[6] In response, once more the frustrated stockholders, many of whom had been complaining that a dividend had not been paid since 1899, appointed a committee to investigate. A similar committee was appointed from the Board of Directors to work with the stockholders' committee and independent accountants were employed to "go over the books."[7]

In May, both committees reported that "the accounts were in good shape and that the officers of the company had conducted its affairs as well as could be expected." The reports agreed that gross earnings for the year had been $21,900 and that, after deducting expenses, the profit was sufficient to allow the payment of modest dividends. Again, however, it had been decided by Elmer Botsford as general mnager and treasurer that, rather than pay a dividend, it was more prudent to reinvest in "further development of the company's property" in Dawson City. No dividends were paid.

At that meeting several new board members were elected: Hon. Smith M. Weed, Katharine M. Ladue, Amasa B. Clarke, of *Clarke and Company*, constructors and builders, New York City (succeeding R. C. Jackson, who had resigned); Albert W. Emery, Charles W. Wells, R. A. Rotche, Willard Brown, William E. Fort, Addis K. Botsford, John A. Sleicher, Elmer F. Botsford, D. W. Cooke, general passenger agent, Erie Railroad; George S. Bixby, A. J. Pierce, and Walter A. Phelan.

In March, Phelan had issued a circular "attacking the management of the company." At the May meeting, after hearing the report of the committees, he made a "public apology" and said he would be forwarding a "letter of retraction to the stockholders."[8]

In late June 1902 Botsford returned to Dawson via the White Pass and Yukon Route Railroad and by riverboat. He was now president and general manager of the Ladue Company. He had also acquired "a large share of the stock."[9] When approached by reporters, he declined to say whether he had a controlling interest, stating only that there were "also other large holdings in Montreal, New York and Philadelphia."

Ever-optimistic and overly enthusiastic writers for *The Klondike Nugget*, more than a year earlier, however, appeared to believe that he already owned the controlling share, referring to his being in Dawson to look after "his flourishing Company."[10] Since the price of the company's stock began to diminish and none could be sold after the loss of the *Morgan City* in the fall of 1899, Botsford could have purchased as many shares as he liked for very little.[11] In fact, after Joe's death, the appraisal made for purposes of probate reflected stock values as ten cents per share of common stock and one dollar for preferred. These valuations revealed the devastating loss suffered by original investors who paid ten dollars per share in 1897 with no distinction between common and preferred stock.[12] One of the Nugget's competitors, the *Yukon Morning Sun*, in its July 6, 1902, edition wrote, "A report has reached the Sun that Elmer F. Botsford has secured a controlling interest in the Ladue Company."[13]

Although he must have been aware of the sluggish condition of business in Dawson, Botsford told the Sun that he planned to expand the company, but was not prepared to give specifics. The Mercantile Department would definitely be "increased" as would the capacity of the sawmill; nine timber berths were leased that year.[14] The Townsite Company, during this period, continued to focus primarily on its rental properties for which Emil Stauf, a "Mining and Financial Broker," served as agent as he had for some time.[15] Although the company still owned 11 and 39 Eldorado, 97 Above and 30 Below Bonanza, it appears that no work had been done on them, the cost of labor and the ten percent royalty still considered too high to allow a reasonable profit.[16]

Elmer Botsford also planned to pursue the possibilities of quartz, believing that Dawson was "slowly changing from a placer to a quartz camp...."[17] During that summer, several tons of ore were brought to the Ladue Quartz Mill from their Eldorado property, but assay results were disappointing.

If assays were to confirm the anticipated value of the company's recently acquired Lepine Creek property, Botsford had plans to install a larger stamp mill at the site. When interviewed by The *Klondike Nugget* in the fall of 1902, Botsford said, "It looks very much as though we have a veritable mountain of ore...and should that prove to be the case no unnecessary time will be lost in establishing a big milling plant on the grounds."

The "big milling plant" he was referring to was a projected 100-stamp mill to process ore from the company's "Murrayville" group, where a large number of Ladue men were already at work. A mill at that site would require an additional investment of $250,000. Had these plans materialized, the operation would have been the first hard-rock mining ever done in the Klondike.[18] The results of the assays conducted on the Lepine Creek ore at the company's Quartz Mill were inconclusive, so Botsford decided to take samples Outside for more thorough testing. He took many photographs of the Lepine Creek area that he planned to use to illustrate addresses to eastern financiers if he received positive assay results. His expectations were further bolstered when R. H. Cavill, "a well-known mining expert," said, after examining the Lepine Creek area, that what he saw "looked good" and expressed the conviction that the district "is likely to be the leader in the Klondike in the development of quartz mining."[19] One of Botsford's final statements to the press in Dawson before leaving on October 3, 1902, was:

> As for myself, I actually believe there will be much doing in quartz before the winter is over. I have seen enough this summer to convince me that the country is fast shifting from a placer to a hard rock camp.[20]

Prior to leaving Dawson that fall Botsford joined most Dawson merchants in switching his accepted medium of exchange from the use of gold dust to currency. It was accomplished by declaring that as of September 1902, they would value gold dust submitted for payment at $13.50 per ounce. The banks were paying $14.50 per ounce.[21] He also ordered placement of an advertisement for the company in a local newspaper:

THE LADUE QUARTZ MILL
is now in operation.
We have made a large number of tests and are
ready to make others.
We have the best plant money can buy and
guarantee all our work in this
mill and also in the
ASSAY OFFICE[22]

The future development of Lepine Creek by the Ladue Company and others was, to a great extent, dependent upon the government's building a 15-mile road between Dawson and the mine site. However, the government was hesitant to make such a significant expenditure until the assays indicated substantial amounts of gold in the quartz outcroppings sampled. The results of the Ladue Company's "more thorough testing" of the ore were ultimately disappointing, however, as were assays done by other groups. A road was never built, and Joe's vision of quartz mining in the Yukon vanished.

In March 1903 Elmer Botsford gave lectures at the Normal School in Plattsburgh and at the Waldorf-Astoria Hotel in New York City. His collection of lantern slides of "every phase of the country, its industries and inhabitants were unquestionably the finest ever gathered." Of particular interest to the Plattsburgh audience was a portrait of Joseph Ladue. A series of slides showed the Ladue Company store from the time it had been constructed to the present. Botsford offered a gold nugget scarf pin to the Normal School student who would write the best essay on Alaska.[23]

Since the summer of 1900 the Ladue Company had made improvements and expansions within its several departments in an attempt to keep up with its competitors. By the end of 1902, however, it became evident that other adjustments would be necessary if the company were to survive. At a meeting of the Board of Directors in Jersey City on April 8, 1903, it was decided that, because of the high corporate tax levied on companies with charters in New Jersey, the company should be dissolved and reincorporated in another state, South Dakota.[24]

Elmer Botsford and George Bixby of Plattsburgh, N.Y., and Roy Dorothy of Pierre, South Dakota, filed Articles of Incorporation. The new corporation retained the name, The Joseph Ladue Gold Mining and Development Company of Yukon, and was licensed to operate as it had since 1897 on the same broad basis in real estate, mining, buying and selling merchandise and operating mills. The Articles of Incorporation were "filed for record" at the Secretary of State's Office in Pierre, South Dakota, April 15, 1903. The new corporation was registered for a period of 20 years and was authorized to issue up to 5,000,000 shares of stock at $1.00 per share.

There were ten members of the Board of Directors: From Plattsburgh, N.Y.: Smith M. Weed, Elmer F. Botsford and Albert W. Emery. From New York City: Willard Brown, Almon J. Pierce and George S. Bixby. From Saranac Lake, N.Y.: Addis Botsford. From Pierre, South Dakota: Roy Dorothy, Harry S. Anderson and Carl Swenson.[25]

When Elmer Botsford returned to Dawson on June 20, 1903, aboard the steamer *Yukoner*, the Ladue Company had 35 employees,[26] but business was slow for all departments except the sawmill which was kept busy turning out lumber, mainly for boats. When the mill opened for business in June, it was considered by the *Yukon Sun* to be "an event in the local industrial world." It had the capacity to produce 16,000 board feet of lumber a day. Earlier in the month, logs cut the previous winter from the company's 13 timber berths had been formed into big "booms" and rafted down from the upper Yukon, the Stewart and Pelly. Edward Smith, mill foreman for the previous three years, was considered locally to be "one of the finest men in the business." The mill had always been a moneymaker for the company and had a reputation for "turning out the best lumber in the territory."[27] It did not operate beyond 1903, the last year its name appeared in tax rolls and there is no record that it was still leasing timber berths. During the preceding year, lumber sales in Dawson had decreased by 2,000,000 board feet. Mining companies were not ordering lumber for sluices and, with Dawson's dwindling population there was little construction. The *Dawson Daily News* reported in its February 3, 1904 issue that the only sawmill operating in Dawson was the *Northern Lumber Company*.

By August 1903, it appears that the Ladue Company had finally given up on the possibility of quartz mining flourishing in the Klondike, and its mill was shut down. Because the city of Dawson continued to assess the mill on a valuation of $10,000, which meant an annual tax of $325, Botsford decided to remove the equipment and abandon the building. In the August 13, 1903 issue of the *Dawson Record*, Botsford stated:

We offered to sell the mill to the government to help encourage the quartz industry, but the government declined to buy. We considered the contribution of $325 a year toward the government for the privilege of maintaining such an enterprise too heavy and are removing the machinery.

The *Record* editorialized in the same issue that:

> The least the government and the city of Dawson could do would be to allow the Ladue quartz mill the free use of a site. It is a shame and a disgrace that this mill must have to be dismantled and removed because of the perversity of the territorial and city governments.

The reason why the Ladue or any stamp mill should be given a free site and freed from taxation of all kinds is because of the present value to the country. It would be far more to the benefit of the territory if a bonus was paid to the quartz mill which would come here and locate and which, more than most other things of the kind, will bring on the era of quartz mining. The era of quartz mining means the era of permanent life in the Yukon.

The September 24,1903 issue of the Dawson Record reported that the hardware department of the Ladue Company store on Front Street was moved to a building rented from Max King on King St. across from the auditorium theater. John J. Rossman from Clinton County, New York, was hired as manager. "The quarters are being put in condition as rapidly as possible and when completed will present an attractive appearance, the front windows being among the largest French plate in Dawson." The Record also reported that beginning with the removal of the hardware department, the Front St. store would operate exclusively as a wholesale outlet and had on hand large quantities of flour, sugar, butter, lard, hams and case-lots of a variety of canned foods.

At 1:00 A.M., January 21, 1904, as the temperature hovered at 40 below zero, the great destroyer that had, on two previous occasions laid low many of the businesses of Dawson, struck the Ladue Company store. Local resident, Peter Vidovich, who was passing the front of the store when the fire broke out, stated that "it looked as though one joint of (stove) pipe was gone and two feet of solid flame was shooting up from the disconnected pipe to the roof of the store." Watchman Dwyer was in the habit of checking the stove every two hours and had last checked it half an hour earlier.[28]

After the fire had been raging for about half an hour Dwyer and two of the company's bookkeepers, J. J. Gately and G. H. Wand, forced their way into the office where they managed to save two daybooks and the stock ledger. From them, the losses were eventually determined.

Several years earlier, Botsford had ordered a custom-built, metal-covered "strong-box" in which the company's most important records were kept along with those of a number of customers. When the box was broken into it was found that "all the papers and documents left in it for safekeeping had been burned to ashes....More than $400 in nuggets and $180 in gold coin...were found in fairly good condition." Among the records lost by the Ladue Company were those of the sawmill that Lyon had placed in the box the previous day.

Store manager J. H. Hughes and company superintendent Walter Lyon speculated that the blaze had originated in the warm storage department, where a stove was kept continuously fueled during the winter to keep certain goods from damage by freezing.

In the days following the fire Lyon was able to determine the value of the ravaged building and its inventory at about $180,000. Insurance covered only one half the loss. One man offered Lyon $4,000 for the contents of the ruins. He refused and, over the next few weeks, he had three crews of men digging through the charred remains. Surprisingly, among the ashes and rubble they found nearly 15 tons of hams, bacon and lard all in good condition. They also found large quantities of butter, soap, "high priced" teas, coffee and dried fruits. Most of these items were sold on-site at a fraction of their wholesale price. But, the two-story building had been well stocked for the winter and much of the inventory was lost. The loss in tobaccos alone was between $6,000 and $7,000.[29]

The Ladue store had operated in Dawson since late August 1898, when Joe arrived aboard the company's steamer *Rideout* with 150 tons of goods. For five and a half years, its location away from the center of town and, the fact that it was sheathed in corrugated metal, had given it greater longevity than most. But in the end it, too, had succumbed to the unrelenting scourge of the North.[30]

The Dawson Daily News reported January 29 that manager Hughes' final estimate of the value of goods in the store was $50,000. Of these, what was not sold on-site, was retrieved from the rubble and stored in Brener's Third Avenue warehouse where the temporary offices of the mercantile department were reopened. None of the stock was sold until insurance company representatives had completed their appraisal. The article also stated that "As the stock (that was) burned, however, only represents about one-quarter of the total stores of the Ladue Company, the fire does not interfere materially with the carrying on of the business of the company the same as before."

But business was not carried on for long and in its March 19, 1904 issue the *Dawson Daily News* carried a fire sale advertisement placed by Hughes:

> FIRE SALE!
>
> Boyle's Wharf, First Avenue on the Water Front.
>
> I have been authorized to take over and sell the goods belonging to the Borden Condensed Milk Company (Creams and Milks).

T.M. Sinclair's Fidelity Hams, Bacon Lards and Kit goods.
Geo E. Turkett & sons Tobacco's, Cigars and Cigarettes.
Castle Bros. Dried Fruits, Honey and Nuts, and other lines of goods formerly handled by Ladue Company
Sale of damaged goods will commence on Monday Morning.
Our frozen Creams are pronounced undamaged. Get our fire sale prices on these goods.
John H. Hughes

On March 22 the News reported that the "ton" of tobacco remaining at the site of the Ladue Company store fire was destroyed in the presence of "a deputy of the internal revenue office." Such action was required in order for the company to avoid payment of government tax.

The stark, gaunt shell of the Ladue Company store was still standing in mid-April and citizens began to complain to the authorities that it was becoming dangerous and should be removed.[31] By early summer the charred remains of Joe's store had been torn down, loaded on wagons, and dumped into the river that had brought Joe into the country 22 years earlier. The lot on which it had stood became a gaping hole on the town site landscape. As the years passed dozens of other buildings would meet the same fate and "Joe's town," as he had known it, faded into history.

What was left of the Ladue Company in Dawson following the fire was the sawmill, The Ladue Company Hardware Store on King St., managed by John T. Rossman of Clinton County, several rental properties and the silent Quartz Mill, its assaying days long past. The placer claims, too, were idle. In September 1904, the hardware store ran the following advertisement in a local newspaper:

PIPE—FITTINGS—HOSE!
EVERYTHING IN HARDWARE

WE HAVE JUST RECEIVED A LARGE SHIPMENT
OF CROCKERY

THE LADUE COMPANY
KING STREET
DAWSON, Y.T.[32]

Elmer Botsford, still the company's president, spent much of the summer of 1904 in Dawson assessing the company's position. On August 23 he left for the Outside aboard the steamer, *Dawson*.[33]

In February 1905 Botsford announced in New York City that the Joseph Ladue Gold Mining and Development Company of Yukon would be dissolved at the annual meeting of the Board of Directors in the spring. Speculation in the *Dawson Daily News* gave the possible reasons for the company's demise as three-fold: stiff competition from the "Pacific Coast" mercantile houses, failure to work its placer properties and the loss of the *Morgan City*. One employee, however, stated that he thought the announcement of dissolution was premature and that it was the intention of Botsford and the shareholders to reorganize rather than to dissolve the company.[34] Unfortunately, the employee was mistaken.

On February 8, Botsford submitted to the department of the Secretary of State in Ottawa, in compliance with the provisions of the Foreign Companies Ordinance of Yukon Territory for filing, the "Annual Report of The Joseph Ladue Gold Mining and Development Company of Dawson, Yukon Territory, Canada." The report recorded only the names and addresses of members of the Board of Directors, the number of shares issued and other basic corporate information. Listed among the board members was "Katherine (sic) M. Ladue."

Other board members were Robert A. Roche of Peekskill, N.Y., Willard Brown, William E. Fort, Dr. George S. Bixsby, Almon J. Pierce and E. Merton Merrihew of New York City, Albert W. Emery, Elmer F. Botsford, C. E. M. Edwards and Corydon S. Johnson of Plattsburgh, Lewis E. Carr of Jersey City, N.J., and L. E. Geoffrion of Montreal, Quebec.

One sad fact related in the report was that 400,000 shares of common stock "is to be issued to Joseph Ladue or his Estate for the purchase price of properties."

The "properties" were nearly everything Joe had acquired during his fifteen years in the Yukon. The company's stocks in 1905 had no value and Joe's estate would receive no further benefits.[35]

At an April 21, 1905 meeting more than two-thirds of the stockholders voted to dissolve the company. In May a committee representing them (Botsford, G. S. Bixby, A. W. Emery, R. A. Rotche, A.

J. Pierce, E. S. Swift and Victor K. Moore) proposed a frantic, last-ditch attempt to "secure from the shareholders ten percent in cash of the stock they own and with this sum it is estimated that the property can be saved." Their plan was use those funds to pay off the outstanding debts and perhaps salvage the company.[36]

Meanwhile, back in Dawson, the sawmill and hardware store, trading with a constantly dwindling population, struggled to survive. In March 1905 the hardware store ran its last advertisement:

WE ARE AFTER YOUR TRADE
We have 40 per cent. Giant Powder, also stumping
Powder in large quantities.
Discount on 1-pound lots.

Wire Rope, 1-2 in. and 3-8 in. A Full Line of Pipe Fittings.
LADUE COMPANY[37]

Arriving in Dawson in mid-June 1905, Elmer Botsford must have recalled just three years earlier *The Klondike Nugget's* reference to "his flourishing company" and stated to the *Dawson Daily News*:

> The directors of the Ladue company...have voted to dissolve the company.... With the loss of the company's river steamer,[38] the burning of our principal store and the depression in Dawson realty the company is in anything but flourishing circumstances for the time.
>
> Just now affairs are in a process of evolution. The outcome is uncertain. The company has a great deal of land, many buildings and other property in Dawson and elsewhere in the Yukon. It will go into the hands of someone, and I trust before long everything will be right side up with care and again sailing serenely.
>
> I shall be in Dawson all summer looking after the affairs of the company, of which I am personally one of the most heavily interested."[39]

Elmer Botsford, still the company's president, did spend much of the summer in Dawson. In the June 26, 27, and 28 editions of the *Dawson Daily News* he placed the following advertisement:

MINING PROPERTIES FOR SALE.
ELDORADO—No. 39.
SULPHUR—Nos. 51, 58, 59, 60, 61, 105, 106, 107, 108, 109, 110, below discovery.
BONANZA—No. 30 above Discovery.
DOMINION—No. 31 below Upper; half int. No. 11 above Upper.
VICTORIA GULCH—Half int. Nos. 11 and 12.
HUNKER—No. 15A below Discovery and 1/4 int. in No. 16 below Disc.
BIG SKOOKUM—No. 1, 5th tier from Bonanza.
1 20 h.p. engine; 1 40 h.p. boiler; 1 60 h.p. boiler; 1 double drum hoist; 1 8-in. centrifugal pump; 1 3-in. centrifugal pump; 1 quartz mill; 1 assay plant complete; 1 sawmill.
E. F. Botsford, The Ladue Company

Only one of the gold claims, 31 Upper Dominion, appears to have been sold that summer. On August 10 it was listed in the *Dawson Daily News* under Mining Records as being sold to Horatio A. Stewart, Arthur L. Stewart and Napoleon J. Huot.

For all of Botsford's public optimism, however, "everything" was never again to be "sailing serenely." Little information regarding the final days of the Joseph Ladue Gold Mining and Development Company of Yukon has been located and it passed quietly into history, as had so many other great ventures in the Klondike.

Epilogue

The legendary towns of Deadwood, Tombstone and Dawson City, where Joe Ladue and other gold seekers searched for precious metals, are now only indistinct shadows of their former glory. The voices of raucous miners and dance tunes from discordant pianos that rang in the streets of Deadwood have been replaced by the sound of slot machines. Nearby, at Mt. Rushmore, the faces of four U.S. presidents carved into the stone look out over the sacred land of the Sioux and serve as a tourist attraction. Tombstone, the "town too tough to die," long ago replaced its hammering stamp mills with daily re-enactments of the "shoot out at the OK Corral" for the benefit of tourism, now its main industry.

A state park at Cumberland Bay commemorates the September 11, 1814, Battle of Plattsburgh—an unexpected victory that occurred when a group of hastily trained American sailors destroyed the superior British fleet on Lake Champlain during the War of 1812. Today, Plattsburgh is a small historical community, and an enjoyable destination for tourists. The naval victory of Commodore Thomas Macdonough is celebrated the first two weeks in September each year and is particularly meaningful to the local chapter of the Daughters of the American Revolution.

It is also home to Plattsburgh State University of New York and the Plattsburgh State Art Museum with its Rockwell Kent Collection showcasing his paintings, prints and illustrations. Plattsburgh is located 300 miles north of New York City, 150 miles north of Albany, and an hour's drive south of Montreal.

In Dawson City, by January 1904, when fire destroyed the Ladue Company store and its warehouse full of stock for the winter, it and many other businesses were struggling to survive. Many proprietors tried to sell their inventories at drastically reduced prices or at auctions. Often, unsold goods were left on shelves, the doors locked, and owners left town on the last boat, never to return. Dawson took on the aura of a ghost town, most of its hotels, stores, cabins and large houses standing in silence, hulking edifices, shells of their glory days when gold was king and the merchants supplied miners from the creeks everything they needed and anything they wanted. With taxes unpaid, and ownership claimed by no one, hundreds of buildings became a convenient source of building materials. For the next six decades they continued to be cannibalized and emptied of their treasures. This trend was reversed when Parks Canada, a federal agency, arrived in 1960 to begin work on many of the structures considered worthy of preservation or replication. Decades ago fires destroyed the old museum on Front Street beside the Bank of Commerce. In 1967 flames engulfed the meeting hall of the Yukon Order of Pioneers, burning many of the original treasures of the Gold Rush era including their banner that had been purchased in San Francisco and brought to Dawson by Jack McQuesten in 1898. Once threatened by permafrost, some of the remaining Victorian buildings have been restored, others replicated, and are maintained as historic sites. Song and dance revues at Diamond Tooth Gerties and the melodramas at the Palace Grand are favorite attractions. The Dawson City Museum, located in the stately old territorial Administration Building, houses extensive history exhibits and the Klondike History Library. The Library is on the upper level and comprises a valuable research facility established in July 1998. It includes an extensive archive of catalogued Klondike and Yukon documents and photographs. Descendants of former Dawsonites and others continue to contribute to the archive. The Lind Gallery at the Dawson City Museum—named for John Lind, a successful miner during the Gold Rush—was funded by his descendants and currently displays artifacts from the pre-Gold Rush period with which Joe Ladue would have been familiar.

Yukon Gold Panning Championships are held every July 1 in Dawson. Residents compete to see who can retrieve the most gold in the shortest time by panning; visitors compete for a separate prize. Tourists also flock to the city on Discovery Day, held in mid-August to commemorate the day gold was discovered in the Klondike; events include a parade, canoe races, ball games, dances and other events. The Tr'ondek Hwech'in (Han) host a biennial gathering at Moosehide, three miles downstream from Dawson.

Although many adventurers enjoy rafting or canoeing the Yukon, the transportation network is much different than it was in Joe's day. The Alaska Highway was built in 1942. In 1953 the Klondike Highway was completed between Dawson and Whitehorse, eliminating paddle-wheeler traffic on the Yukon River.

EPILOGUE

Joe's town, once crowded with men and women from many parts of the world seeking their fortunes in gold, is now visited by thousands of tourists each summer. Fire, floods and the ravages of time have erased most of the original buildings of the gold rush era. Many Gold Rush records were lost when the capital of Yukon was moved from Dawson to Whitehorse in 1953. Residents recall that boxes of documents remained in the attic of the Administration Building. The doors were left unlocked and soon many of those documents disappeared along with the government royalty tax stamp that played such an important role in the lives of miners. Among the records may have been those relating to the fate of the Ladue Company's sawmill, gold claims, hardware store and its rental properties. By the time its New Jersey charter was included on the state of New Jersey List of Certificates in 1911 as "forfeited" for "non-payment of taxes" all the company's activities had ceased. The records of the South Dakota Secretary of State's office contain no documents to indicate that any official dissolution was filed to end the company's charter issued by that state in 1903.

The extensive paper and photo archives of Parks Canada contain the history of many of Dawson's earliest buildings and are available for research. Their storage facilities hold a substantial collection of irreplaceable artifacts from the area. The Keno, one of two sternwheelers remaining in the Yukon, was originally restored for Dawson's Gold Rush Festival in 1962; a second, more thorough restoration, was completed by Parks Canada in 2001. Work on the creeks, where the Ladue Company was so heavily invested, has been curtailed significantly as claims have been worked out and government regulations have, in some instances, made mining unprofitable.

Jack McQuesten's Fort Reliance post ceased operation in the summer of 1886 and was never reopened. The primary signs that the site was ever inhabited are three impressions in the ground, one of which is thought to be the location of the store. The property is part of the Tr'ondek Hwech'in land claims settlement. The exact site of the Indian village of Nuklako has yet to be determined. It is known, however, to have been on the mainland across the Yukon River from Fort Reliance.

The Harper and Ladue trading posts on the river have long-since been abandoned. For many years after the Klondike Gold Rush,

Fort Selkirk was an active community, but gradually faded and came to an end when the riverboats ceased operation in the 1950s with the completion of the road connecting Whitehorse and Dawson. Work done by the Heritage Branch of the Yukon Government and the Selkirk First Nation has made Fort Selkirk an interesting stopping point for travelers on the Yukon River. To the casual passerby no sign remains of Joe's post at Ogilvie that Ellis Turner referred to as "a very plesent place" in 1895. Hay fields that once fed the horses working on the company's numerous timber berths are overgrown. Willows and poplars cover whatever may be left of its many cabins, barns and the store. They disappeared—used as fuel for sternwheelers, or simply fell to the ground. The trading post burned in 1923. It is a lonely place today, devoid of the "ever-smiling" trader and the men who heard his "wonderful tales" about the tributaries of the Sixty Mile and Indian Rivers. Gone, too, is the constant whine of the sawmill, vanished on the wind. It is doubtful if river travelers stop at the island; it is now only one of many along their way.

Gone, too, are the riverboats like the *Yukon*, *New Racket* (*Little Pelley*), *Beaver*, *Arctic*, *Portus B. Weare*, *Willie Irving*, *Dawson*, *Casca*, *Columbian*, *Gold Star*, *Sarah*, *Susie*, *Hannah*, *Julia B*, the Ladue Company's *Rideout* and dozens more that connected Dawson City to the outside world. Until the road to Whitehorse was completed they brought everything the people needed and each arrival was greeted as had been the stagecoaches to the earlier gold camps of California, Colorado, Deadwood, Tombstone and many others. When the whistle of the first steamer of the season announced its arrival from upriver, still out of sight around the bluff at Klondike City, pulses quickened. Residents hurried to the waterfront to meet friends who had wintered Outside. Businessmen anticipated the arrival of goods ordered the previous fall. For decades, much to the delight of tourists, a small group of intrepid Dawsonites, dressed in period costumes, met them as they stepped off the gangplanks. These hardy volunteers were the foundation of today's Klondike Visitors Association. The arrival of each steamer throughout the summer was a time of great excitement; departure of the last boat of the season, often a solemn occasion for many. For seven months they were landlocked, only a few able to afford the fare for the winter stage to Whitehorse.

After Joe's death in 1901, Kittie and their son, Francis, continued to live in the family's gracious Schuyler Falls house. The Grantee's Index of Clinton County records that on November 19, 1901, Kittie purchased 100 acres of land for $1,000 from James H. and Carrie Lobdell and on March 31, 1904, she purchased a small property from Wallace and Aurie F. Turner for $600. Francis spoke of his mother's traveling out with horse and buggy to collect rents on the Ladue properties and the frequent visits she made to the home of Willis Lamay, Francis' biological father.

On October 3, 1907, Kittie surprised her family and friends by marrying Harry Edson Tyler, 31, a wagon and cutter (small sleigh) painter, who lived in nearby Morrisonville. No children were born of this marriage. By May of 1918 the Tylers had sold the Schuyler Falls home and moved to a home on Brinkerhoff Street in Plattsburgh. Later they moved to a modest bungalow on Cordelia Street. Kittie remained active in the Methodist Church, the Daughters of the American Revolution and the Daughters of 1812. But, her heart was in the work of the Women's Christian Temperance Union of which she was a member for more than 50 years. Kittie served as a member of the Ladue Company Board of Directors for a short time and maintained her friendship with Elmer F. Botsford until his death in 1930.

Catharine "Kittie" Marie Mason Ladue Tyler died January 8, 1948, and is buried in the Mason family plot next to Joe. Upon his death in 1956 Harry Edson Tyler was also buried there.

Joe and Kittie's home in Schuyler Falls has changed hands several times. Today it is owned by a young man with historic preservation experience who is renovating it. As layers of wallpaper and plaster were peeled away, a cloth bag from Loren Weaver's Schuyler Falls potato starch factory was found along with remnants of wallpaper chosen by Joe and Kittie in the winter of 1897-1898.

Joe and Kittie's son, Francis, became a factory-trained Cadillac mechanic, married Hannah Ryan in 1923 and remained in the area until his death in 1986. After Kittie's second marriage, Joe was seldom mentioned in the home, but Francis persevered for many years seeking information about his shadowy adoptive father. Kittie gave Francis two large gold nuggets Joe had brought from the Klondike along with an American flag, displaying a field of forty stars, likely flown at Ogilvie post and in 1896 over Joe's cabin in Dawson City.

Francis' children, Joseph III, Kathryn Hannah and Nancy Jane remained in New York State. Ladue III lives approximately a two-hour drive from Joe and Kittie's home. As the custodian of the family's Yukon memorabilia, he retains the flag in his possession, Kittie's scrapbook, Joe's pocket watch and copies of Joe's two books, Klondyke Nuggets and Klondyke Facts. Regrettably, the larger of the two gold nuggets was stolen from the home several years ago.

Joe's three siblings remained in Iowa for several years. Joe's brother Andrew worked in the Black Hills for a time and then returned to Iowa where he married Caroline Floyd and raised a family. Their young son, Walter, is buried in the Center Point Cemetery. Andrew and his family moved to Missouri and later to Salem, Oregon, where he died in November 1942. Almira married James Manley on September 29, 1882, lived in Center Point, Iowa, later Montana and finally joined Andrew in Salem where she died October 6, 1937. Mary married a fellow student from the Iowa School for the Deaf, John A. Hendryx. They lived in the hamlet of Lafayette, Iowa, farming for many years. After John's death in 1934 she moved to Center Point where she died January 8, 1947. She is buried beside John in the beautiful cemetery in Lafayette. No descendants of these three children of and Marie returned to New York State. Their large number of descendants today live in Ontario, Canada, and across the United States and many are in contact with one another.

The children of Francois and Philomen: Clemence, Mary Adele "Ida," Charles and Marian "Minnie" returned to the Plattsburgh area in 1886 or 1887. Mary Adele died October 28, 1890. Philomen Favreau Burke-Laliberte Ladue died April 21, 1902, and is buried in the Old Roman Catholic Cemetery in Plattsburgh next to Mary Adele. Clemence married James Thornton. Charles married Elizabeth Delorme and died November 7, 1937. Marian married James Doyle; she died in Plattsburgh in 1967.

Although quartz mining eluded the Ladue Company, it finally got underway in the Klondike on a small scale in 1911 and continued until 1913. Adits (tunnels leading into the mine) are still visible on the Consolidated Lone Star Mining Company's diggings on Number 7 Pup which runs into Victoria Gulch on Upper Bonanza

Creek. Jerry Byrde works the property today. He owns a steam engine and a crusher from the old mill that was located several hundred yards from the adits. He also has a stamp that came from the assay building behind the Ladue Quartz Mill in Dawson.

In the Yukon today the Ladue name survives in three locations. Robert C. Coutts, in his book, *Yukon Places and Names*, records that two rivers in the Yukon bear the Ladue name: Ladue River, a tributary of the White River, named by Joe in the 1880s while prospecting, and the Ladue Keno River, a tributary to the Stewart River. In Dawson a memorial plaque overlooking his town site was dedicated August 3, 2002, during the city's centennial celebrations, by the family and friends of Joe Ladue who wished to honor him as the founder of Dawson City.

Of the original "Big Four"—Jack McQuesten, Arthur Harper, Alfred Mayo and Joe Ladue, traders, prospectors and promoters of the Yukon Valley—Mayo outlived them all and was the only one to remain in the North. He lived contentedly with his family at Rampart on the middle Yukon and died there July 18, 1923. Arthur Harper "divorced" his wife Jennie and she, and her son Walter, returned to her village on the lower Yukon. When Harper left Dawson in the fall of 1897 for San Francisco he was a wealthy man, but terminally ill. By November he had succumbed to tuberculosis while receiving treatment in Yuma, Arizona. Even six years after his death, on December 15, 1903, his estate contained "excess of assets" of $31,768. His estate had been significantly depleted over the years by withdrawals by his second wife, Erena, prior to her death in 1900 and expenses paid for seven of his eight children who had been enrolled in private schools in San Francisco. The boys borrowed advances from their legally appointed guardians and attorneys, leaving little available at final distribution. Arthur and Jennie's two daughters, Marianne (Jessie) and Margaret, however, who did not apply for advances, graduated from college and became teachers in Alaska. According to the probate file for the estate of Arthur Harper, his children (with the exception of Walter who was not included as a beneficiary in the will) continued to receive small payments from earnings of the Harper and Ladue partnership until 1920. Joe's decision to sell his share of the partnership to the company in 1897 precluded Kittie, as it had Joe, from receiving any income from the partnership.

In 1898, Jack McQuesten, affectionately referred to as the "Father of Alaska," moved with his family to Berkeley, California, overlooking San Francisco Bay. In its June 28, 1978, issue, the Berkeley Independent and Gazette wrote an article for the Berkeley Architectural Heritage Association describing the home. Their "gracious...home...on the north side of Hopkins Street" was "among the first dozen houses constructed in a grand style in Peralta Park." It displayed a complex carpentry and craftsmanship typical of the period. Its exterior architectural details were further emphasized by the "painted lady" Victorian contrast of several complimentary colors—in this case, tan, yellow and white. The house originally had a turret that was removed because of the difficulty of repairing it. Soon after the McQuestens moved in they purchased an adjacent 13-acre lot. The house remains in the McQuesten family and is occupied by one of Jack's great-grandsons.

Jack, as Al Mayo, was happily married to a Native woman. In his first letter to his family in 47 years he wrote: "I don't suppose you boys will think I did very well, when I tell you I have a full-blooded Alaskan Indian wife (I named her Kate), but I never expected to see a white woman again, so I took the best the country afforded, and we have a large family of bright children whom I dearly love." Leona Bean McQuiston included this letter in her genealogical study of the McQuesten family. An unattributed newspaper clipping forwarded to the McQuesten family in 1987 by a family friend, Fanchon L. Tunnard of Lacey, Washington, states that "When Jack died in 1909, twelve charter members of the Yukon Order of Pioneers of which he was one of the first, sent his widow a beautiful clock, ordered from Germany, as an indication of his popularity."

Harold H. Pitts of London, "a man of wonderful character and integrity" who came into the country in 1882 with Joe, purchased the trading post at Fort Selkirk from the Harper Estate and remained there until his death on January 3, 1913, at age 64. He is buried in the Fort Selkirk Cemetery.

The cash journal for the estate of Arthur Harper, deceased, dated 1903 shows that "Sixty Mile Post" and the steamer *New Racket* (Harper's *Little Pelley*) were sold on December 10 of that year for \$1,284—\$575.50 in "gold dust," plus \$708.50 in "currency." Another entry was for $750 paid to the Harper Estate by S. O. Morford. A May 1904 report indicates that another $750 was yet due from him. These amounts were likely payments owed by Morford following the settling of the suit brought against him by Harper and Ladue in the fall of 1898. No record was found of Alexy, Joe's Creole friend and interpreter. It is possible that he assumed the Ladue name and remained in the area for some time. The mortuary records in Dawson City record the death of three-year-old Rachel Ladue of meningitis at St. Mary's Hospital on September 12, 1934. A note in the record states, "child of Joe Ladue," from Fort Selkirk. One First Nation family bearing the Ladue surname resides in the Yukon today.

The Han no longer live at Nuklako or maintain their fish camp (Tr'ochek) at the mouth of the Klondike. They live and work in Dawson year round; some spend time during summer months at their village of Moosehide downriver midway between Dawson and the site of Fort Reliance. Many hunt moose and caribou throughout the area, including in their traditional hunting grounds in the uplands of the Blackstone River and in the Tombstone Mountains. Today, the Han at Dawson prefer to be known as the Tr'ondek Hwech'in and are proud to be recognized as one of Canada's First Nations. Slowly they are recovering from the great changes brought about by the arrival of white men and are in the process of rediscovering and recording the stories and customs of their proud culture.

On April 18, 1906, a devastating earthquake struck San Francisco followed by raging fires. The Alaska Commercial Company headquarters at 310 Sansome Street was among the victims. Lost in the wreckage were the majority of the records of McQuesten, Harper, Mayo, Joe, the Merciers and many others who traded for the company up and down the Yukon River. Fortunately, the rare collection of Indian artifacts gathered by Alaska Commercial Company traders since it began business on the Yukon in 1868 had already been moved to the Ferry Building, which was spared. They remain today as part of the Hearst Collection housed in the Phoebe A. Hearst Museum of Anthropology at the University of California, Berkeley. Carefully catalogued and preserved, the artifacts provide a fleeting glimpse into the past and the lives of Indian people along the Yukon

River who loved and respected men like Jack McQuesten, Arthur Harper, Al Mayo and Joe Ladue.

After Joe's death and by the time most of the other pioneers had left the country, a young bank clerk arrived in the Yukon and over the next several years wrote poems—rhymes he called them—about the land, the people he met and the men who had risked all to search for gold. Many of his rhymes are masterpieces, capturing the imagination, illuminating dreams, speaking of gold and unimaginable wealth, of boundless freedom, unspeakable hardship and bitter disappointment. One wonders how Joseph Ladue, Jack McQuesten, Arthur Harper, Al Mayo, William Moore, Frank Dinsmore, "Slim Jim" Wynn and other earliest of venturers into the Yukon would view the territory, characters and plots in Robert Service's rhymes. Would they have agreed that:

> There's a land where the mountains are nameless,
> And the rivers all run God knows where;
> There are lives that are erring and aimless,
> And deaths that just hang by a hair;
> There are hardships that nobody reckons;
> There are valleys unpeopled and still;
> There's a land—oh, it beckons and beckons,
> And I want to go back—and I will.
> from "The Spell of the Yukon," Robert Service

Ladue Genealogy

Descendants of Francois and Marie Pelletier Ledoux

Francois Ledoux was the son of Gabriel Ledoux and Marie Metevier. Marie Pelletier was the daughter of Andre Pelletier and Charlotte Caron. Francois and Marie were born and married in the Province of Quebec. Their first child, John, was born and died in Quebec. Later Ledoux offspring were born in New York State.

Immigration officials often guessed at the spelling of the names of those crossing borders and entering harbors, or took it upon themselves to change or simplify the names. That may have happened in the case of Francois and Marie. At any rate, variations and interpretations of spellings of the French surname were located in baptismal, funeral and real estate records, census reports, obituaries, on cemetery markers, in Mary Ladue Hendryx's Scrapbook and other sources used for this biography.

Variations of Family Surname

Francois	Ledoux Ladoo Ledou Ladou Ladue La Due
Marie	Pelletier Peletier Pelky

Descendants of Francois Ledoux and Marie Pelletier

Given names (with variations in spelling) of Francois Ledoux and Marie Pelletier's children

Elmire	Elmira Almira Elvira
Joseph	
Celina	Celine Alena Alenza
Pierre	Peter
Andre	Andrew
Francis	Frank
Marie Catherine	Mary
Jean	John

Children of Almira Ladue 1852-1937 and James Manley

Francis E.

Orvil

Silas Lee (later known as Joseph Kepp)

Children of Joseph Kepp (Silas Lee Manley) and Lucy Mae Lusk

Mavis Andrea 1928-

Donna Leigh 1934-

Carl Joseph 1940-

Children of Donna Leigh Kepp and John Tremblay

Gregory Lucien 1954-

Brenda Leigh 1956-

Jocelyn Ann 1958

Gary Robert 1960 (adopted son)

Children of Andrew Melvin La Due 1859-1942 and Caroline Floyd

Archibald Milton 1886-1962

Victor Mason 1887-1981

Mary Frances 1888-1974

John Doble 1891-1944

Walter Floyd 1893-1897

Lloyd Lee 1901-1940

Children of Victor Mason La Due and Ethel Ada Knox

Sarah Caroline 1914-

Melvin Willis 1916-

Maxine Opal 1918-1974

Keith Calvin 1926-

Children of Keith Calvin La Due and Viola Maye Colling

Kevin Randolph 1953-

Cheryl Kathleen 1955-

Rebecca Susan 1958-

Children of Mary Catherine Ladue 1862-1947 and John A. Hendryx

Charles

George

Robert

Richard J.

Walter

Judson

Frank

Flora L.

Given names of Francois Ledoux and Philomen (Philomene, Phileman, Filomen, Filleman) Favreau Burke-Laliberte's Children

Clemence Thais	Climma		Kitine
Mary Adele	Mary	"Ida"	
Marian	Mina	Mimi	Minnie
Charles			

Children of Joseph Francis Ladue 1854-1901 and Catherine Marie "Kittie" Mason

Cecil William Lamay/Joseph Francis Ladue (II) 1899-1986 (adopted son)

Children of Joseph Francis Ladue (II) and Hannah K. Ryan

Joseph Francis Ladue (III) 1924-
Kathryn Hannah 1925-
Nancy Jane 1936-

Children of Joseph Francis Ladue (III) and Anita M. Poissant

Mary Jo (now bearing the married name Goth) 1948-
Stanley 1950-
Lou Ann (now bearing the married name Judge) 1951-
Susan (now bearing the married name Tong) 1955-
Joan (now bearing the married name Veracruse) 1956-
Carol (now bearing the married name Doyle) 1958-
Christine (now bearing the married name Paine) 1959-
Michael 1963-

Given Names of Andre Burke-Laliberte (Laliberte, Liberty) and Philemon Favreau's Children

Philomene	Minna
Rose Delima	Delia
Joseph	
Salomon	

Philomene Burke-Laliberte (daughter) 1855-1935 married William Jasper Denison at Center Point, Iowa.
Rose Delima (Delia) Burke-Laliberte c. 1858 married Hilaire Bouteillier (aka Eli Butler) lived in Beekmantown, New York until her death.
Joseph Burke-Laliberte b. 1859-?
Salomon Burke-Laliberte b. 1862-?

Yukon Chronology

8000 B.C. Native American peoples from Asia have reached the geographic area that will become known as the Yukon.
800 A.D. The Athabaskan culture is well established in the Yukon.
1820 Coastal northern Yukon becomes known to Europeans when British explorer, Sir John Franklin, maps part of the Arctic while seeking the Northwest Passage.
1840 July 19—Hudson's Bay Company trader Robert Campbell first arrives in the Yukon, and names Frances Lake.
1842 August 16—Robert Campbell returns from Fort Halkett and constructs a trading post on Frances Lake. He names it Glenlyon House.
1846 Spring—*Hudson's Bay Company* establishes a trading post (Lapierre's House) on the Bell River, a tributary of the Porcupine. Robert Campbell establishes a trading post at Pelly Banks.
1848 June 1—Robert Campbell, his Indian interpreter, Kitsa, James Stewart, other *Hudson's Bay* employees, their Indian wives and a number of Indian hunters from the Liard River arrive at the junction of the Pelly and Lewes Rivers.
June 30—Fur trading commences.
Early September—construction of post buildings completed at Fort Selkirk...
1852 August 19—Chilkats arrive at the fort and begin looting and destroying buildings.
August 22—Campbell flees downriver; Fort Selkirk is abandoned.
September 6—Campbell leaves via Pelly Banks and Frances Lake for Fort Simpson
1867 March 30—The U.S. purchases Alaska from Russia for $7.2 million.
1869 July 31—Captain Charles Raymond of the U.S. Corps of Engineers arrives at Fort Yukon via the Yukon River to investigate whether the Hudson's Bay post is in American territory. With the departure of *Hudson's Bay Company* the Alaska Commercial Company establishes a trading post at Fort Yukon.
1873 August 15—Jack McQuesten, Arthur Harper, Alfred Mayo, Fred Harte and several others arrive at Fort Yukon via the Mackenzie, Peel and Porcupine Rivers.
1874 August—Jack McQuesten and Frank Banfield establish Fort Reliance (six miles downriver from what would become Dawson City) for the *Alaska Commercial Company*
1882 September 5—Joe Ladue and five other prospectors arrive at Fort Reliance.
1886 August—Fort Reliance abandoned. McQuesten and Company establish Fort Nelson at the mouth of the Stewart River.
September —Coarse gold is discovered on the Forty Mile River.
1887 George M. Dawson explores the northern portion of British Columbia and travels down the Pelly to the site of Robert Campbell's Fort Selkirk. Behind schedule, he returns to the coast via Chilkoot Pass, never seeing the site of Dawson City later named for him by Joe Ladue.
1890 Joe Ladue and Arthur Harper establish trading posts on Sixty Mile Island and at the site of Fort Selkirk.

1894 December 1—The *Yukon Order of Pioneers* is organized at Forty Mile.
1896 August 16—Skookum Jim Mason, Dawson Charlie, George and Kate Carmack travel up Rabbit Creek where gold is discovered in such quantity that Carmack renames the creek Bonanza.
August 24 Joe Ladue marks the perimeter of the Dawson town site
September 1—Ladue begins construction of the first cabin in Dawson.
Ladue moves the Harper and Ladue sawmill from their Ogilvie post to Dawson.
November 6—All uncertainty regarding the richness of Bonanza Creek ends when one pan of dirt nets $3.35. This is soon followed by $18, $22 and finally an $800 pan on Eldorado.
1897 Early June—Dawson's population is about 500; 1,500, including those on the creeks. Most live in tents. Nellie Cashman arrives in Dawson, files on mining claims and establishes a grocery store.
July 15—The steamer *Excelsior* carrying Joe Ladue and other successful Klondike gold miners docks at San Francisco. Two days later, the North American Trading and Transportation Company steamer *Portland* "The Gold Ship," docks in Seattle. The news begins a world-wide stampede to Dawson City and the Klondike.
August— Dawson's population is about 3,000.
1898 Early Summer—Dawson has a population of 30,000 with equal numbers scattered on nearby creeks. Two sawmills work 24 hours a day turning out lumber for houses, businesses and sluice boxes.
June 13—Yukon Territory given Royal Assent.
July 4—William Ogilvie is appointed Commissioner of the Yukon.
August—By the Dominion Act of Parliament, the Yukon Territory is established.
August 27—Joe Ladue returns to Dawson. On September 6 he leaves, never to see his town again.
October 14—A fire burns 40 buildings in the Dawson business district with total losses over a half million dollars.
1899 A fire burns 111 buildings in the Dawson business district with losses estimated at over a million dollars. As the ashes cool they are panned for gold.
May—Steamers, barges, scows, canoes and rafts ply the Yukon. Some bring supplies such as fresh milk, although eggs are still scarce.
June 14—The exodus begins to the new gold strike on the beaches of Nome, Alaska.
July 4—After celebrating Dominion Day on July 1, a gunshot, one minute after midnight announces the Fourth and 10,000 jubilant Americans and Canadians fill the streets to celebrate.
August—In the last week 8,000 leave town.
1898-1900 *White Pass and Yukon Railway*. From 1898 construction is in progress, the rails reaching Whitehorse July 29, 1900.
September- Lewes River Mining and Dredging Company operates the first gold dredge on Cassiar Bar in the Yukon River.
1901 June 27—Joe Ladue dies at his Schuyler Falls home, at age 46. A fire burns Dawson's Second Avenue, destroying all property facing Third Street. Martha Louise

Munger returns to Dawson to manage the family's sawmill and 2-stamp quartz mill.
1902 Yukon Territory selects its first member to the Dominion Parliament with full voting rights.
1905 Robert Service arrives, hired as a ledger keeper in the Canadian Bank of Commerce at Whitehorse where he becomes inspired to write about the human drama of the Klondike Gold Rush.
1907 Robert Service's first book, Songs of a Sourdough, is published.
1908 Robert Service is transferred to the Bank of Commerce in Dawson.
1909 Jack McQuesten dies September 8 in Berkeley, California, at age 73.
The population of Dawson dwindles to 6,000.
1914 At the outbreak of WWI, successful miner Joe Boyle offers to raise a force of men from the Klondike. A machine gun battery fully equipped by Boyle leaves Dawson on board the steamer *Lightning*.
1916 "Skookum Jim," whose legal name was James Mason, establishes in his will the "Skookum Jim Indian Fund." Native people in the Yukon still benefit from Jim's generosity.
1918 October 25—Two weeks before the end of WWI, the *Princess Sophia*, taking northerners Outside for the season, strikes Vanderbilt Reef between Skagway and Juneau, Alaska. All 343 on board perish.
1920 March 20—Kate Carmack dies in Carcross during an influenza epidemic.
1922 June 5—George Carmack dies in Seattle at age 62.
1932 The world-wide Depression reaches Dawson City and, as jobs become scarce; many leave for the Outside.
1935 Martha Louise Munger Black is elected to Parliament as an Independent Conservative from the Yukon.
1942 (during WWII)—About 30,000 American and Canadian workers labor on construction of the Alaska Highway and the Canol Pipeline.
1953 Yukon's capital is moved from Dawson to Whitehorse.
1959 July—Queen Elizabeth II visits the Yukon.
1962 Parks Canada, after constructing a replica of the Palace Grand Theatre and restoring the steamer *Keno*, (the last sternwheeler to travel downriver to Dawson City) begins an ambitious program to preserve Dawson's gold rush sites, artifacts and reference material.
1966 *Yukon Consolidated Gold Corporation* closes its last operating dredge and ceases all activities in the Klondike Valley.
1979 A devastating flood occurs when the Yukon River ice goes out. The government soon constructs the protective dike along Dawson's waterfront.
2001 Dawson's population is 2,059.
2002 August 3—A bronze plaque honoring Joe Ladue as founder of Dawson City, is placed on the river walk overlooking his town site.

Notes

Roots

1 McLellan Cemetery Records of Clinton County; Baptisms, St. Peter's Parish, Plattsburgh, N.Y.,1853-1870, Office of the Clinton County Historian, Government Records.

2 Victor La Due to Francis Ladue, Salem, Orgeon 16 March 1976, Joseph F. Ladue III Collection; Ronald Scott Hendryx: Interview by the authors. Center Point, Iowa, October 2000.

3 St. Peter's Church Census, 1857, Baptisms, St. Peter's Parish,1853-1870; Church Records; Mary Ladue Hendryx scrapbook; no stone for Pierre could be found in the Irish Settlement Cemetery, Schuyler Falls.

4 Mariage de St.-Antoine-sur le Richlieux, 1741-1965, National Archives of Canada; Genealogical records list differing dates: 2/11/1850 and 11/2/1850. The correct reading is "November 2, 1850."

5 Mary Ladue Hendryx scrapbook.

6 U.S. Census 1860, Schuyler Falls, N.Y.; Clinton County Gazetteer for 1862, Office of the Clinton County Historian, Government Records. Francois Ladue's occupation is listed as "bricklayer."

7 *Souvenir Industrial Edition of Plattsburgh*, 1897 (Plattsburgh Press), pp. 18-20.

8 Duane Hamilton Hurd. History of Clinton and Franklin Counties, N.Y., 1880, Office of the Clinton County Historian.

9 *Beers Atlas 1869*, Plattsburgh and Schuyler Falls, Office of the Clinton County Historian, Government Records; Historical Marker, placed by Schuyler Falls, n.d.

10 Baptisms, St. Peter's Parish, 1853-1870; U.S. Census 12 June 1860, Schuyler Falls, New York; Mary Ladue Hendryx scrapbook.

11 Baptisms, St. Peter's Parish, 1853-1870; Grantee's Index A-Z, "Ledoux, Francois from Rock, Joseph, 21 May 1857," vol. 32, p. 58, Clinton County Clerk's Office, Government Records; McMasters, Clinton County's Man in Alaska, Joseph Ladue, North Country Notes, (February 1971), Clinton County Historical Association.

12 "Roy Vaughn of Beckwith Street, now living, says that his father, as a young boy, carried mortar for a Mr. Ladue, father of Joe, while building the Southerland house on Beckwith Street." (in Plattsburgh), stated local historian Emily McMasters in a 1966 interview documenting Francois' work in the Plattsburgh area.

13 Baptisms, St. Peter's Parish.

14 Ibid.

Another son, Salomon, born 20 February 1862, never appeared in the St. Peter's Church census or in the U.S. Census for 1870 or 1880, nor was he listed as a surviving child when Philomen's estate was probated.

15 St. Peter's Church, Marriages 1830-1880, Office of the Clinton County Historian, Government Records.

16 Mary Ladue Hendryx scrapbook records his death as 10 August 1866.

17 Grantee's Index A-Z, 1866, "Ladue, Francois from Brand, James and Fanny," volume 53, p. 546, Clinton County Clerk's Office, Government Records.

18 Baptisms, St. Peter's Parish.

19 Grantor's Index IV, 1865-1875, p. 973, 12 March 1869 "Ladue, Francois and Philomene to Lobdell, Nathan," Clinton County Clerk's Office, Government Records.

20 Article, Center Point Lotus, n.d., in Mary Ladue Hendryx's scrapbook. This biographical article is about Brunson M. Hilliard (then living). Mary had written the date "1926" across the top of the clipping.

21 U.S. Census July 19, 1870, Washington Township, Center Point, Iowa, in Mary Ladue Hendryx's scrapbook.

22 U.S. Census 1870, Schuyler Falls, Clinton County, N.Y.; Beers Atlas 1869.

23 McMasters, "Clinton County's Man in Alaska," *North Country Notes*, Clinton County Historical Association. Although the term "protectory" indicates destitution or delin-

quency, neither the Ladue family nor any other source suggests that Joe was either.

24 Beers Atlas 1869.

25 John Sleicher, "The Original King of the Klondike: Remarkable Career of Joseph Ladue, The Founder of Dawson City," *Leslie's Illustrated Weekly Magazine*, 16 September 1897. If Joe was placed in the care of James Henry Lobdell at "the age of nine," he would have left home prior to his mother's death in 1865. That seems unlikely; the arrangement may have occurred when Francois and Philomen married in April the following year, when Joe was 11. He never stated why "he found some things uncongenial" at home. In 1897 when Sleicher reported it, many years had passed and Joe could easily have been mistaken about his age at the time. When Joe died, neither Philomen nor her children, were listed as surviving family members in his obituary, but neither were his own siblings,], Mary and Andrew.

26 McMasters, "Clinton County's Man in Alaska," *North Country Notes*; Beers Atlas 1869.

27 McMasters, "Clinton County's Man in Alaska," North Country Notes.

28 *Beers Atlas 1869*; U.S. Census, Clinton County, N.Y., 12 August 1870.

29 Ibid.

30 On-site visit, 1999.

31 Hendryx scrapbook.

32 U.S. Census 1860, Schuyler Falls, and Washington Township, Linn County, Center Point, Iowa, 19 July 1870; Hendryx scrapbook.

33 Hendryx scrapbook.

34 U.S. Census 1880, Washington Township, Troy Mills, Iowa; Obituary, Charles Ladue, d.o.d., 7 November 1937, Plattsburgh Sentinel, n.d.

35 Victor La Due to Francis Ladue, Salem Orgeon, 16 March 1976 Ronald Scott Hendryx Interviewed by the authors Center Point, Iowa, October 2000.

36 Iowa Cemetery Records, Benton County, Iowa, Placement Lot 2, Iowa State Historical Society; Victor Ladue to Francis Ladue; Hendryx scrapbook. A stone marker, similar to those made for Marie and her two children in Schuyler Falls, was erected on his grave. His site is located at the far corner of the cemetery. The stone was not listed as an expense to his estate at the time it was administered, and the name of the purchaser is not known.

37 Sleicher, "The Original King," *Leslie's Illustrated Weekly Magazine*, n.d.

38 Linn County Probate, vol. 11, p. 540, 11 February 1875; vol. 3, p. 44, parts 1 and 2; vol. 11, p. 543, 23 February 1875; vol. 13, p. 126, 3 January 1876; vol. 13, p. 252, 29 May 1876; vol. 13, p. 323, 11 August 1876; vol.13, p. 530, parts 1 and 2, June 1877; vol. 13, p. 529, 4 June 1877, Office of the Circuit Court, Linn County, Iowa, Government Records.

39 U.S. Census 1880, Washington Township, Troy Mills, Iowa.

40 Obituary, Charles Ladue, d.o.d., 7 November 1937, Plattsburgh Sentinel, n.d. The obituary stated that when Charles was 16 years old he returned to New York with his family.

41 Clinton County Marriages 1830-1880, Northern New York American-Canadian Genealogical Society. The Society provided the information that "Rose Delima/Delia Born 31 July 1858 Plattsburgh, N.Y. married Hilaire/Eli Bouteillier/Butler, 25 Feb. 1878 Plattsburgh, N.Y."

According to the American Catholic website, "Index of Saints," St. Rose of Lima (Santa Rosa de Lima) lived in Peru from 1586-1617 and was the first canonized saint of the "New World."

Philomen's son, Joseph Laliberte, who was recorded in the U.S. Census for Iowa in 1870 and 1880 disappears from family accounts beyond that date. He did not appear as a surviving child in probate documents at the time of his mother's death in 1902.

42 Victor La Due to Francis Ladue, Salem, Orgeon, 16 March 1976

The American West
The Black Hills: 1876-1880

1 Parker, Gold in the Black Hills, p. 6.

2 Joel Waterland, *The Spawn and the Mother Lode*, p. 10

NOTES

3 Parker, pp. 36-37.
4 Ibid. p.71.
5 Cy and Jeannie Martin, *Gold and Where They Found It*, p. 59.
6 Martha McKeown, *Them Was The Days: An American Saga of the '70s*, p. 169.
7 Bennett, *Old Deadwood Days*, p. 71. Ms. Bennett states the first stage to arrive in Deadwood was September 26, 1876. Anyone entering the Hills prior to that date would have walked, ridden horseback or accompanied a wagon freight train.
8 Ibid. p.71.
9 Marc Simmons, Santa Fe Reporter, 20-26 September 2000. A noted western historian, Dr. Simmons published a column in the weekly Reporter. His column "*Trail Dust*" now appears in the Saturday edition of Santa Fe New Mexican.
10 Dick Lloyd, Outlaw Country: A Map & Guide to the Cheyenne-Blackhills Express Route and the Sydney-Deadwood Trail. Brochures.
11 Bennett, p. 10.
12 Sleicher, "The Original King," *Leslie's Illustrated Weekly Magazine*, n.d.
13 Ibid.
14 Waterland, p. 52.
15 Sleicher, "The Original King."
16 Victor La Due to Francis Ladue.
17 Sleicher, "The Original King." The U.S. Department of Treasury had been printing detailed mining reports since the California gold rush of 1849. Joe may have studied those reports that described methods and production of placer and quartz mining.
18 Parker, *Deadwood: The Golden Years*, p. 226.
19 Ibid. pp. 226-227.
20 Parker, *Deadwood*, photo facing p. 115, source unidentified; Bennett, p. 25. At the Adams Museum in Deadwood there is a photograph on file of the Merchants Hotel in which the sign "Sidney Stage" is clearly visible.
21 Sleicher, "*The Original King*."
22 McMasters, "Clinton County's Man in Alaska," *North Country Notes*.
The confusion about the final destination of Lewis may have occurred since abbreviations at the time for Colorado, Col., and California, Cal., were frequently misread by researchers, particularly when notes appeared in cursive form.
23 Emily McMasters to Ed and Star Jones, Plattsburgh, N.Y. c.1965.
24 Ibid
25 McQuesten, Recollections, p. 11, Yukon Archives.
26 Leonard, *The Gold Fields of the Klondike*, p. 31.
27 Bennett, p. 156. Ms. Bennett writes of a man who gambled to earn a 50 cent fare for the short stagecoach ride from Deadwood to Central City. After the stage had waited half an hour, he was found still "beside the faro table...coppering bets and writing orders on future wages." Joe Ladue's generous salary of $10.00 per day, and the low living costs in shared accommodations leaves historians wondering why he frequently was without funds.
28 Ibid. p. 68.
29 U.S. Census, 1880, Rochford, Pennington, Dakota Territory.
30 Ibid.
31 Bennett, p. 142. While Joe shared a residence with another man, it was common in the Black Hills mining camps for workers to live in boarding houses where inexpensive accommodations were provided. In nineteenth century America boarding houses were available for men who rafted logs down waterways, to miners, drovers, tannery workers and to women laboring in the textile and shoe mills.
32 Parker, *Deadwood*, p. 67, states that "miners' pay days (were) the sixteenth and twenty-sixth of each month."
33 Petition, District Court of Iowa in and for Linn County (Iowa), no docket number, Genealogical Society of Linn County, Iowa; Andrew Ladue Claim against the Estate of Joseph F. Ladue, Clinton County Clerk's Office, Government Records.

New Mexico and Arizona: 1880-1881

34 Victor La Due to Francis Ladue. (year & date?) Victor wrote that Joe was "next heard from in New Mexico and Arizona."

35 Marilyn Butler, Destination Tombstone, pp. 16-18.

36 1878-1880 Pima County (Arizona) Great Register; Cochise County (Arizona) Great Register, Arizona History and Archives Division, Arizona Department of Libraries, Archives & Public Records.

37 State Bureau of Mines and Mineral Resources, Directory of Mines of New Mexico, 1965. (text and map: Metal Mining Districts and Subdistricts, New Mexico.) New Mexico Institute of Mining and Technology, Socorro, New Mexico.

38 Robert Julyan, *The Place Names of New Mexico*, p. 148.

39 Robert W. Eveleth, Senior Mining Engineer New Mexico Bureau of Mines & Mineral Resources, to Ed and Star Jones, [New Mexico], 16 February 1999.

40 *Patent Mining Books: Book 3*, pp. 441-448, 676; Book 4, pp. 35-41, 222-223, 226; Book 5, pp. 33-34, 38-40, 46, 103-104, 181-182, 185, 235-236. Grant County Clerk's Office, New Mexico , Silver City, New Mexico, Government Records.

41 Myrick, *Railroads of Arizona, vol. 1*, The Southern Railroads, p. 58.

42 Alvin M. Josephy Jr., *500 Nations*, pp. 421, 423, 425; Reader's Digest Association, Through Indian Eyes, pp. 322-323; Robert M. Utley, Encyclopedia of the American West, p. 14.

43 Ralph Emerson Twitchell, *The Leading Facts of New Mexican History, vol. 2*, pp. 436-437.

44 *Tombstone Epitaph*, 19 April 1881.

45 Marvin Lewis, *The Mining Frontier*, p. 40.

46 Butler, p. 18.

47 *Tombstone Epitaph*, 26 October 1881.

48 Ledbetter, *Nellie Cashman, Prospector and Trailblazer*, p. 15.

49 Rochlin, "Nellie Cashman: Gold Digger of '77," *Ms. Magazine*, 1973, pp. 282-283.

50 John Clum, *Nellie Cashman: The Angel of Tombstone*. John Clum was a respected man whose various professions included editor and publisher of the Tombstone Epitaph, mayor of Tombstone, Arizona and Indian Agent in Alaska.

51 van Clyde Lake, *Irish Nellie: Angel of the Cassiar*, Alaska Sportsman, (1963).

52 Clum, *Nellie Cashman*.

The Yukon Years: 1882-1898
Wonderful Prospects in Newly-Found Places

1 Wright, "The Yukon Gold Fields," *The Nation*, 5 August 1897, p.105; Jack McQuesten to Al Mayo Forty Mile winter 1886-87, Snow Collection, Yukon Archives. Alexander von Humboldt (1769-1859) was a German aristocrat, natural scientist, explorer, geographer, geologist and archaeologist. Most of the early traders and miners carried in their packs two "bibles," the Holy Bible and a volume of Humboldt's writings. During the long winters the miners frequently met to study and discuss one or both. Humboldt was a prolific writer. The volume carried by the miners was likely *Cosmos, Geognostic Essay on the Trend of Rocks in Two Hemispheres* (1822) or one of the 30 vol. of *Voyages de Humboldt et Bonpland 1799-1804*.

2 Young, Hall Young of *Alaska: An Autobiography*, p. 80.

3 Stein, "The Gold Fields of Alaska," *Review of Reviews*, 13, (June 1896); Wright, The Nation, pp. 105-106.

4 After his return over the Chilkoot Pass the fall of 1875, Holt was employed as a trader for the Alaska Commercial Co. and was killed by an Indian at the Knik trading post in 1885. He is buried in Kodiak next to the Russian Orthodox Church. (Brooks, *Blazing Alaska's Trails*, pp. 321-322).

Ivan Petrof, who conducted the first census of Alaska, wrote in The Population and Resources of Alaska, 1880 that in 1874 a group of miners from British Columbia had crossed over the Chilkoot to the headwaters of the Yukon, descending it for some distance and finding "prospects" of gold in a few localities. Petrof, however, provided no evidence to sup-

port his claim (Petrof, p. 208) and none was located in other sources.
5 *Pacific Coast Pilot*, 1883, Fogler Library, University of Maine, pp. 200-278; Ogilvie, *Early Days on the Yukon*, p. 105.
6 Dominion Lands Surveyor William Ogilvie wrote: "This Territory (Yukon) is bounded on the south by the 60th parallel of latitude, on the east by the watershed between the basins of the Yukon and Mackenzie Rivers, on the west by the 141st meridian west of Greenwich or the International Boundary line, and on the north by the waters of the Arctic Ocean." (Ogilvie, *The Klondike Official Guide*, p. 83)
7 In Ladue's book, *Klondyke Facts*, published in 1897, Willliam Ogilvie, early surveyor of the Alaska/Canadian boundary (later Commissioner of the Yukon) is quoted as saying that "The Tagish (Indians of the interior) are little more than slaves to the more powerful coast tribes, and are in constant dread of offending them in any way." (p. 43)
8 Quinan, Discoverer of the Yukon Gold Fields, *Overland Monthly*, (October 1897).
9 Ibid.
10 *Sitka Post*, 20 October 1876.
11 Dawson, Report on an Exploration in the Yukon District, N.W.T. and Adjacent Northern Portion of British Columbia, 1887, p. 179. Klotz-Kutch (Chartrich) was the Tlingit Chilkat chief of the Wolf clan who led all his tribe on the raid to pillage and destroy the Hudson's Bay Co. post at Ft. Selkirk, (George T. Emmons, *The Tlingit Indians*, p. 39) and perhaps Pelly Banks and Ft. Frances in 1852, although they had been closed for some time. Richard Coutts in *Yukon Places and Names* also states that "local natives later burned the Ft. Selkirk's buildings to get the iron fittings for tools." (p. 102) Ed Ferrell, in *Biographies of Alaska-Yukon Pioneers* mentions one Endi-Ank, his father and brother, Sculdahoo ("the most famous medicine man on the coast") as having been with the raiding party. (Ferrell, *Daily Alaskan*, Volume 2, pp.86-87, Skagway, March 17, 1899).
12 One contributor to the *Snow Collection* wrote that the Chilkats had early
established a large trading & council house on Marsh & another at the head of 30 mile river. When they heard about the new Hudson Bay's Post at Selkirk, they all gathered at the council house on Marsh lake & had a big Pow Wow, winding up with a war dance. A stick indian who happened to overhear the Pow-Wows made his escape in a birch bark canoe & warned the people at Ft. Selkirk that the Chilcats were going to raid their Post. In consequence of which the friendly Stick Indians from different parts of the river gathered at Selkirk to help the white men repel the raiders on the post. They remained there nearly all summer, as the Chilkats did not show up the Sticks came to the conclusion that the raid had been postponed until the following year & as it was getting late in the Season & the salmon were running, they all went down the river to catch their winter supply of fish, but unfortunately it so happened that the second day after their departure the Chilkats arrived in large force, the Ft. being unguarded by a stockade the indians forced their way into the post. After murdering 2 of the inmates, the rest of the white men yielding to the sheer force of numbers fled down the river, leaving the Post to be pillaged by the Chilkats. (Snow Collection, Yukon Archives.)
13 Captain L.A. Beardslee, Report of Commander L.A. Beardslee, USN Relative to the Affairs of Alaska and the Operations of the USS Jamestown, p. 61, New Mexico State Library. Lester Anthony Beardslee was born in Little Falls, New York 1 February 1836. He graduated from the U.S. Naval Academy in 1856, and was promoted through the grades to Rear Admiral. He died in Augusta, Georgia, 10 November 1903 and is buried in Arlington National Cemetery, Arlington, Virginia. (arlingtoncemetery.com/labeard.htm)
14 George Dawson recorded that by the time the party arrived at Lake Lindeman its number had increased to 25. One of the six who joined the original 19 was R. Steel. (*Dawson Report*, p. 179)

"Slim Jim" Wynn and Johnny Mackenzie also crossed the Chilkoot that summer, arriving at Lake Lindeman July 3, one day before the Bean party started out across that lake. Dawson also states, "It is possible that other parties as well entered the country in that year; but if so, I have been unable to trace them." (Dawson, Report, p. 180)

James "Slim Jim" Wynn was born at Cornwall, England in 1840. In 1872 he was prospecting in the Cassiar region of British Columbia. He died in Juneau 24 August 1916. (*Anchorage Daily Times*, 24 August 1916.)

15 Lt. McClellan's instructions were to transport the miners to the "Chilkhat" village and to leave them there only when he was certain that the chiefs would keep their promise to allow them safe passage through their country and over the Chilkoot Pass. He was also instructed to have with him on the launch a gatling gun, and that he and all the men who accompanied him should "wear uniform and sidearm" when "interviewing" the chiefs.(Beardslee, Report, p. 61)

16 Beardslee, Report, p. 61; Pacific Coast Pilot, pp. 200-278; Alaskan Census Records,1870-1907, Rasmuson Library, University of Alaska Fairbanks; Dall, Alaska and the New Gold Fields, *The Forum*, winter, 1897.

Spellings of some names differ with source. Spellings in parentheses were located in Alaskan Census Records, 1870-1907.

17 Whipsawing required the construction of a platform on which logs could be placed. The platform was high enough off the ground to allow for a man to stand under it. With another man on top, the saw was pulled first up, then down to make boards or planks. The lasting quality of many partnerships was tested when whip-sawing was underway and the man below was constantly showered with sawdust.

18 *Dawson Report*, pp. 179-180.

19 *Pacific Coast Pilot*, p. 200.

20 *Dawson Report*, p. 180; Brooks, Blazing Alaska's Trails, p. 325.

21 Dall, *Alaska and its Resources*, pp. 336-338; Lieutenant Zagoskin's Travels in Russian America, 1842-1844, introduction, pp. 275, 355; Brooks, *Blazing Alaska's Trails*, p. 220.

St. Michael's Island is about 17 miles long, 13 miles wide and is separated from the mainland by a narrow, shallow channel. It has a rolling, barren surface with no trees. There is no harbor there nor any true harbor along the entire coast of Norton Sound, but St. Michael's does shelter the nearest anchorage from most of the prevailing winds.(*Reconnoissance of the Yukon River, Alaska Territory*, pp. 21,30; Raymond, *Reconnaissance of the Yukon River, Alaska Territory*, July to September 1869, pp. 14, 25-26.

22 Dall, *Alaska and Its Resources*, pp. 338-339; Whymper, *Travel and Adventure in the Territory of Alaska*, p. 169; Schwatka, *A Reconnaissance of the Yukon Valley*, 1883, p. 322; Ogilvie, *Early Days*, p. 20; Raymond, "The Yukon River Region, Alaska," *Journal of the American Geographical Society of New York*, p. 173; Raymond, *Report of a Reconnaissance of The YukonRiver*, July to September, 1869, p. 15. New Mexico State Library.

No evidence was located to indicate that the Russian American Co. ever traded at Ft. Yukon or traveled farther upriver than Nuklukayet. One of its employees, Ivan Simonsen Lukin, a Creole, did travel to Ft. Yukon in 1863 posing as a defector from the Co. to observe the trade the Hudson's Bay Co. was carrying on with Indians in that section of the river. (Raymond, *Reconnaissance*, July to September 1869, p. 15; Brooks, *A Reconnaissance in the White and Tanana River Basins*, p. 437; Pierce, p. 73) Captain Charles Raymond, Chief of Engineers of the U.S. Corps of Topographical Engineers, reported that William Dall, who had been Director of the Scientific Corps of the Western Union Telegraph Expedition in Alaska from 1865-1868, had given him the same date for Lukin's visit to Ft. Yukon. (Raymond, "*The Yukon River Region, Alaska*," p. 160); see also, George M. Dawson, *Historical Note on Events in the Yukon District, Northwest Territories*, in Review of Historical Publications Relating to Canada, p. 178)

According to George Adams, a member of the Western Union Telegraph Expedition from 1865-1867, Lukin was "very intelligent" and had been "taken to Sitka when young and educated as an assistant to the "Greek Catholic Church;...he could read and write Russian perfectly and besides the Eskimo, spoke two of the Indian languages fluently, one of which was Ingalik...." (Pierce, p. 34.)

23 Allen, *A Military Reconnoissance of the Copper River Valley*, p. 452. This annual trading event was started in 1861 by Strachan Jones, the Hudson's Bay Company. trader at Ft. Yukon.

(Brooks, *Blazing Alaska's Trails*, p.242.)

24 Dall, "Reminiscences of Yukon Exploration, 1865-1868," p. 135, *Popular Science Monthly*, August 1906.

25 Shepard Krech III, "On the Aboriginal Population of the Kutchin," *Arctic Anthropology*, 15 [1], 1978; pp. 89-104; see also, Krech, The Ecological Indian: Myth and History, Norton, 1999. Dr. Ruth Goddard, Yukon Archaeologist concurs with Dr. Krech's estimate. Dr. Krech to the authors, 2003., stated that although he believes his analysis of data obtained in 1978 has not been supplanted; "If I were to revisit this analysis today, I might be even more cautious."

Dr. Krech is Director of the Haffenreffer Museum of Anthropology, Brown University, Bristol, Rhode Island. Dr. Krech's population analysis was limited to the Athabaskan Kutchin whose various groups extended from the Mackenzie River Flats and the Peel River on the east to Yukon Flats on the south and to western Alaska. His estimate does not include the Han or Tutchone.

26 Dall, *Alaska and Its Resources*, pp. 338-339.

The treaty of sale was agreed upon March 30, 1867. It was ratified by the U.S. 28 May 1867. The treaty of sale was exchanged and proclaimed by the President of the U.S. 20 June 1867. On October 18 the territory, i.e., all the public property, was formally "ceded" by Russia to the U.S. Private property of the Russian-American Co. remained in the hands of its owners and was sold to Hutchinson/Kohl Co. of San Francisco, that soon, through mergers and acquisitions, became the Alaska Commercial Co. (Dall, *Alaska and Its Resources*, pp. 266, 359)

27 Journal of Robert Campbell, pp. 43-45, Manitoba Provincial Archives; see also, George M. Dawson, Historical Note on Events in the Yukon District, Northwest Territories, p. 178.Robert Campbell was born in Glen Lyon, Scotland, 21 February 1808, and spent his early years helping his father on their sheep farm. By 1830 he had immigrated to Canada and was hired that year by the Hudson's Bay Co. as an assistant to Chief Factor James McMillan on an experimental farm at Red River, Manitoba. Tiring of farm work he requested a position as a fur trader and in 1834 was employed as a clerk and directed to open a post at Dease Lake, British Columbia. In 1839, an agreement between the Russian American Co. and Hudson's Bay Co. allowed the latter to lease the Alaska panhandle. The effect was an end to competition along the coast and inland to Dease Lake. Campbell was directed to continue the company's earlier explorations along the branches of the Liard River. His 1840 expedition, consisted of ten Hudson's Bay Co. employees and four Indians.

Two years later he returned and on Frances Lake constructed a "rough shanty" he named Glenlyon House, the first building of what would later be known as the Hudson's Bay Co.'s Frances Lake post. This was the beginning of ten years of trading in the Yukon. (Two Journals of Robert Campbell, p. 60; see also, *Dictionary of Canadian Biography*, pp.155-156)

In 1848, officials of the Hudson's Bay company, relying upon speculation of Arrowsmith's map of the northwest, believed that the Lewes was a tributary of the Pelly which emptied into the Artic Ocean. The origins of the Yukon were unclear, but Campbell believed that Ft. Selkirk and Ft Yukon were both on the Yukon. It was only in the mid-twentieth century that the name Yukon was officially applied to the Lewes, its headwaters determined to be in Lake Lindeman.

In 1851 Campbell descended the Yukon from Ft. Selkirk to Ft. Yukon, thus proving the connection of the Pelly River with the Yukon. From Ft. Yukon he ascended the Porcupine and followed Alexander Murray's route to Ft. Simpson. Finding this route easier for delivering trade goods to the Yukon basin than the Liard, he closed the Hudson's Bay post at Pelly Banks in 1850 and Ft. Francis in 1851. (Johson, Llewellyn and Dominique Legros, pp. 104-120)

Campbell had heard rumors in the spring of 1852 that the Chilkats, who had a council house on Lake Lebarge were planning a raid on Ft. Selkirk. The local natives remained nearby for most of the summer. Soon after they left downriver to catch their winter supply of fish, the Chilkats descended on the fort. Campbell and his few men were unable to provide any resistance, but were not harmed. All the food, clothing and other trade goods, however, were either destroyed or taken back upriver by the attackers. Campbell traveled up the Pelly and set out overland on a journey that ended at Crow Wing, Minnesota. From there he traveled to London where he met with Sir George Simpson, the overseer of the Hudson's Bay Company's Rupert Land operations to request that he be allowed to reopen Ft. Selkirk. His request was denied and Robert Campbell's work in the Yukon came to an end. (George M. Dawson, *Historical Note of Events in the Yukon, Northwest Territories*, p.177. Review of Historical Publications Relating to Canada, Vol.II, 1897)

Campbell was assigned to Ft. Liard, N.W.T. in the Swan Lake District, and in 1897 was named Chief Factor. His tenure with the company came to an end in 1871 when he was abruptly dismissed. Some of hie remaining years he spent in Scotland and finally settled on a ranch in Manitoba. He died there in 1894. *Dictionary of Canadian Biography*, pp. 155-156)

28 McConnell, Report on an Exploration in the Mackenzie and Yukon Basins, in Dawson, Report, p. 224; Murray, *Journal of the Yukon*, 1847-1848, p. 6.

29 Canham, "The Diocese of Selkirk: Its Work and Workers," Church Missionary Intelligencer, pp. 16-21, Yukon Archives; Kirkby, "A Journey to the Youcon, Russian America," pp. 416-420, *Smithsonian Annual Report*, Yukon Archives; see also, Sarah Simon "Long Long Ago Story" in Sax and Linklater, GIKHYI, p. 10.

The earliest missionaries to the Yukon were sent by the Church of England. Reverend William W. Kirkby came into the country in 1861, (Sax and Linklater, p. 14) "carrying the Gospel to numerous tribes hitherto strangers to the joyful sound...they need something that shall raise them, raise them from the death of sin to a life of righteousness..." (Canham, pp. 16, 19, "The Diocese of Selkirk," *Church Missionary Intelligencer*) The Catholics were not far behind, and when Anglican Archdeacon Robert McDonald arrived at Ft. Yukon in 1862 he was surprised to see that Father Jean Seguin OMI was already there proselytizing among the Indians. (Sax and Linklater, p.14)

30 Ogilvie, *The Klondike Official Guide*, p. 86. The fact that there was coarse gold in the "Alaska District" was known to the outside world as early as 1864. On October 2 of that year a Hudson's Bay Co. employee wrote from Ft. Yukon in a letter to his father in Ontario that: "There is a small river not far from here that the minister, the Revd.(sic) McDonald saw so much gold on a year or two ago, that he could have gathered it with a spoon." (Ogilvie, *Early Days*, p. 86) In *The Klondike Official Guide*, Ogilvie recorded that: "It was mainly through the direction of the Canadian Missionary, the Venerable Archdeacon McDonald, that this field (Birch Creek) was opened." (p. 87). See also, Peake, "Robert McDonald: The Great Unknown Missionary of the Northwest," Journal of the Canadian Church Historical Society, Yukon Archives

31 Mercier, *Recollections of the Youkon*, Alaska Historical Society, p. 66.

32 Johnston, *Alaska Commercial Co.*, 1868-1940, p. 7; Hubert H. Bancroft, *History of Alaska, 1730-1888*, p. 637.

33 Trading posts built by both the Russian-American Co. and the Hudson's Bay Co. were not only called forts, but were surrounded by stockades as high as 20 feet, and had corner blockhouses or lookout turrets. Conversely, the A. C. Co.'s posts had neither fortifications nor weapons for defense. (Mercier, Recollections, pp. xi, 1-3)

34 Petrof, p. 258.

35 McQuesten to McKay, Berkeley, CA, July 1, 1905, Alaska State Historical Collections.

36 McQuesten, *Recollections, Yukon Archives*, p. 2; McQuesten to McKay.

37 Mercier, p. 28.

Monsignor Clut and another priest, Rev. A. Lecorre, arrived at Ft. Yukon 13 October 1873 via the Mackenzie, Peel and Porcupine Rivers. There they remained until the following June with the Alaska Commercial Co. trader, Moise Mercier. That summer, Rev. Clut traveled to St. Michael where he met Francois Mercier, "Chief Agent" of the company. It was during this meeting that Clut made his recommendation of Jack McQuesten as "a very honest man and a good fur trader." (Barnum, Account of the Journey of Bishop Clut to Alaska, 7 June, 1906, Foley Center Library, Gonzaga University; Mercier, p. 38)

In his Recollections, McQuesten wrote that "How we came to go to the Yukon in 1871 there was three of us wintering on the head waters of Hay River, trapping and trading with the Indians. We had prospected the Peace River from its head down to Athabaska and could find nothing that would justify working. We had heard a great deal about the Yukon River from men that were in the H.B. (Hudson's Bay) company employ, and we concluded we would go and see for ourselves what the country was like.... We arrived at Fort Yukon on the 15th August 1873." In late June 1874 McQuesten was employed by the Alaska Commercial Co. and headed upriver to establish the company's first trading post on the upper Yukon. (pp. 1, 4)

Jack's grandfather, William McQuesten, had first emigrated from Scotland to Londonderry in northern Ireland and by 1730 was in New Hampshire, U.S.A. His son James was born in Litchfield in 1761. James' son, Leroy Napoleon "Jack" McQuesten, was born 1 July 1836. Soon after Jack's birth the family moved to Portland, Maine. His long life of adventure on the frontier began when he joined the California gold rush. There he mined a few years with his older brother, Varnum, before leaving to fight in the "Oregon War" against the Walla Wallas. By the time he left the military in 1858 to prospect for gold on the Fraser River in British Columbia, he had been promoted to the rank of Quartermaster. (James McQuiston, McUisdean, p. 139; See also Fairbanks Weekly Times, 23 October 1909; Seward Gateway, 11 September 1909; McDonald, "Leroy Napoleon McQuesten, Father of Alaska," The Highlander; Leona Bean McQuiston, The McQuiston, McCuiston, and McQuesten Families 1620-1937, pp. 116-118.)

38 Ogilvie, *Early Days*, p. 87.

39 Adjutant General Records- Muster Roll for Illinois Regiments in Civil War. Illinois State Library.

Mayo was among the earliest prospectors to arrive in the Yukon and would be the only one of that group to remain in the north. He died at his home in Rampart, Alaska July 18, 1923. (*Alaska Weekly*, 10 August1923.)

40 Ogilvie, "The Yukon District," *The Scottish Geographical Magazine*, July 1898, pp. 337-346.

41 Ogilvie, Lecture on the Yukon Gold Fields, p. 10.

Frederick Washington Harte was born in Ireland in 1835 and studied medicine at the University of Dublin. When he arrived in Canada he became a trapper, hunter and prospector and is not known to ever have practiced medicine in the Yukon, or elsewhere. Harte arrived at Ft. Yukon in August 1873 with Arthur Harper. During that winter and perhaps the next he, McKnieiff (sic) (McNipp, McNiff), Arthur Harper and George Nickelson (also referred to as Samuel Wilkinson) (McQuesten, Recollections, p. 4; Ogilvie, Early Days, p. 88) prospected on the White, Forty Mile and Sixty Mile Rivers. In 1875 Harte returned to Ireland. In 1887 he was back in the Yukon. He never found gold, and worked for McQuesten, Harper and Mayo as a store clerk at Forty Mile and perhaps later at Circle City. (Mercier, p. 17)

When the Yukon Order of Pioneers was organized in 1894, Harte was one of its charter members. When he died in Dawson 12 November 1897 he had recently returned from Ireland where he had visited his two unmarried sisters. He was the first member of the organization to be buried in its Eighth Avenue Cemetery. President Thomas W. O'Brien, another charter member, presided over the funeral. Harte's large stone monument can still be seen in the cemetery. (Mayo Historical Society, Gold and Galena, p. 19; Wells, Magnificence and Misery, pp. 115,124.)

42 Mercier, pp. 26, 34; See also Ogilvie, *Early Days*, pp. 96-99; Brooks, *Blazing Alaska's Trails*, p. 435; McQuesten, *Recollections*, pp. 2-3; Callahan, "A Yukon Auto-biography," *Alaska Journal*, p. 128; McQuesten to McKay; place & date? McQuesten manuscript, Snow Collection, Yukon Archives.

43 McQuesten to McKay; McQuesten, *Recollections*, p. 3; McQuesten manuscript; Mercier, p. 26.

44 Mercier, p. 1; McQuesten to Mckay.

45 McQuesten, *Recollections*, p. 4.

William Ogilvie's later writing on results of Harper, Harte and Finch's prospecting during the summer and fall of 1873 and the summer of 1874 differed from McQuesten's Recollections: They "found very good indications in the vicinity of the mouth of the Stewart. But the shortage of provisions prevented their taking advantage of these discoveries. On their way up they ascended the Forty Mile River two or three miles prospecting, and found very good prospects, but the Indians whom they met on that river scared them away by telling them that there was a very dangerous and impassable canyon some distance farther on." (Ogilvie, Lecture on the Yukon Gold Fields, p. 10) There was, indeed, a dangerous canyon and it would take the lives of many miners in years to come.

46 Ibid. Francois Mercier was born in St. Paul l'Emmite, Quebec in 1838. Among his relatives were Honore Mercier, Prime Minister of Quebec, 1887-1891 and Joseph Royal, Lt. Governor of the North West Territories, 1888-1893.

He arrived in Alaska in 1868 with the Pioneer Co., which had been formed by his brother, Moise, Napoleon Robert and Francois. When the company failed, he served for several years as "general agent" for the Alaska Commercial Co. at St. Michael, leaving them in 1877 to work as a trader for the Western Fur & Trading Co,. which entered the Yukon River valley that year. When the A. C. Co. bought out its rival in 1883 Mercier returned to trade for them again until 1885 when he left the Yukon and returned east to make his home in Montreal. Sometime after his return he was received at the Vatican by Pope Leo XIII in recognition of his work to facilitate the ability of Catholic missionaries to evangelize among the Indian people of Alaska. (Mercier, pp. xi-xiii)

47 Mercier, p. 26.

James Wickersham in *Old Yukon, Tales, Trails and Trials* states that "Harper and Bates, were...the first white men to explore the Tanana." This is the only mention of Bates in all the early records reviewed. (p. 313)

48 Mercier, pp. xiv, 26.

49 The 10 by 35 foot river steamer was brought to St. Michael from San Francisco in 1869, lashed to the deck of the brig Commodore. It was owned by Parrott and Co. and when it was launched 1 July, 1869, it was the first steam-driven boat to travel the Yukon River. (Raymond, *Reconnoissance of the Yukon River*, 1869, pp. 21-23; Raymond, "*The Yukon River Region, Alaska*," p. 168; Mercier, p.71.) For the next few days men were busy loading two barges with trade goods and winter provisions for new American trading posts to be established on the Yukon by Parrott and Co. at Anvik, Nulato and Ft. Yukon.

On July 4 the little steamer, pulling the two barges, started across Norton Sound headed for the Aphoon mouth of the Yukon with "dipping of flags and the firing of guns." On board were Captain Benjamin Hall, the "Commander," Frederick Smith, Superintendent of Parrott and Co., Thomas Williams, pilot, John R. Forbes, engineer, Captain Charles P. Raymond of the U.S. Corps of Topographical Engineers, John J. Major, Raymond's assistant, Private Michael Foley of the Ninth U.S. Infantry, Raymond's "bodyguard," the cook, McIntire, three traders: Frederick Westdahl, John Godfrey, Robert Bird and two trappers. Captain Raymond was traveling under orders of the Commanding General of the Military Division of the Pacific to determine whether the Hudson's Bay Co. post at Ft. Yukon was in American territory. It was found to be 80 miles west of the boundary and the company moved its operations up the Porcupine River to a location they named Rampart House. (*Alaska-Yukon Gold Book*, p. 14.) In 1890 J. H. Turner of the U.S. Coast Survey found it, too, was in U.S. territory and in 1891 Hudson's Bay Co. moved it 20 miles farther upriver. (Ladue, *Klondyke Nuggets*, p.15)

The two earliest river steamers to arrive at St. Michael, the *Lizzie Horner*, a motor "launch" and the *Wilder*, a sternwheeler, were brought by the ocean vessel *Nightingale* in 1865 and 1866 respectively. They were the property of Western Union Co. that had plans to run a telegraph line from southern British Columbia through Alaska along the Yukon River, across the Bering Strait and along the Amur River in Russia to St. Petersburg. The *Wilder*, captained by Everett E. Smith, was used only on Norton Sound to transport supplies between St. Michael and Unalakleet, considered impractical for the Yukon River because of its limited power. The *Lizzie Horner*, due to mechanical difficulties was never put into service. Lt. George Adams, wrote in his diary that "the engineer of our launch was unable to get the engine to work. The interior of the motor engine was a new patent and quite intricate, which the engineer had taken apart to ship and he had forgotten the combination....On a trial trip the following day, when out on the bay, the safety valve blew out with a loud report and volume of steam. Two Eskimos who were on board with us as helpers, promptly jumped overboard and swam to a near-by canoe. We soon had the trouble repaired, but the Eskimos refused to risk their lives again on the 'devil Kiyak' as they called the launch. This was the first and last trip that the launch ever made in the northern waters....Our little steamer is a failure we can not make it go. And our intended expedition up the Kvikpak is broken up." The expedition was greatly hampered by the "useless" steamers that were intended to transport expedition members on an exploratory trip up the Yukon River to Ft. Yukon and Ft. Selkirk. (Pierce, pp. 27-2, 101-102, 119, 206-207, 169, 183.)

William H. Dall, Director of the Scientific Corps attached to the Western Union Telegraph Expedition, said of the steamers:

They were shaped much like an old-fashioned flat-iron, and were just about as valuable for the purposes required; being unable to tow anything, or to carry any freight, while in a breeze of any strength it was no easy matter to steer them.

(Dall, *Yukon Territory*, pp. 7, 24; see also: Raymond, "*The Yukon River Region, Alaska*," p. 168; Petrof, p. 203.)

50 McQuesten manuscript; McQuesten, *Recollections*, p. 4.

51 McQuesten, *Recollections*, p. 5.

52 McQuesten manuscript; See also McQuesten to Albert McKay; McQuesten, *Recollections*, p. 5. Mercier stated in his "Recollections of the Youkon" that he established Ft. Reliance. His reason for establishing it was that "the Indians of the upper Yukon, and the more numerous Indians of the upper Tanana, were obliged in order to exchange their furs to take them to Fort Youkon or the Nookelakayet Station, situated several hundred miles from their hunting grounds (500 or 600) miles."(p.1)

The main building was 25 by 30 feet. "The others (outbuildings) were even smaller and more roughly constructed." (Mercier, p.1; see also, Donald W. Clark, Fort Reliance, Yukon: An Archaeological Assessment, p. 31) In 1883, a year when the post was closed, Lt. Frederick Schwatka, conducting a reconnaissance of the Yukon River for the U.S. Army, passed Ft. Reliance and described it as "a dilapidated-looking place of two or three houses, a main store nailed up and three others, cellar-like and semi-subterranean in character." (Schwatka, *A Reconnaissance*, p. 311)

53 McQuesten, Recollections, p. 11.

54 Wickersham, *Old Yukon, Tales-Trails-and Trials*, p. 313; Osgood, *The Han Indians*, p. 32 indicates that Fetutlin was at Forty Mile.

55 Schwatka, *A Reconnaissance*, pp. 311-312; Osgood, p. 11; Stuck, *Voyages on the Yukon and Its Tributaries*, p. 82; Baker, *Geographic Dictionary of Alaska*, p. 170; Petrof, p. 68; Murray, p. 51; See also Schmitter, *Upper Yukon Native Customs and Folk-Lore*.

56 Allen, *A Military Reconnoissance*, p. 445; See also, Schwatka, *A Reconnaissance*, pp. 340-344, 362.

57 Schmitter, p. 3.

58 Schwatka, *A Reconnaissance*, p. 340.

59 Ibid. p. 311.

60 Ibid. p. 312.

61 Osgood, pp. 98-114.

62 Sim, in Letters and Papers of the Church Missionary Society, National Archives of Canada; See also, Westbrook, *A Venture into Ethnohistory: the Journals of Rev. V. C. Sim*.

63 McQuesten to McKay.
64 Ogilvie, "Story of the Yukon," *Scientific American*; Ogilvie, Lecture, p. 11.
65 In McQuesten's Berkeley letter to McKay and in his manuscript in the George T. Snow Collection he refers to a partnership with Al Mayo and Arthur Harper. He states that "Harper went to Sixty Mile River prospecting in Sept. 1875. He found prospects that he thought would pay to work. The next year we sent for a tank of quicksilver to work the mine. It was our intention to all go to Reliance, one to keep the store and two to work in the mine." As it worked out, however, McQuesten spent the winter of 1875-76 at Ft. Yukon; Harper and Mayo and their families went to Ft. Reliance where they spent the next three years. (McQuesten to McKay, 1 July 1905.)
66 Ogilvie, *Early Days*, p.101; Ogilvie, "Story of the Yukon," *Scientific American*, p. 11; Ogilvie, Lecture, p.11.
67 McQuesten, *Recollections*, p.9; See also McQuesten manuscript. If McQuesten's information was correct regarding the arrival of Dinsmore and Wynn on the upper river in 1880, they may have been among the six men who joined the Bean expedition at Lake Lindeman.
68 Turner, *Contributions to the Natural History of Alaska: Results of Investigations Made Chiefly in the Yukon District and the Aleutian Islands*, p.8.
69 Johnston, *Alaska Commercial Co.*, p. 62. University of Washington Library.
70 Mercier, p. 35; McQuesten, *Recollections*, p. 7.
71 Mercier, pp. 3, 5.
72 McQuesten manuscript; See also, McQuesten, *Recollections*, p. 7.
73 Murphy, Haigh, *Gold Rush Women*, p. 22.
Creoles in Alaska were the children of Russian fathers and Aleut, Eskimo or Athabascan mothers. Today they are seldom mentioned in historical accounts, generally forgotten. When the Americans purchased Alaska in 1867, they had little respect for Creoles. However, the research of historian Dee Longenbaugh of Juneau reveals that among the Russians from 1790-1867, Creoles were highly valued, "so all the children were given a sound education and the brighter ones educated to the level of their abilities... Promising boys (and several girls) were sent for higher education." Many attended school in New Archangel (Sitka) where, in the fall of 1860, the "All-Colonial College" was opened and available to all children who were "academically qualified." Creole men became the "premier explorers of the jagged coasts of Alaska and the vast interior." They were "surveyors, charters, journal-keepers and cartographers." Longenbaugh points out, however, that in Alaska as elsewhere it was "a man's world," but the women were "taught basic reading and writing and numbers." They "could all waltz skillfully, dance the French Quadrille gracefully...." (Longenbaugh, "Creole Cartographers," *Terrae Incognitae*, 1999, vol. 31, pp. 61, 63.) Men and women often became interpreters for the early traders and miners, including Joseph Ladue.
74 Murphy, Haigh, p. 22.
Marriages were conducted both according to Athabaskan custom and later by an Anglican minister. (Callahan, "A Yukon Autobiography," *The Alaska Journal*, Autumn 1975, p. 128.)
75 Callahan, p. 128.
Among the Indians in the Ft. Yukon area and across Alaska, most females married young—usually as soon as they reached menarche and had undergone puberty seclusion. The Rev. William W. Kirkby, the first missionary to visit the area, wrote that in 1861 "All that is requisite is the sanction of the mother of the girl and often it is a matter of negotiation between her and the suitor when the girl is in childhood. The father has no voice in the matter whatever, nor any other of the girl's relatives." (Kirkby, "A Journey to the Youcon, Russian America," *Smithsonian Annual Report*, 1864, p. 419.)
76 Murphy, Haigh, p. 22.
77 *Fairbanks Weekly Times*, 23 October 1909; Seward Gateway, 11 September 1909
The Mayo children were Clinton, Arthur, Selina, Charles, Martha, Benjamin, Leroy (Lee), Kitty, Antoinette and Annette (twins), Florence and a baby who died. Harper children were Alfred, Frederick, Charles, Marianne (Jessie), Samuel, Margaret, Andrew and Walter.

The 12 McQuesten children were Henry, Crystal, June (Julia), Alfred, DeWitt, Mary Louise, Charles, Elizabeth, Walter, Richard, William and Leroy. (Callahan, p. 128; See also Harper-Haines, *Cold River Spirits*, p. 65.)

78 Murphy, Haigh, pp. 22-25, 84-85.

79 Teacher and Nicholls, eds., *The Unabridged Jack London*, pp. 112-113.

80 McConnell, *Report on an Exploration in Dawson Report*, p. 233.

81 McQuesten, *Recollections*, p. 13.

82 Mercier, p. 72.

83 Petrof, p. 61.

Petrof traveled from St. Michael to Nuklukayet with Jack McQuesten the summer of 1880. He traveled no farther inland; instead he collected census data on the upper river given to him by McQuesten and other traders. (Mercier, p. 61)

84 McQuesten, *Recollections*, pp. 8-9.

85 Ibid. p 9.

Mrs. Lorenz, wife of the A.C. Co. agent at St. Michael, was with the party on the first trip of the new steamer *Yukon*. Mercier recorded that she traveled to the mouth of the White River, the first white woman to travel that far upriver. (Mercier, p. 22)

McQuesten, in his Recollections, differed with Mercier stating that in the summer of 1882 "Mr. Lawrence (Lorenz) the agent and wife came up, we went up that year within 25 miles of Pelly River. It was the first time the steamer had been above Reliance." (McQuesten, *Recollections*, p. 10) The discrepancy between Mercier's and McQuesten's estimate of how far upriver the Yukon traveled is about 80 miles.

86 The "District" in this instance refers to the "St. Michel" district which, to the A. C. Co., meant all of its trading area along the Yukon River including the Yukon District of the Canadian North West Territories. (Mercier, p. 28)

87 Harold Harris Pitts was born in London, England in 1848 to John Henry and Mary Hopkins Pitts. (Pigot & Co. *A Directory of London and its Suburbs*, September 1839, p. 319, Great Britain, General Register Office, marriage certificate; Family information provided by Charles Kristian Pitts.) By 1864 the family was in San Francisco and later that same year arrived in Victoria, British Columbia. In 1864 Harold attended the Collegiate School and participated in its scholarly competitions in June. "Master Pitts" was winner of prizes for Algebra, Scripture and the Astonomy. (*Victoria Daily Colonist*, June 24, 1864).

The next year Harold, now 17, was a telgrapher for Western Union Telegraph Company in Barkerville, B.C. where he also served as secretary of the Reed (Mining) Company on nearby Conklin Gulch. Western Union transferred him to Olympia, Washington Territory in 1869. (Rosemary Neering, *Continental Dash*, pp. 40-48) In 1878 Pitts "went over to Victoria...intending to go up into the Cariboo and engage in merchandizing." (*Victoria Daily Colonist*, May 24, 1878). No further information of his whereabouts could be located until Joe Ladue mentioned him as being among his party starting from San Francisco for the Yukon in 1882. (*New York World*, August 6, 1897)

Pitts left the Yukon at the end of the 1883 mining season. No record of his return to the Yukon could be located, but he is known to have been at Ft. Selkirk in June 1897 when Dr. Luella Day stopped there on her way to the Klondike. She later wrote that "Mr. Pitt" was "a man of wonderful character and integrity, which endeared him to whites and Indians alike." (Day, *Tragedy of the Klondike*, p.57)

Records of the Harper Estate indicate that in March 1898 Pitts purchased Harper's trading post at Ft. Selkirk for $1,500. (Assets and Debts, Estate of Arthur Harper) Each spring, after the ice left the river, he traveled the 175 miles downstream to Dawson in his distinctive hide boat constructed according to the design previously used by the Northern Tutchone. (*Dawson Daily News*, August 14, 1900)

At 5:45 p.m. January 3, 1913 Thomas Jeffries, noticing that no smoke was coming from Pitts' stovepipe, entered the cabin and found him unconscious. When the symptoms were described to Dr. LaChapelle in Dawson by telegraph he diagnosed the symptoms as those of a stroke. Pitts could not be revived and was buried at Ft. Selkirk. (*Dawson Daily News*, January 4, 1913) His gravemarker is still readable.

Joe's traveling companion, William Domingo Moore, was born in Callao, Peru, the son of Captain William "Billy" Moore. Captain Moore was one of the best known early British Columbia pioneers. In 1887 he joined the party of Dominion Land Surveyor, William Ogilvie, the Canadian assigned to determine the U.S./Canadian boundary below Forty Mile. In 1896, at age 73, Billy Moore secured a contract from the Canadian Government to carry mail from Juneau to Forty Mile. Moore early established a townsite at Skagway, Alaska, believing that a big gold strike was imminent and his town would become the main gateway to the Yukon. His son, William D., spent many years in the Yukon and he, too, was often referred to as "Captain" causing some confusion as to which Captain Moore was involved in certain events. (Hacking, *Captain William Moore: B.C.'s Amazing Frontiersman*)

88 *New York World*, 6 August 1897. On the trail, as in finding gold, the Indians of the coast and the interior were vital to the success of the miners. They were stronger than most white men, carrying packs of up to 200 pounds. Even Indian women carried as much as the average white man.

89 Ibid. Secretan, *To Klondyke and Back*, p. 75.

90 Wilson, *Glimpses of Alaska*, p. 25.

Miles Canyon was named for Brigadier General Nelson A. Miles, commanding the U.S. Army Department of the Columbia. Lt. Frederick Schwatka gave the canyon its name when he first saw it on July 2, 1883. (Schwatka, *A Reconnaissance*, pp. 285, 302)

91 Ogilvie, in Ladue, *Klondyke Facts*, p. 56.

In early June 1897, J. H. E. Secretan and his party trekked over the Chilkoot, traveled through the chain of lakes and started down the Yukon. They successfully passed through Miles Canyon, but decided to portage around White Horse Rapids after observing the results of an experiment to see what would happen to a log they rolled into it at the upper end. Secretan later wrote: "I tried putting a log through this chaos of waters, just to see what it would do, with most discouraging results. The log sailed gracefully through the centre, riding serenely over the heavy swells at about forty miles an hour, and, just as I had concluded it was all safe and easy, the log suddenly stood up straight on end, and, looking me in the face, plunged out of sight into some subterranean passage which was not laid down on the chart, disappearing for ever." (Secretan, p. 90.)

92 Wilson, p. 24.

93 *New York World*, 6 August 1897.

94 Whymper, *Travel and Adventure in the Territory of Alaska*, pp. 210-211.

95 McQuesten, *Recollections*, p. 11; Ogilvie, *Early Days*, p. 110; Ladue, *Klondyke Facts*, p. 203; *New York World*, 6 August 1897.

96 McQuesten, *Recollections*, pp. 6, 11.

97 *New York World*, 6 August 1897.

98 McQuesten, *Recollections*, p. 11.

99 McQuesten to McKay.

George Frederick Spangenberg was one of many pioneer merchants in Tombstone, Arizona. He was a gun dealer and locksmith and in 1880 operated a store at 212 Fourth Street. A fire in 1881 destroyed most of Tombstone, including Spangenberg's store.

During his time in Tombstone he was a member of the Turn Verein, a gymnastics and social club that had its origins in Germany. In the summer of 1881 the club held a "Grand Ball" at their hall on Fremont St. Spangenberg was assigned to the "Arrangements" committee. (Fischer, *The Jewish Pioneers of Tombstone*, p. 18; Traywick, *Historical Documents and Photographs of Tombstone*, p. 160)

By 1882 rumors of gold in the Yukon District reached the miners in southeastern Arizona. Joe Ladue, George Spangenberg and others decided that summer to try their luck in yet another remote part of the frontier west. Although the grand opening of his new store was planned for July 19, Spangenberg sold his building to Wells Fargo and was among the party of prospectors who followed Ladue over the Chilkoot Pass and down the Yukon to Ft. Reliance where they were greeted by Jack McQuesten in early

September. (Ben Traywick; *Tombstone Epitaph*, 19 July 1882)

100 *New York World*, 6 August 1897.

101 Clark, Ft. Reliance, p. 48.

From archaeological signs found at the site in 1983 and 1991, Donald Clark, a curator of archaeology at the Canadian Museum of Civilization tentatively concluded that "the miners actually were living at Ft. Reliance." No cabin sites were found on level areas around the trading post, but a total of seven cabins were found at the north end of the main site. (p. 13.)

102 Ladue, *Klondyke Nuggets*, p. 86.

103 Sonnikson, *The Klondike Nugget*, 11 March 1899.

104 Moore, *Report Upon the Yukon Country*, Yukon Archives; see also Bell and Sullivan, *A Cultural Resource Inventory of the Fortymile River*, p. 14.

105 McQuesten, *Recollections*, p.11.

George Spangenberg, having been a member of a gymnastics club in Tombstone, likely amazed everyone present with his acrobatic skills during the blanket toss.

Throughout much of the twentieth century it was often written that Al Mayo had been an acrobat with a circus. No clear evidence to support that assertion has been located. It appears likely that the originator of the story may have confused Mayo with Spangenberg.

In 1874 there were only 32 whites in the district called "St. Michel," which extended from the mouth of the Yukon in Alaska to Ft. Reliance in the Yukon District of the North West Territories. There were 13 posts. The closest to Ft. Reliance was Ft. Yukon, about 365 miles north. (Mercier, pp. 13-14)

106 *New York World*, 6 August 1897.

107 McQuesten, *Recollections*, p. 11.

108 Ibid. p. 12; *New York World*, 6 August 1897.

109 McQuesten, *Recollections*, p. 11.

Mercier established "Belle Isle" post in 1880 while in the employ of the Western Fur and Trading Company, naming it "for one of his Canadian friends in San Francisco" (Mercier, p. 3)

110 Mercier, p. 32.

111 Ibid.

112 *New York World*, 6 August 1897; McQuesten, Recollections, p. 12; Mercier, p. 32.

113 *New York World*, 6 August 1897. This statement appears to be inconsistent with Joe's later comment in the same article: "We had the usual miner's kit—blankets, picks, shovels, gold pans, rockers, rocker irons, nails, whipsaws, hand saws etc."

This is also inconsistent with Frederick Schwatka's report of meeting Joe much farther downriver in July, 1883. Statements made in interviews with "old timers" many years after events happened frequently are found to be in conflict with earlier comments or with known facts.

114 Alaskan Census Records, 1870-1907; anonymous account, Snow Collection, Yukon Archives. Preston Cloudman was with the Bean party that crossed the Chilkoot in 1880. His name appeared on the list of participants as "Preston Uontenman." "Thomas Curney" may have been Thomas Kernan, also with that party.

115 Dawson, Report, p. 180.

116 Ibid.; Sherwood, *Exploration of Alaska*, p. 80; Schwatka, *A Reconnaissance*, p. 306.

117 Butler, p. 107; Brooks, *Blazing Alaska's Trails*, p. 327.

Edward Lawrence Schieffelin was born on the family farm in Pennsylvania on 8 October 1847. At 19 he left home to work in the gold camps along the Rogue River in Oregon. In the early 1870s he traveled to Pioche, Nevada to search for silver. Over the next three years he explored much of Nevada, southwestern Utah and northwestern Arizona. By 1877 Schieffelin was prospecting in southeastern Arizona Territory. The following year he discovered a rich silver vein, naming his first mines the Lucky Cuss and the Toughnut. That same year he formed the Tombstone Mining District and soon the town of Tombstone grew up nearby. In the early 1880s Schieffelin sold his mining interests and began planning his trip to Alaska. He traveled to St. Michael and up the Yukon River to Nuklukayet where he prospected that fall and the following spring. Not finding gold in promising quantities, he decided "to abandon the country" and returned to Alameda, California, where he and his wife, Mary, purchased a home. Periodically throughout the remainder of his life he continued to prospect. In 1897 Ed Schieffelin "was found dead in a lonely cabin about 20 miles from Canyonville, Oregon, where he had gone prospecting." (Butler, p. 8; See also Burns, Tombstone)

118 Charles Ogilvie Farciot was born in Corgemont, Switzerland, in 1840 and became a U.S. citizen in 1858. Farciot was an inventor, steamship engineer and photographer. Among his patented inventions were an Automatic Recording Compass (1889) and a Burglar Alarm Attachment for Alarm Clocks (1890). When Farciot met Ed Schieffelin he operated a photography gallery in Tombstone or nearby Charleston, Arizona Territory in 1881 (Charles O. Farciot Collection, Consortium Library, University of Alaska Anchorage) and joined the prospecting party to Alaska. When Ed Schieffelin left Alaska in 1883, Farciot stayed behind, according to McQuesten, "not to prospect but to work on some of his invention."(sic) (McQuesten, *Recollections*, p. 12.) He did prospect, however, and in 1884 was one of several men working on the Stewart River. (Mercier, p. 35) In 1886 Farciot returned to San Francisco where he opened a photography shop. (Charles O. Farciot Papers and Photographs, 1858-1986, Consortium Library, University of Alaska Anchorage)

McQuesten, in his *Recollections*, referred to Farciot as "C. Lancier," (p. 12); Mercier referred to him as Charles Farcint. (Mercier, p. 30)

119 Jacobsen, *Alaska Voyage, 1882-1883,* pp. 3, 83, 215.

Johan Adrian Jacobsen was employed by the Royal Berlin Museum to report on the Indians of northwestern North America and to collect and send back to the museum ethnographic specimens: "clothing, household implements, weapons and handicrafts." Jacobsen hired Pitka Pavaloff as interpreter for his trip up the Yukon to Nuklukayet and return. He wrote that he "was forced to pay a high wage." (pp.86, 103.)

120 Butler, p. 102. William Ogilvie wrote that an article about the Yukon River was published in the *San Francisco Bulletin*, 18 September 1887. No copy of the article was located. If De Wolfe did write about his journey it would have been limited to his experiences on the lower river since he traveled only as far as a point between Anvik and Nulato before returning to the coast. (Jacobsen, p.99.)

121 Brooks, *Blazing Alaska's Trails*, p. 327.

The machinery for the *New Racket* was built by the Main-Street Iron Works in San Francisco. The boat was registered as a "stern wheeler, weighing 15 tons, 53 feet long," 12 feet wide and "drawing 15 inches of water." It had "two engines 8-inch cylinder with a 24-inch stroke." (Butler, pp. 98, 109.) One observer wrote that it had "a fire-box boiler which burns two-foot wood. Average speed from eight to nine miles per hour." (Moore, *Report Upon the Upper Yukon Country*, p. 49, Yukon Archives.) Al Mayo, who was the boat's captain, in later years claimed that it could make ten miles per hour in dead water. Surveyor William Ogilvie described the boat as being "wholly taken up with engine and boiler, the berths for the crew being over the engine room." (Ogilvie, *The Klondike Official Guide*, p. 58.) It was unique, having been equipped by its original owner, Edward Scheiffelin, with machinery for both placer mining, which meant its engines could be used to pump water for sluicing, and quartz mining, and that it had machinery for crushing ore. (Bettles, "Some Early Yukon River History," in *Sourdough Sagas*, 1885, p. 119; McQuesten *Recollections*, p.12; Allen, *A Military Reconnoissance*, p. 452; Moore, *Report on the Yukon Country*, pp. 495-501.)

122 Butler, pp. 102, 103,13; See also: Jacobsen, p. 88; Burns, *Tombstone*, p. 22.

123 Bettles, "Some Early Yukon River History," in *Sourdough Sagas*, p. 119.

Gordon Charles Bettles had first heard of the Yukon from George "Tuck" Lambert in the late fall of 1886 while in Sand Point, Idaho. Lambert told him about the coarse gold he, Howard Franklin and others had found on the Forty Mile and Bettles began planning a trip to the north. Crossing Chilkoot Pass, he arrived at Forty Mile in early summer 1888.

When he found many of the miners discouraged with the area he continued downriver to St. Michael, prospecting along the way. At one point he joined a group of miners (among them Joe Ladue) from Forty Mile who were on their way downriver to find and hang an Indian who had murdered John Bremner, a miner, the previous summer. That gory task completed, Bettles soon started working as a trader on the middle Yukon River and later at Koyukuk on the lower river. In 1893 he married Sophie Kokrine, a Creole. On January 1, 1894 he published the first edition of the Yukon Press, the first newspaper on the Yukon. (*Seattle Sunday Times*,11 July 1937.)

124 Mercier, p. 28.

125 Mercier, p. 30; See also Brooks, *Blazing Alaska's Trails*, p. 328, Schwatka, *A Reconnaissance*, p. 321; Allen, *A Military Reconnoissance*, p. 452; Ogilvie, *Early Days*, p. 70; *Alaska-Yukon Gold Book*, p.15.

In the summer of 1883 the total Yukon fleet consisted of three small steamers: the *St. Michael* (one of the assets acquired by the A. C. Co. from the Western Fur & Trading Co. that summer), the A. C. Co.'s new *Yukon*, and the *New Racket*, now owned by McQuesten and Co. (Mercier, p. 30; See also, Schwatka, *A Reconnaissance*, p. 313.)

The *Yukon* was 20 feet wide and from 75 feet to 80 feet in length. It had nine 36-inch cylinders, could carry 25 tons of freight and had a speed of 8 to 9 miles per hour. (Moore, *Report*, p. 500.) It was brought to St. Michael the summer of 1882 and was the second of the same name to be owned by the Alaska Commercial Co. Schwatka's comment on the steamer *St. Michael*, when he saw it in 1883, was that it was "comparatively worthless."(Schwatka, *A Reconnaissance*, p. 321.)

126 Curtin, *Yukon Voyage*, pp. 277-278.

127 Allen, *A Military Reconnoissance*, p. 453.

128 Mercier, pp. 35, 71; See also Jacobsen, p. 99; Schwatka, *A Reconnaissance*, p. 313; *San Francisco Examiner*, 30 August 1885.

Schwatka wrote that during his 1883 reconnaissance of the Yukon River he camped the night of July 24 "alongside of a small river steamer called the *St. Michael*, which during the spring freshet, while descending the river, had grounded on this bar, and, being unable to get off was abandoned, her keel being now some 6 or 7 feet above the level of the present stage of water." The boat belonged to the Western Fur & Trading Co. "recently bought out by the Alaska Commercial Co." (Schwatka, *A Reconnaissance*, p. 313.)

129 Mercier, p. xi; McQuesten manuscript.

130 McQuesten, *Recollections*, p. 11; Mercier, pp. 3, 32, 71.

131 Petrof, pp. 69, 133.

132 *New York World*, 6 August 1897.

133 Schwatka, *A Reconnaissance*, pp. 312-313.

134 Schwatka, *A Summer in Alaska*, pp. 262-271.

135 Ibid.

136 *New York World*, 6 August 1897.

137 McQuesten, *Recollections*, p. 13.

138 Once established in Canada, the "Episcopal" Church of England took the name Anglican.

139 Sim, Letters and Papers of the Church Missionary Society,1884, National Archives of Canada; See also "Exploration on the Upper Yukon River" in Sheldon Jackson, *Report on Education in Alaska, 1886*, pp. 52-53; Westbrook, *A Venture into Ethnohistory: The Journals of Rev. V.C. Sim: Pioneer Missionary on the Yukon*, p. 36.

140 Canham, "The Diocese of Selkirk: Its Work and Workers," *Church Missionary Intelligencer* p. 19; Jan Harper-Haines, p. 63.

141 McQuesten to McKay; See also Brooks, *Blazing Alaska's Trails*, pp. 326-328; *The Alaska Yukon Gold Book*, p. 24.

142 McQuesten, *Recollections*, p. 12; Ogilvie, *Early Days*, p.110.

143 McQuesten, *Recollections*, p. 12; Schwatka, *A Summer in Alaska*, p. 266.

144 Brooks, p. 326; Ogilvie, *Early Days*, p. 108.

145 *New York World*, 6 August 1897.

146 McQuesten, *Recollections*, p. 13.
147 Brooks, *Blazing Alaska's Trails*, pp 326-328.
148 McQuesten to McKay.
149 Ibid.
150 Brooks, *Blazing Alaska's Trails*, p326.
151 Tollemache, *Reminiscences of the Yukon*, pp. 132-135.
152 McQuesten, *Recollections*, p.13; McQuesten to McKay.
153 McQuesten to McKay; Allen, *A Military Reconnoissance*, p. 453.
154 Carmack, *My Experiences in the Yukon*, p. 10. Snow Collection, Yukon Archives.
155 Allen, *A Military Reconnoissance*, p. 452; See also, Turck, Trading Posts Along the Yukon River: Noochuloghooyet Trading Post in Historical Context, *Arctic*, 1 March 1992, pp. 51-61.

Two of the earliest prospectors in the interior of Alaska were Pete Johnson and John Bremner. They entered via the Copper and Tanana Rivers, traveling with Lt. Allen. (Bettles, "Some Early Yukon River History," in *Sourdough Sagas*, p. 119.)

156 Allen, *A Military Reconnoissance*, p. 452.

Allen, as many other early white men on the Yukon River, may have been mistaken in describing the vocalizations of the Indians as merely shouts. Most music produced by Indians, then and now, often sounds discordant, without harmony, to those who understand neither the nature of the music they are hearing nor the language of the singers. To most people, exposed to primarily three, and sometimes, four-part harmony, Native singing is incomprehensible. It was Frederick Schwatka's opinion that the Indians from the mouth of the Yukon to Nuklukayet had learned from the Russians to fire guns whenever visitors approached the shore. (Schwatka, *A Reconnaissance*,p. 311.)

157 Raymond, *Reconnaissance of the Yukon River*, 1869, p. 38.
158 Allen, *A Military Reconnoissance*, p. 453.

The Alaska Commercial Co.'s post at Nuklukayet, operated for several years by Arthur Harper, was located on the right bank of the Yukon several miles downriver from the trading grounds at the mouth of theTanana, known as Nuclerai. (Allen, *A Military Reconnoissance*, p.452.)

159 In his *Recollections*, McQuesten indicated "about fifty tons of miners' supplies landed at Ft. Reliance on 10 August." (p. 13) In his 1905 letter to McKay he "had brought in 30 tons of miners' supplies, the first to come into the country, arriving at Reliance on August 20."
160 McQuesten to McKay; Allen, *A Military Reconnoissance*, p. 453.
161 It appears that one reason for the limited number of posts was due to information given to Indians along the river by Creoles that the prices charged by the traders were exorbitant, which resulted in their being furious and threatening to the traders. (Allen, *A Military Reconnoissance*,p. 454.)

At Ft. Yukon, in particular, the traders had good reason to avoid any direct contact with the Indians. The chief of the Kutcha-Kutchin, who inhabited the area between the Yukon and Porcupine Rivers and north to the Rat River, was a man named Sakhnite, or Senate (Sen-a-te), nicknamed "Old Thunder." Trader Francois Mercier described him as a "man of extraordinary stature and strength, of braveness, or more than that, ferocity, and duplicity which one rarely encounters even among the savages. He was not only the terror of the people of his tribe, but above all, of other neighboring tribes, whom he rarely left in peace, and whom he massacred each in their turn for the least reason, or for the love of carnage." (Mercier, p. 54.)

Lt. Frederick Schwatka, however, who met Senate in 1883 saw a leader who was "respected by the various tribes." (Schwatka, *A Reconnaissance*, p. 345.) Perhaps what Schwatka interpreted as respect was, rather, the carefully masked fear typical of those who live under the iron rule of a despot.

162 Dawson, *Report*, p. 25.
163 McQuesten to McKay; See also, *Alaska-Yukon Gold Book*, p. 25.

164 Mike to J.M.Vanderbilt, Ft. Reliance, *Sitka Alaskan*, 28 November 1885; See also, *Alaska-Yukon Gold Book*, p. 25.

165 McQuesten, Recollections, p. 14.

Some of the prospectors and miners on the Stewart River between 1883 and 1888: Joseph Laduc, Benjamin Beach, Joe Beaudreau, Berndt, Jeremiah "Jerry" Bertrand, Thomas Boswell, Frank Bowker, John Chapman, Steven Custer, Al Day, Hugh Day, Frank Dinsmore, Howard Franklin, John Fraser, Arthur Harper, Frederick Harte, Mike Hess, John Hughes, Joe Macheal, Henry Madison, George Marks, George Matlock, Alfred H. "Captain Al" Mayo, Charles McCoskey, Alexander McDonald, Leroy Napoleon "Jack" McQuesten, George F. "Buckskin" Miller, Francis "Frank" Morphat (Moffat), John Nelson, Walter H. Pierce, Richard "Dick" Poplin, Charles Powell, Ike Powers, George T. Snow, Chris Sonnickson (Sonnikson), "Black Mike" Sullivan, Hank Summers, Peter "Pete" Wyborg, Tom Williams, "Slim Jim" Wynn, Hare. (Mayo Historical Society, *Gold and Galena*, p. 28; Chris Sonnikson manuscript, Snow Collection, Yukon Archives); See also, *Alaska-Yukon Gold Book*, p. 25.)

166 McQuesten, *Recollections*, p. 14; McQuesten to McKay; See also, Brooks, *Blazing Alaska's Trails*, p. 326.

167 Dawson, *Report*, p. 181.

168 McQuesten, *Recollections*, p. 13; See also: *New York World*, 6 August 1897; *Seattle Daily Times*, 22 July 1897; McQuesten to McKay.

169 McConnell, *Report on an Exploration, in Dawson, Report*, p. 236.

170 Jarvis, *The Great Gold Rush: A Tale of the Klondike*, p. 145.

171 *San Francisco Examiner*, 30 August 1885.

172 Mercier, p. xii.

173 McQuesten to McKay.

174 Nelson, Snow Collection, Yukon Archives.

175 Ogilvie, *The Klondike Official Guide*, p. 76; Ogilvie, Lecture, p. 11; McQuesten to McKay; *Alaska-Yukon Gold Book*, pp. 25-26.

176 *Sitka Alaskan*, 30 October 1886.

177 Clark, Ft. Reliance, Yukon, p. 130. Ft. Reliance today is owned by the Han (Tr'ondek Hwech'in) of Dawson.

178 *Seattle Daily Times*, 22 July 1897; See also: *New York World*, 6 August 1897; Ogilvie, *Early Days*, p. 118; McQuesten to McKay.

The Indians Joe traded with at Belle Isle that winter were the Han from Nuklako, and Johnny's Village about one mile upriver from the post.

As trader for McQuesten and Co. at Belle Isle the trade goods Joe had to offer were shotguns, rifles, pocket knives, white flannel shirts, red flannel shirts, calico shirts, prints, heavy cloth, shawls, cotton drill, bullets (28 to the pound), #4 shot, butcher knives, tin pans of various sizes, tin cups, metal buttons, pearl buttons, linen thread, silk handkerchiefs, Paris neckties, English belts, Canadian belts, gunpowder and wide and narrow ribbon. (Raymond, *Reconnaissance of the Yukon River*, 1869, pp. 38-39.)

179 Schwatka, *A Summer in Alaska*, pp. 284-285.

180 Raymond, *Reconnaissance of the Yukon River*, 1869, pp. 38-39.

181 *New York World*, 6 August 1897.

182 Annual Report of Inspector Constantine, Ft. Constantine, Cudahy P.O., Upper Yukon, 20 January 1896, p. 11, Yukon Archives.

183 *New York World*, 6 August 1897.

184 Ogilvie, *The Klondike Official Guide*, p. 69.

185 McQuesten, *Recollections*, p. 12.

186 Ogilvie, *The Klondike Official Guide*, p. 69.

187 McConnell, "Report on an Exploration," in Dawson, *Report*, p. 236.

188 Ogilvie, *Early Days*, p. 111.

189 Jarvis, p. 146; *New York World*, 6 August 1897; *Dawson Daily News*, 31 August 1906.

190 *Dawson Daily News*, 31 August 1906.

Other writers, including Ladue, have reported that the members of the party were Franklin, O'Brien, Tuck Lambert, George Madison, Jim Adams and Bill Hartz, and that the discovery was on Franklin Gulch. (McQuesten to McKay; Jarvis, p. 146; *New York World*, 6 August 1897; see also *Alaska-Yukon Gold Book*, p. 26.

191 Dawson, *Report*, p. 181; Josiah E. Spurr, Through the Yukon Gold Diggings, p. 109; Ogilvie, "The Yukon District," *The Scottish Geographical Magazine*, pp. 337-346; Ogilvie, Some Notes on Gold Mining in the Yukon Territory, National Archives of Canada; *Alaska-Yukon Gold Book*, p. 26.

192 The community of Forty Mile was established on "a flat of about four or five hundred acres in area." (Ogilvie, *The Klondike Official Guide*, p. 60) On July 20, 1883, when Schwatka first saw what later became known as the Forty Mile River, he named it Cone Hill River because of a "conspicuous conical hill in its valley near the mouth." (Schwatka, *A Reconnaissance*, p. 311.)

193 Clark, *Ft. Reliance*, p. 130.

194 Buteau, "My Experiences in the World," in *Sourdough Sagas*, p. 96.

195 *New York World*, 6 August 1897.

196 McQuesten to McKay.

An unidentified account in the Snow Collection, apparently written by a miner on site at the time, indicates there were 50 men at Stewart camp the winter of 1886-87.

197 Sonnikson manuscript, Snow Collection, Yukon Archives.

198 Buteau, "*My Experiences*," p. 117.

Frank Buteau was born in Quebec, July 29, 1856. From there his family moved to Lewiston, Maine. In 1879 he was living in Merrill, Wisconsin. In 1882 he traveled to the west coast and soon took up residence in Kamloops and later Vancouver, British Columbia. On July 11, 1886 he joined 21 other men headed for the Yukon. They left Dyea in late August, crossed over Chilkoot Pass and traveled down the Yukon, arriving at Forty Mile October 13, 1886. There, he and several others built cabins on an island at the mouth of the Forty Mile River. They named their island "The Sixteen Liars Island."(Buteau, "*My Experiences*," pp. 93-96.)

199 Lewis Gerstle, President of A. C. Co. to Mr. Lorenz, agent at St. Michael, May 7, 1886, in *Klondyke and Alaska Gold Fields 1898*, p. 8, (American Jubilee Publishing Co,);See also, Johnston, *Alaska*, pp. 58-59.

200 Anonymous account, Snow Collection, Yukon Archives.

201 Burlingame, "John Healy's Alaskan Adventure," *Alaska Journal*, autumn, 1978, p. 311; Brooks, *Blazing Alaska's Trails*, p. 331; Spurr, *Through the Yukon Gold Diggings*, pp. 109-110; Sonnikson, Snow Collection, Yukon Archives; See also, *Alaska-Yukon Gold Book*, p. 26.

202 Buteau, "My Experiences," in *Sourdough Sagas*, p. 98; *New York World*, 6 August 1897.

203 Ogilvie, Lecture, p. 11.

204 Davis, "Recollections," in *Sourdough Sagas*, p. 50.

205 Ogilvie, *The Klondike Official Guide*, p. 78.

1887 was the first year the Canadian Government demonstrated interest in the north-western portion of its possessions. (For a detailed account of the early history of the Yukon, see Canada, Department of the Interior, *The Yukon Territory: Its History and Resources, 1907*, pp. 1-16, and 1916, pp. 1-12, Yukon Archives.)

206 John Nelson (Nielsen) had been Joe's partner prospecting on the Klondike River in 1886. Thomas O'Brien would later be involved in establishing the Klondike Mines Railway that ran from Front Street in Dawson to Grand Forks at the junction of Bonanza and Eldorado creeks. "Skiff" Skiffington Samuel Mitchell came to the Yukon in 1886. He made little from mining on the Forty Mile, but in 1896 bought discovery claim on #1 Eldorado from prospector Jay Whipple. He worked that and other claims successfully until his death April 12, 1904.

Nelson was a charter member of the Yukon Order of Pioneers and is buried in the Yukon Order of Pioneers 8th Avenue Cemetery in Dawson City. His surname on a tall granite marker is spelled Nielsen, which is its proper spelling in his homeland of Denmark.

207 Davis, "Recollections," in *Sourdough Sagas*, p. 50.
208 The Klondike District did not extend to Forty Mile, which later became known as the Forty Mile District.
209 *New York World*, 6 August 1897.
210 McConnell, "Report on an Exploration," in Dawson, *Report*, p. 233.
211 Ogilvie, The Klondike Official Guide, p. 76; Dawson, *Report*, p. 182.
212 Schwatka, *Along Alaska's Great River*.
213 Ogilvie, *The Klondike Official Guide*, p. 78.
214 Bettles, "Why I Came to Alaska," *Fairbanks News-Miner*, fall, 1995.

"Dutch Kate" Wilson was described as "one of those poor, fallen women, who are often found casting their miserable lot with the mining class." Evidence indicates that she was poor, but not necessarily "fallen." When that brave and adventurous woman failed to find gold at Forty Mile she went with a number of miners who were leaving the Yukon via St. Michael in the fall of 1888. Having no money or gold she could not afford passage on any of the steamers and was forced to remain the winter, depending completely on the generosity of the Indians and missionaries. The following spring the captain of a sealing ship gave her free passage and she eventually reached San Francisco. (*Sitka Alaskan*, 23 November 1889)

215 Adney, "Who Discovered the Klondike?", *Harper's Weekly*, 1 April 1899.
216 *Sitka Alaskan*, 19 March 1889.
217 Goodrich, "History and Conditions of the Yukon District to 1897" in Spurr, *Geology of the Yukon District, Alaska*, pp. 103-133; Stone, "Atomistic Order and Frontier Violence: Miners and Whalemen in the Nineteenth-Century Yukon," *Ethnology*, 23, no. 4, 1983, pp. 327-339; *Sitka Alaskan*, 9, 16 March and 13 October 1894; Steffens, "Life in the Klondyke Gold Fields: Personal Experiences of the Founder of Dawson City," *McClure's Magazine*, p. 965.

It appears that out of the early miners' meetings at Forty Mile evolved a Miners' Association. When the N.W.M.P. arrived in 1895, as the duly appointed representatives of law and order, one of the Association's members took the organization's banner Outside, apparently for safekeeping. It is now in possession of a bookstore owner in the state of Nevada. The banner measures 44 by 63 inches. The background material appears to be dark blue velvet. Near the top, on an image of a sash, are the words "Miner Association." Near the bottom is another sash with the word "Yukon." In the center is a light blue circle showing two miners shaking hands. A gold pan, pick and shovel are in front of them. Behind them is a creek and in the distance a snow-capped mountain range. A bald eagle flies above, carrying a white banner with the words E Pluribus Unum (out of many, one) in its beak.

218 Palmer, "Government and Society in the Klondike," *The Forum*, p. 604.

In 1907, during a visit to Dawson, Andrew Hunker told a *Dawson Daily News* reporter that even as late as August 1896 he trusted the men he met on the creeks. He stated that when he made his discovery on the creek that bears his name, "A man named Peterson was with me. We picked up partners in those days with a feeling of security that almost was impunity, and I did not even ask Peterson his first name, and do not know it today." (*Dawson Daily News*, 5 April 1907.)

219 Stone, "The Mounties as Vigilantes," in *Law and Society*, p. 88; See also Stone, "Atomistic Order," pp. 325-339; Palmer, "Government and Society," *The Forum*, pp. 603-605.
220 Buteau, "My Experiences," pp. 98-99.
221 Jarvis, pp. 147-148.

In 1895 when the North West Mounted Police had established themselves near Forty Mile, they, in at least one instance, resorted to banishment as the solution to criminal activity. Inspector Constantine recorded in his diary for August, 1895 that an accusation had been brought by "Walker" against "Williams" for theft of a diamond stud valued at $60. The case was dismissed for lack of evidence, but Williams was, nevertheless, "ordered to leave the country" by Inspector Constantine, "as was a bad character." ("Constantine

Diary," Records of the Royal Canadian Mounted Police.) The decision of the Miners' Association would likely have been the same.

222 Webb, "The River Trip to the Klondike," *New Century Illustrated Magazine*, March 1898, p. 682.

223 Heller, ed., *Sourdough Sagas*, p. 4.

224 Time-Life Books, 1976 *The Miners*, p. 208.

225 Jarvis, p. 24.

Francois Mercier's opinion of the Han-Kutchin was in stark contrast: "They were, then, true hypocrites(sic) who would not have wanted to shoot a rifle on Sunday nor eat the meat of an animal because their minister told them not to, but who meanwhile would steal from you this day or any other day of the week. They were sharp, shrewd men who would kill their women with work and of a revolting cruelty toward their poor dogs." (Mercier, p. 57)

Robert Kennicott, the original director of the Scientific Corps, assigned to the Western Union Telegraph Expedition in 1865 made equally negative comments regarding the Ft. Yukon Kutcha-Kutchin, writing: "They treat their women a little worse than their dogs, and the killing of female infants, to avoid the care of them, is not, or was, of very rare occurrence." (Dall, "Robert Kennicott," *Chicago Academy of Science Transactions 1867-69*, pp.133-226.)

226 Dall, "Reminiscences," *Popular Science Monthly*, pp. 136-137.

227 *Sitka Alaskan*, 26 March 1892.

For a more detailed account of observations made of the Indians inhabiting the area between the Peel River and the Yukon River see also Hardisty, "The Loucheux Indians," pp.311-320; and Jones, "The Kutchin Tribes," pp. 320-327, in *Smithsonian Institution Annual Report*, 1866, Yukon Archives.

228 Steffens, "Life," *McClure's Magazine*, pp. 957-958.

229 Ogilvie, Lecture, p. 29.

230 Steffens, "Life," *McClure's Magazine*, pp. 964-965; Pike, Through the Sub-Arctic Forest, pp. 220-221.

231 Callahan, p. 128.

The murdered John Bremner was the same man who entered the interior of Alaska in 1885 in company with Lt. Henry Allen. (Bettles, "Some Early Yukon River History," in *Sourdough Sagas*, p. 119.)

Schwatka, reporting on his 1883 reconnaissance of the Yukon River valley, stated that the Indians at the mouth of the Koyukuk "have the worst reputation of any from Ft. Yukon to the mouth of the Yukon." (Schwatka, *A Reconnaissance*, p. 322.)

232 The men in the party were Joseph Ladue, Hank Wright, Jim Bender, Frank Dinsmore, Tom Evans, George Cary, Frank Hawley, Captain Billy Moore, Old Herman, Jim Stafford, George Newman, Jim Baker, John and Jim McPike, Tuck Lambert and Gordon Bettles.(Bettles, "Some Early Yukon River History," in *Sourdough Sagas*, p. 121; *Sitka Alaskan*, 13 October 1888.

Jim Bender in his memoirs, "Early Days in Alaska," which appears in *Sourdough Sagas*, also listed in the party: Nick Lambert, Matt Hall and Henry Davis. (p. 87.) An article in the *Sitka Alaskan* indicated there were 25 men in the "lynching party," but did not list their names. (*Sitka Alaskan*, 13 October 1888.)

233 *Sitka Alaskan*, 13 October 1888.

Gordon Bettles, one of the miners, wrote that the steamer they borrowed was named the *Explorer.* (Bettles, "Some Early Yukon River History," p. 121.)

By 1888, the Alaska Commercial Co. had two steamers on the lower Yukon, the *Explorer* and the *Pioneer*. The *Explorer* was used primarily by their trader, Aneasum Belkof, at Russian Mission. (*Sitka Alaskan*, 13 October 1888) The *Pioneer* was a steam launch originally brought to St. Michael in 1865 (Pierçe, Diary, p. 206.)

234 Callahan, p. 128.

235 The murderer, ignorant of the judicial system, said he had shot Bremner believing he

would be sent to San Francisco and paid $700. His misconception was based on an event the previous year when another Indian, Sneataw, was sent to San Francisco to testify against a man named Fuller who had allegedly murdered Archbishop Seghers. (*Sitka Alaskan*, 13 October 1888.)

236 Bettles, "Some Early Yukon River History," pp. 121-122; *Sitka Alaskan*, 13 October 1888; Davis, "Recollections," p. 55, Jim Bender, Indian Hanging on Koyukuk, 1888, Snow Collection, Yukon Archives.

Such vigilantism was not new to gold camps. Historian H.W. Brands wrote in *The Age of Gold* that when gangs from New York City and Australia arrived in the gold fields of California in the 1850s they were dealt with by Committees of Vigilance. The charters of the committees pledged their members to "the maintenance of the peace and good order of society, and the preservation of the lives and property of the citizens" While they were bound to uphold civil law that was present in the form of sheriffs, they were determined "that no thief, burglar, incendiary or assassin shall escape punishment, either by the quibbles of the law, the insecurity of prisons, the carelessness or corruption of the police, or a laxity of those who pretend to administer justice." (p. 265.)

237 Adney, *The Klondike Stampede*, pp. 241-242; Ogilvie, Lecture, p. 21.

"Drifting," i.e., tunneling to follow the pay-streak after having reached bedrock was first tried successfully by O.C., Miller on Forty Mile. The practice was not generally understood and, therefore, not widely used until a few years before the Klondike Gold Rush. In the Yukon, drifting required thawing the ground with small wood fires then hoisting the dirt to the surface where it was piled on a "dump." The dirt was sluiced the following spring when water was flowing in the streams. One of the hazards of burning was carbonic acid created by the fires. Many miners used a rude ventilating machine that was a hand-made windmill. (Adney, *The Klondike Stampede*, p. 243; Dall, "Alaska and the New Gold Field," *The Forum*, p.23; Ladue, *Klondike Facts*, p. 99)

238 Buteau, "My Experiences," pp. 102-103.

Al Mayo, from whom Joe purchased the borax to be used by Buteau and John Nelson in their blacksmithing business, likely did similar work himself at Ft. Nelson. At the time of his enlistment in the U.S. Army in 1863 Mayo was a "blacksmith's apprentice." (Adjutant General Records- Muster Roll for Illinois Regiments in Civil War, Illinois State Library)

In 1899 Buteau was again making miners' picks. A brief advertisement in the October 25 issue of The Klondike Nugget reads: "Frank Buteau's own make of miner's picks for sale at A.C. Co. or Frank Buteau's blacksmith shop, Klondike City; thirteen years experience. $5.25 without handle. $6 with handle. Name stamped on every pick." Buteau's first blacksmithing in the Yukon was in 1886 when he and John Nelson repaired the points of miners' picks.

239 Buteau, "My Experiences," p. 106.

240 McConnell, "Report on an Exploration," in Dawson, *Report*, p. 232.

241 *New York Times*, 28 October 1888.

242 *Seattle Daily Times*, 22, July 1897.

243 Ibid.; Sullivan Papers.

244 Ogilvie, *Early Days*, pp. 79-80.

245 Buteau, "My Experiences," pp. 104-105, McQuesten to McKay.

246 It is likely that many of the men were actually on a scow or barge the *Little Pelley* had in tow. None of the smaller steamers pushed their freight barges.

247 Bettles, Why I Came to Alaska, *Fairbanks News-Miner*, fall 1995; McQuesten to McKay; Spurr, *Through the Yukon Gold Diggings*, p. 114.

248 Ogilvie, *Early Days*, p. 67. No indication has been found that there was a breach of friendship among the three men. It seems likely that Harper, from his many years of prospecting on the rivers of the upper Yukon, believed that there was much gold yet to be found in that area, an opinion McQuesten and Mayo may not have shared.

249 Davis, "Recollections," p. 71.

250 Ogilvie, *Early Days*, p. 118.

251 Adney, *The Klondike Stampede*, p. 277.
252 Ibid., pp. 276-77; Adney, "Who Discovered the Klondike; *New York World*, 6 August 1897; Adney, Interview with Joe Ladue, Dartmouth College Library.
253 Hayes, "An Expedition Through the Yukon District," *National Geographic Magazine*, 15 May 1892, pp. 121-122.

In the spring of 1891, a syndicate of U.S. newspapers organized an expedition to explore a portion of the southern Yukon District. On June 28, 1891 the expedition party, comprised of three white men (Charles W. Hayes, a geologist with the U. S. Geological Survey, Lt. Frederick Schwatka of the U.S. Army and a prospector, Mark Russell) arrived at Ft. Selkirk. There they reported they saw "a store...recently...established on the site of old Ft. Selkirk," and that "The trader, Mr. Harper, was down the river...." (Hayes, "An Expedition Through the Yukon District," *National Geographic Magazine*, p.121)

Harper had actually "established" his store on the second site of Ft. Selkirk, which was under construction in August 1852 when it was pillaged and destroyed by Chilkats from the coast. The original site of Ft. Selkirk, constructed in 1848 by Robert Campbell was on the left bank of the Pelly River. The site was, at times of high water, an island.

254 Juneau Business Directory, 1895, Alaska State Library Historical Collections; See also *New York World*, 6 August 1897; Davis, *Recollections,* p. 71; *Yukon Press*, 1 January 1896.

Frank Buteau, who was mining in the Yukon at the time, stated that "In the summer of 1891, Harper established a trading post at Ft. Selkirk." (Buteau, "*My Experiences*," p. 115)

Ladue's new partner was born in County Antrim, Ireland in 1835. He arrived on the Atlantic coast of the United States as a young boy and soon made his way west. In the late 1860s he worked as a miner in British Columbia. Finding little success there, and believing with many others that North America's goldfields extended farther north, he made he made his way to the Mackenzie River, and floated down to its mouth with four companions; George Finch, Andrew Kansellar, Frederick Harte and George Wilkinson. Following the route laid out by the Hudson's Bay Co. in the 1840s, they traveled up the Peel River, over McDougal Pass and finally down the Porcupine to the Alaska Commercial Co. post at Ft. Yukon, arriving in August, 1873. Harper spent that fall and the following spring prospecting on the Forty Mile, Sixty Mile and White rivers, returning to the Yukon River via the Tanana. There he again met Leroy Napoleon "Jack" McQuesten and his party who had also arrived at Ft. Yukon the previous summer. Harper, McQuesten and Alfred Mayo formed a partnership to work as traders on the river for the Alaska Commercial Co., a partnership that would last nearly fifteen years. (Ogilvie, *Early Days*, pp. 87- 97.)

255 Ogilvie, Lecture, p. 27.
256 Fickett, *Meteorology*, p. 489; Schwatka, *A Reconnaissance*, p. 319.
257 McQuesten to McKay.
258 *New York World*, 6 August 1897.
259 Adney, *The Klondike Stampede*, p. 277; Adney, "Who Discovered the Klondike?" *Harper's Weekly*; *New York World*, 6 August 1897.
260 Wilson, p. 36.
261 Ogilvie, Lecture, p. 11.
262 Adney, *The Klondike Stampede*, p. 277; Adney, Interview with Joe Ladue.
263 *New York World*, 6 September 1897.
264 Adney, *The Klondike Stampede*, p. 456.
265 *Sitka Alaskan*, 31 August 1895.
266 *New York World*, 6 August 1897.

Miller Creek is a tributary of the Sixty Mile River, which flows into the Yukon from the west and is not in the Klondike District.

267 Stein, "The Gold Fields of Alaska," *Review of Reviews*, p. 697.
268 Ogilvie, *Early Days*, p. 113.
269 Davis, "Recollections," p. 73.
270 *The Klondike Nugget*, 25 November 1900.
271 Ogilvie, *Early Days*, p. 120.

272 Ibid., pp. 36, 67-68.
273 Pike, *Through the Sub-Arctic Forest*, pp. 216-217.
274 Henderson, *The True Story of the Discovery of the Klondike by Bob Henderson*, pp. 12, 16.
275 Ogilvie, *Early Days*, p. 67; Ogilvie, Lecture, p. 12.
276 Ogilvie, Lecture, p. 29.
277 John Jerome Healy had operated a trading post at Dyea, Alaska for about seven years when he decided to explore opportunities in the interior of the Yukon and Alaska. With the financial backing of the Cudahy Meat Packing Co. of Chicago, plans were made to start trading at Forty Mile in 1892. In late July he stated to a reporter of the Seattle Post Intelligencer: "Now as to what we propose doing. We have gotten together out here all the timbers, machinery, boiler and everything for a steamer about the size of the (ocean-going) 'State of Washington.' We have chartered the steamer *Alice Blanchard* at Tacoma and expect her here by Saturday to carry our boat up in the mouth of the Yukon, where we will put it together. We are also taking up mill machinery, mining pumps and a general stock of supplies and, if everything goes as I feel it will we will establish headquarters in Seattle after a time and run a regular line of boats.

"Our steamer will be named the *P.B. Weare*. We expect to run her up the Yukon at least 1600 miles. (*Seattle Post Intelligencer*, 26 June 1892; Burlingame, "John Healy's Alaskan Adventure", p. 310 ff.)
278 Stein, "The Gold Fields of Alaska," *Review of Reviews*, p. 697.
279 Although prices did drop quickly with the opening of the N. A. T. & T Co. store, John Healy, as its manager made few friends in the Yukon and by October about half the supplies he had brought in on the company's steamer *P.B. Weare* remained unsold. (Ogilvie, *Early Days*, p. 68; *Sitka Alaskan*, 14 October 1893.)

John Jerome Healy was born in 1840 in County Cork, Ireland. In 1853 he,his father, Thomas, his mother and his five siblings (Thomas, Maurice, Anselm, Joseph and Mary), arrived at Ellis Island. Healy left New York in 1857 to join the U.S. Army and was soon assigned to duty in Utah "to control the mormons." In 1860 he received his discharge from the Army and "began taking up the more adventurous life of a frontiersman." In 1863, he married Mary Francis Wilson of New York City. In 1871 Healy moved north to the province of Alberta and established Ft. Whoop-up where he carried on fur trading and whiskey peddling. By 1881 he was back in Montana where he served as sheriff of Choteau County. At Dyea, Alaska he and a partner, Edgar Wilson, a Civil War veteran, built a trading post in 1886. His business ventures in the Yukon began in 1893 with the establishment of Ft. Cudahy near the mining camp of Forty Mile. He died September 15, 1908, in Los Angeles at age 68 and was eventually buried in Lakeview Cemetery in Seattle beside his first wife, Mary, his only son, Thomas and his granddaughter, Regina Mary. (Hunt, *Whiskey Peddler*, pp. 4-9, 48-49, 115, 231, 144.)
280 Murphy, Haigh, p. 84.
281 Callahan, p. 128; Ogilvie, *Early Days*, p. 113; Murphy, Haigh, p. 20.
282 McQuesten to McKay.
283 Callahan, pp. 127-128.
284 Anonymous account, Snow Collection, Yukon Archives; Ogilvie, *Early Days*, p. 113; Mercier, p. 18; Callahan, p. 128.
285 Adney, *The Klondike Stampede*, p. 458; *Alaska-Yukon Gold Book*, p. 26.
286 Palmer, "Government and Society," *The Forum*, pp. 603-604.
287 George Washington Carmack arrived in the Yukon in 1885 via the Chilkoot Pass. He soon married a Tagish woman and began to follow the Indian way of life. When his wife died in the early 1890s he married her sister Shaaw Tlaa (Kate). In 1893 George and Kate traveled down the Yukon River to a point about 20 miles above Five Finger Rapids to establish a trading post for John Healy who operated a store at Dyea, Alaska. The short-lived venture was known among miners as "McCormick's Post." (Adney, *The Klondike Stampede*, p. 282)

In the fall of 1894 he left his post and traveled downriver to Ladue's Ogilvie post where he spent the winter. The following summer when Joe returned from his extended trip back to his hometown of Schuyler Falls, New York, he hired Carmack to work at his sawmill. In the fall he traveled upriver to Ft. Selkirk on his way to Big Salmon River. When the steamer arrived it was too late for it to go farther and Carmack remained at Ft. Selkirk for the winter of 1895-96 and looked after the Harper and Co. trading post while Harper was Outside on business. (Carmack, *My Trip to the Yukon*, p. 13; for biographical information see *Alaska-Yukon Gold Book*, pp. 32-33.)

288 Carmack, *My Trip to the Yukon*, p. 13.

289 Leonard, p. 138; Lyons, *Glimpses of Alaska*, p. 26; Adney, *The Klondike Stampede*, p. 282.

290 Adney, *The Klondike Stampede*, p. 283; Adney, "Who Discovered the Klondike?" *Harper's Weekly*.

Carmack's daughter, Graphie Grace, described him as "fair, blue eyes," and "always wore a mustache because he said his nose was so large he said that if he had a mustache it kinda hid his nose, you know. He'd kid about it." (*Gold: A Human Story of All That Glitters Told by Sourdoughs Who Were in it*, Capitol Records, Ed and Star Jones Collection.)

Among the papers of George Snow, historian for the Yukon Order of Pioneers, is a statement by George Carmack that later, in the summer of 1895, he went upriver aboard the N. A. T. & T. Co.'s steamer, Arctic to Ft. Selkirk "to look after the post at that place for Mr. Harper as Mr. Harper was coming later on another boat, but the other boat did not arrive until late in the fall, so again I could not get back to my post up the river." (George Carmack, *My Trip to the Yukon*, p. 13, Snow Collection, Yukon Archives; See also, Cruikshank, "Discovery of Gold on the Klondike: Perspectives from Oral Tradition," in Brown and Vibert, Reading *Beyond Words: Contexts for Native History*, p. 445.) Carmack left his store in the summer of 1894, but wasn't able to get back. (Carmack. *My Experiences in the Yukon*, Snow Collection, Yukon Archives.)

291 New York World, 6 August 1897.

292 Chapman, "Mining Life on the Yukon," *The West Shore*, vol. 12, 1886, p. 359.

293 Prior to a winter journey, beans were cooked and spread into thin sheets, usually on the roofs of cabins where they froze. Broken into small chunks carried in canvas bags, they could quickly be prepared in a pot over a camp fire.

294 Chris Sonnikson, *Klondike Nugget*, 19 March 1899.

295 Bobillier, *Madame Emilie Tremblay: A Pioneer Woman of the Yukon*, unpublished Joanne Sanchez Collection.

296 Minutes of the first meeting of the Yukon Order of Pioneers, December 1, 1894, Yukon Archives.

297 Davis, "Recollections," p. 75; see also: Buteau, "My Experiences," p. 114; Steffens, "Life," *McClure's Magazine*, September 1897, p. 965-6.

298 Steffens, "Life," *McClure's Magazine*, September 1897, pp. 965-6.

299 Interview with Kittie Ladue, unidentified New York City newspaper late December 1897; Sullivan Papers.

300 McMasters, "Clinton County's Man in Alaska," North Country Notes.

301 Kittie Ladue scrapbook.

302 *Alaska Sights and Scenes for the Tourist*, Union Pacific System, Omaha, Nebraska, 1894 (brochure), Ed and Star Jones Collection. (This brochure was carried to the Yukon by Ellis Turner in 1895.)

303 Ellis Turner to Turner Family, 18 March 1895, Turner Family Collection.

304 Ibid. 19 March 1895.

305 Ibid. 20 March 1895.

306 Ibid. 19 March 1895.

307 Joe Ladue to his friend Willie Lobdell 25 March 1895, Joseph F. Ladue III Collection.

308 Ellis Turner to Turner Family, 25, March 1895.

309 Ibid., 28 March 1895.

310 Ibid., 29 March 1895.

311 Joe later referred to her as "a pioneer of pioneers." (Ladue, *Klondike Facts*, p. 147; *New York*

World, 2 August 1897)

312 Ellis Turner to Turner Family, 20 May 1895.

313 McMasters, "Clinton County's Man in Alaska," *North Country Notes*.

314 Ellis Turner to Turner Family, 20, May 1895.

315 Schwatka, *A Summer in Alaska*, p. 274.

316 Note, Joseph Ladue III Collection.

317 Ellis Turner to Turner Family, 19 May 1895.

318 Ibid., 9 June 1895.

319 Ibid., 19 May 1895; 16 June 1895.

320 Ibid., 21 July 1895.

321 Joe Ladue to *Plattsburgh Sentinel* from Ogilvie, N.W.T., 22 July 1895, Dawson City Museum/Klondike History Library.

322 Bishop Bompas' concern was primarily related to the effect the presence of white men was having on Indians. He stated that "the miners coming down from the mines to pass the long winter, in British Territory (Forty Mile) crowd the traders' houses. They, I am told have the usual accompaniments of a miner's encampment, dancing saloon, gambling and drinking, in which I suppose they persuade the Indians who work for them at the mines to join. But, it is also said that the miners are manufacturing illicit whiskey and that the Indians are learning to do the same. It is thus I fear the Indians will be demoralized...I do not know that injury to the Indians could be wholly avoided but it might probably be partially at least, abated by a little provident government interference, such as I doubt not might be cheerfully received by yourself if the matters were in your hands." (Bishop Wm. Bompas to the Lieutenant Governor of British Columbia, Buxton Mission on a Yukon River island near Forty Mile, 1 August 1892, National Archives of Canada.)

323 Annual Report of Inspector C. Constantine, Ft. Constantine, Cudahy P.O., Upper Yukon, 20 January 1896, Yukon Archives.

324 Hayne, *The Pioneers of the Klondyke*, p. 45.

325 Baird, *Sixty Years in the Klondike*, p. 9; see also Ladue, *Klondyke Nuggets*, p. 18; Ellis Turner to Turner Family, 24 July 1895.

326 Hayne, pp. 48, 61, 65, 66, 128.

327 Ladue, *Klondyke Nuggets*, p. 19.

328 *Seattle Daily Times*, 22 July 1897.

329 *Plattsburgh Sentinel*, 4 August 1895.

330 Hayne, p. 2.

331 William Ogilvie to "Mr. Wilson," Forty Mile, 22 May 1897, National Archives of Canada.

332 Annual Report of Inspector C. Constantine, Ft. Constantine, Cudahy P.O., Upper Yukon, 20 January 1896, pp. 12-13.

333 Joe Ladue to the editor of the *Plattsburgh Sentinel*, 4 August 1895, Dawson City Museum/Klondike History Library.

334 Ellis Turner to Turner Family, 1 August 1895.

335 Ibid., 29 December 1895.

336 Hayne, p. 47.

337 Stein, "The Gold Fields of Alaska," *Review of Reviews*, p. 697; see also Ogilvie, *Early Days*, p. 68.

338 Ellis Turner to Turner Family, 29 December 1895; see also *Henderson, The True Story*, p. 12.

339 Celina Bompas, *Spirit of Missions Magazine*, June 1895; Johns, *The Early Yukon, Alaska, and the Klondike Discovery as They Were Before the Great Klondike Stampede Swept Away the Old Conditions by one Who Was There*, p. 85, Yukon Archives.

340 Crystal McQuesten Morgan, *A Human Story of All That Glitters Told by Sourdoughs Who Were in it*, Ed and Star Jones Collection.

341 Callahan, p. 127.

342 J.C. Hestwood, *London Daily Mail*, 28 August 1897.

343 Ellis Turner to Turner Family, 28 January 1896.

344 Hayne, p. 51.
345 Ellis Turner to Turner Family, 29 December 1895.
346 Chapman, "Mining Life on the Yukon," *The West Shore*, p. 359.
347 Ellis Turner to Turner Family, 5 January 1896.
348 Ibid., 27 October 1895.

William Ogilvie wrote: "A few words about the mosquitoes. During the summer, and until September, they are a veritable plague. They seem to feed on smoke. As to fire—they appear to revel in it. The only way to escape them is to cover one's self with mosquito netting. Indeed, it is impossible to prospect in the summer time unless a man be an old miner and well hardened, for all day long, and twenty-four hours in the day, those mosquitoes are after you. It is no use trying to get rid of them." (Ogilvie, Lecture, p. 23)

William Dall wrote: "Mosquitoes, the pest of the North, appear in clouds. Except in midstream, or where a brisk breeze is blowing, life without a net and leather gloves is misery. The Indians smear their faces with a mixture of grease and charcoal, and paddle with a smudge on a square turf in the bows of their birch canoes. The caribou, moose, and bear, driven from the thickets, plunge into the river, for a temporary respite." (Dall, "Alaska and the New Gold Field," *The Forum*, September 1897, p. 19.

349 Willis Lamay left Forty Mile sometime after July 1, 1896 when he signed as a witness to a document written by Arthur Harper on that date. (Declaration, Arthur Harper, Department of the Interior, Ottawa, 1 July 1896, National Archives of Canada)
350 Ellis Turner to Turner Family, 7 June 1896.
351 *New York World*, 6 August 1897.
352 Joseph Ladue, to his friend Willie Lobdell, from "Wrangle Narrows, Alaska," 3 March 1896, Joseph F. Ladue III Collection.
353 Henderson, *The True Story*, p. 16.
354 *Yukon Press*, 1 January 1896. When the Beaver arrived at St. Michael in the summer of 1896, Harper employed Stewart Menzies to take her upriver to Fort Selkirk. (McCurdy, Marine History of the Pacific Northwest, p. 9) Menzies later worked as auditor fo the Alaska Commercial Company in Dawson and made application for a parcel of land adjacent to the Harper and Ladue townsite. It is still known as the Menzies addition. Manzies is buried in the Hillside Public Cemetery in Dawson.
355 *New York World*, 6 August 1897.
356 Ellis Turner to Turner Family, 7 June 1896; Bobillier, *Madame Emilie Tremblay*, p. 26; Buteau, "My Experiences," p. 115; *Yukon Press*, June 1896.

Hugh Day and his brother Al were among the early miners in the Yukon. In 1884 they prospected on the upper river; the summers of 1885 and 1886 they mined the bars of the Stewart and were among the few men who did extremely well on that river. Over the next few years they mined on the Forty Mile and Sixty Mile. Hearing of the strike on Bonanza in 1896 they soon had two claims, 30 and 31 Below Discovery on that creek and No. 11 on Bear Creek. The brothers also made application for land that became known as the Day Addition to the Harper and Ladue Townsite. (*Klondike Nugget*, Anniversary Number, November 1, 1899) Hugh Day died in Douglas, Alaska, December 31, 1914. (*Douglas Island News*, 6 January 1915.)

357 The *Bella* was one of the largest and most powerful ships on the Yukon in 1896. It was 30 feet wide by 145 feet long, had 350 horsepower engines, could carry 200 tons and towed two barges, each carrying 300 tons. (Ellis Turner to Turner Family, 20 October 1896 from aboard "The Steamer *Bella*.")
358 Ellis Turner to Turner Family, 8 September 1896.
359 Ibid., 20 October 1896.
360 Ogilvie, *Early Days*, p. 119.
361 Henderson, *True Story*, preface, pp. 8, 12, 19; *Alaska-Yukon Gold Book*, p. 27.
362 Ogilvie, *Early Days*, p. 120.
363 Adney, *The Klondike Stampede*, pp. 277-278.
364 *New York World*, 6 August 1897.

There were at least 18 other men working on Quartz Creek the summer of 1896. They had entered the Yukon that spring and were told of Henderson's find. (*Alaska-Yukon Gold Book*, p. 29)

365 Henderson, *The True Story*, p. 19.

Other men had already tried their luck on the creek Henderson named Gold Bottom. In a letter to Tappan Adney, dated 19 December 1898, he wrote: "thair was two men on Gold Bottom before I was and found gold but not enough to pay. thair names is Munson and Ed Nelson. I tried harde to get them to go over to the creek with me but thay would not go so I went by my Self and Staid five days prospecting on the creek..." (Robert Henderson to Tappan Adney, Dartmouth College Library.)

366 Adney, *The Klondike Stampede*, p. 279; Robert Henderson to Tappan Adney.

367 Henderson, *The True Story*, p. 17.

368 *New York World*, 6 August 1897; see also Henderson, *The True Story*, p. 19.

369 Joe stated to the *New York World* that at Ogilvie he had "two American horses which I bought of Jack Dalton." Perhaps he had obtained two others from another source. (*New York World*, 6 August 1897) Tappan Adney recorded from his interview with Ladue that he "sent over two horses and packs." (Tappan Adney, Interview with Joe Ladue)

The first horse was brought over the Chilkoot Pass and to the Yukon River in 1893 by Bill McPhee. McPhee said that bringing in the horse was the proudest thing he had done in the Yukon. It was still alive in 1899 and the property of Belinda Mulrooney. McPhee announced it was his intention to "purchase the animal, no matter what the cost, take him in a palace car to Southern California and pension him for life." (*Dawson Daily News*, Special Mining Edition, midsummer, 1899, p. 28.)

370 Sleicher, "The Original King,"; *Henderson, The True Story*, p. 19; *New York World*, 6 August 1897; Tappan Adney, Interview with Joe Ladue.

371 Johnson, Carmack, pp. 58-59, 63, 84; Cruikshank, "Discovery…," in *Reading Beyond Words*, pp. 442-448.

Kate Carmack was the sister of Skookum Jim; Tagish Charlie and Patsy Henderson were Jim and Kate's nephews. Because of his involvement at Dawson, and the fact that there was already a man in his village known as Tagish Charlie, Charlie's name was changed to Dawson Charlie. It seems odd that Carmack would have given Patsy the name Henderson. All were Tlingits. Carmack and Kate named their daughter Ah-gay, but changed it to Graphie Grace because her Indian name was considered by white men to be quite difficult to pronounce. The new name was after a character Carmack found in a book he had borrowed from Rev. T. H. Canham at Ft. Selkirk. Carmack would later abandon Kate and in July 1901 she returned to her village at Carcross, taking Grace with her. (Cruikshank, "Discovery…," in Brown and Vibert, *Reading Beyond Words*, p.132; Johnson, George Carmack, pp. 80-81,141, 145.) Kate died of influenza March 29, 1920 and is buried in the Carcross cemetery. (Backhouse, *Women in the Klondike*, p. 10.)

372 Carmack, *My Experiences in the Yukon*, p. 9.

373 Henderson, *The True Story*, p. 19; see also *Alaska-Yukon Gold Book*, pp. 32-33.

374 *New York World*, August 6, 1897; see also, Adney, Interview with Joe Ladue.

375 Carmack, *My Experiences in the Yukon*, p. 13.

Carmack apparently felt it was pre-ordained that something uncommon was going to happen to him the summer of 1896. His story is that "One very early morning in the latter part of May 1896, I was sitting on the bank of the river at Ft. Selkirk...Over the palisades the morning star was drowsily blinking... As I watched the flaming banners thrust forth their streams of scintillating fire above the mountains I felt my blood begin to tingle with new life and strength. I had a premonition that something unusual was going to take place in my life. Right then and there I made up my mind to take action on that hunch at once, so, taking a silver dollar out of my pocket I flipped it into the air. It was to be heads up the river and tails down the river. It came out tails." (Carmack, My Experiences in the Yukon, p. 6.) George Snow recorded that on July 1, 1896, Carmack was at Forty Mile completely broke, having in his pocket "only about $5.00 in dust and a silver dollar in chee-cha-Co money which he carried...for a souvenir lucky piece (he was very superstitious). At Forty Mile he asked McQuesten for an outfit so he could go on a fishing and prospecting trip. McQuesten gave him $130 worth of provisions and he headed upriver for the Klondike." Seven weeks later his prospecting trip paid off. (George Snow, Snow Collection, Yukon Archives.)

376 Armstrong, *Yukon Yesterdays*, pp. 29-30.

377 *Seattle Daily Times*, July 24, 1897.

378 Glave, "Pioneer Packhorses in Alaska," *Century Illustrated Monthly Magazine*, September-October, 1892; *Seattle Daily Times*, 24 July 1897.

379 *Dawson Daily News*, May 13, 1904; *Alaska-Yukon Gold Book*, p. 31.

380 Nelson, Snow Collection, Yukon Archives.

381 Adney, "A Winter's Work in the Klondike," *Harper's Weekly*, 1 October 1898.

382 Ogilvie to Wilson.

383 *New York World*, 6 August 1897.

384 Carmack, *My Experiences in the Yukon*, p. 14; Ogilvie, Lecture, p. 13; Berton, *Klondike: All That Glitters, 1896-1899*, p. 45.

James Albert Johnson, in his book *Carmack,* mentions George Carmack meeting Alphonse Lapierre and George Remillard at the mouth of the Klondike before he started for Forty Mile to register his discovery claim on Bonanza. Johnson's references were primarily a number of letters written by Carmack that he found at a bookstore in Seattle. The letters had come from the library of Judge James Wickersham who served in Eagle, Alaska, for a number of years and wrote *Old Yukon, Tales, Trails and Trials*.

Jeanne Pomerleau, in Les chercheurs d'or, Des Canadians francais epris de richesse et d'adventure, wrote that Alphonse Lapierre of Quebec, and one of his friends heard about Bonanza from George Carmack when he was on his way to Forty Mile to register his claim. He told them to return and choose a claim on Bonanza. They had been prospecting "infructueuses" (fruitlessly) for nine years, their faces were sunburned, [they were] hungry and more dead than alive. They doubted Carmack's word, but returned to Bonanza and "Ils y firent fortune," there they found their fortune. (pp. 107-108.)

385 Ogilvie, *Early Days*, pp. 130-131; Fritz Kloke, Application for Grant for Placer Mining, #21; Harry Waugh, Application for Grant for Placer Mining, #35; David McKay, Application for Grant for Placer Mining, #37; Dan McGillivary, Application for Placer Mining, #297. (Mining Records Book, Dawson City Museum/Klondike History Library.)

Ogilvie's statement that Dave Edwards staked No. 16 Below Discovery differs from Mining Records Book at the Klondike History Library in the Dawson City Museum, which indicates that Dan McGillivary filed on it October 23, 1896.

386 Adney, *The Klondike Stampede*, p. 289.

387 Jarvis, pp. 167-68.

388 Application and Affidavit for Placer Mine, Numbers 136, 138 and 139, Yukon Archives.

389 Hayne, p. 136; Spurr, *New York Times*, 7 August 1897; Ogilvie, Lecture, p. 13; *Yukon Press*, April 1897.

390 Ogilvie, in Ladue, *Klondyke Facts*, p. 178; Letter, Ogilvie to Wilson.

391 *New York World*, 6 August 1897.

392 Ladue, *Klondyke Facts*, p. 152; see also Sleicher, "The Original King "; Leonard, pp. 47-48.

When Joe arrived at the mouth of the Klondike two men, Jack Moffatt and Theo Anderson who were just starting up the Klondike for Bonanza Creek "called out to Ladue of the strike that had just been made." (Adney, Interview with Joe Ladue.)

393 Joseph Ladue's application to the Minister of the Interior to purchase Dominion Land, 27 August 1896, Yukon Archives; Adney, Interview with Joe Ladue.

394 Adney, Interview with Joe Ladue; New York World, 6 August 1897; Adney, *The Klondike Stampede*, p. 181.

The first structure in the area, though perhaps not within the perimeters of the townsite laid out by Joe, was a fish-drying shed belonging to Fritz Kloke. Two other white men were also nearby, Dan Monahan and Joseph Cooper. (Adney, *The Klondike Stampede*, p.

283) Across the mouth of the Klondike was Tr'ochek, the traditional fish camp of the Tr'ondek H'wech'in, one of several groups of the Han living along that section of the Yukon River. When the men of the gold rush arrived in 1898 the Han were moved to a site three downriver from Dawson, and the site of their former camp was inhabited by prostitutes. Its new name was Lousetown. Later, when the area became an industrial center, the name was changed to Klondike City (*Tr'ochek, The Archaeology and History of a Han Fish Camp*. Government of Yukon, Department of Tourism, Heritage Branch, 2001, Government Records.)

395 *New York World*, 8 August 1897.

396 Adney, Who Discovered the Klondike?, *Harper's Weekly*; Archibald, *A Substantial Expression of Confidence*, p. 12.

397 *New York World*, 6 August 1897.

398 Adney, *The Klondike Stampede*, pp. 288-89.

399 Burlingame, pp. 310 ff.; *New York World*, 6 August 1897.

400 *New York World*, 6 August 1897.

401 Sleicher, "*The Original King*."

402 Index of Original Locators, Placer Claims, 1896-1903, Yukon Archives; Mining Records Book, Dawson City Museum/Klondike History Library.

403 *New York World*, 6 August 1897.

404 Ibid. George Westbrook, a native of the state of Georgia, remained in Dawson for the remainder of his life, dying 30 September, 1954.

405 Ogilvie, *Early Days*, pp. 216-17, 272.

406 O'Connor, *High Jinks on the Klondike*, p. 176.

407 Winslow, p. 143.

408 Ogilvie, *Early Days*, p. 272.

409 Hamlin, *Old Times on the Yukon*, p. 11.

410 Tollemache, *Reminiscences*, p. 53.

411 O'Connor, p. 176.

412 *New York World*, 6 August 1897.

413 Ibid.

414 Memorandum, E. Deville, Surveyor General, 4 November 1898, Topographical Surveys Branch, Department of the Interior to the Deputy Minister of the Interior, National Archives of Canada; Ogilvie, *Early Days*, p. 159.

415 Ogilvie, Field Notebook No. 5, 1896-1897, p. 67, Canadian National Archives; Commissioner Ogilvie to "Mr. Justice Dugas," 3 December 1898; Memorandum, W. H. Matthews, Department of Geology, University of British Columbia, Yukon Archives.

416 Plan of Dawson and Klondike Townsites, Yukon District—NWT, Surveyed by James Gibbon DLS, 1897 and 1898, Dawson City Museum/Klondike History Library.

417 Commissioner Ogilvie to C. M. Woodworth, Department of the Interior, 8 February 1899; Commissioner Ogilvie to the Minister of the Interior, 28 June 1899, Yukon Archives.

418 Ladue, *Klondyke Facts*, p. 152.

419 *Seattle Daily Times*, 22 July 1897.

420 Ogilvie, *Early Day*, p. 67.

421 *Seattle Daily Times*, 22 July 1897.

422 Ogilvie, *Early Days*, pp. 195-197.

423 Hamlin, pp. 21-22.

424 Dunham, *The Alaskan Gold Fields*, p. 33; Webb, "The River Trip to the Klondike," pp. 684-5, *Century Illustrated Monthly Magazine*; Tollemache, *Reminiscences*, p. 66; Lynch, *Three Years in the Klondike*, p. XXVIII.
Samuel C. Dunham was an employee of the U.S. Department of Labor. He was sent on assignment to the Klondike to determine "Opportunities They Offer for Capital and Labor."

425 Craig, p. 60.

426 Martinsen, *Black Sand and Gold*, p. 93; *New York World*, 6, 11 August 1897.

427 Next door to the Harper and Ladue sawmill in 1897 was Dawson's first ladies' shop, a building 12x24 feet. It had no sign and all the goods "lay in pufft heaps on a bare rough board counter." (Hamlin, p. 16) All the lumber for the shop came from the Harper & Ladue sawmill.

428 *Seattle Daily Times*, 22 July 1897.

429 *New York World*, 6 August 1897; Hamlin, p. 10.

430 Dunham, *The Alaskan Gold Fields*, p. 31.

431 Hayne, p. 51.

432 Hamlin, p. 10; see also Ogilvie, *Early Days*, p. 159; *New York Times*, 12 January 1898; Bettles, Why I Came to Alaska, *Fairbanks News-Miner*, fall, 1995; Annual Report of Superintendent C. Constantine, Commanding Yukon District,1897, p. 309, Royal Canadian Mounted Police Historical Branch, Ottawa, Ontario.

433 Teacher and Nichols, *The Unabridged Jack London*, p. 57.

434 *Yukon Press*, 1 January 1896.

435 Harper/Ladue Partnership Agreement, 19 November 1896,Yukon Archives.

436 *Klondike News*, 1 April 1898. Ed and Star Jones Collection.

437 Dunham, p. 25.

438 Hayne, p. 153; see also Ogilvie to Wilson; Ogilvie, Some Notes on Gold Mining in the Yukon Territory.

439 Ogilvie, Lecture, p. 15.

440 *London Times*, 11 November 1897.

441 Application from Arthur Harper for 18 acres, Nov. 17, 1896,Yukon Archives.

442 Francois Xavier Gosselin, Land and Timber Agent,to the Secretary of the Department of the Interior, Ottawa, 14 September 1901,Yukon Archives; Memorandum, E. Deville, Surveyor-General of the Topographical Surveys Branch of the Department of the Interior to the Deputy Minister of the Interior, 4 November 1898,Yukon Archives.

There were several additional acreages applied for and surveyed in the Dawson area. F. Atkins applied for 14.3 acres. Napoleon Dupras applied for 160.67 acres at the mouth of Bonanza Creek. H.C. Gingg applied for 32 acres on an island at the mouth of Bonanza. 159.6 acres were applied for by Johnson, Fortier and Morgan on the west side of the Yukon across from Dawson City. B. C. Sprague applied for 79.5 acres, which was "Lot 10," and another 12.33 acres "adjoining Lot 10," also in west Dawson. The Government held two parcels of land: 40 acres on which the compound was constructed and another 42.59 acres. Two other parcels of land were the riverfront on 1st Avenue and 26.18 acres in Klondike City (Memorandum, 4 November 1898 from E. Deville, Surveyor-General of the topographical Surveys Branch to the Deputy Minister of the Canadian Department of the Interior,Yukon Archives)

443 Application from Joseph Ladue to the Minister of the Department of the Interior for 480 acres of land, 20 November 1896,Yukon Archives.

444 Department of the Interior to Francois X. Gosselin,Yukon Lands and Timber Agent, Dawson City, 6 December 1901,Yukon Archives.

445 Applications from Arthur Harper to the Minister of the Department of the Interior for 480 acres of land and 160 acres of land at Ft. Selkirk, 30 June 1896,Yukon Archives.

446 Ibid.

447 Ibid.

448 Ibid.

449 Richardson, *Winter Conditions Along the Yukon, 1899*, p. 748.

450 Burlingame,"John Healy's Alaskan Adventure," *The Alaska Journal*, p. 310 ff.

451 Walden, a dog-team freighter, wrote that he had "helped to carry the first word" down to Circle City in January 1897. Still others have been credited with bringing the news of the Klondike strike to the men at Circle.

The *New York Times* ran an article in which they stated: "authentic news was carried to Circle City by J.M. Wilson of the Alaska Commercial Co. and Thomas O'Brien, a trader." (Walden, *New York Times*, 17 July 1897, p. 69.)

452 Adney, *The Klondike Stampede*, p. 294.
453 Hayne, pp. 139, 151.
454 Ibid., pp. 151-152; see also Adney, *The Klondike Stampede*, pp. 294-298; Ogilvie, Lecture, p. 14; Richardson, Winter Conditions, 1899, p. 748.
455 *Yukon Press*, April 1897.
456 Ogilvie, "Story of the Yukon," *Scientific American*.
457 Adney, *The Klondike Stampede*, pp. 297-98; Ogilvie, Lecture, p. 14; Walden, pp. 152-153.
458 Ellis Turner to Turner Family, 20 October 1896.
459 *New York World*, 11 August 1897.
460 *New York World*, 2 August 1897.
461 Ibid.; see also Charles J. Judge, p. 184; Ogilvie, in Ladue, *Klondike Facts*, p. 133. During an interview in August 1897 Joe stated that there were "1,500 men...in the vicinity of Dawson City when the snow began to go off..." (*New York World*, 6 August 1897.)
462 Ogilvie to Wilson. New York World, 2 August 1897.
463 *Dawson Daily News*, 11 February 1904.
464 Ogilvie to Wilson; see also, Ladue, *Klondyke Facts*, pp.133-134.
465 *New York Times*, 3 August 1897; *Klondyke News*, 17 July 1897.
466 Ogilvie to Wilson.
467 Ogilvie to Wilson; *Yukon Sun*, 7 September 1902.
468 Adney, *The Klondike Stampede*, p. 298.
469 Berton, *Klondike*, p. 83.
470 *New York World*, 6 August 1897.
471 Ladue, *Klondyke Facts*, pp. 136, 138-39.
472 *New York World*, 6 August 1897.
473 Ibid.; *New York Times*, 8, 17 August 1897; Palmer, "Government and Society," *The Forum*, p. 607; Richardson, *Winter Conditions Along the Yukon, 1899*, p. 748.
474 Ladue, *Klondyke Facts*, p. 187; see also Ogilvie to Wilson; Dunham, *The Alaskan Gold Fields*, p. 25; Ogilvie, *Some Notes on Gold Mining in the Yukon Territory*.
475 Mrs. J.T. Wills was born in Iowa, raised three daughters in Missouri, divorced her husband then traveled west to pioneer in New Mexico, Colorado and Washington. In Tacoma she married J.T. Wills, a blacksmith, gunsmith and locksmith whose name appeared in the Tacoma City Directory in 1895, but who suffered from rheumatism and was not able to work at his trade. His shop had been at 1121 Pacific Avenue. Their residence was at 3307 Mason Avenue. When Mrs. Wills heard stories of gold being found in the Yukon she set out for Alaska in March 1895 where she met Joe Ladue, Ellis Turner and Willis Lamay at Dyea and traveled with them over Chilkoot Pass and down the Yukon. For the next year she operated a bakery and laundry at Circle City. When she heard news of the strike in the Klondike she immediately went upriver and either staked or bought a claim. When she left the Klondike in the summer of 1897 her mining property was valued at $250,000. (*New York World*, 2 August 1897.)
476 *New York World*, 2 August 1897; Ladue, *Klondyke Facts*, pp. 147-48; Haskell, *Two Years in the Klondike and Alaskan Gold Fields*, pp. 399-403.
477 *New York World*, 6 August 1897.
478 Anglican Church Burial Records, #1; Bill of Sale, Victoria Faulkner Collection, Yukon Archives.
The lot Felcht purchased was "Lot 9, in Block A. being 50 x 100 feet..." ("Bill of Sail" [sic] Dawson, 18 October 1896. Dawson City Museum/Klondike History Library.
An "unknown man" committed suicide in the Klondike "during the winter" of 1897. (*Klondike Nugget*, 16 July 1898) This information was apparently not known in Dawson prior to Ladue's departure in June 1897.
479 *New York World*, 6 August 1897.
480 Tollemache, pp. 66-67.
481 The Third Avenue Cemetery is completely overgrown with willow, spruce and shrubs. Most of the original wood markers have long since fallen to the ground and disintegrat-

ed; some have been stolen. One stone monument marks the resting place of Irol Totten; it was placed there by the "Woodmen of the World" for the Totten family that still resides in Sherman, Texas. Its poignant inscription reads: "Our dear boy, Irol Totten, Son of Joseph and Lavinia Totten of Sherman, Texas. Born March 25, 1871, Died Aug. 25, 1898." Totten was one of the many buried in this cemetery who died from typhoid fever.

482 Dunham, p. 31.

483 Hunt, *The Whiskey Peddler*, p. 182.

484 Judge, p. 184.

485 Ladue, *Klondyke Facts*, p. 186; Steffens, "Life," *McClure's Magazine*, p. 962; Judge, p. 184.

486 Secretan, p. 110.

487 Dunham, p. 31.

488 Smyth, p. 6; Davis, *Sourdough Gold: The Log of a Yukon Adventure*, p. 177; Bankson, *The Klondike Nugget*, pp. 107, 127-146; Palmer, "Government and Society," The Forum, pp. 609-612; Trelawney-Ansell, *I Followed Gold*, p. 173.

489 Walden, p. 86.

490 Annual Report of Superintendent Charles Constantine Commanding Yukon District, 1897 in 18 January 1898. Report of the Commissioner of the North West Mounted Police, 1898, Royal Canadian Mounted Police Historical Branch, Ottawa, Ontario; see also Johns, "News from the Klondike," *Harper's Weekly*, 20 November 1897.

In anticipation of the potential lawlessness of the flood of stampeders who descended upon Dawson the summer of 1898, the Government of Canada sent the Yukon Field Force to augment the North West Mounted Police. The Force, comprised of "two hundred and three uniformed soldiers in scarlet jackets and white helmets," officers and men from the Royal Canadian Rifles, the Royal Canadian Dragoons and the Royal Canadian Artillery arrived at Dawson September 11, 1898. (Smyth, p. 7; Berton, p. 215.)

491 Woodside, "Dawson As It Is," *The Canadian Magazine of Politics, Science, Art and Literature*, May-October 1901, p. 407.

492 Sullivan, *A Woman Who Went to Alaska*, pp. 38-39.

493 Glenn Wright, Staff Historian, Royal Canadian Mounted Police Historical Branch, 23 February 1999. Ed and Star Jones Collection.

494 *Plattsburgh Republican*, 16 October 1897.

495 *New York World*, 6 August 1897.

496 *Seattle Daily Times*, 18 July 1897.

497 *Victoria Daily Colonist*, 8 July 1897; *Plattsburgh Republican*, 4 September 1897; *Seattle Daily Times*, 18 July 1897; *San Francisco Examiner*, 15 July 1897.

Among those who came down the gangplank that day were several other members of North West Mounted Police whom Inspector Constantine had given permission to take time off to stake claims during the early days of the Klondike. Those who "brought out good money" were Sergeant P.C. Engel, Sergeant Murray Henry Edward Hayne, Constable H.N. Jenkins, Constable Telford and Corporal E. Newbrook. Inspector Strickland had "between $44,000 and $130,000!" Others of the police who came out later that summer were S.R. Churchill who owned 52 Above on Bonanza; James Murry, who owned 1/2 of claim 34 on Eldorado, 11 Below on Hunker Creek and 53 Above on Bonanza; A. Ward, who owned 38 Above on Bonanza; A.P. Zeller who "has sold his claim on Bonanza for a large sum." Several other policemen, Pinkerton, Thornton, Webster, Sinclair and Gowler all had claims worth at least $20,000. (*Seattle Daily Times*, 11 September 1897; *San Francisco Examiner*, 15 July 1897; *Victoria Daily Colonist*, 18 July 1897.)

498 MacDonald, "Seattle, Vancouver and the Klondike," *The Canadian Historical Review*, September 1968; Berton, p. 93.

499 *New York World*, 6 August 1897.

Another Trip East

1 Winslow, *Big Pan Out*, p. 143.

2 Archibald, *A Substantial Expression of Confidence: The Northern Commercial Co. Store, Dawson, 1897-1951*, pp. 11-12; Gordon Newell, ed. H.W. McCurdy *Marine History of the Pacific Northwest, 1895-1965*, p.27.

3 Mining Records Book. Dawson City Museum/Klondike History Library.

4 S. O. Morford was born on a farm in Trumbull County, Ohio in 1849. He graduated from State Normal School in Edinborough, Pennsylvania. Later he took a course in law at the Hastings Law College in San Francisco where he was admitted to the bar. For a period of time he taught in a Lake County Public School, then served as Superintendent of Schools for one year, 1878, in the same county. He practiced law for four years in San Francisco, then moved to Yakima County, Washington and worked as a lawyer and probate judge for nearly 12 years. In 1895 he started for the Yukon over the Taku Trail. It was a very difficult trip, taking several months. In the fall of 1896, while prospecting up the Klondike River, he was caught in an early winter storm that nearly resulted in his death. For 36 hours, without blankets or food and with temperatures below zero, he struggled against the weather. He had extensive mining interests in the Klondike (Polk & Co. 1888 *Puget Sound Directory*, Alaska State Library Historical Collections; *Klondike News*, 1 April 1898, Dawson City Museum/Klondike History Library.) and mined successfully on Dominion Creek for several years.

In 1904 he was involved in extremely controversial litigation regarding a divorce and the division of real property consisting of three farms in Yakima, Washington where the Morfords had resided. The courts ruled in favor of his former wife, Pearl. (*Dawson Daily News*, 29 July 1904.)

One positive comment about Morford was made by Eugene C. Allen of *The Klondike Nugget* who referred to him as "my friend, Judge Morford, who had done so much to get me started." (Bankson, *The Klondike Nugget*, p. 119.)

Morford died December 1919 at age 70. (Alaska Daily Empire, 22 December 1919.)

5 Power of Attorney, Joseph Ladue to S. O. Morford, Dawson City Museum/ Klondike History Library.

6 Bankson, *The Klondike Nugget*, p. 85; *Klondike News*, 1 April1898

7 *New York World*, 6 August 1897; *San Francisco Examiner*, 15 July 1897; *Victoria Daily Colonist*, 18 July 1897.

8 *New York Herald*, 24 July 1897.

9 *New York World*, 6 August 1897.

10 *New York World*, 17 September 1897; *Butte Miner*, 16 September 1897.

11 *Seattle Daily Times*, 22 July 1897.

12 Steffens, "Life," *McClure's Magazine*, pp. 958-959.

13 Ogilvie, *Plattsburgh Republican*, 4 September 1897.

14 *Seattle Daily Times*, 15 July 1897.

15 *Klondyke and the Gold Fields of Alaska*, American Jubilee Co., 1 October 1897.

16 *Los Angeles Herald*, 14 August 1897; see also *Seattle Daily Times*, 22 July 1897.

17 *New York World*, 26 July 1897.

18 McMasters, "Clinton County's Man in Alaska," *North Country Notes*; see also *Plattsburgh Republican*, 7 August 1897.

19 Steffens, "Life," *McClure's Magazine*, pp. 957-967. For further information on the Chilkoot Trail see William Ogilvie, "The Geography and Resources of the Yukon Basin," *The Geographical Journal*, The Royal Geographical Society, vol. 12, July-December 1898, pp. 21-24.

20 Sleicher, "The Original King."

21 *New York World*, 6 August 1897. This was a curious remark considering the fact that in 1895 Joe had wanted to marry Kitty Mason and take her back to the Yukon.

22 Spurr, *Through the Yukon Gold Diggings*, p. 103.

23 Davis, *Sourdough Gold*, p. 97.

24 *Plattsburgh Republican*, 31 July 1897.

25 *Plattsburgh Sentinel*, 16 July 1897.

26 *Royal Baking Powder Co., Camp Cookery*, p. 4.
27 *New York World*, 26 July 1897.
28 Ibid.
29 At about the same time *Klondyke Nuggets* was being published in New York, it was also published in Montreal by John Lovell & Son, 23 Nicholas St.
30 *Plattsburgh Sentinel*, 13 August 1897.
31 Allen, "Dawson, Yukon Territory," *American Journal of Industry*, 1901, p. 48.

All That Glitters
The Joseph Ladue Gold Mining and Development Company of Yukon

1 *New York World*, 11 August 1897.
2 Ogilvie to Wilson.
3 Elmer Francis Botsford was born in Burke, Franklin County, New York in 1861. At the time he became associated with Joe Ladue in August, 1897 he was "one of the rising young lawyers of Clinton County, having already established a high reputation as a careful adviser and shrewd financier. "In 1886 he graduated from Dartmouth College with a Bachelor of Arts degree."

In 1894 his alma mater conferred upon him an honorary Master of Arts degree. Botsford and George Henry Beckwith established their law firm in Plattsburgh, New York in 1892. Beckwith separated from the firm in 1896, opening offices in New York City, but Botsford appears to have continued his law practice under the company name of Beckwith and Botsford for some years until he took a new partner and the name was changed to Botsford and Merrihew.

Botsford was a founding member and trustee of the Plattsburgh Institute in 1893. The purpose of the Institute was "to cultivate a more general interest in the history of Plattsburgh and vicinity, and to perpetuate the memory of many important historic events of the Champlain Valley. (*Souvenir Industrial Edition of Plattsburgh, 1897*, pp. 41- 42, 75-76)

On October 23, 1897 Joe gave a broadly-based power of attorney to Botsford to conduct his personal affairs in New York. (Registered Documents, Department of the Interior, 23 October 1897, Yukon Archives.)

4 The eight-story Murray Hill Hotel, located at the corner of Park Avenue and Fortieth Street, was in "one of the most quiet and refined, as well as the most accessible portions of the city." Among its guests over the years were J. P. Morgan, Mark Twain, P. T. Barnum and President McKinley. The 62-year-old landmark was closed April 24,1947 and demolished soon thereafter. (Murray Hill Hotel brochure, George B. Corsa Hotel Collection, The New York Historical Society; *New York Herald-Trubune*, 25 April, 5 May 1947.)
5 *New York City Directory, 1897-98*, New York State Historical Society; New York World, 11 August 1897.
6 *New York Times*, 17 August 1897.
7 *Selkirk Journal*, 27 August 1897; Botsford Affidavit, 16 April 1902,Dawson City Museum/Klondike History Library; Klondike News, 1 April 1898.
8 *Washington Times*, 21 September 1897.
9 Official Prospectus of the Joseph Ladue Gold Mining and Development Co. of Yukon, Alaska State Library Historical Collections; *Klondike News*, 1 April 1898; *Dawson Daily News, Special Mining Edition* (Timber and Resources), September, 1899; Report of the Committee Appointed by the Stockholders Present at the Annual Meeting Held in New Jersey, 4 February 1901, Dawson City Museum/Klondike History Library; *Klondike News*, 1 April 1898.
10 Sleicher, "The Original King."
11 Honorable Smith M. Weed was a prominent citizen of Clinton County and had a reputation throughout New York State "second to none as a lawyer, a political leader who has done excellent service as a legislator, and an enterprising, successful business man to whom must be accredited full honors, his success in life being entirely self-acquired." Weed was born in Belmont, Franklin County, New York in 1833, attended public schools

and began studying law with Judge Beckwith in Plattsburgh. He later attended Harvard Law School and graduated with an LL.B. degree.

He was immensely popular and well-respected, and served six terms in the New York State legislature. He served on the boards of many community organizations, was a "foe of political corruption" and an abolitionist. (*Souvenir Industrial Edition of Plattsburgh*, pp. 67-68; Official Prospectus.)

12 Official Prospectus.

13 *Seattle Daily Times*, 28 August 1897.

14 *Klondike Nugget*, 16 June 1898; *Klondike News*, 1 April 1898.

15 *Klondike News*, 1 April 1898.

16 Official Prospectus; see also *Klondike News*, 1 April 1898; *Adirondack News*, 2 April 1898.

17 Memorandum of Association of the Golden Wedge Mining Co., Ltd., 8 November 1896, British Columbia Archives.

The company was owned by Charles H. McIntosh and J. Nesbitt Kirchoffer, members of the Ladue Co. Board of Directors. On paper, the Golden Wedge Mining Co., Ltd. looked substantial.

18 Counter Receipt The Joseph Ladue Gold Mining and Developmen Co. of Yukon, 1901, Dawson City Museum/Klondike History Library.

19 Telegram, Western Union Telegraph Co., 17 September 1897, Dawson City Museum/Klondike History Library.

20 Ibid., 20 September 1897. Dawson City Museum/Klondike History Library.

21 *Plattsburgh Republican*, 21 September 1897; *Adirondack News*, 2 April 1898; *The Life of William McKinley*, p. 37.; *New York Times*, September 22, 1897.

22 *Plattsburgh Press Republican*, 25 September 1897.

23 The machine that was supposed to be able to travel over a winter route from the coast to Dawson, was known as Glover's Locomotive and "The Snow Conqueror." Built by a Vermont man, George T. Glover, it slid over the ground on runners and had spiked driving wheels for traction on lake and Yukon River ice. The first passenger trip was scheduled to leave Ft. Wrangel about January 20, 1898. The fare to Dawson was $200, which covered food and sleeping berths in one of 26 heated cars. Passengers were required to sign an agreement that in the event of an emergency along the trail, they would be willing to do whatever work might be required. Tickets were sold, but "The Snow Conqueror" never made the trip to Dawson. (unidentified Washington, D.C. newspaper, 18 December 1897; *Explore.com*: "Historical Vignettes of the North.")

24 *Plattsburgh Daily Press*, 5 March 1898.

25 Assets and Debts, Estate of Arthur Harper, Yukon Archives; Ogilvie, *Early Days*, p. 101.

26 *Dawson City Glacier*, 23 December 1897, Yukon Archives.

27 McConnell, "Gold Values in the Klondike 1907" in *The Yukon Territory: Its History and Resources, 1916*, p. 33.

28 Circular No. 9 to stockholders from the Joseph Ladue Gold Mining and Development Co. of Yukon, April 4, 1898, Alaska State Library Historical Collections.

29 *Plattsburgh Daily Press*, 5 March 1898.

30 Bonner, "Competition for the Klondike Trade," *Leslie's Illustrated Weekly Magazine*, 30 December 1897.

31 *Plattsburgh Republican*, 5 March 1898.

32 "The Best Route to the Northern Gold Fields," *Overland Monthly*, June 1898, p. 577.

33 Historic Photographs & Ships Plans, National Museum of Britain; *Plattsburgh Daily Press*, 3 March 1898; *A History of Morgan City, Louisiana*, pp. 65-66, Morgan City Historical Society.

34 Wheeler, *The Railroaders*, p. 37.

35 Certificate of Registry, Puget Sound Maritime Historical Society. The length of the Morgan City was reported in *Overland Monthly*, June 1898 as "350 feet."

The "master" of the *Morgan City* at the time of its purchase was John Leach. It had a "crew space of 100."

36 Certificate of Registry; Mills, Canadian Coastal and Inland Vessels, 1809-1930, Steamship Historical Society of America, Inc.; McCurdy, in Newell, ed.

The McCurdy Marine History of the Pacific Northwest, 1895-1965, pp. 36, 78; see also "The Best Route to the Northern Gold Fields," *Overland Monthly*, June 1898; Annual Report of the Joseph Ladue Gold Mining Co. of Yukon, 1901, Dawson City Museum/Klondike History Library.

37 Wright, ed., *Lewis and Dryden's Marine History of the Pacific Northwest*, p. 376; Mills, Canadian Coastal and Inland Steam Vessels, 1809-1930, p. 32, The Steamship Historical Society of America, Inc.

The estate administrator in India was Fazalbhai Joomabhoy. Captain William Webster brought the *Cutch* across the Indian Ocean to the China Sea, and from there to Vancouver, British Columbia where she traveled between Nanaimo and other ports until purchased by the Ladue Co. in 1898.

The *Cutch* was equipped with "compound engines twenty-five and forty- eight by thirty inches" and had "a nominal speed of twelve miles per hour on a coal consumption of twelve tons in twenty-four hours." (Wright, *Lewis and Dryden's Marine History of the Pacific Northwest*, pp. 366-377)

38 Customs Records, Wrecks, Merchant Vessels of the United States, June 30, 1900, p. 303, U.S. National Archives and Records Administration, Pacific Alaska Region, Anchorage, Government Records.

39 Armstrong, *Yukon Yesterdays*, p. 123.

40 Thirty-second Annual List of Merchant Vessels of the U.S., 1900, The Mariners' Museum, Newport News, Virginia.

41 U.S. Customs Service, Wrecks Reports, 1875-1905, U.S. National Archives and Records Administration, Pacific Alaska Region, Anchorage, Government Records.

42 "The Best Route to the Northern Gold Fields," *Overland Monthly*, June 1898, pp. 577-578.

43 Thirtieth Annual List of Merchant Vessels of the United States, 1898, pp. 222, 243, 284, 207, 240, 291; Thirty-Second Annual List of Merchant Vessels of the United States, 1900, The Mariners' Museum Library, Newport News, Virginia; "The Best Route to the Northern Gold Fields," pp. 577-580; Mills, *Canadian Coastal and Inland Steam Vessels, 1809- 1930*; Affleck, *Affleck's List of Sternwheelers Plying the Yukon Waterways*, pp. 27, 49, Rasmuson Library, University of Alaska Fairbanks; Eldredge Collection Notebooks. The Mariners' Museum, San Francisco.

44 "Best Route to the North Goldfields," *Overland Monthly*, p. 578.

45 Brochure, Ladue-Yukon Transportation Co., Candy Waugaman Collection.

46 McConnell, "Gold Values in the Klondike, 1907," in *The Yukon Territory: Its History and Resources, 1916*, p. 38. Dawson City Museum/Klondike History Library.

47 *Yukon Sun*, 6 June 1899.

48 Eldredge Collection Notebooks.

49 Affleck, *Affleck's List of Sternwheelers Plying the Yukon Waterways*, p. 28.

50 Eldredge Collection Notebooks.

51 Affleck, pp. 27, 49.

52 Eldredge Collections Notebooks.

53 *Plattsburgh Sentinel*; *Plattsburgh Daily Press*, 11 February 1898.

54 *Plattsburgh Daily Press*, 17 February, 7 March, 23 April 1898.

55 Ibid., April 23, 1898.

56 Young, *History of the War with Spain*, U.S. Army Military Research Collection, U.S. Army War College and Carlisle Barracks, Carlisle, Pennsylvania, p. 316, Government Records; The Dodge Commission Assesses the Work of the Quartermaster Department in the War with Spain, Center of Military History, U.S. Army, Washington, D.C., Government Records; *The Spanish American War Centennial* website; *Idaho Statesman*, 26, 27 June 1898; *Lewiston Morning Tribune* (Idaho), 5 February 1939.

57 Report, Board of Survey, San Francisco, 7 November 1898, U.S. Army Military Research Collection, U.S. Army War College and Carlisle Barracks, Carlisle, Pennsylvania,

Government Records.

58 Correspondence Relating to the War with Spain...from 15 April 1898 to 30 July 1902, pp. 868-871, 996, 1023, 1063-1064, U.S. Army Research Collection, U.S. Army War College and Carlisle Barracks. Government Records.

59 *Plattsburgh Republican*, 18 November 1899.

60 *Yukon World*, 11 February 1905.

61 U.S. Customs Service, *Wrecks Reports, 1892-1905*, p. 91, U.S. National Archives and Records Administration, Pacific Alaska Region, Alaska, Government Records; Preliminary Inventory of the Records of the Office of U.S. Local Inspectors, Seattle Bureau of Marine Inspection and Navigation, U.S. National Archives and Records Administration, Seattle, Washington, Government Records; Eldredge Collection Notebooks, Tornfelt and Burwell, *Shipwrecks of the Alaskan Shelf and Shore*, p. 90, New Mexico State Library.

62 U.S. Customs Service, *Wrecks Report, 1875-1905*, district of Alaska, Subport of Wrangel, Alaska, U.S. National Archives and Records Administration, Pacific Alaska Region, Anchorage, Government Records; Annual Report of the Joseph Ladue Gold Mining and Development Co. of Yukon, 14 February 1901, Dawson City Museum/Klondike History Library.

63 McCurdy, in Newell, *The McCurdy Marine History*, p. 102. The waters at the mouth of the Columbia are among the most treacherous in the world.

64 Thomas Ward Kirkpatrick was the superintendent of the Joseph Ladue Gold Mining and Development Co. of Yukon from its inception in August 1897 and was involved with Joe and Harper in establishing the Dawson townsite. By August 1898 he was part owner of a number of the gold claims held by the Ladue Co. on several creeks in the Klondike. Kirkpatrick was an excessively modest man, which made it difficult for local newspapers to develop a biographical sketch of him. "He flies from a newspaper man like an eastern tourist in a California earthquake."

He was, however, recognized as "a man of affairs; one who handles large transactions daily and with consumate (sic) ease. Nothing seems to worry him or frustrate him, and he moves on in the even tenor of his way as calm as a spring morning, while others, with one-eighth of his business cares, fly around with feverish haste and accomplish nothing."

The *Klondike News* in its first edition described him as a man who not only responded when opportunity knocked at his door, "he took the door from its hinges and threw it into the Yukon." They thought him the consummate business man: "Every detail of the company's immense business, from the value of a dump to the number of feet of lumber in a saw log, he is thoroughly familiar with, and might be termed an all-round business athlete." (*Klondike News*, 1 April 1898.)

Kirkpatrick's great-nephew, George has indicated that Thomas and his family left the Yukon about 1917 for Berkeley, California. Later, they moved to Saskatchewan where he opened a trading post in a remote area. His wife, Rose, and their three daughters, Wynonna, Eulalai and Libby soon returned to Berkeley. Thomas froze to death at the trading post, probably during the winter of 1919; his body not found until the following spring. Kirkpatrick to authors 20 January 2003.

65 *Plattsburgh Daily Press*, 17 December 1897.

66 Ladue Finds A Treasure Here, unidentified New York City newspaper, 18 or 19 December 1897; Sullivan Papers.

67 *Plattsburgh Press Republican*, 18 December 1897; unidentified Troy, New York newspaper article, n.d., Sullivan Papers.

68 Ladue Finds a Treasure Here.

69 McMasters, "Clinton County's Man in Alaska."

70 Grantee's Index, A-Z, vol. 7, 1896-1905, and recorded in Deeds, vol. 96, 15 January 1898, p. 165, Clinton County Clerk's Office. Government Records.

71 On-site visit, 1999.

72 "The Best Route to the Northern Gold Fields," *Overland Monthly*, June 1898; Notice of Annual Meeting of the Joseph Ladue Gold Mining and Development Co. of Yukon, 10

January 1898, Alaska State Library Historical Collections; *Klondike News*, 1 April 1898.
73 McMasters, "Clinton County's Man in Alaska." *Plattsburgh Daily Press*, 5 March 1898.
74 *Plattsburgh Sentinel*, 11, 18 March 1898.
75 Grantee's Index, A-Z, vol. 7, 1896-1905 and recorded in Deeds, vol. 96, p. 316. Clinton County Clerk's Office. Government Records.
76 Kittie Ladue scrapbook.
77 *Plattsburgh Sentinel*, 13 May 1898.
78 *Plattsburgh Sentinel*, 27 May 1898.
79 Whipple, *The Story of the White House and its Home Life*, p. 46.
80 McMasters, "Clinton County's Man in Alaska."; Kittie Ladue scrapbook.
81 *Plattsburgh Sentinel*, 17 June 1898.
82 *Klondike News*, 1 April 1898.
83 *Plattsburgh Daily Press*, 3 March 1898. In the Yukon, however, the title "King of the Klondike," belonged solely to Alexander McDonald.
84 *Klondike Nugget*, 9 July 1898.
85 Baird, *Sixty Years in the Klondike*, pp. 4, 10-11.
86 *Klondike News*, 1 April 1898; Sullivan Papers.
87 *Klondike Nugget*, 10 August 1898.
88 *Klondike Nugget*, 28, 31 August 1898.

When Joe arrived in Dawson, August 31, 1898 aboard the *Rideout*, it was the only remaining riverboat of his original fleet of nine. The *Rideout* had been advertised in *Klondike Nugget* newspaper as "The swiftest and most powerful steamer on the Yukon. Passenger accommodations for two hundred and fifty first-class passengers." In June 1899, *New York Times* printed an article that the *Rideout* arrived at Circle City with a story about the suffering and deaths of three men whose bodies were found 17 miles from the mouth of Old Man Creek. They were Michael Daly of Providence, R.I.; Victor Edair of Woonsocket, R.I.; and M. Provost of Brockton, Massachusetts. Daly's partially eaten body was found on a stove inside a tent, the doorway to which had been tied from the outside. The bodies of the other two men were found about five miles away. The writer concluded that "Daly's body had not been eaten by animals." It appears that the *Rideout* was sold by the Ladue Yukon Transportation Co. in early June 1899 to the California-Yukon Trading Co., and was taken off the "up-river service" and sent to St. Michael. (*New York Times*, 20 June 1899; *Klondike Nugget*, 1 July 1899; *Yukon Sun*, 6 June 1899.)

89 *Klondike Nugget*, 31 August 1898.

While it is clear that Joe appointed Walter Lyon superintendent and general manager before his departure from Dawson in early September1 898, Botsford, in the company's Annual Report for 1901, recorded having received "a letter dated September 14th, 1898 from S.T. Conkling the company's General Manager at Dawson" in which he announced the purchase of $36,000 worth of real estate on which the store warehouse and mill then stood. (Annual Report, 1901.)

90 There was no Ladue store in Dawson after the goods brought down from Ogilvie were sold in the late summer of 1896 until September 1898. Tappan Adney wrote that the original cabin was used as a bakery the summer of 1897, but no corroborating information was located. (*Klondike Nugget*, 9 September 1898.)

Dr. T. Bates Cook, a graduate of Dartmouth Medical College, had lived in Plattsburgh, New York, and was in charge of the Hagey Institute, which offered what was called the "Keeley Cure" for "inebriety and morphinism." Patients at the institute were given the "Hagey Double-Chloride of Gold" treatment for diseases resulting from excessive use of alcohol, morphine, cocaine and tobacco. (*Souvenir Industrial Edition of Plattsburgh*, p. 80.)

Dr. Cook died in Pasadena, California at 70, having retired there at age 55. (McMasters, "Clinton County's Man in Alaska.")

Walter H.B. Lyon resided in Plattsburgh, New York, the son of Dr. E. M. Lyon, and a brother-in-law of Elmer F. Botsford. Relatives of Lyon still reside in Plattsburgh.

Another man from Plattsburgh who worked as a laborer for the Ladue Co. was George

Light, whose nephew was at one time a member of the Plattsburgh City Council.

Barney of Plattsburgh was proprietor of the Gold Saloon in Dawson. The bar was of solid mahogany, and was used to construct his coffin when he died in Nome, Alaska. During his time in the north he sent furs to relatives in Cadyville and Morrisonville. Prior to his death he arranged to have a stone monument to himself placed in the Paris, New York cemetery.

Joe Puttraw of Plattsburgh made a big gold strike on Eldorado. He was so well liked by his employees and the miners in general that he was often referred to as the "Klondike Prince." Other Clinton County men who went to the Klondike were Sam Merchant, Parsons, Emery, Clark and John T. Rossman. (McMasters, "Clinton County's Man in Alaska.") From the twenty-first Infantry stationed at Plattsburgh: Sergeant Reiner and Private Lowery. From Rouses Point: Titus Shedden, M. Sheets, C. Fitch, Charles Weeks, F. Crook and John Bowron. From Clinton Mills: A. Oldham. From Ellenburgh: William Brennan and A. B. Oldham. (*Yukon Sun*, 16 June 1903; *Plattsburgh Daily Press*, 5 February 1898.)

91 Judge, p. 240.

92 *Klondike Nugget*, 31 August 1898.

93 Hitchcock, *Two Women in the Klondike*, pp. 242-243.

94 Ibid., pp. 291-292; McMasters, "Clinton County's Man in Alaska." ; see also *Klondike Nugget*, 31 August 1898.

95 Hamlin, p. 21.

96 The properties in question were:

1/3 interest in Placer Mining Claim No. 39 Eldorado

1/2 interest in Placer Mining Claim Nos. 1 and 17, French Gulch

1/4 interest in Placer Mining Claim No. 4, French Gulch

7/12 interest in Placer Mining Claim No. 12 Discovery on Bonanza Creek

7/24 interest in Placer Mining Claim No. 9 Below Discovery on Bonanza Creek

1/3 interest in the upper half of Placer Mining Claim No. 11 Below Discovery on Bonanza Creek

1/2 interest in Placer Mining Claim No. 50 Below Discovery on Last Chance Creek

1/2 interest in Placer Mining Claim Fraction A 19 _____ Discovery on Hunker Creek

1/3 interest in Placer Mining Claim Nos. 17 and19 Below Discovery on Hunker Creek

1/6 interest in Placer Mining Claim Nos. 18 and 20 Below Discovery on Hunker Creek

1/9 interest in Placer Mining Claim No. 25 Below Discovery on Hunker Creek

1/3 interest in Placer Mining Claim No. 30 Above Discovery on Hunker Creek

1/3 interest in Placer Mining Claim Fraction No. 17A, Below Discovery on Hunker Creek

1/6 interest in Placer Mining Claim No. 20 Above the mouth of Gold Bottom Creek

(All in the "Torandyk" (Klondike) Mining Division of the Yukon Territory.)

Interest in the Moosehide Mining Division of the Yukon Territory (1/4 interest in Placer Mining Claim No. 4 Above Discovery on Moosehide Creek)

Interest in the Indian Creek Mining Division of the Yukon Territory.

1/4 interest in Placer Mining Claim No. 11 Above Upper Discovery on Dominion Creek.

Revocation of Power of Attorney, Joseph Ladue to S. O. Morford, Dawson City, 29 August 1898, Dawson City Museum/Klondike History Library; Lis Pendens, In the Territorial Court of the Yukon Territory, 19 August 1898, Dawson City Museum/Klondike History Library; Mining Records Book, Dawson City Museum/Klondike History Library.

97 *Klondike News*, 1 April 1898.

98 *Klondike Nugget*, 16 July 1898.

99 Ibid.

100 Power of Attorney, Joseph Ladue to J.E. Hansen, 6 September 1898, Dawson City Museum/Klondike History Library.J.E. Hansen, referred to as "Captain," was employed by the Alaska Commercial for several years and was the company's manager in Dawson

at the time he accepted responsibility for the activities of the Harper and Ladue partnership outlined in the Power of Attorney. When the A. C. Co. later merged with another company, he became manager of its mercantile department, Northern Commercial Co. Prior to 1905 he left Dawson and accepted a position as captain of the oceangoing fleet of the Northwest Fisheries Co. in Alaska. In May 1905 he committed suicide by jumping from the deck of the company's steamer Dolphin while enroute to Seattle. (*Dawson Daily News*, 10 May 1905.)

101 Although the court file relating to this action is incomplete, since Joe acted to revoke Morford's power of attorney immediately upon his arrival in Dawson, he undoubtedly was aware, prior to that time, that there was some question regarding the management of Harper & Ladue's original gold claims and those transferred, bought and sold during the previous 14 months. Morford had mining interests of his own, separate from the company, which further complicated an accurate and timely accounting. Some kind of liability on Morford's part is evidenced by an entry in the probate file of the estate of Arthur Harper, indicating the executor of his estate and the company "settled" with Morford for $1,500 "on a debt." However, it was not until August 26, 1901 that payment was made. It was divided equally between Harper's Estate and the Ladue Co., each netting $750. (Assets & Debts, Estate of Arthur Harper, Yukon Archives.)

102 *New York World*, 6 August 1897.

103 Ogilvie to Wilson.

104 Davis, *Sourdough Gold*, p. 185.

105 Johns, "News from the Klondike," *Harper's Weekly*, 20 November 1897; Dunham, *The Alaskan Gold Fields*, pp. 31-34.

106 *Seattle Daily Times*, 20 July 1897.

107 Curtis, "The Rush to the Klondike Over the Mountain Passes," *Century Illustrated Magazine*, March 1898, p. 697; see also U.S. Department of the Interior Annual Report, 1898, p. 213. Yukon Archives.

108 Curtis, "The Rush Over the Mountain Passes," *Century Illustrated Magazine*, p. 697.

109 Secretan, p. 1.

110 The Oxford Companion to United States History, pp. 183-184; Carruth, What Happened When, p. 564.

111 Nicols, "Advertising and the Klondike," *Washington Historical Quarterly*, vol. 13, 1922.

112 *Seattle Post Intelligencer*, 11 March 1898.

113 Bonner, "The Competition for the Klondike Trade," *Leslie's Illustrated Weekly Magazine*, 30 December 1897; Craig, *Glimpses of Sunshine and Shade in the Far North*, p. 62; *Seattle Post Intelligencer*, 11 March 1898.

114 *Sitka Alaskan*, 26 March 1892.

115 *New York World*, 30 August 1897.

116 Falconberg, *Gold, A Human Story of All That Glitters: Told by Sourdoughs Who Were in it*, Record, Capitol Records, Ed and Star Jones Collection.

117 Berton, *Klondike: All That Glitters, 1896-1898*, pp. 197-200; Margeson, *Experiences of Gold Hunters in Alaska*, pp. 86-93; Brookfield, *Across Valdez Glacier*, p. 596; Preston, *Across Valdez Glacier with Sleds Drawn by Hand*, pp. 599-601; Lowe, *From Valdez Inlet to Belle Isle, on the Yukon*, p. 591.

There were actually three trails available to those who chose the All-American route to the Klondike. The trail over Valdez glacier began at the community of Valdez at the head of Prince William Sound. Those who chose to cross the Malaspina glacier entered it from Yakutat Bay. Another trail followed the Matanuska Valley from a point at the head of Cook Inlet. All three were deadly. Lt. J.C. Castner, who made a reconnaissance of the latter trail, wrote of the experience that "Without food, firearms, shoes, coats, or blankets, we gathered around a fire of driftwood...Without covering, we lay shivering in the snow. The pus-running sores on our feet closed at night, only to cause additional pain as we stumbled along next morning over the hard, frozen ground, which broke them open again...As my men often said, it would be impossible to make others understand what we suffered those days. No tongue or pen could do the case justice." (Castner, U.S. Fourth Infantry, A Story of Hardship and Suffering in Alaska, p. 691.)

118 Miller, "Stampedes on the Klondike. How I Missed Being a Millionaire," *Overland Monthly*, December 1897.

119 Russell Bankson, author of *The Klondike Nugget*, the story of the early Dawson newspaper by that name, described the stampeders of 1898 he saw on the streets during the summer. "The thing that impressed me the most was the aimlessness of the stampeders. These men—and a few women—had fought death almost every step of the way over that 600-mile trail in a frantic race to get to the source of the wealth. And now all they appeared to do was to mill around like a band of sheep without a leader, winding and twisting in and out of the saloons and dance halls and gambling dens along the street.

"Stricken with the gold fever, most of them had rushed blindly northward, without definite plans, and only a vague idea that once in the Klondike, they would take a shovel, go out along some creek, and start digging up the gold and sacking it. And when they had all they could get away with, they would load it on a boat and start for the 'outside' and home again.

"The cold, hard facts seemed to have left them stunned and helpless, I gathered after talking to many of them. They didn't know how to go about making their dreams come true. Naturally, the region had been pretty thoroughly staked by the summer of 1898—most of it by the sourdoughs from Forty Mile, Circle City and other parts of the interior of Alaska and Canada, beginning in the fall of 1896 after the first strike." By the end of June 1898 10,000 claims had been recorded in the Klondike District. (Bankson, pp. 69-70; Davis, *Sourdough Gold*, p. 185)

120 Dawson in 1898, *New York Times,* 6 August 1897.

121 *Klondike Nugget*, 30 July 1898.

122 Ft. Herchmer, built in the summer of 1897, was named for Commissioner Herchmer, commanding officer of all the NWMP in Canada. It covered about one square acre of ground and was enclosed by a high stockade of cottonwood logs. At the end of 1897 it was far from complete. The guard room was used as a jail. Eventually there would be a separate jail and a hospital. Frederick Palmer, a writer for The Forum, who was on-site in the summer of 1898 thought the barracks and stockade were "ridiculously large, considering the size of the flat which constitutes the townsite."

In his Annual Report, Inspector Constantine, promoted to superintendent in 1897, does not comment on what presence the force may have had in Dawson during the winter of 1896-97. On June 12, 1897 Inspector W. H. Scarth arrived with 19 replacements for Constantine's dwindling force, many of whom had come to the end of their two year enlistment and were among those who staked claims on Bonanza or Eldorado. In October, Inspector Harper arrived with 20 more men, but "without any food" for the winter, which put an even greater strain on Constantine's already short supply. (Palmer, "Government and Society," *The Forum*, p. 611; see also Annual Report of Superintendent Constantine, Commanding Yukon District, 18th January, 1898, Royal Canadian Mounted Police Historical Branch, Otttawa, p. 308, 310; *Klondike Nugget*, 5 July 1898)

123 *Klondike Nugget*, 5 July 1898.

124 Joe's cabin was removed from the middle of Front Street sometime during the summer of 1898 following an announcement in the June 17 issue of *Klondike Nugget* by J. Morrow Walsh, Executive Officer of the Yukon:

"Notice is hereby given that the officer commanding the Northwest Mounted Police at Dawson, has been requested by me to carry out the following instructions: All logs, timber, lumber, cordwood, and other obstructions must at once be cleared from Front Street." (Adney, "Who Discovered the Klondike?" *Harper's Weekly*, 1 April 1899; see also Davis, *Sourdough Gold*, p. 98; Dunham, p. 25; Ladue, *Klondike Nuggets*, p. 152; Hamlin, p. 10.)

Walsh was appointed Chief Executive Officer of the Government of the Yukon Territory August 17, 1897. He did not arrive in Dawson City until May 21, 1898, his position discontinued when William Ogilvie was appointed Commissioner of the Yukon on July 4.

(Smyth, *The Yukon's Constitutional Foundations: The Yukon Chronology*, p. 6.)

125 Adney, *The Klondike Stampede*, pp. 178-181; Judge, pp. 235, 239-40; *Klondike Nugget*, 30 July 1898.

126 Dunham, p. 33; Craig, p. 61.

127 Walden, *A Dog-Puncher on the Yukon*, p. 145.

128 Judge, pp. 239-240.

129 Walden, p. 146.

130 Palmer, "Government and Society"; *The Forum*, p. 608.

131 Ibid., p. 607.

132 *Klondike News*, 1 April 1898.

133 Palmer, "Government and Society," *The Forum*, p. 612; Bankson, *The Klondike Nugget*, pp. 127-129.

Three months before Fawcett left the Territory, Judge Dugas wrote from Dawson to L. O. David, June 29, 1899, his frustrations regarding the Gold Commissioner: "He is a good man, meaning well, but entirely lacking in administrative capacity. In all his dealing with the public, he...reminds me of the girl in that song the 'Chimes of Normandy' who 'never says yes and never says no.' He seems anxious to please everybody and pleases nobody." (Dugas to L. O. David, Sifton Papers, vol. 64, p.46760. National Archives of Canada)

134 Smyth, p. 6.

135 Bankson, *The Klondike Nugget*, p. 127.

136 Three days after Ogilvie's appointment an order was passed in the Privy Council in Ottawa appointing four men to Territorial Council: F.C. Wade, legal advisor; J.E. Girouard, Register of Lands; T.H. McGuire, Territorial Court Judge; and Samuel B. Steele, Officer Commanding the North West Mounted Police. (Smyth, p. 6.)

137 Margaret Ogilvie, *Gold, A Human Story of All That Glitters: Told by Sourdoughs Who Were in it*, Record, Capitol Records, Ed and Star Jones Collection.

138 *Klondike Nugget*, 30 July 1898.

139 *Klondike Nugget*, 14 December 1898.

140 Commissioner Ogilvie to C.M. Woodworth, 8 February 1899, Yukon Archives.

141 James A. Smart, Deputy Minister, Dept. of the Interior, to Commissioner Ogilvie, 10 October 1898; Elmer F. Botsford, Attorney for the Harper and Ladue Townsite Co., to Alex McLeod, 22 August 1899, Yukon Archives.

142 Lynwode Pereira, Asst. Secretary of the Dept. of the Interior to Joseph Ladue, 24 December 1897; Clifford Sifton, Secretary of the Dept. of the Interior to Commissioner Ogilvie, 24 August 1898; James M. Wilson and Elmer F. Botsford to Secretary of the Interior, 1 September 1899; James M. Wilson and Elmer F. Botsford to Commissioner Ogilvie, 30 September 1899; Commissioner Ogilvie to Elmer F. Botsford, 4 August 1899; Elmer F. Botsford to Commissioner Ogilvie, 4 August 1899; Commissioner Ogilvie to "Agent," Harper & Ladue Townsite Co., 17 August 1899. Yukon Archives.

143 Elmer F. Botsford to Alex McLeod, Dept. of the Interior, 22 August 1899; Commissioner's Office to Harper and Ladue Townsite Co., 17 August 1899, Yukon Archives.

144 *Klondike Nugget*, 17 January 1900.

145 Dominion Lands Grant No. 3751, Yukon Archives.

146 Memorandum, H. W. Newlands, Legal Advisor to the Dept. of the Interior to J.N.E Brown, Territorial Secretary, Dawson, 14 January 1902, Yukon Archives.

147 The first gave Ladue and Wilson title to lots 2-6 and 8 in Block K. The second gave them title to Lots 7-9 in Block P, and lot 10 in Block Q. The third grant was the south half of lot 2 and part of lot 16 in Block Y. The fourth grant gave title to lots 9 and 12 and parts of lots 10 and 11 in Block HA, and the fifth grant gave title to the east half of lots 1 and 2, and part of lot 3, both in Block H. ("Dominion Lands Grants" Numbers 5509, 5510, 5511, 5512 and 5513; Certificate of Title, No. 28 "C" to J.L. Wilson, 1901, Yukon Archives.)

148 Commissioner Ogilvie to the Minister of the Department of the Interior, 28 June 1899; see also F.W. Clements to the Minister of the Interior, 29 March 1899, Yukon Archives.

149 Elmer F. Botsford to Commissioner Ogilvie, 2 August 1899, Yukon Archives.

150 Commissioner Ogilvie to Deputy Minister of the Interior, 23 November 1899, Yukon Archives.

151 F.W. Clements to the Department of the Interior, 29 March 1899, Yukon Archives.

152 James M. Wilson, Executor of the Harper Estate and J.A. Hansen, agent for Joseph Ladue, to Commissioner Ogilvie, DC, N.W.T., 8 October 1898, Yukon Archives.

153 *Klondike Nugget*, 10 May 1899.

Emil Stauf had arrived in Dawson the summer of 1898 with no experience in mining and low on funds. He soon established himself as a real estate broker and by May 1899 he was agent for the Harper and Ladue Townsite Co. By the time he left Dawson the fall of 1904, he had not only considerable earnings from real estate but also an inheritance from Erena Harper, Arthur Harper's second wife. Stauf continued his real estate partnership in Dawson with attorney, Dufferin Pattullo, and formed the Stauf-Berghausen Liquor Co. with offices in California, Chicago and New York City. (*Dawson Daily News*, 9 May 1905.)

154 1897-1898 New York City Directory, New York Historical Society; *Plattsburgh Press Republican*, 29 April 1899.

155 *Plattsburgh Republican*, 15 March 1899.

156 *Plattsburgh Republican*, 11 February 1899.

157 Affidavit, Elmer F. Botsford, 16 April 1902.

158 Grantee's Index A-Z, 1896-1905, recorded in Book of Deeds, vol. 99, p. 134, Clinton County Clerk's Office, Government Records.

159 Grantee's Index, Book 84, pp. 379-386, Clerk of Warren County, New York, Government Records.

160 McMasters, "Clinton County's Man in Alaska."

161 *Malone Palladium*, 2 March 1899.

162 Annual Report of Inspector Samuel B. Steele, Commanding North-West Mounted Police in the Yukon Territory, 10th January, 1899, p. 21, Royal Canadian Mounted Police Historical Branch, Ottawa, Ontario.

163 *Dawson Daily News* Special Mining Edition, September 1899. In January 1899 Dawson's population was estimated by the Klondike Nugget at "between 5,000 and 6,000 people..." When word was received that gold had been found on the beaches of Nome, Alaska Dawson's population plummeted as thousands of men left downriver. The steamer, Rideout, no longer owned by the Ladue Co., left Dawson in July 1899 with 797 passengers "who fought to get aboard her and her barges."(Davis, *Sourdough Gold*, p. 162.)

Regardless of the mass exit of miners for Nome, *Klondike Nugget*, in its "Anniversary Number" 1 November 1899 reported that: "The Dawson of today presents an appearance of stability and permanence which few of those who landed in the country two years ago thought would ever be possible for it to attain. In place of the rough log shacks which originally occupied the business portion of the townsite there are now long blocks of substantial buildings, erected not only with a view to utility, but also with some consideration given to architectural beauty."

164 William Ogilvie shared Joe's belief in the potential for quartz mining in the Yukon. He stated in his 24 January, 1897, report on a geological survey conducted for the Canadian Government that, "A quartz lode showing free gold has been located on one of the creeks. The quartz, I understand from a reliable source, is rich as it tested over $100 to the ton." In a letter to a Mr. Wilson, 27 May 1897, Ogilvie stated that he felt sure quartz mining would be "prosecuted with profit." (Ogilvie, in Hayne, p.162; Ogilvie to Wilson.)

165 *Klondike Nugget*, 15 April 1899.

166 Ibid., 29 July 1900.

167 Ibid., 21 June, 26 July, 9 August, 13 October 1900; *Dawson Daily News*, 1 August 1900.

168 *Klondike Nugget*, 9 September 1900.

169 Mary Jane Wells is buried in the Lamay family plot in the Peasleeville, New York Cemetery. The grave marker reads: "Willis Lamay 1869-1940, His Wife Mary J. Wells,

1863-1900." On-site visit by authors.

170 Adoption Agreement and Order, 8 May 1900, recorded 25 June 1901, Clinton County Court, Government Records.

171 McMasters, "Clinton County's Man in Alaska." Among the McMasters papers was a notation written by Margaret Lunt of Plattsburgh, New York, that Kittie's mother, Mrs. Martha Bates Mason traveled with them to Colorado Springs and may have remained there until their return in May 1901.

172 At the time of the report the officers of the company were: Joseph Ladue, President, Smith M. Weed, Vice-President, Elmer F. Botsford, Secretary and Treasurer, and William E. Fort., Assistant Secretary/Treasurer. The members of the Board of Directors were: Smith M. Weed, Richard C. Jackson, Charles W. Wells, R. A. Rotche, Willard Brown, Walter A. Phelan, Albert W. Emery, Addis Fort., John A. Sleicher, Elmer F. Botsford, Almon J. Pierce, H.F. Hatch and George Bixby. (Annual Report of the Joseph Ladue Gold Mining and Development Co. of Yukon, 4 February 1901, Dawson City Museum/Klondike History Library.)

173 Ibid.

174 Photo, with inscription First passenger train over White Pass and Yukon Route to Summit, 29 Feb. 1899. Yukon Archives Smyth, p. 7; Brooks, *A Reconnaissance in the Tanana and White River Basins, Alaska in 1898*, p. 32, New Mexico State Library; *Plattsburgh Daily Press*, 3 March 1898.

175 *Klondike Nugget*, 25 December 1901.

176 Annual Report, 4 February 1901.

177 *Klondike Nugget*, 12 August 1900.

178 Ibid., 13 May 1900.

179 Carter, A History of the Use of Wood in the Yukon to 1903, Canadian Dept. of the Interior Reports, Timber Berths, 1899, Appendix G vi; p. 311; Timber Berths, 1900, Appendix G ix, Dawson City Museum/Klondike History Library.

180 Annual Report, 4 February 1901.

181 *Klondike Nugget*, 11 January 1900.

182 A counter receipt of the "Joseph Ladue Gold Mining and Development Co. of Yukon" dated 16 November 1901, indicates a "Branch at St. Michaels." Another counter receipt appearing to also be dated 1901 indicates "Branches: St. Michael, Dall River." The branch at St. Michael was likely a warehouse. (Dawson City Museum/Klondike History Library.)

183 Annual Report, 4 February 1901; Report of the Committee Appointed by the Stockholders Present at the Annual Meeting Held in Jersey City, 4 February 1901, Dawson City Museum/Klondike History Library.

184 Annual Report, 4 February 1901.

185 The Canadian government charged a ten percent royalty on all gold taken from the ground after the initial $2,500 had been removed. A mining license was $15. The government also took for its own purposes each alternate claim on all creeks after the original claims were filed on Bonanza, Eldorado, Hunker and Gold Bottom. (Bankson, *Klondike Nugget*, p. 125; Palmer, "Government and Society," *The Forum*, p. 609; see also U.S. Department of the Interior Annual Report, 1898, p. 214. Yukon Archives.)

As early as January 1898, the Superintendent of the North West Mounted Police reported that "the expenses of working mines here are very great; on some of the richest claims it has cost more to take gold out than its value." (Annual Report of Inspector C. Constantine, Commanding the Yukon District, January 18, 1898.)

In Ladue's book, *Klondyke Facts* (pp. 105-106) he records: "Toronto, July 28. The Globe's Ottawa special says: 'At a Cabinet Council yesterday the Yukon was again under consideration, and it was decided that the royalty to be levied on the gold taken out of that country would be 10 per cent on all amounts taken out of any one claim up to $500 a week, and after that 20 per cent." Botsford never referred to having had to pay a 20 percent royalty.

186 John Gould, Dawson City historian.

187 Annual Report, 4 February 1901.

188 Coutts, *Yukon Places and Names*, p. 154.
189 Annual Report, 4 February 1901.
190 Ibid.; Affidavit, Elmer Botsford, 16 April 1902.
191 Report of the Committee Appointed 4 February 1901.
192 The steam yacht *Yale* was built in 1890 in Piermont, New York. Its dimensions were 10 by 51 feet. In 1900 the Ladue Co. purchased it from the New York Safety Steam Power Co. No record was found to indicate when or why the yacht had been purchased or that it was wrecked, but such may have been the case since its value, when sold, was less than $800. (Records of Alaska Customs Houses, Press Copies of Letters; Letters sent from St. Michaels, 1902-1906, National Archives and Records Administration, Pacific-Alaska Region, Anchorage, Government Records.)
193 Report of the Committee Appointed 4 February 1901.
194 Johnston, *Alaska*, p. 17.
195 *Klondike Nugget*, 18 April, 19 May, 28 August 1901.
196 Carter, A History of the Use of Wood, p. 316: Appendix G xi, Canadian Dept. of the Interior Report, Timber Berths, 1901,
197 Martha Black, *Martha Black: Her Story from the Dawson Gold Fields to the Halls of Parliament*, Flo Whyard, ed., p. 61ff, Whitehorse, Yukon: Wolf Creek Books, 2003.
198 *Klondike Nugget*, 10 July 1901.
199 *Dawson Waterfront, 1898-1908*, 3/3, Yukon Archives.
200 McMasters, "Clinton County's Man in Alaska."
201 *Plattsburgh Daily Press*, 28 June 1901.
202 *Klondike Nugget*, 6 July 1901.
203 Petty sketch, Day Family scrapbook. Office of the Town Historian, Chazy, New York; Plattsburgh Daily Press, 3 July 1901.
204 Joe's year of birth was 1854. U.S. Census 1900 for Clinton County, New York.
205 *Plattsburgh Sentinel*, 12 March 1903.
206 *Plattsburgh Daily Press*, 3 July 1901; Day Family scrapbook, Office of Chazy Town Historian.
207 Baptisms, St. Peter's Parish, 1853-1870; U.S. Census Schuyler Falls, New York, 2 June 1860. The State of New York Department of Health, which maintains records of deaths, issued in 1999 a "No Record Certification," document, State of New York, Government Records.
208 Will, Joseph Ladue, Clinton County, New York, Surrogate's Court, Government Records.
209 Ibid.
In November 1905 Kittie Ladue sold her 1/4 interest in 16 Above Upper Dominion to Charles G. Fernie and M.G. McDiernan. (*Dawson Daily News*, 18 November 1905.)
210 Affidavit, Victor C. Mason, Clinton County, New York, Surrogate's Court, Government Records.
211 Estate of Joseph Ladue, Account for Judicial Settlement, Clinton County, New York, Surrogate's Court, Government Records.
212 In the Account for Judicial Settlement for Ladue there is a discrepancy between Schedules A and H—Personal Property, in relation to the value of the 10,687 shares of common stock. Schedule A shows the value to be $1,068. Schedule H shows the value as $1,850. Schedule A is correct. Nevertheless, the court accepted the documents as presented. (Estate of Joseph Ladue, Income and Real Property; Account for Judicial Settlement.)
213 Affidavit, Elmer F. Botsford, 16 April 1902.
214 Estate of Joseph Ladue, Account for Judicial Settlement; Petition, September 1902, Linn County, Iowa, district court, Government Records.
215 Estate of Joseph Ladue.

Dawson and the Ladue Company after Joe's Death

1 Thompson, "The Year 1901 in the Klondike," *Scientific American*, 18 January 1902.

2 *Klondike Nugget*, 9 October 1901.
3 Ibid., 31 August, 21 December 1901; 15 November 1902.
4 *Dawson Daily News* Special Mining Edition, September 1899; Klondike Nugget, 19 July 1902.
5 Carter, *A History of the Use of Wood*, pp. 316-317, Canadian Dept. of the Interior Report, 1901, Timber Berths.
6 Members of the committee appointed by the Board of Directors were Walter H. Phalen, Almon Pierce, Willard Brown and John Sleicher. The shareholders committee was composed of J. G. Howell and Lewis and John Meyers. The two committees worked together with accountants, reviewing the records of the company. Some members may have visited the Dawson operations. (*Plattsburgh Sentinel*, 7 March 1902.)
7 Ibid.
8 *Plattsburgh Sentinel*, 16 May 1902.
9 *Yukon Morning Sun*, 6 July 1902.
10 *Klondike Nugget*, 22 June 1901.
11 Affidavit, Elmer F. Botsford, 16 April 1902.
12 The 24,700 shares Joe had been given in partial payment for his holdings in the Klondike had a value in 1897 of $2,470,000. In 1901 their value would have been no more than $4,818. Kittie may have sold his shares to Elmer Botsford for that amount.
13 *Yukon Sun*, 6 July 1902.
14 Carter, *A History of the Use of Wood*, p. 325: Canadian Dept. of the Interior Report, 1903, Timber Berths, Appendix G (xix).
In October 1902 there were four sawmills in Dawson: Canadian-Yukon, Ladue, Yukon, and Klondike (N. A. T. & T. Co.). Five million board feet of lumber were sold during the first ten months of the year. There was considerable demand from the creeks, but the majority of the lumber was utilized in Dawson where hundreds of new buildings were constructed and many older ones repaired. The four mills employed 400-500 laborers, the majority of which were engaged in cutting logs and rafting them to Dawson from upriver. (*Yukon Sun*, 27 June, 1 October 1902)
15 *Yukon Sun*, 9 November 1902.
16 *Dawson Daily News* "Golden Clean-up Edition," 1902, Alaska State Library, MS 49-7-1.
17 *Yukon Morning Sun*, 6 July 1902.
18 *Yukon Sun*, 7 September 1902.
19 *Klondike Nugget*, 2 October 1902, 12 September 1902.
20 *Yukon Sun*, 4 October 1902.
21 *Klondike Nugget*, 8 September 1902.
22 Ibid., 17 September 1902.
23 Ibid., 10 March 1903.
24 *Yukon Sun*, 3, 9 April 1903.
25 Articles of Incorporation, 15 April 1903, Office of South Dakota Secretary of State, Government Records.
26 Frank Agnew, Laborer; W.H. Allen, Laborer; G. Bates, Laborer; Samuel L. Bates, Laborer; Elmer F. Botsford, President of the Joseph Ladue Gold Mining and Development Co. of Yukon; J. Clusian, Machine Operator; P. Coffey, Laborer; Dr. T. Bates Cooke, Manager of the Mercantile Dept.; William N. Couch, Warehouseman; Henry T. Deal, Salesman; Peter D. Deiser, Cabinetmaker; J. J. Delay, Laborer; John F. Ewing, Engineer; Rhett W. Ford; Clerk, R. Fox, Laborer; J. Fritz, Laborer; Olaf Hansen, Laborer; Z. Harris, Laborer; L.S. Johnson, Laborer; George Light, Laborer; W. Lotka, Planerman; Walter H.B. Lyon, General Manager of the Joseph Ladue Gold Mining and Development Co. of Yukon; John R. Maltby, Accountant; Dana B. Neal, Bookkeeper; J. Ritchie, Edgerman; John T. Rossman, Clerk; William Seaborn, Laborer; Joseph F. Seller, Foreman, Harper & Ladue Sawmill; Joseph Shull, Boomman; Edward A. Smith, Sawyer; James Stewart, Filer; John J. Toughill, Laborer; Gustave H. Wand, Bookkeeper; George B. Wilcox and Ernest G. Zeller, Laborers. (*Yukon Sun*, 17 June 1903; Polk's Gazetteer, 1903 Directory.)

27 Carter, *A History of the Use of Wood*, p. 325: Canadian Dept. of the Interior Report, Timber Berths, 1903, Appendix G (xix); 17 *Yukon Sun*, June 1903.
28 *Dawson Daily News*, 21, 22, 23 January 1904; *Plattsburgh Sentinel* and *Clinton County Farmer*, 22 January 1904.
29 *Dawson Daily News*, 22 January 1904; Yukon Sun, 21 January1904.
30 Bankson, *The Klondike Nugget*, pp. 241-244, 246-253.
Several days after the Ladue Co. Store fire, the *Dawson Daily News* reported that fire chief, Joe Bingham, and several other members of the Fire Department had suffered injuries while attempting to extinguish it.

Bingham was the most seriously injured. The *News* reported that "Bingham was dragging a line of hose through the burning rubbish and did not have time to pick his way. Not being able to see where he stepped he planted his left foot squarely on a big spike, with considerable force. The spike cut a deep gash in the flesh, but the fireman did not consider the injury serious enough to interfere with his work and went on about his duties.

"Through neglect of the wound or from some foreign matter having been on the nail, blood poisoning set in the cut and Bingham had quite a serious injury by the time he thought it necessary to visit a physician. Dr. Catto is attending him." Bingham referred to the fire as "the most difficult fire-fight he ever put up in Dawson."(*Dawson Daily News*, 27 January 1904)

Some of the merchandise in the Ames Mercantile Co. store next door to the Ladue store was damaged by water. In the February 20 issue of the Dawson Daily News the company advertised a fire sale:

AMES' FIRE SALE

Ladies and gentlemen will find it to their interest to look over this list carefully, mark the selections and cut the ad. out. Bring it with you so you will not experience unnecessary delay at the store. We have put on an extra force in order to handle the crowds. We are in our former store next to the remains of the Ladue building on Front St. The fire did not penetrate our building, consequently the only damage to the goods was by water, the majority of them not even wet.

The insurance companies' loss is your gain.

31 *Dawson Daily News*, 12 April 1904.
32 Ibid.,10 September 1904.
33 Ibid., 5 August 1905.
The results of Botsford's assessment are not known. The Placer Mines Department, however, continued to be inactive and for the same reasons the company's numerous claims had never been developed, the government royalty tax. In February 1904, one miner on Gold Run, complaining about the taxes stated "I am becoming tired of the situation. They have nearly killed the whole thing. Grubstakes and office fees seem the best I can do in this camp. I begin to realize in no mistaken manner that it is time for a change."
34 *Yukon World*, 11, 24 February 1905.
35 Annual Report of the Joseph Ladue Gold Mining and Development of Yukon, 8 February 1905, National Archives of Canada.
36 *Dawson Daily News*, 14 June 1905.
37 Ibid., 6 March 1905.
38 No record was located to indicate that the Ladue Co. owned a riverboat after the *Rideout* was sold in late 1898.
39 *Dawson Daily News*, 16 June 1905.

Bibliography

BOOKS

Adney, Edwin Tappan. *The Klondike Stampede.* New York: Harper, 1899.

Ansell-Trelawney, E. C. *I Followed Gold.* New York: Lee Furman, 1939.

Archibald, Margaret. *A Substantial Expression of Confidence: The Northern Commercial Co. Store, Dawson, 1897-1951.* National Historic Parks and Sites Branch, Parks Canada. Environment Canada, 1982.

Armstrong, Neville A. D. *Yukon Yesterdays: Thirty Years of Adventure in the Klondike. Personal Memories of the Famous Klondike Gold Rush.* London: John Long, 1937.

Atwood, Fred N., ed. *Alaska-Yukon Gold Book.* Seattle: Sourdough Stampede Association, 1930.

Backhouse, Frances. *Women of the Klondike.* Vancouver/Toronto: Whitecap Books, 1995.

Baker, Marcus. Geographic Dictionary of Alaska. 2d ed. Prepared for U.S. Geological Survey Bulletin 299. Washington, DC: Government Printing Office, 1906.

Baird, Andrew. Sixty Years on the Klondike. Vancouver, BC: Gordon Black Publications, Ltd., 1965.

Bancroft, Hubert Home. History of Alaska. 1886. Reprint, Darien, Connecticut: Hafner Publishing Co., 1970.

Bankson, Russell A. The Klondike Nugget. Caldwell, Idaho: Caxton Printers, Ltd., 1935.

Basque, Garnet, ed. Frontier Days in the Yukon. Langley, BC: Sunfire Publications, Ltd., 1991.

Bell, Wendell, and Michael Sullivan. A Cultural Resource Inventory of the Fortymile River. Prepared for the Bureau of Land Management, Fortymile Resource Area, Tok, Alaska, 1976.

Bennett, Estelline. Old Deadwood Days. Lincoln, Nebraska: University of Nebraska Press, 1987.

Berton, Pierre. Klondike: All That Glitters 1896-1899. Toronto: McClelland and Stewart Ltd., 1972.

———. The Wild Frontier. Toronto: McClelland and Stewart, 1978.

Boyer, Paul S. The Oxford Companion to United States History. New York: Oxford University Press, 2001.

Brands, H. W. The Age of Gold: The California Gold Rush and the New American Dream. New York: Random House, 2002.

Brooks, Alfred Hulse. Blazing Alaska's Trails. Caldwell, Idaho: Caxton Printers, Ltd., 1953.

Brown, Jennifer S. H., and Elizabeth Vibert, eds. Reading Beyond Words: Contexts for Native History. Vancouver, BC: University of BC Press, 1996.

Burns, Walter Noble. Tombstone. Garden City, New York: Doubleday, Doran & Co., Inc., 1929

Butler, Marilyn. Destination Tombstone: Adventures of a Prospector; Edward Schieffelin, Founder of Tombstone. Mesa, Arizona: Royal Spectrum Publishing Co., 1996.

Cantwell, Margaret. North to Share. Victoria, British Columbia: Sisters of St. Ann, 1992.

Carruth, Gorton. What Happened When: A Chronology of Life and Events in America. New York: Harper & Row, Publishers, Inc. 1991.

Chase, Will H. Reminiscences of Captain Billy Moore. Kansas City: Burton Publishing Co., 1947.

Clark, Donald W. Fort. Reliance, Yukon: An Archaeological Assessment. Hull, Quebec: Canadian Museum of Civilization, 1995.

Coutts, Robert C. Yukon Places and Names. British Columbia: Gray's Publishing Limited, 1980.

Craig, Lulu Alice. Glimpses of Sunshine and Shade in the Far North. Cincinnati: The Editor Publishing Co., 1900.

Curtin, Walter R. Yukon Voyage. Caldwell, Idaho: Caxton Printers, Ltd., 1938.

Dafoe, John W. Clifford Sifton in Relation to his Times. Toronto: The Macmillan Company of Canada Limited, 1931.

Dall, William Healy. Alaska and Its Resources. Boston: Lee and Shepard, 1870.

———. The Yukon Territory: the Narrative of W.H. Dall, Leader of the Expedition to Alaska in 1866-1868. London: Downey & Co., 1898.

Davis, Mary Lee. Sourdough Gold: The Log of a Yukon Adventure, Boston: W.A. Wilde Company, 1933.

Day, Luella. The Tragedy of the Klondike. New York: privately printed, 1906.

Dawson, George Mercer. Review of Historical Publications Relating To Canada, 1897 vol. II. Historical Notes on Events in the Yukon District, Northwest Territories. Toronto: The University of Toronto(Librarian) 1898.

———. Report on an Exploration in the Yukon District, N.W.T. and Adjacent Northern Portion of British Columbia, 1887. Ottawa: S. E. Dawson, Queen's Printer. 1898.

BIBLIOGRAPHY

Dictionary of Canadian Biography,Volume XII, 1891 to 1900.Toronto: University ofToronto Press, 1990.

Dunham, Sam C. The Alaskan Gold Fields. 1898. Reprint. Anchorage, Alaska: Alaska Northwest Publishing Company, 1983. .

Emmons, George Thornton, ed., with additions by Frederica de Laguna.The Tlingit Indians. New York: American Museum of Natural History(N.Y), Anthropological Papers, No. 70. Seattle: University ofWashington Press, 1991.

Ferrell, Edward, ed. and comp. Biographies of Alaska-Yukon Pioneers, 1850-1950,Volumes 1,2 and 3. Bowie, Maryland: Heritage Books, Inc., 1997.

Ferry, Eudora Bundy.Yukon Gold. New York: Exposition Press, Inc., 1971.

Fischer, Ron W. The Jewish Pioneers of Tombstone and Arizona Territory. Tombstone, Arizona: Ron W. Fischer Enterprises, 2002.

Goodrich, Harold B. "History and Condition of the Yukon Gold District to 1897," in Josiah E. Spurr, Geology of the Yukon Gold District,Alaska.Washington, D.C.: Government Printing Office.1897

Hacking, Norman. Captain William Moore: B.C.'s Amazing Frontiersman. Surrey, B.C.: Heritage House Publishing Co. Ltd., 1993.

Haines, Jan Harper. Cold River Spirits: The Legacy of an Athabaskan-Irish Family from Alaska's Yukon River. Kenmore, Washington: Epicenter Press, 2001.

Hamlin, Charles S. Old Times on the Yukon. Los Angeles, CA: Wetzel Publishing Co, Inc., 1928.

Haskell,William B.Two Years in the Klondike and Alaskan Gold Fields. Hartford, Connecticut: Hartford Publishing Co., 1898.

Hayne, Murray Henry Edward. The Pioneers of the Klondyke. London: Sampson Low, Marston and Co., 1897.

Heller, Herbert L. Sourdough Sagas: The Journals, Memoirs, Tales and Recollections of the Earliest Alaskan Gold Miners, 1883-1923. Cleveland: World Publishing Company, 1967.

Henderson, Henry. True Story of the Discovery of the Klondike by Bob Henderson. Edmonton, Alberta: H. H. Hull Printing Co., n.d.

Hitchcock, Mary E.Two Women in the Klondike. New York and London: G. P. Putnam's Sons, 1899.

Hunt,William R.The Whiskey Peddler. Missoula, Montana: Mountain Press Publishing Co., 1993.

Jacobsen, Johan Adrian. Alaska Voyage, 1882-1883: an Exploration to the Northwest Coast of America. Chicago: University of Chicago Press, 1977.

Jackson, Ronald Vern, and Gary Ronald Teeples, comps. Alaskan Census Records, 1870-1907. Bountiful, Utah: Accelerated Indexing Systems, Inc., 1976.

Jarvis, W. H. P. The Great Gold Rush: A Tale of the Klondike. Toronto: MacMillan Co. of Canada, Limited, 1913.

Johnson, Albert James. George Carmack: The Mystery Man Who Set off the Klondike Gold Rush. Vancouver, B.C.: Whitecap Books, 2001.

Josephy, Alvin M. Jr. 500 Nations. New York: Alfred A. Knopf, 1994.

Judge, Charles J. An American Missionary: Re vWilliam H. Judge. S. J. New York: Catholic Foreign Mission Society of America, 1907.

Julyan, Robert. The Place Names of New Mexico. Albuquerque:University of New Mexico Press, 1996.

Klondyke and the Gold Fields of Alaska. London: American Jubilee Co., 1897.

Ladue, Joseph F. Klondyke Facts: Being a Complete Guide Book to the Gold Regions of the Great Canadian Northwest Territories and Alaska. New York: American Technical Book Co., 1897.

———. Klondyke Nuggets: Being A Brief Description of the Famous Gold Regions of The Great Canadian Northwest and Alaska. New York: American Technical Book Co., 1897.

Ledbetter, Suzann. Nellie Cashman, Prospector and Trailblazer. El Paso, Texas: Texas Western Press, 1993.

Leonard, John. The Gold Fields of the Klondike. Whitehorse, Yukon: Clairedge, 1994.

Lewis, Marvin, ed. The Mining Frontier. Norman, Oklahoma: University of Oklahoma Press, 1967.

Life of William McKinley, The. New York: P. F. Collier & Son, 1901.

Lynch, Jeremiah. Three Years in the Klondike. Chicago: R. R. Donnelley & Sons Co., 1967.

Lyons, Esther, comp. Glimpses of Alaska: A Collection of Views of the Interior of Alaska and the Klondike District. Chicago: Rand, McNally & Co., 1897.

Margeson, Charles Anson. Experiences of Gold Hunters in Alaska, Published by the author, 1899.

Martin, Cy, and Jeannie Martin. Gold and Where They Found It: A Guide to Ghost Towns

and Mining Camps Sites. Corona del Mar, California: Trans-Anglo Books, 1974.
Martinsen, Ella Lung. Trail to North Star Gold. Portland, Oregon: Metropolitan Press, 1969.

———. Black Sand and Gold. Portland, Oregon: Binford & Mort Publishers, 1956.

Mayo Historical Society. Gold and Galena. Altona, Manitoba: 1999: Mayo Historical Society, 1999.

McConnell, Richard G. Report on an Exploration in the Mackenzie and Yukon Basins, 1887-88 in Dawson: Report on an Exploration in the Yukon District, N.W.T. and Adjacent Northern Portion of British Columbia, 1887Ottowa: SE.Dawson, Queens Printer, 1898.

McKeown, Martha. Them Was the Days: An American Saga of the '70s. New York: Macmillan, 1950.

McQuiston, James A. McUisdean. Privately printed, North East, Pa, 2002.

McQuiston, Leona Bean. The McQuiston, McCueston, and McQuesten Families 1620-1937. Louisville: Standard Press, 1937.

Michael Henry N., ed. Lieutenant Zagoskin's Travels in Russian America, 1842-1844: The First Ethnographic and Geographic Investigations in the Yukon and Kuskokwim Valleys of Alaska. Toronto: University of Toronto Press, 1967.

McConnell, R. G. Gold Values in the Klondike 1907. Ottawa: Government Printing Office, 1907.

Moir, George T. Sinners and Saints. Victoria, BC: privately printed, 1947.

Myrick, David. Railroads of Arizona. Vol. 1, The Southern Railroads. Berkeley, CA: Howell-Nroth Books, 1975

Murphy, Claire Rudolf, and Jane G. Haigh. Gold Rush Women. Anchorage, Alaska: Alaska Northwest Books, 1997.

Newell, Gordon, ed. The McCurdy Marine History of the Pacific Northwest, 1895-1965. Seattle: Superior Publishing Co., 1966.

O'Connor, Richard. High Jinks on the Klondike. New York: Bobbs-Merrill Co., Inc., 1954.

Ogilvie, William. Early Days on the Yukon, and the Story of Its Gold Finds. Toronto: Bell & Cockburn, 1913.

———. Lecture on the Yukon Gold Fields. n.d. Delivered at Victoria, B.C: Victoria, B.C., The Colonist Press, 1897.

———. The Klondike Official Guide. Toronto: Hunter, Rose Co., 1898.

Orth, Donald J. Dictionary of Alaska Place Names. Geological Survey Professional Paper No.

567. Washington, DC: Government Printing Office, 1967.
Osgood, Cornelius. The Han Indians: A Compilation of Ethnographic and Historical Data on the Alaska-Yukon Boundary Area. New Haven, Connecticut: Department of Anthropology, Yale University, 1971.

Page, Elizabeth. Wild Horses and Gold. New York: Farrar & Rinehart, Inc., 1932.

Parker, Watson. Deadwood: The Golden Years. Lincoln, Nebraska: University of Nebraska Press, 1981.

———. Gold in the Black Hills. Pierre, South Dakota: State Publishing Co., 1966. Windsor Associates 1997.

Pierce, Richard A., ed. Life on the Yukon, 1865-1867 (The Western Union Telegraph Expedition I), by George R. Adams. Kingston, Ontario: Limestone Press, 1982.

Pike, Warburton. Through the Sub-Arctic Forest. New York: Edward Arno Publishers, 1896.

Pomerleau, Jeanne. Les chercheurs d'or: Des Canadiens francais epris de richesse et d'aventure. Quebec: J. C. Dupont, 1996.

Reader's Digest Association. Through Indian Eyes. Pleasantville, New York: Reader's Digest Association, 1995.

Royal Baking Powder Company. Camp Cookery: A Practical Manual for Miners, Lumbermen, Ranchmen, Sportsmen, Yachtsmen and for All Out-door Cooking. New York: Royal Baking Powder Company, 1902.

Sax, Lee, and Effie Linklater. GIKHY:, The True Story of the Arctic Kutchin Christian Leaders. Whitehorse, Yukon: Diocese of Yukon, 1997.

Schmitter, Ferdinand. Upper Yukon Native Customs and Folk-Lore. Washington DC: Smithsonian Institution, 1910.

Schwatka, Frederick. A Summer in Alaska. St. Louis, Missouri: J. W. Henry, 1893.

Secretan, J. H. E. To Klondyke and Back . London: Hurst and Blackett, 1898.

Senate Committee on Military Affairs. Across Valdez Glacier in Compilation of Narratives of Explorations in Alaska, report prepared by Lt. R. M. Brookfield, Second Infantry., 56th Cong., 1st Session, S. Rept. 1023, Washington, D.C.: Government Printing Office, 1900.

———. Across Valdez Glacier with Sleds Drawn by Hand in Compilations of Narratives of Explorations in Alaska. report prepared by Lt. Guy H. Preston, Ninth Cavalry. 56th Cong., 1st Session. S. Rept. 1023. Washington, D.C.: Government Printing Office, 1900.

———. A Military Reconnoissance of the Copper River Valley; 1885 in Compilation of Narratives of Exploration in Alaska, report prepared by Lt. Henry T. Allen, Second Cavalry. 56th Cong., 1st session, S. Rept. 1023. Washington, D.C.: Government Printing Office, 1900.

BIBLIOGRAPHY

———.A Reconnoissance of the Yukon Valley, 1883 in Compilation of Narratives of Explorations in Alaska. report prepared by First Lt. Frederick Schwatka, Third Cavalry., 56th Cong., 1st Session. S. Rept. 1023, Washington: Government Printing Office, 1900.

———. A Story of Hardship and Suffering in Alaska in Compilation of Narratives of Exploration in Alaska, report prepared by Lt. J. C. Castner, Fourth Infantry. 56th Cong., 1st Session, S. Rept. 1023. Washington, D.C.: Government Printing Office, 1900.

———. From Valdez Inlet to Belle Isle, on the Yukon in Compilation of Narratives of Explorations in Alaska, report prepared by Lt. P. G. Lowe, Eighth Infantry. 56th Cong., 1st Session, S. Rept. 1023, Washington, D.C.: Government Printing Office, 1900.

———. Meteorology in Compilation of Narratives of Explorations in Alaska., report prepared by Fred W. Fickett, U.S. Army Signal Corps, 56th Cong., 1st Session, S. Rept. 1023. Washington DC: Government Printing Office.1885

———. The Population and Resources of Alaska, 1880 in Compilation of Narratives of Explorations in Alaska, report prepared by Ivan Petrof. 56th Cong., 1st Session. S. Rept. 1023. Washington, D.C.: Government Printing Office, 1900.

———. Reconnoissance of the Yukon River, 1869 in Compilation of Narratives of Explorations in Alaska. report prepared by Charles P. Raymond, Engineer Corps, 56th Cong., 1st Session. S. Rept. 1023, Washington, D.C.: Government Printing Office, 1900.

———. Winter Conditions Along the Yukon: 1899, in Compilation of Narratives of Explorations in Alaska report prepared by, Captain Wilds P. Richardson, Eighth Infantry. 56th Cong., 1st Session. S. Rept. 1023. Washington, D.C.: Government Printing Office, 1900.

Sherwood, Morgan B. Exploration of Alaska. New Haven, Connecticut: Yale University Press, 1965.

Smyth, Stephen. The Yukon's Constitutional Foundations. Vol. 1, The Yukon Chronology. Whitehorse, Yukon: Northern Directories, 1991.

Spurr, Josiah Edward. Through the Yukon Gold Diggings. Boston: Eastern Publishing Co., 1900.

———. Geology of the Yukon District, Alaska. USGS Eighteenth Annual Report, 1896-97, Part III, Economic Geology. Washington, D.C.: Government Printing Office, 1897.

Stearns, Peter N. The Encyclopedia of World History. New York: Houghton Mifflin Co., 2001.

Steele, Colonel S. B. Forty Years in Canada. Toronto: McClelland, Goodchild, Stewart, 1918.

Stuck, Hudson. Voyages on the Yukon and its Tributaries: A Narrative of Winter Travel in Interior Alaska. New York: Charles Scribner's Sons, 1917.

Sullivan, Mary Kellogg. A Woman Who Went to Alaska. Boston: James H. Earle & Co., 1903.
Teacher, Lawrence, and Richard Nicholls, eds. The Unabridged Jack London. Philadelphia: Running Press, 1997.

Time-Life Books. The Miners. New York: Time-Life Books, 1976.

Tollemache, Stratford. Reminiscences of the Yukon. London: Edward Arnold, 1912.

Traywick, Ben T. Historical Documents and Photographs of Tombstone. Tombstone, Arizona: Red Marie's Bookstore, 1994.

———, ed. Tombstone Clippings. Tombstone, Arizona: Red Marie's Bookstore, 1994.

Twitchell, Ralph E. The Leading Facts of New Mexican History. Albuquerque, New Mexico: Horn & Wallace, 1963.

Two Journals of Robert Campbell, 1808 to 1853. Seattle: The Shorey Book Store, 1958.

Utley, Robert M., ed. Encyclopedia of the American West. New York: Wings Books, 1998.

Walden, Arthur T. A Dog-Puncher on the Yukon. Boston: Houghton Mifflin Co., 1928.

Waterland, Joel. The Spawn & The Mother Lode: The Story of the Placer, Conglomerate and Precambrian Mines of the Central City, Lead and Deadwood Area. Rapid City, South Dakota, 1987: Grelind PhotoGraphics & Typesetters, 1897.

Wells, E. Hazard. Magnificence and Misery. Garden City, N.Y.: Doubleday & Co., 1984

Wheeler, Keith. The Railroaders. New York, NY: Time, Inc., 1973.

Whipple, Wayne. The Story of the White House and its Home Life. Boston: Dwinell-Wright Co., 1937.

Whymper, Frederick. Travel and Adventure in the Territory of Alaska. London: John Murry, 1868.

Wickersham, James. Old Yukon, Tales, Trails and Trials. St. Paul, Minnesota: West Publishing Co., 1938.

Wilson, Veazie. Guide to the Yukon Goldfields: Where They are and How to Reach Them. Rev. ed. Seattle: Calvert Co., 1897.

Winslow, Kathryn. Big Pan Out. New York: Norton & Co., 1951.

Wright, E. W., ed. Lewis and Dryden's Marine History of the Pacific Northwest. New York: Antiquarian Press, 1961.

Young, Samuel Hall. Hall Young of Alaska: An Autobiography. New York: Fleming H. Revell

Co., 1927.

Young, Samuel Hall. The Klondike Clan. New York: Fleming H. Revell Co., 1916.

ARTICLES

Adney, Tappan. "A Winter's Work in the Klondike." Harper's Weekly, 1 October 1898.

———. "Who Discovered the Klondike?" Harper's Weekly, 1 April 1899.

"Alaska and the Klondike." Popular Science Monthly, May-June 1899.

Allen, A.S. "Dawson, Yukon Territory." American Journal of Industry, 1901.

Bonner, John. "Competition for the Klondike Trade." Leslie's Illustrated Weekly Magazine, 30 December 1897.

Burlingame, Virginia S. "John Healy's Alaskan Adventure." The Alaska Journal, autumn 1978.

Callahan, Erinia Pavaloff Cherosky. "A Yukon Autobiography." Alaska Journal, vol. 5, 1975.

Chapman, John. "Mining Life on the Yukon." The West Shore, vol. 12, 1886.

Clum, John P. "Nellie Cashman: The Angel of Tombstone." The Arizona Historical Review, January 1931.

Curtis, Edward S. "The Rush to the Klondike Over the Mountain Passes." Century Illustrated Monthly Magazine, March 1898.

Dall, William Healey. "Robert Kennicott." Chicago Academy of Science Transactions 1867-69.

———. "Alaska and the New Gold-Field." The Forum, September 1897.

———. "A Yukon Pioneer, Mike Lebarge." National Geographic Magazine, September 1898.

———. "Reminiscences of Yukon Exploration, 1865-1868." Popular Science Monthly, August 1906.

Glave, E.J. "Pioneer Packhorses in Alaska." Century Illustrated Monthly Magazine, vol. 44, September-October 1892.

Hayes, Charles Willard. "An Expedition Through the Yukon District." National Geographic Magazine, 15 May 1892.

Johns, William D. "News from the Klondike." Harpers Magazine, 20 November 1897.

Krech, Shepard III. "On the Aboriginal Population of the Kutchin." Arctic Anthropology, 15 [1], 1978.

Lake, Ivan Clyde. "Irish Nellie, Angel of the Cassiar." Alaska Sportsman, October 1963.

Longenbaugh, Dee. "Alaska's Own Cartographers." Terrae Incognitae: The Journal for the History of Discoveries, vol. 31, 1999.

MacDonald, Norbert. "Seattle, Vancouver and the Klondike." The Canadian Historical Review, vol. 49, no. 3, September 1968.

"Makers of the New Klondike." Alaska-Yukon Magazine. February 1910.

McDonald, W. N. "Leroy Napoleon McQuesten, Father of Alaska." The Highlander, vol. 22, no. 3, May-June 1984.

McClellan, Catharine. "Indian Stories about the First Whites in Northwestern America." Ethnohistory in Southwestern Alaska and the Southern Yukon, University Press of Kentucky, 1970.

Miller, Joaquin. "Stampedes on the Klondike: How I Missed Being A Millionaire." Overland Monthly, December 1897.

"Mission Work on the Upper Yukon." Canadian Church Magazine, Spirit of Missions, vol. 60, June 1895.

Nichols, Jeanette. "Advertising and the Klondike." Washington Historical Quarterly, 13, 1922

Ogilvie, William. "The Yukon District." The Scottish Geographical Magazine, vol. 14, July 1898.

———. "Story of the Yukon." Scientific American Supplement No. 1152, 29 January 1898.

———. "The Geography and Resources of the Yukon Basin." The Geographical Journal, vol. 12, July-December 1898.

Palmer, Frederick. "Government and Society in the Klondike." The Forum. September 1898, February 1899.

Quinan, Lt. W.R. "Discoverer of the Yukon Gold Fields." Overland Monthly, October 1897.

Raymond, Charles W. "The Yukon River Region, Alaska." Journal of the American Geographic Society of New York, 1873.

Rochlin, Harriet. "Nellie Cashman: Gold Digger of '77." Ms. Magazine, 1973.

Sleicher, John A. "The Original King of the Klondike: Remarkable Career of Joseph Ladue, The Founder of Dawson City." Leslie's Illustrated Weekly Magazine, 16 September 1897.

Steffens, Lincoln. "Life in the Klondike Gold Fields." McClure's Magazine, September 1897.

Stein, Robert. "The Gold Fields of Alaska." United States Geological Survey, Review of Reviews, vol. 13, June 1896.

Stone, I. Thomas. "The Mounties as Vigilantes: Perceptions of Community and the Transformation of Law in the Yukon, 1885-1897." Law & Society Review, vol. 14, 1979.

———. "Atomistic Order and Frontier Violence: Miners and Whalemen in Nineteenth Century Yukon." Ethnology, vol. 23, no. 4, October 1983.

"The Best Route to the Northern Gold Fields." Overland Monthly, June 1898.

Thompson, Harold T. "The Year 1901 in the Klondike." Scientific American, January 18, 1902.

Turck, Thomas J., and Diane L. Lehman Turck. "Trading Posts Along the Yukon River: Noochuloghoyet Trading Post in Historical Context." Arctic, vol. 45, no. 1, March 1992.

Wade, Mark S. "The Clondyke Gold Fields." The Fortnightly Review, September 1897.

Webb, John Sidney. "The River Trip to the Klondike." Century Illustrated Monthly Magazine, March 1898.

Westbrook, Mary E. "A Venture into Ethnohistory: the Journals of Rev. V. C. Sim, Pioneer Missionary on the Yukon." Polar Notes, no.9, May 1969: 34-35.

Williams, E. "Klondike—A Study in Booms." The Living Age, September 1889.

Woodside, Henry J. "Dawson as It Is." The Canadian Magazine of Politics, Science, Art and Literature, (Toronto) vol. 17, May 1901-October 1901.

Wright, G. Frederick. "The Yukon Gold Fields." The Nation, 5 August 1897.

NEWSPAPERS

Alaska

Alaska Daily Empire
Alaska Weekly
Anchorage Daily Times
Douglas Island News
Fairbanks News-Miner
Fairbanks Weekly Times
Seward Gateway
Sitka Alaskan
Sitka Post
Yukon Press (Ft. Adams)

Arizona

Tombstone Epitaph

British Columbia

Victoria Daily Colonist

California

Los Angeles Herald
San Francisco Chronicle
San Francisco Examiner

England
London Daily Mail
London Times

Idaho
Idaho Daily Statesman (Boise)
Lewiston Morning Tribune

Iowa
Center Point Lotus

Manitoba
Selkirk Journal

Montana
Butte Miner

New Mexico
Santa Fe New Mexican
Santa Fe Reporter

New York State
Adirondack News
Malone Palladium
New York Herald
New York Herald-Tribune
New York Times
New York World
Plattsburgh Daily Press
Plattsburgh Press Republican
Plattsburgh Republican
Plattsburgh Sentinel
Plattsburgh Sentinel and *Clinton County Farmer* (Souvenir Industrial Edition of Plattsburgh, 1897. *Plattsburgh Daily Press*, Reprint, CornerStone Book Shop, 1978)

South Dakota
Black Hills Times

Washington DC
Washington Star

Washington State
Seattle Daily Times
Seattle Sunday Times
Seattle Post-Intelligencer

BIBLIOGRAPHY

Yukon

Clarion (Dawson City)
Clondyke News
Dawson City Glacier
Dawson Daily News
Dawson Record
Klondike News
Klondike Nugget, The
Yukon Catholic
Yukon Sun
Yukon World

ARCHIVAL SOURCES

British Columbia Archives

Memorandum. Association of the Golden Wedge Mining Co., Ltd. 8 November 1896. "company files." Company # (1890) - 0000456, Microfilm #B4413.

Manitoba Provincial Archives

Journal of Robert Campbell, 1808-1851. MG1 D8.

National Archives of Canada

Annual Report of the Joseph Ladue Gold Mining and Development Co. of Yukon, submitted to the Secretary of State, Ottawa, Ontario, Canada. 8 February 1905. R.G., vol. 117, File 451.

Annual Report of the Joseph Ladue Gold Mining & Development Co. of Dawson, Yukon-for filing. R.G. 6, Volume A-1, 117, Numbers 398-507.

Application. Joseph Ladue to the Minister of the Interior to Purchase Dominion Lands. 27 August 1896. GOV 2085.

Application. Joseph Ladue to the Minister of the Department of the Interior for 480 acres of land at Ft. Selkirk. 20 November 1896. R.G. 91, vol. 3, File 173, microfilm M-2828.

Constantine Diary. Records of the Royal Canadian Mounted Police. R.G. 18, vol. 1345, file 190-1895.

Declaration. Arthur Harper. 1 July 1896.

Dictionnaire Genealogigue des familles du Quebec des origines a 1730. Rene Jette. Montreal: University of Montreal Press, 1983.

Judge Dugas to L. O. David, 29. June 1899. Papers of Clifford Sifton. vol. 64, p. 46760.

Letterhead, The Joseph Ladue Gold Mining and Development Co. of Yukon. 16 February 1899. Yukon Territorial Records. R.G. 91, vol. 14, file 2877.

Mariage de St-Antoine-sur-Richelieux, (1741-1965) compiled and published by B. Pontbriand, Agronome.

Murray, Alexander Hunter. "Journal of the Yukon 1847-48." Ottawa, Ontario: Government Printing Bureau, 1910.

Ogilvie, William. Field Notes: Yukon District, 1896-1897, Book No. 5. William Ogilvie fonds, MG 30, B22, file 2.

———. Some Notes on Gold Mining in the Yukon Territory, 1905. William Ogilvie Manuscripts, 1905. R.G. 30, vol. B-22, file V.1.

Sim, Vincent C. Letters and Papers of the Church Missionary Society, London, 1884. MF Reel A-22.

William to Mr. Wilson. Forty Mile. 22 May 1897. R.G. 30, vol. B-22, file 1, William Ogilvie Correspondence. 1873, 1889-1912.

Reverend William C. Bompas, Bishop of Selkirk District to the Lieutenant Governor of British Columbia. 1 August 1892. R.G. 6, Vol. 81, File 4991-5582 (5425).

Royal Canadian Mounted Police Historical Branch, Ottawa, Ontario

Annual Report of Inspector Samuel Steele, Commanding the Yukon District. 10 January, 1899.

Annual Report of Inspector C. Constantine, Commanding the Yukon District, 18 January 1897. Report of the Commissioner of the North West Mounted Police, 1898.

Yukon Archives

Alaska Commercial Co. 1898, to the Klondike Gold Fields and Other Points of interest in Alaska. PAM 1898-33.

Annual Report of Inspector C. Constantine, Ft. Constantine, Cudahy P.O., Upper Yukon. 20 January 1896. PAM 1895-6.

Annual Report of Inspector C. Starnes, Dawson, Y.T. 1 December 1901. The Officer Commanding, North-west Mounted Police. Yukon Territory.

Application and Affidavit for Placer Mine, Numbers 136 and 139. Pam, 1896-1.

Application from Arthur Harper to the Minister of the Department of the Interior for 160 acres of land at Ft. Selkirk. Yukon Territorial Records, R.G. 91, vol. 7, file 956.

Application from Arthur Harper to the Minister of the Dept. of the Interior for 480 acres of land at Ft. Selkirk. 30 June 1896. Yukon Territorial Records. R.G. 91, vol. 7, file 956.

Application from Arthur Harper to the Minister of the Interior for 160 acres of land at Ft. Selkirk. 30 June 1896. Yukon Territorial Records. R.G. 91, vol. 7, file 956.

BIBLIOGRAPHY

Application from Arthur Harper for 18 acres. 17 Nov. 1896. Yukon Territorial Records. R.G. 90, vol. 14, file 2877.

Application from Joseph Ladue to the Minister of the Department of the Interior for 480 acres of land at Ft. Selkirk. 30 June 1896. Yukon Territorial Records, R.G. 91, vol. 1, file 173.

Assets and Debts. Estate of Arthur Harper. GOV 1444, Series 11, file 2, 4/40.

Bompas, Mrs. C.S. "Mission Work on the Upper Yukon." Spirit of Missions, vol. 60, June 1895. PAM 1895-2.

Brooks, Alfred Hulse. "A Reconnaissance from Pyramid Harbor to Forty Mile River, Alaska." Science, vol. II, May 25, 1900. No. 282. PAM 1900-1

Canadian Department of the Interior. Registered Documents. MF Roll No.4.

Canadian Department of the Interior to Francois X. Gosselin, Land and Timber Agent, Dawson City, December 6, 1901. Yukon Territorial Records, R.G. 91, vol. 1, file 173.

Canham, Rev. Thomas H. "The Diocese of Selkirk: Its Work and Workers." Church Missionary Intelligencer, No. 23, January 1898. PAM, 1898-130.

Carmack, George. My Trip to the Yukon. Snow Collection.

Celina Bompas. June 1895. vol.60, PAM, 1895-2.

Clifford Sifton, Minister of the Interior to Commissioner William Ogilvie. 24 August 1898. R.G. 91, vol.14, file 2877.

Commissioner William Ogilvie to the Canadian Department of the Interior. 28 June 1899. Yukon Territorial Records. R.G. 91, vol. 14, file 2877.

——— to C.M. Woodworth, Dept. of the Interior. February 8, 1899. Yukon Territorial Records, R.G. 91, vol. 14, file 2877.

——— to "Mr. Justice Dugas." 3 December 1898. Yukon Territorial Records. R.G. 91, vol. 14, file 2877.

——— to Minister of the Interior. 28 June 1899. Yukon Territorial Records. R.G. 91, vol. 14, file 2877.

——— to Deputy Minister of the Interior. 23 November 1899. Yukon Territorial Records. R.G. 91, vol. 14, file 2877.

— to Elmer F. Botsford. 4 August 1899. Yukon Territorial Records. R.G. 91, vol. 14, file 2877.

——— to T.G. Rothwell, Acting Deputy Minister of the Dept. of the Interior. Dawson, Y.T.

20 January 1902. Yukon Territorial Records. R.G. 91, vol. 14, file 2877.
Dawson Waterfront, 1898-1908. GOV 1684, 3/3.

Dominion Lands Grant No. 3751. Yukon Territorial Records. Dominion Lands Grant Numbers 5509, 5510, 5511, 5512 and 5513.
E. Deville, Surveyor General to the Minister of the Department of the Interior. 4 November 1898. Yukon Territorial Records. R.G. 91, vol.14, file 2877.

Elmer F. Botsford, Attorney for the Harper and Ladue Townsite Co. to Mr. Alex McLeod. 22 August 1899. Yukon Territorial Records. R.G. 91, vol. 14, file 2877.

——— to Mr. A. McLeod, Dept. of the Interior. 22 August 1899. Yukon Territorial Records. R.G. 91, vol. 14, file 2877.

——— to Commissioner William Ogilvie. 2 August 1899. Yukon Territorial Records. R.G. 91, vol.14, file 2877.

——— to Commissioner William Ogilvie, Dawson. 4 August 1899. Yukon Territorial Records. R.G. 91, vol. 14, file 2877.

——— to Commissioner Ogilvie. 8 October 1898. Yukon Territorial Records. R.G. 91, vol. 14, file 2877.

Francois Xavier Gosselin, Land and Timber Agent, to the Secretary of the Department of the Interior. Ottawa, Ontario. 14 September 1901. Yukon Territorial Records. R.G. 91, vol. 1, file 173.

F. W. Clements to Minister of the Interior. 29 March 1899. Yukon Territorial Records. R.G. 91, vol. 14, file 2877.

Hardisty, William Lucas. "The Loucheux Indians." Smithsonian Institution Annual Report, 1866. PAM 1866-2.

Harper/Ladue Partnership Agreement. 19 Nov. 1896. R.G. 91, vol. 14, file 2877.

Index of Original Locators, Placer Claims, 1896-1903.

Interim Receipt No. 387 attached to "My Experiences in the Yukon" by G.W. Carmack. MF, Snow Collection.

James A. Smart of the Department of the Interior to Commissioner Ogilvie. 10 October 1898. R.G. 91, vol. 14, file 2877.

James M. Wilson, Executor of the Harper Estate and J.E. Hansen, agent for Joseph Ladue, to Commissioner Ogilvie. 30 September 1899. Yukon Territorial Records. R.G. 91, file 2877.

——— and Elmer F. Botsford to Clifford Sifton, Minister of the Interior. 1 September 1899. Yukon Territorial Records. R.G. 91, vol.14, file 2877.

Johns, William Douglas. Coutts Collection, 78/69, box F-89, folders 20 and 21, n.d.

Jones, Strachan. "The Kutchin Tribes." Smithsonian Institution Annual Report, 1866. PAM 1866-1.
Kirkby, William W. "A Journey to the Youcon, Russian America." Smithsonian Annual Report. PAM, 1864-1.

Leroy Napoleon "Jack" McQuesten to McKay, Berkeley, California, 1 July 1905. MS 13, Box 5, #5.

Lyndwode Periera, Assistant Secretary of the Department of the Interior, to Joseph Ladue, Esq. 24 December 1897. Yukon Territorial Records. R.G. 91, vol.14, file 2877.
McQuesten, L.N. Manuscript. 1884-1947. George Snow Collection, Microfilm, #80/13, MF #47, 80/89, 1871-1923.

Memorandum, W. H. Mathews, Dept. of Geology, University of British Columbia, Vancouver, BC. n.d., Coutts Collection, 78/69, Pt. l, Folder F.

Memorandum, H. W. Newlands, Legal Advisor, Dept. of the Interior to J. N. E., Brown, Territorial Secretary. Dawson. 14 January 1902. Yukon Territorial Records. R.G. 91, vol. 14, file 2877.

Memorandum. W.H. Mathews, Department of Geology, University of British Columbia. n.d., Robert C. Coutts Collection, 78/69 pt. 1, Folder F.

"Minutes of the first meeting of the Yukon Order of Pioneers. 1 December 1894." COR 221 f.1 #82/454.

Moore, William. "Report Upon the Yukon Country, April 25, 1888." William Moore. Sessional Papers of British Columbia Lands and Works Dept. PAM, 1888-1.

Ogilvie, William. The Geography and Resources of the Yukon Basin. Vol. 12, 7-1898. PAM 1898-29.

Peake, F.A. "Robert McDonald, the great unknown missionary of the northwest." Journal of the Canadian Church Historical Society. vol. 27, no. 3. September 1975. PAM 1975-0263.

Recollections of Leroy N. McQuesten. PAM 1952-0003, Coutts Collection.

Registered Documents. (Canadian) Department of the Interior, MF Roll No. 4.

Sim, Rev. Vincent C. Exploration of the Upper Yukon River. Washington: Government Printing Office, 1886. PAM, 1824-1947.

U.S. Department of the Interior Annual Report, 1898. PAM 1898-4.

Victoria Faulkner Collection. Yukon Archives. MSS 141, Folder 50

Whymper, Frederick. Russian America or 'Alaska': The Natives of the Youkon River and

Adjacent Country. PAM 1869-1.

Yukon Territorial Court Records.

LIBRARY COLLECTIONS

Alaska State Library Historical Collections

Circular No. 9: to stockholders from the Joseph Ladue Gold Mining and Development Co. of Yukon. 4 April 1898. MS 16B.

Dawson Daily News Golden Cleanup Edition. 1902. MS 49-7-1.

George Snow Papers on microfilm, folder 1, Boxes 3, 4.

Notice of Annual Meeting of The Joseph Ladue Gold Mining and Development of Yukon. 10 January 1898. MS 16B.

Official Prospectus of The Joseph Ladue Gold Mining and Development Co. of Yukon. MS 16B.

Polk's 1888 Puget Sound Directory.

Juneau Business Directory. 1895.

Report of the Operations of the U.S. Revenue Steamer Nunivak on the Yukon River Station, Alaska, 1899-1901. First Lieutenant J. C. Cantwell. Washington, D.C.: Government Printing Office, 1904.

Arizona State Library

1878-1880 Pima County Great Register.

1881-1884 Cochise County Great Register.

California Historical Society Library

A.C. Co. Minutes of Meetings. MSS (2 volumes).

Consortium Library, University of Alaska Anchorage

Charles O. Farciot Collection.

Dartmouth College Library, Rauner Special Collections Library: Archives, Manuscripts, Rare Books

Robert Henderson to Tappan Adney. 18 December 1898. Edmund Tappan Adney Collection.

Tappan Adney Interview with Joe Ladue. n.d., Edmund Tappan Adney Collection.

BIBLIOGRAPHY

Dawson City Museum/Klondike History Library

Affidavit. Elmer Francis Botsford. 16 April 1902. Vertical files.

Annual Report of the Joseph Ladue Gold Mining and Development Co. of Yukon. 4 February 1901. Vertical files.

"Bill of Sail." (sic) Dawson City, Yukon. 18 October 1896. Vertical files.

Carter, Margaret. A History of the Use of Wood in the Yukon to 1903. National Historic Sites Service, 1973. MF.

Counter Receipt. The Joseph Ladue Gold Mining and Development Co. of Yukon. 1901. Vertical files.

Carmack, George. My Experiences in the Yukon. Vertical files.

Indenture made 2 September 1899 between James M. Wilson and Joseph Ladue. Vertical files.

Lis Pendens. Demand made on S. O. Morford for accounting. Dawson City, Yukon Territory. 29 August 1898. Registered Documents, MF, Roll #4.

Memorandum. W. H. Mathews. Origin of the name of the Yukon City of Dawson, by whom and why. n.d. Vertical files.

Mining "Records Book." MF Roll No. 8.

Notice of Annual Meeting of the Joseph Ladue Gold Mining and Development Co. of Yukon. 10 April 1898. Fred Caley Collection.

Plan of Dawson and Klondike Townsites, Yukon District—NWT. Surveyed by James Gibbon DLS. 1897 and 1898.

Power of Attorney. Joseph Ladue to S. O. Morford. 22 June 1897. Registered Documents, MF, Roll # 4.

Power of Attorney. Joseph Ladue to Elmer F. Botsford. Plattsburgh, New York. 23 October 1897. Registered Documents, MF, Roll #4.

Power of Attorney. Joseph Ladue to J. E. Hansen. Dawson City, Yukon Territory. 6 September 1898. Registered Documents, MF, Roll #4.

Report of the Committee Appointed by the Stockholders Present at the Annual Meeting. New Jersey. 4 February 1901. Vertical files.

Revocation of Power of Attorney. Joseph Ladue-S. O. Morford. Dawson City, Yukon Territory. 29 August 1898. Registered Documents, MF, Roll # 4.

Telegram. U.S. Adjutant General's Office to Joseph Ladue. 17 September 1897. Vertical files.

Telegram. Joseph Ladue Gold Mining and Development Co. of Yukon to U.S. Adjutant General's Office. 17 September 1897. Vertical files.

The Yukon Territory: Its History and Resources, 1907. Canada, Department of the Interior.

The Yukon Territory: Its History and Resources, 1916. Canada, Department ofthe Interior.

Yukon Territory and Alaska, Directory and Gazeteer. 1901. Maria L. Ferguson.

Fogler Library, University of Maine

Pacific Coast Pilot, Alaska. Washington DC: 1883. Microfiche No. 15817.

Geology of the Yukon District, Alaska. U.S. Geological Survey, Eighteenth Annual Report, 1896-97, Part III, Economic Geology. Washington, D.C.: Government Printing Office, 1897.

Foley Center Library, Gonzaga University

Francis Barnum, S.J. Account of the Journey of Bishop Clut to Alaska. New York, June 7, 1906.

Illinois State Library

Adjutant General Records— Muster Rolls for Illinois Regiments in Civil War.

Marriott Library, University of Utah

Grinnell, Joseph. Gold Hunting in Alaska. Edited by Elizabeth Grinnell. Elgin, Illinois: David C. Cook Co., 1901. Microfilm.

New Mexico Institute of Technology Library

File, Lucien. Directory of Mines of New Mexico. State Bureau of Mines and Mineral Resources, 1965.

New Mexico State Library

Brooks, Alfred Hulse. A Reconnaissance in the Tanana and White River Basins, Alaska, in 1898. Twentieth Annual Report of the USGS to the Secretary of the Interior, 1898-99, Part VII, Explorations in Alaska in 1898. Washington, D.C.: Government Printing Office, 1900. SUDOCS# I 1.1: 898-99, Part VII.

Goodrich, Harold B. "History and Condition of the Yukon Gold District to 1897." Geology of the Yukon Gold District, Alaska by Josiah E. Spurr USGS, Eighteenth Annual Report, 1896-97, Part III, Economic Geology. Washington, D.C.: Government Printing Office, 1898. SUDOCS # I 1.1: 896-7, Part III.

Raymond, Captain Charles W., Chief Engineer, U.S. Corps of Engineers. Report of a Reconnaissance of the Yukon River, Alaska Territory, July to September 1869. 42nd Cong., 1st Sess. Washington, D.C.: Government Printing Office, 1871. S. Executive Document No. 12 (42-1) 1466.

Report of Captain L.A. Beardslee, USN Relative to the Affairs in Alaska and the Operations of the U.S.S. Jamestown. 47th Cong. 1st Sess. Washington, D.C.: Government Printing Office, 1882. S. exec. doc., vol. 4. no. 71. Microfilm #1.

Tornfelt, Evert E. and Michael Burwell. Shipwrecks of the Alaskan Shelf and Shore Anchorage, Alaska: U.S. Department of the Interior, Minerals Management Service, Alaska OCS Region. 1992. SUDOCS # 1 72.12/3: 92-0002.

Rasmuson Library, University of Alaska Fairbanks

Affleck, Edward. Affleck's List of Sternwheelers Plying the Yukon Waterways, 1995.

Everette, Willis. Willis Everette Scrapbook Collection. No. 76-91.

Jackson, Sheldon. Report on Education in Alaska, 1886. Report to the 49th Cong., 1st Sess. Washington, D.C.: Government Printing Office, 1886. Exec. doc. No. 85.

Jackson, Ronald V., and Gary R. Teeples, comps. Alaskan Census Records, 1870-1907. Bountiful, Utah: Accelerated Indexing Systems, 1976.

The Mariners' Museum Library, Newport News, Virginia

Thirtieth Annual List of Merchant Vessels of the United States... for the Year Ending June 30, 1898. Washington, D.C.: Government Printing Office, 1898.

Thirty-second Annual List of Merchant Vessels of the United States...for the Year Ended June 30, 1900. Washington, D.C.: Government Printing Office, 1900.

Certificate of Registry, No. 17, S.S. Morgan City.

University of Washington Library

Johnston, Samuel P, ed. Alaska Commercial Co., 1868-1940, A More or Less "Documented" History: Evidenced by Papers from Governmental Files and Books; By Old Letters From Company Files; By Newspaper Articles; By Memories of Officials and Employes of Long Standing. N.p., n.d.

Shwinkin, Anne D., Elizabeth F. Andrews, Russell H. Sackett and Mary V. Kroul. Ft. Egbert and the Eagle Historic District: results of archaeological and historic research, summer 1977. Tok, Alaska: Bureau of Land Management-Alaska Technical Report 2, Fortymile Resource Area.

Zimmerman Library, University of New Mexico

Turner, Lucien M. Contributions to the Natural History of Alaska: Results of Investigations made chiefly in the Yukon District and the Aleutian Islands; Conducted under the auspices of the Signal Service, U.S. Army, extending from May 1874 to August 1881. Washington, D.C.: Government Printing Office, 1886.

HISTORICAL SOCIETIES

Alaska Historical Society

Mercier, Francois Xavier. Recollections of the Youkon. Linda Finn Yarborough, trans., ed. and annotated. Anchorage, Alaska, 1986.

Clinton County Historical Association

McMasters, Emily. "Clinton County's Man in Alaska, Joseph Ladue." North Country Notes. 2 February 1971.

Iowa State Historical Society

Iowa Cemetery Records, St. Mary's Cemetery, Benton County, Iowa.

Morgan City (Louisiana) Historical Society

A History of Morgan City, Louisiana. 1960.

New York State Historical Society

1897-1898 New York City Directory.

George B. Corsa Hotel Collection

The Steamship Historical Society of America, Inc.

Mills, John M. Canadian Coastal and Inland Steam Vessels, 1809-1930. Providence, RI, 1979.

MUSEUM COLLECTIONS

National Maritime Museum of Britain

Historic Photographs & Ships Plans.

The Mariner's Museum, San Francisco

Eldredge Collection Notebooks.

U.S. Signal Corp Museum, Georgia

Collector of Customs, St. Michael, Alaska, 1900.

BIBLIOGRAPHY

PRIVATE COLLECTIONS

Bob Majni, Macedonia, Ohio
Candy Waugaman, Fairbanks, Alaska
Day Family Scrapbooks, Plattsburgh, New York
Donald and Katie Miller, Lake Oswego, Oregon
Donna Tremblay, Barrie, Ontario
Ed and Star Jones, Santa Fe, New Mexico
Jeffrey Hunston, Whitehorse, Yukon
Joanne Sanchez, Arlington, Washington
Joan Vericruse, Cold Spring, New York
Joseph F. Ladue III, Highland, New York
Keith La Due, Salem, Oregon
Kittie Ladue Scrapbook (Joseph F. Ladue III Collection)
Mary Ladue Hendryx Scrapbook (Ronald Scott Hendryx Collection), Center Point, Iowa
Ronald Scott Hendryx, Center Point, Iowa
Sullivan Papers, (Mrs. Benjamin F. Sullivan), Office of the Town Historian, Town of Chazy, New York
Turner Family, Velma Newton, Plattsburgh, New York

GOVERNMENT RECORDS
Clinton County, New York

Account for Judicial Settlement. Surrogate's Court. Plattsburgh.

Adoption Agreement and Order. May 8, 1900. County Court. Plattsburgh.

Affidavit. Victor Mason. Surrogate's Court. Plattsburgh.

Andrew La Due Claim Against the Estate of Joseph F. Ladue. Clinton County Clerk's Office.

Baptisms St. Peters Parish. Book One. Plattsburgh, New York. 1853-1870. Comp. by William H. Marquis, Jr. Office of the Clinton County Historian.

Beers Atlas 1869, Plattsburgh and Schuyler Falls. Office of the Clinton County Historian. Historical Marker, Town of Schuyler Falls, New York. n.d.

Clinton County 1862 Gazeteer. Office of the Clinton County Historian. Plattsburgh.

Estate of Joseph Ladue, Income and Real Property. Surrogate's Court. Plattsburgh.

Grantee's Index A-Z, 1866. Clinton County Clerk's Office. Plattsburgh.

Grantee's Index, 1896-1905. Clinton County Clerk's Office. Plattsburgh.

Grantor's Index IV, 1865-1875. Clinton County Clerk's Office. Plattsburgh.

McLellan Cemetery Records of Clinton County, with index. Office of the County Historian. Plattsburgh.

Notarized acknowledgement by Joseph Ladue that he had executed the power of attorney to S. O. Morford. 23 October 1897. County Clerk's Office. Plattsburgh.

Probate Records, Estate of Philomen Ladue. Clinton County Clerk's Office. Plattsburgh.

St. Peter's Catholic Church Census Records, 1860. Office of the Clinton County Historian. Plattsburgh.
St. Peter's Catholic Church. Marriages 1830-1880. Plattsburgh.

Will. Joseph Ladue. Surrogate's Court. Plattsburgh.

Grant County, New Mexico

Great Britain Entry of Birth, Harold Harris Pitts General Resiter Office, London.

Patent Mining Book. Grant County Clerk's Office. Silver City.

Linn County, Iowa

Petition. Linn County, Iowa. September 1902. District Court.

New Jersey

Corporations of New Jersey, List of Certificates to 31 December 1911. State of New Jersey. Department of State, Division of Archives and Records Management.

South Dakota

Articles of Incorporation. Recorded with the South Dakota Secretary of State. 15 April 1903. Recorded in vol. 3, p. 342. Record of Domestic Corporations.

State of New York

State Department of Health, No Record Certification.

U.S. Army Military Research Center Collection

Correspondence Relating to the War with Spain...from April 15, 1898 to July 30, 1902. Volume 2 U.S. Army War College and Carlisle Barracks, Carlisle, Pennsylvania. Government Printing Office, 1902.

Report of Board of Survey. San Francisco, California. 7 November 1898. U.S. Army Research Collection.

The Dodge Commission Assesses the Work of the Quartermaster Department in the War with Spain. In United States Army Logistics, 1775-1992, An Anthology, Volume 2. Charles R. Shrader, ed. Center of Military History. U.S. Army. Washington, D.C.: 1997.

Young, James Rankin. History of our War with Spain including Battles on Sea and Land. U.S. Army War College and Carlisle Barracks, Carlisle, PA.

U.S. CENSUS

1860 Census, Schuyler Falls, Clinton County, New York.
1870 Census, Schuyler Falls, Clinton County, New York.
1870 Census, Washington Township, Center Point, Iowa.
1880, Census, Rochford, Pennington, Dakota Territory.
1880, Census, Washington Township, Troy Mills, Iowa.
1900, Census, Schuyler Falls, Clinton County, New York.

U.S. National Archives and Records Administration

Customs Records, Wrecks, Merchant Vessels of the United States. 30 June 1900. National Archives & Records Administration, Pacific Alaska Region. Anchorage, Alaska. Washington, D.C.: Government Printing Office, 1900.

Records of the U.S. Customs Service, "Wrecks Reports, 1892-1905, U.S. Customs Service, District of Alaska, Subport of Wrangell, Alaska. National Archives-Pacific Alaska Region (Anchorage). R.G. 36, 06/08/09 (4).

Records of Alaska Customs Houses, Press Copies of Letters. Letters sent from St. Michael's, 1902-1906. #AR23, Micro-copy # T1189, Roll 70. National Archives, Pacific-Alaska Region, Anchorage, Alaska.

Williams, John William. Preliminary Inventory of the Records of the Office of U.S. Local Inspectors, Seattle Bureau of Marine Inspection and Navigation. General Services Administration. National Archives and Records Service, Archives Branch Federal Archives and Records Center. Seattle, Washington. 1979. RG 41.

Warren County, New York

Grantee's Index. Book 84. Clerk of Warren County.

Yukon

Tr' ochek: The Archaeology and History of a Han Fish Camp. Heritage Branch, Whitehorse. n.d.

GENEALOGICAL SOCIETIES

Genealogical Society of Linn County, Iowa.

Petition, Linn County Iowa, September 1902. District Court.

Linn County Probate. Volumes 3, 11, 13. Office of the Circuit Court, Linn County, Iowa.

Northern New York American-Canadian Genealogical Society.

Clinton County Marriages, 1830-1880.

BOOKLETS/BROCHURES

Alaska Commercial Co. September, 1868-1898, to the Klondike Gold Fields and Other Points of Interest in Alaska, 1898. Alaska Commercial Co..

Fielder, Mildred, ed. Lawrence County. Sponsored by Lawrence County (South Dakota) Centennial Committee. Lead, SD: Seaton Publishing Co., 1960.

Ladue-Yukon Transportation Co. L.Y.T. Co., Gold Pick Line, Johnson-Locke Mercantile Co., General Agents. Candy Waugaman Collection.

Lloyd, Dick. Outlaw Country, A Map & Guide to the Cheyenne-Blackhills Express Route and the Sydney-Deadwood Trail. Alliance, Nebraska.

Sights and Scenes for the Tourist. Union Pacific Railroad, Omaha, Nebraska, 1894. Ed and Star Jones Collection.

Sydney, Nebraska. Cheyenne Historical Association. Cheyenne County Visitor Committee.

Toms, Donald, ed. The Gold Belt Cities. (Deadwood and Environs). Lead, SD: G.O.L.D., Unlimited, 1988.

CHURCH RECORDS

Anglican Church Burial Records. Record #1. St. Paul's Anglican Church. Dawson City, Yukon.

Births and Baptisms. St. Peters Church. Plattsburgh, New York.

St. Peters Church Census, 1857. Plattsburgh, New York.

St. Peters Church Census, 1865. Plattsburgh, New York.

INTERVIEWS

Ronald Scott Hendryx, Center Point, Iowa.
Joseph Frances Ladue III.
Keith La Due, Salem, Oregon
Donna Tremblay, Barrie, Ontario
Barbara Nelson, North Pole, Alaska
Ben Traywick, Tombstone, Arizona

WEBSITES

American Catholic/Index of Saints.
The Spanish American War Centennial.
Explore.com (Historical Vignettes of the North)
Arlingtoncemetery.com/labeard.htm
Nlc-bnc.ca, The North-Western Territory and Rupert's Land- Canadian Confederation

Index

INDEX

INDEX

INDEX